Soft Despotism, Democracy's Drift

SOFT DESPOTISM, DEMOCRACY'S DRIFT

Montesquieu, Rousseau, Tocqueville & The Modern Prospect

Paul A. Rahe

Yale University Press
New Haven & London

Published with assistance from the Annie Burr Lewis Fund.

Set in Electra and Trajan types by The Composing Room of Michigan, Inc.
Printed in the United States of America.

Library of Congress Cataloging-in-Publication Data

Rahe, Paul Anthony.
Soft despotism, democracy's drift : Montesquieu, Rousseau, Tocqueville, and
the modern prospect / Paul A. Rahe.
p.   cm.
Includes bibliographical references and index.
ISBN 978-0-300-14492-5 (hardcover : alk. paper)   1. Democracy.   2. Republicanism.
3. Montesquieu, Charles de Secondat, baron de, 1689–1755.   4. Tocqueville, Alexis de,
1805–1859.   5. Rousseau, Jean-Jacques, 1712–1778.   I. Title.
JC423.R246   2009
321.8 — dc22
2008039281

A catalogue record for this book is available from the British Library.

This paper meets the requirements of ANSI/NISO Z39.48–1992 (Permanence of Paper).
It contains 30 percent postconsumer waste (PCW) and is certified by the Forest
Stewardship Council (FSC).

10 9 8 7 6 5 4 3 2 1

Laura T. Rahe

I would like to imagine with what new traits despotism could be produced in the world. I see an innumerable multitude of men, alike and equal, who turn about without repose in order to procure for themselves petty and vulgar pleasures with which they fill their souls. Each of them, withdrawn apart, is a virtual stranger, unaware of the fate of the others: his children and his particular friends form for him the entirety of the human race; as for his fellow citizens, he is beside them but he sees them not; he touches them and senses them not; he exists only in himself and for himself alone, and, if he still has a family, one could say at least that he no longer has a fatherland.

Over these is elevated an immense, tutelary power, which takes sole charge of assuring their enjoyment and of watching over their fate. It is absolute, attentive to detail, regular, provident, and gentle. It would resemble the paternal power if, like that power, it had as its object to prepare men for manhood, but it seeks, to the contrary, to keep them irrevocably fixed in childhood; it loves the fact that the citizens enjoy themselves provided that they dream solely of their own enjoyment. It works willingly for their happiness, but it wishes to be the only agent and the sole arbiter of that happiness. It provides for their security, foresees and supplies their needs, guides them in the principal affairs, directs their industry, regulates their testaments, divides their inheritances. . . .

After having taken each individual in this fashion by turns into its powerful hands, and after having kneaded him in accord with its desires, the sovereign extends its arms about the society as a whole; it covers its surface with a network of petty regulations—complicated, minute, and uniform—through which even the most original minds and the most vigorous souls know not how to make their way past the crowd and emerge into the light of day. It does not break wills; it softens them, bends them, and directs them; rarely does it force one to act, but it constantly opposes itself to one's acting on one's own; it does not destroy, it prevents things from being born; it does not tyrannize, it gets in the way: it curtails, it enervates, it extinguishes, it stupefies, and finally it reduces each nation to nothing more than a herd of timid and industrious animals, of which the government is the shepherd.

—*Alexis de Tocqueville*

CONTENTS

ACKNOWLEDGMENTS

I am indebted, as always, to James W. Muller of the University of Alaska at Anchorage, who first steered me to Montesquieu, and to my former colleague Michael A. Mosher of the University of Tulsa, in whose company I first read *The Spirit of Laws* from beginning to end, and with whom I have had innumerable enlightening conversations concerning the French philosophe. I am indebted as well to David W. Carrithers of the University of Tennessee at Chattanooga; Catherine Larrère of the University of Paris (I); Stuart D. Warner of Roosevelt University; Henry C. Clark of Canisius College; Diana J. Schaub of Loyola University, Baltimore; Cecil Patrick Courtney of Christ's College, Cambridge; and Eldon Eisenach and Joseph C. Bradley of the University of Tulsa, who were generous with their time and expertise on a multitude of occasions.

Daniel Gordon and Will Morrissey read and commented on the manuscript as a whole; Victor Gourevitch read and commented on the chapters dealing with Rousseau; and John Robertson, Peter Ghosh, Istvan Hont, Michael Mosher, Robert Eden, Joseph C. Bradley, R. J. Pestritto, Terence Marshall, and Jon Fennell read and commented on various parts of the manuscript. My wife, Laura, to whom this book is dedicated, more than once went over every word.

While on sabbatical from the University of Tulsa in the spring of 1999 at Clare Hall, Cambridge, I began this project in earnest. Later in 2005–6, while on sabbatical again, I received generous support from the Research Office at the University of Tulsa; from Thomas Benediktson, dean of Henry Kendall College of Arts and Sciences at that institution; and from the Earhart Foundation, to which over the years I have come to owe a very large debt. I had the privilege of spending Michaelmas Term in 2005 and Hilary Term in 2006 in congenial company at All Souls College, Oxford—where, as a visiting fellow, I took ample advantage of library facilities unequaled anywhere else in the world and had the opportunity to meet Ms. Ursula Haskins Gonthier, then of Worcester College, Oxford, and to read in various drafts the chapter in her dissertation dedicated to Montesquieu's *Considerations on the Causes of the Greatness of the Romans and their Decline*. In response to her argument, I made various small changes to the first part of the first book contained within this volume regarding the subtextual significance of Montesquieu's attack on Augustus, the incendiary character of the praise that Montesquieu bestowed on England's parliamentary regime, and the precise dates of that work's publication in English and in French. To her, to the warden and fellows of All Souls College, and to the librarians at the Taylorian Institution and the Bodleian Library, I am especially grateful.

The spring and early summer of 2006, I spent in similarly congenial company at the American Academy in Berlin, where once again I was free to devote myself full time to this project; and I did the same in the fall of 2006, when I was on leave from the University of Tulsa on a fellowship from the National Endowment for the Humanities. I owe a special debt to the director and the members of his staff at the American Academy, who were helpful in a great many ways; to the National Endowment for the Humanities and the University of Tulsa for their generosity; and to Marc Carlson, Ann Blakely, Tamara Stansfield, and the staff at the interlibrary loan office at the McFarlin Library at the University of Tulsa, who performed miracles.

Earlier and shorter versions of Book One, Chapters One and Two, appeared as Paul A. Rahe, "Soft Despotism: Democracy's Drift," in *Foundations of American Civilization*, ed. T. William Boxx and Gary M. Quinlivan (Latrobe, PA: Center for Economic and Policy Education, 1999), 15–54, and as Rahe, "Forms of Government: Structure, Principle, Object, and Aim," in *Montesquieu's Science of Politics: Essays on the Spirit of Laws (1748)*, ed. David W. Carrithers, Michael A. Mosher, and Paul A. Rahe (Lanham, MD: Rowman & Littlefield, 2001), 69–108. A great deal of material from these is reprinted here with the permission of the Center for Economic Policy at Saint Vincent College and Rowman & Littlefield Publishers. An earlier and slightly longer version of Book Two, Chapter One appeared as Rahe, "The Enlightenment Indicted: Rousseau's Response to Montesquieu," *Journal of the Historical Society* 18:2 (June 2008): 273–302. Much of it is reprinted here with the permission of the editor.

INTRODUCTION

Fortunately for all of us, the Cold War ended not with a bang but with a whimper. It is surprising, however, that its cessation inspired so little elation. Of course, there was a moment of euphoria and rejoicing when the Berlin Wall quite suddenly ceased to be a barrier. It seemed a miracle, and in a sense it was. But that moment quickly passed; and where one might have expected opinion leaders in the West to celebrate what was, after all, an astonishing and historically unprecedented victory, involving the utter defeat and ultimate dissolution of a powerful and threatening adversary in the absence of a major war, one encountered at best a cautious optimism and at worst a sense of resignation.[1] It was as if liberal democrats everywhere mourned the enemy they had known and were in fear of an enemy who had not yet appeared.

The French worried about the consequences of German reunification; the Germans fretted about its costs. In Czechoslovakia, the Velvet Revolution was followed by the Velvet Divorce. The revival of ancient religious and ethnic hatreds gave rise to armed struggle within and between some of the successor states to the Soviet Union and Yugoslavia. Throughout Eastern Europe, people were less inclined to speak of revolution than of transition; and in many a country, the old communists with a name change and a face-lift were soon returned to power by a newly liberated electorate nostalgic for a past offering in predictability what it had denied in the way of opportunity. Then, on the first occasion that presented itself, the French, the Germans, the Belgians, and many others within a Western Europe that had once been liberated from fascism by the United States and that had later been protected from communism by that same power turned on their former benefactor and set out to put as much distance as possible between themselves and that country, denouncing its policies, demonizing its leaders, and venting great rancor against its people and their way of life.

If, in and soon after 1989, the prevailing mood was nonetheless one of relief, it was not unmixed with sadness, discontent, and a measure of world-weariness. When Francis Fukuyama announced "the end of history" and suggested that we may have entered the era of Nietzsche's "last man," he struck a nerve and caused a sensation—not just in the United States, but in France and in the rest of Europe as well.[2] A similar spirit pervaded Samuel P. Huntington's quite different—one might even say, contrarian—observations concerning the likelihood that there would be a great "clash of civilizations," wherein, as critics noted, there was more than a hint of the profound cultural pessimism that once suffused Oswald Spengler's *The Decline of the West*.[3]

When Ned Lebow and Janice Stein informed their fellow political scientists that "we all lost the Cold War,"[4] their claim was not immediately dismissed as preposterous. When Tony Judt denounced John Lewis Gaddis for focusing narrowly on grand strategy in a book charting the history of the Cold War, sneering that Gaddis had treated "the 'third world' as a sideshow, albeit one in which hundreds of thousands of performers got killed,"[5] no one from among his fellow historians stepped forward to point out that, from the perspective of grand strategy, the proxy wars that occurred within the Third World really were a sideshow, and no one bothered to ask whether Professor Judt knew of a comparable epic struggle between rival coalitions lasting more than four decades in which the collateral damage had been less.[6] In keeping with the prevailing mood, triumphalism was also notably absent from the great outpouring of literature on liberal democracy and its prospects that appeared in the wake of the Soviet Union's collapse.[7]

There was also evidence of growing popular disaffection. In 2004, when a pollster named Scott Rasmussen asked Americans whether their country was "generally fair and decent," roughly a quarter of those planning to vote in the presidential election disagreed; and, when the Pew Trust asked whether American "wrongdoing" might have "motivated" the terrorist attacks in New York and Washington on 11 September 2001, a similar proportion of those who responded were persuaded that this might, indeed, have been the case. Even more to the point, polls taken that year revealed that something like a quarter of the American population doubted that the world would be better off if other nations were more like their own.[8] In February and March 2008, when the wife of a presidential aspirant repeatedly asserted in her stump speech that Americans are "cynical" and "mean" and have "broken souls" and that the lives "that most people are living" have "gotten progressively worse since I was a little girl," she caught the sour mood of this segment of the American electorate.[9]

In Europe, there have also been indications of the emergence of a deep sense of popular malaise. In February 2002, a Convention on the Future of Europe was convened to great acclaim under the chairmanship of former French president Valéry Giscard d'Estaing to draft a constitutional frame for the European Union. The following year a document, more than 450 pages in length, was placed before the public; and in June 2004, an amended version of the original draft was presented to the union's member nations for ratification. A year later, however, when the first referenda were held, despite the fact that the political class throughout the European continent was virtually unanimous in enthusiastic support for the constitutional project, the ordinary people of France and the United Provinces, founding members of the Common Market and leading members of the European Union, promptly and decisively rejected the proposal.

There is something altogether odd and not a little unsettling about these developments, for they leave us wondering where to turn. That the chattering classes should be inclined to sneer is hardly a matter needing extended comment: sneering is the coin in which the modern intellectual trades. But world-weariness and profound popular disaffection are something else again. Perhaps, however, the sobriety with which statesmen, peoples, and scholars have greeted liberal democracy's sudden and unexpected achievement of a seemingly unchallenged hegemony is entirely appropriate. After all, this sobriety jibes well with a conviction which informed the establishment of the modern world's first unequivocally liberal, undeniably republican regime: that an experiment of doubtful resolution had then been set in train. Perhaps, Americans and their European cousins can still echo the words that George Washington wrote to the governors of America's states in early June 1783 on the eve of his retirement as general of the armies — that "it is yet to be decided whether the [American] Revolution must ultimately be considered as a blessing or a curse: a blessing or a curse, not to the present age alone, for with our fate will the destiny of unborn Millions be involved."[10] If there is even a hint of justification for our strangely melancholy response to a set of events that seem, finally, to have made the world safe for democracy, it is worth pondering anew whether liberal republicanism, for all its many obvious virtues, displays certain inherent defects as well.

For reflections of such a sort, there may be no occasion more appropriate than the interval between the 250th anniversary of the death of Charles-Louis de Secondat, baron de La Brède et de Montesquieu, and the 150th anniversary of the death of his disciple Alexis de Tocqueville, when this volume was brought to completion. The latter needs no introduction. The pertinence of his work to the study of modern liberal democracy is well-known, and the same claim can arguably be made for Jean-Jacques Rousseau, whose contributions to democratic theory and to the study of bourgeois society will be discussed in this volume as well. The importance of their teacher Montesquieu may, however, require a brief word of explanation.

That the author of *The Spirit of Laws*, which first appeared in 1748, was a great man, graced with a comprehensive vision of the political setting within which liberal republicanism first emerged, was once a fact well-known. In *The Federalist*, James Madison called him an "oracle," and both Madison and Alexander Hamilton spoke of him as "the celebrated Montesquieu."[11] They knew what subsequent scholarship has shown to be true: that no political writer was more often cited and none was thought to be of greater authority in the era of American constitution-making.[12] They knew, moreover, that in England and on the continent of Europe, he was thought to be of similar stature. Indeed, having carefully read his *Spirit of Laws* themselves, they knew why, throughout the Christian West, he was held in such regard.

If Montesquieu was so often consulted and cited by their contemporaries, it was largely because, in *The Spirit of Laws*, he had announced his discovery, on the very doorstep of his native France, of a new form of government more conducive to liberty and graced with greater staying power than any polity theretofore even imagined. As Madison put it: "The British constitution was to Montesquieu, what Homer has been to the didactic writers on epic poetry. As the latter have considered the work of the immortal Bard, as the perfect model from which the principles and rules of the epic art were to be drawn, and by which all similar works were to be judged; so this great political critic appears to have viewed the constitution of England, as the standard, or to use his own expression, as the mirrour of political liberty; and to have delivered in the form of elementary truths, the several characteristic principles of that particular system."[13] Students of the form of political liberty peculiar to modern republics may still have something to learn from considering what Montesquieu had to say a quarter of a millennium ago concerning the constitution of England—for, James Madison to the contrary notwithstanding, Montesquieu did not profess for "the particular government of England" an "admiration bordering on idolatry."[14] He was, in fact, a critic as well as an admirer, as sensitive to the imperfections inherent in the English form of government as he was to its many virtues; and, as we shall in due course see, the defects he discerned in that polity and the propensities that arise therefrom are pertinent to understanding the political psychology of all modern republics and to tracing the sources of our present discontents.

If, then, we wish to understand whither we are tending, we would be well-advised to reacquaint ourselves with a forgotten form of political science and to read with care Montesquieu and then those, such as Rousseau and Tocqueville, who closely followed his lead and expanded in crucial regards upon what he had to say. This is, however, easier said than done. For Montesquieu, in particular, wrote in a time now largely forgotten and unfamiliar, and he couched his arguments with an eye to an immediate public that has long since disappeared. Moreover, he lived in an age of censorship, and he composed his works in conformity with unwritten rules of discretion, intimating that which could not with profit openly be said. It would be patronizing for us to suppose him a "man of his time," condemned to think as his contemporaries thought; and it would be a grave error as well, for it would deprive us of the capacity to appreciate fully the force and the originality of what he had to say. But it is nonetheless true that to make himself understood Montesquieu had to make use of the vocabulary and the idioms spoken by his compatriots and redeploy them in a fashion suited to conveying what was novel in his reflections. In consequence, the challenge we face if we are to understand his thinking is not just intellectual, it is also literary, and it is unavoidably historical. One might even call our task archaeological. Before we can hope to be able to return to our own age; to rethink our situation in light of the penetrating analysis offered by Montesquieu, Rousseau, and Tocqueville; and to recognize it for what it is for the first time, we must undertake a journey into the past, to Montesquieu's day and, then, to that of his greatest successors, . . . in search of treasure that is buried there.

Journeys of this kind, whether through space or time, can be a liberation. Archaeologists of the ordinary sort may find it necessary to pack a great deal of luggage and equipment. Intellectual archaeologists generally do the opposite. As they proceed, they tend to lose the baggage that they have brought with them—and not to mind a bit. They find themselves jettisoning preconceptions, abandoning prejudices, and setting aside, at least for the length of the ride, their current pressing, confining concerns. Freed from the burden of present-mindedness and from the anxieties to which it gives rise, they enter imaginatively into ways of thinking that are decidedly foreign; and in the process, more often than not, they open themselves to possibilities that they had never before even contemplated, and they secure for themselves a vantage point from which to view their own world. Such was the experience of Voltaire and of Montesquieu when they journeyed through space to England in the late 1720s; such was the experience of Rousseau when he sojourned in Paris in the late 1740s and the 1750s; and such was the experience of Tocqueville when he traveled with Gustave de Beaumont through Jacksonian America in the early 1830s. Moreover, when Montesquieu journeyed through time and gave himself over to Homer and Vergil; to Plato and Aristotle; to Herodotus and Thucydides; to Plutarch, Polybius, and Livy; and to Montaigne, Hobbes, Pascal, Locke, Mandeville, and a great many others, he had much the same experience—not just once, but repeatedly—as did Rousseau when he first read Plutarch and first studied Montesquieu's *Spirit of Laws*, and Tocqueville also, when on a daily basis he entered into conversation with Pascal, Montesquieu, and Rousseau. Such, I hope, will be the experience of those who are led by this work to view the world, at least for a fleeting moment, through the eyes of Montesquieu, Rousseau, and Tocqueville.

Our intellectual odyssey we will begin, as is only proper, at the beginning—some three hundred years ago, at the moment when the world's first fully modern, first fully commercial republic first made its presence felt in the world and first demonstrated its viability in the sphere where aspiring polities meet their first, most decisive, and most grueling test—on the field of the sword. Then, after briefly considering the effect on the young Voltaire and on his slightly older contemporary Montesquieu of Great Britain's victories over France in the War of the Spanish Succession, we will set out on our way, as those two young men did on theirs. Our journey we will make in stages, pausing at discrete intervals to dig deeply into the thinking of Montesquieu, Rousseau, and Tocqueville.

In the case of Montesquieu, to whom I have devoted a separate volume designed to provide a full account of his thinking concerning modernity, we will start by glancing at his provocative analysis of the novel character of modern geopolitics and of the peculiar place occupied within that system by Great Britain. Then, we will take up his regime typology—above all else, his description of the political psychology regnant within the various and strikingly different forms of government that existed in ancient and modern times and his account of the circumstances, practices, laws, and policies that sustain and subvert each polity—and, with an eye to the account of fallen man in Pascal's *Pensées* and to that of man in general in Montaigne's *Essays* and in Locke's *Essay concerning Human Understanding*, we will tease out the implications of Montesquieu's regime typology for the virtues, the vices, and the long-term prospects of Great Britain and of the colonies it established on the North American continent. Our ruminations on Montesquieu we will then conclude with a glance at his penetrating and prescient assessment of the trajectory that European and world history were likely to take.

When we have finished this, we will pause briefly to consider Montesquieu's influence on his contemporaries. Then, we will turn to his greatest admirer and most astute critic, Jean-Jacques Rousseau, and we will ponder the significance of the profound debt the latter owed his predecessor's analysis of the political psychology of the modern liberal republic. In this light, we will consider the substance of Rousseau's attack on the Enlightenment, his contention that progress in the sciences and the arts is likely to corrupt human beings and intensify their misery, and his suggestion that bourgeois society and popular enlightenment pose a threat to intellectual integrity and freedom. Then, we will examine in detail the foundations of the savage critique he directed on other grounds at the commercial societies emerging in his time and weigh the eloquent argument that he made on behalf of intense civic engagement.

It is against this background that we will undertake the last stage of our journey—the one that will bring us home. Therein we will consider Tocqueville's application of the psychological insights of Pascal, the political science of Montesquieu and Rousseau, and that of Aristotle to the strange new world that emerged in the wake of the American and French revolutions. Here, once again, our focus will be first and foremost psychological, and we will examine the cast of mind promoted by the democratic social condition, the new species of despotism to which that condition gives rise, and the salutary remedies applied in the America that Tocqueville visited in the early 1830s. Then and only then will we return to our own time and, in light of what we have learned from Montesquieu, Rousseau, and Tocqueville, trace the trajectory of France, the European Union, and the United States; ponder whether the world's modern republics are on the right course; and face up to what must be done if we are to recover from the profound sense of malaise to which we are now prone.

ABBREVIATIONS

In the notes, I have adopted the standard abbreviations for classical texts and inscriptions and for books of the Bible provided in *The Oxford Classical Dictionary*, 3rd edition revised, ed. Simon Hornblower and Antony Spawforth (Oxford, UK: Oxford University Press, 2003), and in *The Chicago Manual of Style*, 15th edition (Chicago: University of Chicago Press, 2003), 15.50–53. Where possible, the ancient texts and medieval and modern works of similar stature are cited by the divisions and subdivisions employed by the author or introduced by subsequent editors (that is, by book, part, chapter, section number, paragraph, act, scene, line, Stephanus page, or by page and line number). Cross-references within this volume refer to book, part, and chapter and specify whether the material referenced can be found above or below.

In citing particular works by Machiavelli, to render my citations more precise, I have added, in some instances, the paragraph numbers provided in Niccolò Machiavelli, *Discourses on Livy*, tr. Harvey C. Mansfield and Nathan Tarcov (Chicago: University of Chicago Press, 1996), and the sentence numbers provided in Niccolò Machiavelli, *Art of War*, ed. and tr. Christopher Lynch (Chicago: University of Chicago Press, 2003).

In citing Montesquieu, wherever possible, I have employed the splendid new critical edition being produced by the Société Montesquieu: Charles-Louis de Secondat, baron de La Brède et de Montesquieu, *Œuvres complètes de Montesquieu*, ed. Jean Ehrard, Catherine Volpilhac-Auger, et al. (Oxford, UK: The Voltaire Foundation, 1998–), which I cite as VF. For works as yet unavailable in this edition, I cite Montesquieu, *Œuvres complètes de Montesquieu*, ed. Roger Caillois (Paris: Bibliothèque de la Pléiade, 1949–51), as Pléiade; and Montesquieu, *Œuvres complètes de Montesquieu*, ed. André Masson (Paris: Les Éditions Nagel, 1950–55), as Nagel.

I cite Jean-Jacques Rousseau, *Œuvres complètes de Jean-Jacques Rousseau*, ed. Bernard Gagnebin and Marcel Raymond (Paris: Bibliothèque de la Pléiade, 1959–95), as JJR; and Rousseau, *Correspondance complète de Jean-Jacques Rousseau*, ed. Ralph A. Leigh (Oxford, UK: Voltaire Foundation, 1965–1998), as CCJJR. Those who want to read Rousseau's works in English may wish to consult *The Collected Writings of Jean-Jacques Rousseau*, ed. Roger D. Masters and Christopher Kelly (Hanover, NH: University Press of New England, 1990–). Some, but not all, of the works by Rousseau cited in this volume are also available in fine translations in Rousseau, *The Discourses and Other Early Political Writings*, ed. and tr. Victor Gourevitch (Cambridge, UK: Cambridge University Press, 1997); in Rousseau, *The Social Contract and Other Later Writings*, ed. and tr. Victor Gourevitch (Cambridge, UK: Cambridge University Press, 1997); and in Rousseau, *Emile, or On Education*, tr. Allan Bloom (New York: Basic Books, 1979).

I cite Alexis de Tocqueville, *Œuvres, papiers et correspondances*, ed. J.-P. Mayer et al. (Paris: Gallimard, 1951–) as ATG, and Tocqueville, *Œuvres*, ed. André Jardin et al. (Paris: Bibliothèque de la Pléiade, 1991–2004) as ATP.

For modern works frequently cited, the following abbreviations and short titles have been employed:

Montesquieu, *CEC*   Charles-Louis de Secondat, baron de La Brède et de Montesquieu, "Essai sur les causes qui peuvent affecter les esprits et les caractères" (ca. 1736), ed. Pierre Rétat, cited by line, in VF IX 219–70. For this work, there are two accessible English translations, see Montesquieu, "An Essay on the Causes That May Affect Men's Minds and Characters," tr. Melvin Richter, *Political Theory* 4:2 (May 1976): 139–62, and Montesquieu, "An Essay on Causes Affecting Minds and Characters," tr. David W. Carrithers, in Montesquieu, *The Spirit of Laws: A Compendium of the First English Edition*, ed. David W. Carrithers (Berkeley: University of California Press, 1977), 417–54.

——, *CR*   Charles-Louis de Secondat, baron de La Brède et de Montesquieu, *Considérations sur les causes de la grandeur des Romains et de leur décadence* (1734), ed. Françoise Weil and Cecil Courtney, cited by chapter and, where appropriate, line from VF II 89–285.

——, *EL*   Charles-Louis de Secondat, baron de La Brède et de

Montesquieu, *De l'Esprit des lois* (1757), cited by part, book, chapter, and, where appropriate, page from Pléiade II 225–995.

——, *LP*   Charles-Louis de Secondat, baron de La Brède et de Montesquieu, *Lettres persanes* (1721), ed. Edgar Mass, cited by number and, where appropriate, line from VF I 137–569—followed, where appropriate, by a backslash and the new number assigned the pertinent letter in the posthumous edition of this work published in 1758, which is reprinted in Pléiade I 129–373.

——, *MP*   Charles-Louis de Secondat, baron de La Brède et de Montesquieu, *Mes pensées*, cited by number and, where appropriate, page from Nagel II 1–677, who follows the enumeration provided by Montesquieu in the manuscript. This is the order that will be followed in VF XIV–XV and in the English translation by Henry Clark scheduled for publication by Liberty Fund. This is also the order followed in Montesquieu, *Pensées, Le Spicilège*, ed. Louis Desgraves (Paris: Laffont, 1991), who provides a table of concordance, specifying the number assigned each corresponding entry in *Pensées et fragments inédits de Montesquieu, publiés par le baron Gaston de Montesquieu*, ed. Henri Barckhausen (Bordeaux: Publications de la Société des Bibliophiles de Guyenne, 1899–1901), and later reprinted in Pléiade I 971–1574, where the entries have been rearranged in topical order and renumbered.

——, *NA*   Charles-Louis de Secondat, baron de La Brède et de Montesquieu, *Notes sur l'Angleterre* (ca. 1729–31), cited by page from Pléiade I 875–84.

——, *RMU*   Charles-Louis de Secondat, baron de La Brède et de Montesquieu, *Réflexions sur la monarchie universelle en Europe* (1734), ed. Françoise Weil, cited by chapter and line from VF II 339–64.

Rousseau, *C*   Jean-Jacques Rousseau, *Les Confessions* (1770), ed. Bernard Gagnebin and Marcel Raymond, cited by book and page from JJR I 1–656.

——, *CP*   Jean-Jacques Rousseau, *Considérations sur le gouvernement de Pologne et sur sa réformation projettée* (ca. 1771), ed. Jean Fabre, cited by the chapter numbers supplied by the editor and by page from JJR III 951–1041.

——, *CS*   Jean-Jacques Rousseau, *Du Contrat social; ou, Principes du droit politique* (1762), ed. Robert Derathé, cited by book and chapter and, where appropriate, page from JJR III 347–470.

——, *D*   Jean-Jacques Rousseau, *Dialogues: Rousseau, juge de Jean Jacques* (ca. 1772), ed. Robert Osmont, cited by number and page from JJR I 657–992.

——, *DEP*   Jean-Jacques Rousseau, *Discours sur l'économie politique* (1755), ed. Robert Derathé, cited by page from JJR III 239–78.

——, *DOI*   Jean-Jacques Rousseau, *Discours sur l'origine et les fondemens de l'inégalité parmi les hommes* (1755), ed Jean Starobinski, cited by page from JJR III 109–223.

——, *DR*   Jean-Jacques Rousseau, "Dernière Réponse de J.-J. Rousseau de Genève," ed. François Bouchardy, cited by page from JJR III 71–96.

——, *DSA*   Jean-Jacques Rousseau, *Discours sur les sciences et les arts* (1751), ed. George R. Havens (New York: Modern Language Association of America, 1946), cited by page and line.

——, *É*   Jean-Jacques Rousseau, *Émile, ou De l'Éducation* (1762), ed. Charles Wirz, cited by book and page from JJR IV 239–868.

——, *EOL*   Jean-Jacques Rousseau, *Essai sur l'origine des langues* (ca. 1750–66), ed. Jean Starobinski, cited by page from JJR V 373–429.

——, *Julie*   Jean-Jacques Rousseau, *Julie, ou La nouvelle Héloïse* (1761), ed. Henri Coulet, cited by the divisions made by the author and, where necessary, by page from JJR II 1–745.

——, *LM*   Jean-Jacques Rousseau, *Lettres écrites de la montagne* (1764), ed. Jean-Daniel Candaux, cited by number and page from JJR III 683–897.

——, *LS*   Jean-Jacques Rousseau, *Lettre à M. d'Alembert sur les spectacles* (1758), ed. Bernard Gagnebin, cited by page from JJR V 1–125.

——, *PC*   Jean-Jacques Rousseau, *Projet de constitution pour la Corse* (ca. 1760–69), ed. Sven Stelling-Michaúd, cited by page from JJR III 899–950.

——, *PN*   Jean-Jacques Rousseau, "Préface a *Narcisse*" (1753), ed. François Bouchardy, cited by page from JJR II 959–74.

——, *RPS*   Jean-Jacques Rousseau, *Les Rêveries du promeneur solitaire* (1777), ed. Marcel Raymond, cited by number and, where appropriate, page from JJR I 993–1099.

Tocqueville, *DA*   Alexis de Tocqueville, *De la Démocratie en Amérique*, ed. Eduardo Nolla (Paris: Librairie Philosophique J. Vrin, 1990), cited by tome, part, chapter, and, where appropriate, page.

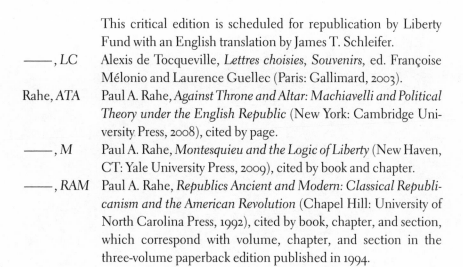

This critical edition is scheduled for republication by Liberty Fund with an English translation by James T. Schleifer.

——, *LC*   Alexis de Tocqueville, *Lettres choisies, Souvenirs*, ed. Françoise Mélonio and Laurence Guellec (Paris: Gallimard, 2003).

Rahe, *ATA*   Paul A. Rahe, *Against Throne and Altar: Machiavelli and Political Theory under the English Republic* (New York: Cambridge University Press, 2008), cited by page.

——, *M*   Paul A. Rahe, *Montesquieu and the Logic of Liberty* (New Haven, CT: Yale University Press, 2009), cited by book and chapter.

——, *RAM*   Paul A. Rahe, *Republics Ancient and Modern: Classical Republicanism and the American Revolution* (Chapel Hill: University of North Carolina Press, 1992), cited by book, chapter, and section, which correspond with volume, chapter, and section in the three-volume paperback edition published in 1994.

Book One

THE MODERN
REPUBLIC EXAMINED

Battles are the principal milestones in secular history. Modern opinion resents this uninspiring truth, and historians often treat the decisions in the field as incidents in the dramas of politics and diplomacy. But great battles, won or lost, change the entire course of events, create new standards of values, new moods, new atmospheres, in armies and in nations, to which all must conform.

— *Winston S. Churchill*

PREFACE

Roughly three hundred years ago, on 13 August 1704, an event took place that is today little remembered and even more rarely remarked on—though it signaled the beginning of a political and an ideological transformation that was arguably no less significant than the one marked in our own time by the fall of the Berlin Wall and the dismemberment of the Soviet Union.[1] In the late spring and summer of that fateful year, two armies made their way from western to central Europe. The first, led by the comte de Tallard, marshal of France, aimed at upsetting the balance of power on the continent of Europe; at establishing Louis XIV's hegemony over the Holy Roman Empire by installing a French nominee on its throne; and at securing the acquiescence of the Austrians, the English, the Dutch, and every other European power in a Bourbon succession to the Spanish throne. The second army, led by John Churchill, then earl, later duke of Marlborough, with the assistance of Prince Eugene of Savoy, sought to preserve the existing balance of power, defend Hapsburg control of the imperial throne, and deprive Louis of his Spanish prize.

At stake, so Louis's opponents with some reason supposed, was the establishment of a universal monarchy in Europe and French dominion in the New World. At stake for Englishmen, Scots, Irish Protestants, and Britain's colonists in the Americas were the supremacy of Parliament, the liberties secured by the Glorious Revolution in 1688 and 1689, the Protestant succession to the English crown, and Protestant hegemony in the British Isles and in much of the New World. James II, who had been ousted so unceremoniously from the English throne in 1688, had died in 1701. His Protestant daughter Anne was queen. But waiting in the wings, ready to claim his birthright when he came of age, was the French nominee—her fiercely Catholic younger brother James, known in France as the chevalier de Saint George.

There was every reason to suppose that Louis would attain for himself and his heirs the predominance within Europe that had been the object of his ambition during the entirety of his adult life. After all, on the field of the sword, France then enjoyed a preeminence that no one dared deny. The French had occasionally been checked, but on no occasion in the preceding 150 years had an army of France suffered a genuinely decisive defeat. It thus came as a shock when all of Europe learned that the army commanded by Marlborough and Prince Eugene had annihilated the French force and captured Marshal Tallard.

Of course, had the battle of Blenheim been a fluke, had it been a genuine anomaly, as everyone at first assumed, Louis's defeat on this particular occasion would not have much mattered. At most, it would have marked a temporary, if severe setback for French arms. In the event, however, this great struggle was but the first of a series of French defeats meted out by armies captained by Marlborough, and it foreshadowed a series of setbacks that would bedevil monarchical France as the century wore on. It is in light of this bold claim that we must read Voltaire's *Philosophical Letters* and Montesquieu's *Considerations on the Causes of the Greatness of the Romans and their Decline* and consider their subsequent careers. For although it would be a gross exaggeration to say that, in comparison with the battle of Blenheim, the French Enlightenment and the French Revolution were little more than aftershocks, there can be no doubt that Marlborough's stirring victories over Louis XIV's France exposed the weakness of the *ancien régime* and occasioned the first efforts on the part of the philosophes to rethink in radical terms Europe's political trajectory.

Charles-Louis de Secondat, baron de La Brède et de Montesquieu, was born in 1688; François-Marie Arouet, whom we know best by his pen name Voltaire, was born in 1694. Both came of age during the War of the Spanish Succession. Both emerged as critics of what we now call the *ancien régime*. Both journeyed to Great Britain in search of political understanding. Both mastered the English language, and both penned works in which the political practices of the English, their mores, manners, and ways were used as a foil for the purpose of criticizing the French monarchy.

There was this difference. Voltaire published his *Lettres philosophiques* in 1734 and suffered the consequences. His printer was arrested; his book was burned by the public hangman at the order of the Parlement de Paris; and he was driven into exile. Montesquieu, who had published his own philosophical letters, the *Lettres persanes*, in 1721 at a time when censorship was lax, was more astute. Initially, he had intended to publish within the covers of a single volume his *Considérations sur les causes de la grandeur des Romains et de leur décadence*, his

Réflexions sur la monarchie universelle en Europe, and an essay on England that he had begun drafting in 1733. Upon reflection, he set aside unfinished the third part of this triptych. The first two parts he had set in type. Then, when Voltaire's audacious eulogy of England stirred up a storm, Montesquieu balked. Fearing that his *Reflections on Universal Monarchy in Europe* would be "interpreted ill," he relegated to his personal archives the printed copy sent him for review by his printer in Amsterdam. His *Considerations on the Causes of the Greatness of the Romans and their Decline* he then published on its own. To that essay there could be no objection. To all and sundry, it seemed as if his aim were to present the world with a philosophical history of ancient Rome.

Had Montesquieu published his triptych as originally planned, this would not have been the common opinion. The triptych would have been read, as was intended, as a savage critique of Roman policy and of the Roman political model, as an attack on the modern quest for universal monarchy, and as an argument that English policy and the English form of government better suited the circumstances of eighteenth-century Europe than the policy pursued and the form of government established in France.

Montesquieu begins his *Considerations on the Romans* in the manner of Niccolò Machiavelli—by depicting the early Roman republic as a martial polity intent on conquest and expansion—and he insists throughout that Rome never became a commercial state. If the republic is to be admired—and he clearly considers it a wonder—it is for the single-mindedness with which it pursued aggrandizement, training its citizens in the military virtues, pretending to befriend those to whose aid it came, and conducting its foreign policy with a ruthlessness and cunning unprecedented and never since excelled. For their success in this enterprise, as Machiavelli had acknowledged, the Romans paid with their liberty. The wealth they acquired by conquest corrupted them. Moreover, to achieve victory, they had to increase their manpower; and, to this end, they admitted the most loyal and formidable of their allies to citizenship. Eventually, as their empire grew, they found themselves forced to extend citizenship to everyone in Italy; and Rome thereby lost its ethos as a civic republic of virtue capable of inspiring in its citizens an all-encompassing love of the laws and the fatherland. In addition, to sustain its rule outside the Italian peninsula, Rome had to station large armies abroad, and this required both that it confer on generals and governors stationed far afield for extended periods something approaching despotic power and that it enroll as soldiers propertyless men with no material stake in the existing republican order who were willing to serve in distant parts for long periods of time. That there would be civil wars, that Rome's generals would recruit these soldiers as clients and deploy them against the republic, and that a despotic polity would eventually emerge—this was, Montesquieu leads his readers to recognize, a foregone conclusion.

To these observations, Montesquieu added a stout denial that the "dreadful Tyranny of the Emperors" was in any way an anomaly. It "stemmed," he argues, "from the general spirit of the Romans. Because they fell all of a sudden under an arbitrary Government, & because there was almost no interval between their being in command & their servitude, they were not at all prepared for the transition by a softening of mores. Their ferocious humor remained; the Citizens were treated as they themselves had treated the Enemies they vanquished, & they were governed on the same plan." It was, he suggests, "the continual sight of Gladiators in Combat" that had "made the Romans" so "ferocious." "Accustomed," as they were, "to making sport of human nature in the person of their Children & their Slaves, the Romans could hardly be cognizant of that virtue which we call Humanity" (*CR* 15.16–32).

In his *Considerations on the Romans*, Montesquieu asks us to contemplate "the spectacle of things human," and he invites us to feast our imaginations on the grandeur that had so inspired Machiavelli. "How many wars do we see undertaken in the course of Roman History," he asks, "how much blood being shed, how many Peoples destroyed, how many great actions, how many triumphs, how much policy, how much sagacity, prudence, constancy, courage!" But then, after giving classical Rome its due, Montesquieu asks us to pause and reexamine, with a more critical eye, the trajectory of the imperial republic: "But how did this project for invading all end—a project so well formed, so well sustained, so well completed—except by appeasing the appetite for contentment [*à assouvir le bonheur*] of five or six monsters? What! This Senate had caused the disappearance of so many Kings only to fall itself into the most abject Enslavement to some of its most unworthy Citizens, and to exterminate itself by its own Judgments? One builds up one's power only to see it the better overthrown? Men work to augment their power only to see it, fallen into more fortunate hands, deployed against themselves?" (15.83–92). Gradually, unobtrusively, in this fashion, Montesquieu weans us from the enticement of Rome—as our admiration gives way to horror and disgust. And gradually and unobtrusively, at the same time, he lays the groundwork for the argument that he intended to advance in his *Reflections on Universal Monarchy.*

"It is a question worth raising," Montesquieu writes in the very first sentence of the second part of his triptych, "whether, given the state in which Europe actually subsists, it is possible for a People to maintain over the other peoples an unceasing superiority, as the [ancient] Romans did." For this question, Montesquieu has a ready answer—that "a thing like this has become morally impossible," and in support of this bold and unprecedented conclusion he gives two reasons: first, "innovations in the art of war," such as the introduction of artillery and firearms, "have equalized the strength [*forces*] of all men & consequently that of all Nations" so that none can achieve a permanent advantage; and second, "the *Ius Gentium* has changed, & under today's Laws war is conducted in such a manner that by bankruptcy it ruins above all others those who [initially] possess the greatest advantages" (*RMU* 1.1–9).

The second reason offered needs explication. In Machiavelli's *Art of War*, when the dialogue's protagonist, Fabrizio Colonna, laments the decline of martial virtue in Europe, he traces its disappearance to ancient Rome's elimination of the republics that had once flourished there. Europe's failure to recover after the fall of the Roman empire he explains partly with regard to the difficulty involved in restoring something that has been spoiled. Then he mentions a second, no less salient cause: "the fact that the mode of living today, as a consequence of the Christian religion, does not impose the necessity for self-defense that existed in ancient times." In antiquity, he explains, those conquered were either massacred or enslaved, their territories were seized and sold. In modern times, none of this is done, and victory impoverishes not only the vanquished but the victor as well.[2]

That which Machiavelli regrets Montesquieu celebrates as an historic achievement, guaranteeing that, in modern times, imperial expansion tends to eliminate the conditions prerequisite for the imperial venture's success (1.10–19). To this he adds that commerce has greatly expanded in modern times; that, Machiavelli to the contrary notwithstanding, money has become the sinews of war; and that, by interrupting and obstructing their commerce, war weakens belligerents (2). The remaining chapters of his little treatise Montesquieu devotes to listing and analyzing the abortive attempts made at the achievement of universal monarchy since classical antiquity—including the enterprise of Louis XIV (3–25). It is easy to see why Montesquieu feared that his *Universal Monarchy* would be "interpreted ill."

The point that Montesquieu intended to make is clear enough. We should not want to imitate the Romans, and in his *Considerations on the Romans* he shows us why. And even if for some perverse reason we wanted to imitate the Romans, he then demonstrates in his *Universal Monarchy*, we could not succeed. We are left to wonder what alternative to the policy hitherto followed by states there might in fact be, and it is at this point that Montesquieu for a time intended to direct our attention to the polity that had recently emerged on the other side of the English Channel.

We are not certain how far Montesquieu got in composing what his son later described as his "book on the government of England."[3] We know that his son was correct in asserting that he worked on it in 1733, for much of what later appeared as a chapter in his *Spirit of Laws* under the title "The Constitution of England" (*EL* 2.11.6) survives in manuscript in the handwriting of a secretary who worked for him at that time. It cannot, however, have been Montesquieu's intention to stop where this chapter ends. As we have seen, the common focus of his *Considerations on the Romans* and his *Universal Monarchy* was empire. To round out and finish a work of which they were to form so signal a part, Montesquieu would have had to discuss at some point the imperial policy adopted by the English. He would have been required to demonstrate that, by the very nature of its polity, England was committed to a foreign policy that was, in modern circumstances, viable in a way that the Roman policy consistently followed by the continental powers clearly was not; and, at some point prior to the production of a clean copy of the manuscript of *The Spirit of Laws* in 1741–42, he set out to do just that in a second essay aimed at showing the degree in which English mores, manners, and character derived from England's fundamental laws (3.19.27). When one puts the two essays together, as an enterprising Edinburgh publisher did in English translation some two years after *The Spirit of Laws* first appeared in French,[4] one has an account of eighteenth-century England perfectly suited to what Montesquieu had in mind when he first designed his triptych. Although less historical and consequently much shorter than his essay on Rome, Montesquieu's two-part analysis of the English constitution and of the mores, manners, and character it inspired is no less ambitious in aim and equally comprehensive in scope.

Among other things, in the latter of the two chapters (3.19.27, pp. 577–80), Montesquieu demonstrates that England is — or, at least, ought to be — free from the "malady" that so threatens the powers on the continent with bankruptcy and ruin. In it, he allows us to comprehend how it is that, in modern times, a well-ordered Carthage, such as England, "whose principal strength consists in her credit and commerce," could "render fictive wealth real," equip "her Hannibal" with "as many men as she could buy," and "send them into combat," while Louis XIV's ill-ordered French Rome, "in a spirit of vertigo," patiently awaited "the blows" solely "in order to receive them" and fielded "great armies" only "to see" her "fortresses taken" and her "garrisons deprived of courage, and to languish in a defensive war for which" she had "no capacity at all" (*MP* 645). In it, he also demonstrates that England's prime concerns are its liberty and its commerce, that it has no interest in territorial aggrandizement for its own sake, that its aim in

Europe is to sustain a balance of power, and that its colonial enterprise is aimed almost solely at the extension of its commerce.

If, in 1734, circumstances conspired to prevent Montesquieu from spelling out in full detail the true focus of his critique of the imperial aspirations inspired by Roman grandeur, if they ruled out his making clear the depth of the admiration that he harbored for the peculiar species of commercial republicanism that had emerged in England in the course of the seventeenth century, they did not stop him from doing so in the slightly more relaxed political atmosphere of 1748, when the French philosophe included within his *Spirit of Laws* much of the material that he had suppressed on that earlier date and even contrived therein to juxtapose his beloved England with Rome.[5] Montesquieu published this material in his magnum opus in the hope that he might persuade his compatriots and their neighbors on the continent to abandon the Roman model and imitate England, but he did not succeed. Under the Bourbon monarchs, their republican successors, and Napoleon Bonaparte, France continued along the trajectory that Louis XIV had set out for it; and when France could no longer sustain the quest for universal monarchy, the Germans, then the Russians took up the cause.

The simple fact that Great Britain withstood Napoleon proves, nonetheless, the prescience of Montesquieu. Despite its diminutive size, its limited resources and population, Britain was able to put together, fund, and lead the various coalitions that ultimately inflicted on that would-be Caesar a defeat even more decisive than the one suffered by Louis XIV. Moreover, in 1940, Montesquieu's England stood up to Hitler, and for a time it did so alone. If, in the end, Great Britain did not put together, fund, and lead the coalition that eventually defeated the Nazi colossus, if it did not put together, fund, and lead the alliance that later contained, wore down, and ultimately dismembered the Soviet empire, it was because the British came to be overshadowed by another commercial people, which took "shape," as Montesquieu had predicted, "in the forests" of the New World, a great people endowed by Britain with a "form of government, which brings with it prosperity" (*EL* 3.19.27, p. 578).

This people finds itself compelled to follow the path opened up in the wake of the Glorious Revolution by the nation that contained Louis XIV, defeated Napoleon, and stood up to Hitler. In the Cold War with the Soviet Union—despite the propensity for "inconstancy" and "internal agitation" natural to a polity distinguished, as was its mother country, by a distribution of powers (3.19.27, pp. 579–80), and despite its inclination "to make its political interests give way to the interests of its commerce" in the manner of England (4.20.7)—the United States proved steadfast. Whether today it still possesses the spiritual resources, the prudence, and the resolve requisite if it is to play the role that circumstances have conspired to confer upon it remains an open question. In the last three hundred years, Carthage has repeatedly defeated Rome, but this need not always be the case. After all, at the outset, it was not a foregone conclusion that Louis XIV, Napoleon, Hitler, and Stalin would go down in defeat. On more than one occasion, what Montesquieu described as "morally impossible" very nearly took place.

Such thoughts are sobering. They serve as a timely reminder that we have no grounds for the complacency that we so often evidence. They suggest, moreover, that Montesquieu's assessment of the English polity is a matter of more than mere antiquarian interest. It is in light of what the French philosophe stopped short of saying in 1734 that we should read and ruminate on what he actually said fourteen years thereafter in the masterpiece for which he is generally remembered today.

One

PRINCIPLES

We see next to nothing pertaining to justice & injustice that does not change in quality with a change in climate. Three degrees of Latitude overthrows all jurisprudence. A Meridian decides the truth; with a few years of possession the fundamental laws change. Right has its epochs. It is a ridiculous justice that has a river or a Mountain as its boundary. Truth on this side of the Pyrenees, error on that.

— *Blaise Pascal*

The first eight books of the work that Montesquieu entitled *De l'Esprit des lois* have one distinctive feature.[1] It was there — after a brief introduction dealing with the problematic character of man's place in the universe and with the foundations of man-made law (*EL* 1.1.1–3) — that the French *philosophe* first introduced his novel typology of political forms. His stated purpose for doing so was to trace the *esprit* — the spirit, the mindset, the motive, the impetus, the purpose, the intention, the object, as well as the logic — behind the "infinite diversity of laws & mores" which are to be found in the larger world: his aim thereby was to refute skeptics and cynics inclined to agree with Blaise Pascal,[2] and to demonstrate to the satisfaction of all that there is a method to this apparent madness and that human beings "are not conducted solely [*uniquement*] by their fantasies" when they opt against "uniformity" and do not in every time and place adopt the same weights, the same measures, the same laws, and the same religion (Préf., 6.19.18).

To this end, at the beginning of the second book of this great work, Montesquieu distinguishes, with regard to "nature," three species of government — republics, in which "the people as a body, or only a part of the people, hold the sovereign power"; monarchies, in which "one governs alone, but by laws fixed &

established"; and despotisms, in which "one alone, without law & without regulation [*règle*], draws everything in train by his will & by his caprices" (1.2.1). As Montesquieu's argument unfolds in the course of that book (1.2.2–3), he complicates this assertion by further differentiating aristocratic republics, in which a part of the people hold the sovereignty, from democratic republics, in which the people hold the sovereignty themselves.

The typology deployed by Montesquieu is peculiar in two regards. On the one hand, it abstracts from questions of moral character. Where Xenophon, Plato, Aristotle, Polybius, and their medieval and Renaissance admirers had distinguished kingship from tyranny, aristocracy from oligarchy, and well-ordered popular government from the regime variously called democracy, anarchy, or mob rule and had done so chiefly with an eye to the character of the ruling individual or group,[3] Montesquieu insists that "the form of the constitution" is alone determinative; and when discussing one-man rule, he therefore treats as "accidental" matters such as "the virtues or vices of the prince" and as "external" questions such as "usurpation" and "the succession" (2.11.9).

At the same time, however, that Montesquieu jettisoned the contrast between aristocracy and oligarchy and that between well-ordered and ill-ordered popular government, he reasserted that between well-ordered one-man rule and tyranny. He had long been sensitive to the fact that, with regard to their subjects, European monarchs exercised a species of self-restraint unknown in the Orient (*LP* 99–100/102–3), and he soon came to recognize that this was rooted in the fact that they did not themselves exercise the judicial power (*CR* 16.37–47). In consequence, where Thomas Hobbes had explicitly rejected regime distinctions of the sort espoused by the ancients as not just illusory but dangerous in the extreme,[4] Montesquieu insisted on restoring in the case of monarchy alone something like the classical understanding. But where the ancients and their medieval and Renaissance admirers had juxtaposed the lawful rule of an individual over willing subjects in the interest of those ruled with the lawless rule of an individual over unwilling subjects solely in the interest of the ruler himself, Montesquieu abandoned the focus on interest and consent while reemphasizing the rule of law. If he ultimately eschewed political moralism, he was nonetheless a constitutionalist of sorts; and although he appears at one stage to have been inclined to criticize Machiavelli for confusing despotism and monarchy,[5] in the end, it was from the Florentine, who teaches that one should attend solely to "the effectual truth of the matter," that he took his cue.[6] As he saw it, monarchical government is distinguished from despotism solely by the presence of corporate bodies (*corps*) possessing the privilege of self-government, which is to say, by "the prerogatives of the lords, the clergy, the nobility, & the towns"—above all, by the prerogatives accorded the "powers intermediary, subordinate, & dependent" which cause the monarch to "govern by the fundamental laws." There is, he contends, a sense in which "the nobility" with its esprit de corps "enters . . . into the essence of monarchy," for the "fundamental maxim" of this form of government is: *"no monarch, no nobility; no nobility, no monarch."* Where there is one-man rule in the absence of such a nobility, "one has a despot" on one's hands (*EL* 1.2.4).

PRINCIPES

In the third book of his encyclopedic work, Montesquieu puts flesh on these constitutional bones by introducing a "distinction" which he thinks "very important" and which he describes as "the key to an infinity of laws." There is, he suggests, a "difference between the nature of the government & its principle [*principe*]: its nature is that which makes it such as it is, & its *principe*, that which makes it act. The one is its particular structure, & the other is the human passions that set it in motion" (1.3.1). The principle of democracy is virtue; that of aristocracy is moderation; that of monarchy is honor; and that of despotism is *la crainte* or fear (1.3.2–11). If Montesquieu rivals Aristotle as an analyst of political regimes, it is because he attends to the procedure Plato followed in the eighth and ninth books of *The Republic* and supplements his strictly institutional analysis with an attention to political psychology which gives to his political science a suppleness, a flexibility, a subtlety, and range elsewhere unexcelled in modern times. The bulk of the first eight books of *The Spirit of Laws* is devoted to a consideration of the manner in which the laws and customs reigning within a polity must be framed with an eye not only to the structure of that polity but to the passions setting it in motion (1.4–8). As Montesquieu explains when he first introduces the notion, the "principle" of a polity has "a supreme influence over the laws," and one can see them "flow from it as from a spring [*source*]" (1.1.3).

We would therefore expect that, when Montesquieu suddenly and without warning complicates his typology further by introducing yet another species of government, he would not only discuss the structure of that government but take care to specify its principle and examine in detail the consequences that arise therefrom. After all, in mounting a defense of his *Spirit of Laws* against the charges laid against it by the faculty of theology at the Sorbonne, Montesquieu would later insist that his account therein of "the principles" distinguishing the various forms of government is "of a fruitfulness [*fécondité*] so great" that it can justly be said that these principles "give form to my book almost in its entirety."[7] But when the time comes and Montesquieu turns his attention to the question of "political liberty" in the eleventh book of *The Spirit of Laws*, he has nothing to say concerning the principle animating the new species of government that he describes therein.

His focus is what he terms elsewhere "a republic concealed under the form of a monarchy" (1.5.19, p. 304), and he prefaces its discussion by introducing a category of distinction to which he has hitherto barely alluded (1.4.8): the "object" peculiar to each political community. That "all states have the same object in general, which is to maintain themselves," Montesquieu readily concedes. But he insists as well that "each state has an object that is particular to it."

> Aggrandizement was the object of Rome; war, that of Lacedaemon; religion, that of the Jewish laws; commerce, that of Marseilles; public tranquillity, that of the laws of China; the carrying trade [*navigation*], that of the laws of the Rhodians; natural liberty was the object of public administration [*la police*] among the savages; in general, the delights of the prince was its object in despotic states; his glory & that of the state, its object in monarchies; the independence of each individual is the object of the laws of Poland, & what results from this is the oppression of all.

"There is also," he then adds, "one nation in the world which has for the direct object of its constitution political liberty," and he promises "to examine the principles [*les principes*] on which" this constitution "is founded" (2.11.5). This promise he keeps in the very next chapter by launching into an elaborate discussion of the "beautiful system" constituted by the pertinent nation's constitution and laws (2.11.6, especially p. 407). But neither here nor anywhere else does he tell us what is *the* "principle" and what are "the human passions that set in motion" what turns out to be the government of England.

It is difficult to know what to make of this. It is possible that, when he deals with England's constitutional monarchy in the eleventh book, Montesquieu abandons the mode of analysis that he had made extensive use of when he discussed democracy, aristocracy, monarchy, and despotism in Books Two through Eight. He may, in fact, be implying that it makes no sense to analyze the English polity in terms of "the human passions that set it in motion." But it is equally possible that Montesquieu has deliberately left it to his readers to discover on their own "the principle" exercising "a supreme influence over the laws" of England, which he had himself left unmentioned. At the end of the eleventh book of his magnum opus, Montesquieu remarks that "it is not necessary always to so exhaust a subject that one leaves nothing for the reader to do. The task is not to make him read but to make him think" (2.11.20). To properly explore these two possibilities, we will have to return to the first eight books of *The Spirit of Laws* and consider Montesquieu's political typology as a whole.

VIRTUE AS A PRINCIPLE

If, as Montesquieu more than once suggests, the English polity really is "a republic" of some sort (1.5.19, p. 304; 1.6.3; 2.12.19), and if, as he clearly implies, its government has a popular cast (1.2.4), it should be set in motion by virtue—the principle that animates democratic republics. This seems, however, not to be the case. To begin with, Montesquieu never attributes political virtue to the English: he touches on the subject only in referring to the brief republican experiment that took place after the execution of Charles I. The "impotent efforts" of the English "to establish among themselves democracy" on this occasion he regards as "a fine spectacle," noting that those "who took part in affairs had no virtue" and that the ambition that fueled their rivalries and gave rise to faction produced so "much of movement" and so "many shocks & jerks" that "the people," unable "to find anywhere" the democracy that "they were seeking," eventually "found repose in the very government that had been proscribed" (1.3.3).

Moreover, Montesquieu nowhere suggests that political liberty is the object pursued by democracies and aristocracies. Indeed, he contends that these republics "are not in their nature free states" (2.11.4). And he warns that it is a mistake to look for liberty "in democracies" where "the people seem pretty much to do what they wish" since to do so would be to "confound the power of the people with the liberty of the people" (2.11.2), for "political liberty does not at all consist in doing what one wants" (2.11.3). It is, in any case, "not to be found except" in what he calls "moderate governments"—and not always there. Political liberty, he observes, "is not present except where there is no abuse of power, & it is an eternal experience that every man who has power is drawn to abuse it; he proceeds until he finds the limits." It is in alluding to the human propensity for the abuse of power that he pointedly adds: "Who would say it! Even virtue has a need for limits" (2.11.4).

This claim should give us pause. If virtue has a need for limits, it is because the principle of democratic republicanism can itself become a motive for the abuse of power. It is "a misfortune attached to the human condition," Montesquieu later observes, but one cannot deny the fact:

> Great men who are moderate are rare; & as it is always easier to follow one's strength [*force*] than to arrest it, within the class of superior people, one may

perhaps with greater facility find people extremely virtuous than men extremely wise.

The soul tastes so much delight in dominating other souls; even those who love the good love themselves so strongly that there is no one who is not so unfortunate as to still have reason to doubt his own good intentions: &, in truth, our actions depend on so many things that it is a thousand times easier to do good than to do it well. (6.28.41)

In this passage, Montesquieu describes one dimension of the problem: there is something inherently immoderate and perhaps even tyrannical at the heart of all forms of political idealism and public spiritedness. The other dimension of the problem stems from the nature of political virtue itself.

When Montesquieu speaks of democratic republics, he nearly always has foremost in his mind ancient Rome and the cities of classical Greece. His analysis of these communities and of their customs and laws in terms of constitutional structure and political psychology is, in one crucial regard, at odds with their self-understanding. As I have tried to demonstrate in fine detail elsewhere, the Greeks—and the Romans as well—took political rationality to be the fundamental principle of the classical republican regime. To be precise, their institutions and practices embodied the presumption that, with the proper civic education, human beings can rise to the task of sorting out through public deliberation the character of the advantageous, the just, and the good; and a quarter of a millennium before Aristotle fully articulated what this entailed, they evidenced that they were quite conscious of the fact.[8] Montesquieu stands opposed to the ancients and to those of their civic-minded, humanist admirers in the communes of Renaissance Italy who entertained similar presumptions concerning man's capacity for rational, public speech—for, like Machiavelli,[9] he has next to nothing to say concerning public deliberation. When he speaks of virtue, he is not interested in those qualities of character and intellect that enable the very best citizens (and perhaps even the ordinary citizens at their very best) to transcend petty, private concerns and engage in public deliberation concerning the dictates of justice and the common good. Nor is he concerned with the liberation of reason from passion. In stark contrast with the citizens of the ancient republics, the classical philosophers, and their disciples the Christian theologians,[10] he doubts whether "reason" ever "produces any great effects on the minds of men" (3.19.27, p. 577). In this spirit, he has his protagonist Usbek suggest in the *Persian Letters* that it makes far more sense "to treat man as feeling [*sensible*] than to treat him as reasonable" (*LP* 31.22–34/33). As one would then expect, when Montesquieu mentions virtue, he has in mind the fostering of an irrational, unreasoning passion for equality—for, in his judgment, it is this passion that sets the democratic republic in motion (*EL* 1.5.2–7).

This passion in no way depends on, gives rise to, or is subordinate to anything resembling moral, Christian, or even philosophical virtue as interpreted by Aristotle and his Christian successors, and it is at odds with what Montesquieu calls "moderate" government. It is perfectly possible for a republic to adopt some of the institutional safeguards that the French *philosophe* considers essential to "political liberty"; and as he demonstrates, something of the sort actually happened in classical Rome, which benefited for a time from a distribution of powers between the Senate, the people, and the magistrates highly favorable to a correction of abuses of power, to a tempering and confinement of magisterial authority, and to constitutional government and the rule of law (*CR* 8.92–94, 11.29–31; *EL* 2.11.12–19). But this cannot alter the fact that the democratic republic is not in its "nature" moderate. Popular government is rendered problematic by the fact that, in such a polity, the rulers are subjects at the same time. In a monarchy, and surely also in "a republic concealed under the form of a monarchy" such as the polity which Montesquieu found established in England, "he who causes the laws to be executed" by appointing a public prosecutor "judges himself above the laws," and "one needs less of virtue than in a popular government where he who causes the laws to be executed senses that he must submit to them himself & that he will bear their weight" (1.3.3, 6.8, 2.11.6, pp. 396–99). In a democracy, if civic virtue is lacking among the populace as a whole, the laws will not be enforced—for, in the absence of self-discipline, there will be no discipline at all.

The difficulty arises from the fact that self-discipline is, in Montesquieu's judgment, unnatural. Virtue is not onerous at the outset and then somehow satisfying in the end. It is not what it was for Aristotle—a completion of nature's work, a perfection of the soul.[11] Nor is virtue anything like what Homer (*Il.* 6.208, 9.443) and his successors took it to be: the product of self-assertion on the part of a man who strives "always to be the best [*aristeúein*] and to be superior to others." It, in fact, requires doing violence to oneself: "political virtue" is not an assertion, writes Montesquieu, it "is a renunciation of self"—and this is never pleasant, never satisfying. Virtue is "always a very painful thing" (*EL* 1.4.5).

According to Montesquieu, republican virtue is grounded in a "love of the laws & the fatherland"; it demands "a continual preference for the public interest over one's own"; in its emphasis on equality, which Montesquieu describes as "the soul" of the democratic state, it "restricts ambition to a single desire, to the sole happiness of rendering to the fatherland greater services than the other citizens." To produce this love, to so restrict the scope of ambition, and to inspire in the citizens of a republic the requisite spirit of self-renunciation, one must deploy "the complete power of education" (1.4.5, 5.3, 5). In practice, this tends to require what Montesquieu calls "singular institutions"—of the sort established by the Greeks on Crete and in Thessaly, by the Spartans in Lacedaemon, by William Penn in Pennsylvania, by the Jesuits in Paraguay, by Plato in *The Republic* (1.4.7, 4.23.17), and by the Jews, the early Romans, and, we are told, the Chinese.[12]

The "singular institutions" that Montesquieu has in mind "shock all the received usages by confounding all the virtues," and they "confound" as well "things naturally separate" such as "laws, mores, & manners." By way of illustrating what this entails, Montesquieu invites us to admire "the extent of genius" found in the Spartan lawgiver Lycurgus who, by means of "harsh institutions," instilled a "warlike spirit" into the Lacedaemonians; rendered them "grave, serious, dry, taciturn"; and produced a "people always correcting or being corrected, always giving instruction or being instructed, equally simple & rigid," more inclined "to exercise the virtues among themselves than to accord them [genuine] respect."

> By mixing larceny with the spirit of justice, the harshest slavery with extreme liberty, the most dreadful sentiments with the greatest moderation, he gave stability to the city. He seemed to deprive it of all resources—the arts, commerce, silver, walls: there, one had ambition without the hope of improvement; there, one possessed the natural sentiments without being a child, husband, or father; modesty itself was denied to chastity. By these roads Sparta was conducted to grandeur & glory—& with such an infallibility attending its institutions that one achieved nothing against it by winning battles if one did not succeed thereby in depriving it of its *police* (1.4.6, 3.19.7, 16, 21).

When established in democracies, Montesquieu observes, "singular institutions" of this sort are incompatible with "the confusion, the negligence, the extended affairs of a great people" situated on an extended territory; they find their "place" only "in a petty state" like the cities of ancient Greece where "all the citizens pay a singular attention to one another" and where "one can provide a general education & rear a people as a family" (1.4.7). In "small republics" such as these, especially in those graced with "singular institutions" dictating public supervision of affairs no less private than "the marriages" which take place "between the children of citizens," their "love of the public good can be such that it equals or surpasses every other love" (4.23.7). As Montesquieu had observed in his *Considerations on the Romans*, "there is nothing so powerful as a Republic in which the Laws are observed not out of fear, not because of reason, but by way of passion, as was the case at Rome & Lacedaemon—since there to the wisdom of good Government was joined all the force that faction can possess" (*CR* 4.60–64).

In a large republic, Montesquieu adds in his *Spirit of Laws*, "interests become particular; a man senses then that he can be happy, great, glorious without his fatherland; & soon that he can be great solely on the ruins of his fatherland." One consequence of such a republic's size is that "the common good is sacrificed to a thousand considerations; it is subordinated to the exceptions; it depends on accidents." The situation "in a small" republic is more favorable: there, "the public good is more fully felt, better known, closer to each citizen; the abuses are less extensive there & as a consequence less well protected" (*EL* 1.8.16). Republics, if they are successfully to deploy shame as a reinforcement for the spirit of self-renunciation, must be comparatively simple and exceedingly small.

In such a republic, Montesquieu observes, it is particularly important that the women be closely supervised. "In a popular state," he explains, one ought to look "on public incontinence as the final evil indicating the certainty of a change in the constitution." In consequence, "good legislators there have demanded of women a certain gravity in mores. They have proscribed from their republics not only vice but even the appearance of vice. They have banished even that commerce of gallantry which produces laziness—which causes the women to corrupt even before they have themselves been corrupted, which gives a price to every nothing & lowers the value of what is important, & which causes one to base one's conduct solely on the maxims of ridicule that women understand so well how to establish." In this particular, republics are opposed to monarchies, where women take up "the spirit of liberty" associated with the court, become the arbiters of taste, and cause "vanity" and "luxury" to come into their own. In republics, though "free by law, women are held captive by mores; luxury is banished & with it corruption & vice" (1.7.8–9, 14, 3.19.5–6, 8–9, 12, 14–15, 6.28.22).[13]

Montesquieu takes care to underline the alien character of classical republican institutions, and, like Machiavelli,[14] he traces the change to the rise of Christianity. When the virtue of the ancients was "in full force," he reports, "they did things that we no longer see & which astonish our little souls." If his contemporaries are unable to rise to the same level, it is, he suggests, because the "education" given the ancients "never suffered contradiction" while "we receive three educations different" from and even "contrary" to one another: "that of our fathers, that of our schoolmasters, that of the world. What we are told in the last overthrows the ideas imparted by the first two." In short, there is now "a contrast between the engagements" which arise "from religion" and those which arise "from the world" that "the ancients knew nothing of." This is apparently why the moderns possess such "little souls" (1.4.4).

As should be obvious, here, as in his *Considerations on the Romans*, Montesquieu evidences that he has much in common with his Florentine predecessor. Like Machiavelli, he wants his readers to stand in awe of the spiritedness and the ambition exhibited by the ancients. This is why he writes: "One can never leave the Romans behind. So it is that still today, in their capital, one leaves the new palaces to go in search of the ruins; so it is that the eye which has taken its repose on the flower-strewn grasslands loves to look at the rocks & mountains" (2.11.13). But, in contrast to the author of the *Discourses on Titus Livy*, Montesquieu is also intent that his readers recoil in horror and distaste at the price that the ancients paid for having what he regarded as great souls. "It is necessary," he observes in one chapter, "to regard the Greeks as a society of athletes & warriors." The exercises that they engaged in were "suited to making men harsh & savage." They "excited" in the citizens "but one species of passion: severity, anger, cruelty" (1.4.8). Later, he may begin by remarking that the "love of the fatherland" fostered by the ancient republics "is conducive to goodness in mores" and that "goodness in mores leads to a love of the fatherland," but he goes on to clarify what "goodness in mores" involves by invoking a disturbing analogy: "The less we are able to satisfy our private passions, the more we abandon ourselves to those of a more general nature. Why are monks so fond of their order? Precisely because of those things which make it insupportable. Their rule deprives them of all the things on which the ordinary passions rest: there remains, then, only that passion for the rule which torments them. The more austere the rule, that is, the more it curbs their inclinations, the more strength [*force*] it gives to the one inclination which it leaves them with" (1.5.2). Classical virtue has something in common with Christian virtue: in both cases, Montesquieu contends, the self-renunciation required contains within itself the seeds of an ugly fanaticism. Montesquieu may accept in its broad outlines Machiavelli's account of ancient citizenship and of the aggrandizement that he regarded as its raison d'être — but this does not make him an unabashed admirer of the severity, the cruelty, and the ferocity to which, both agree, it inevitably gives rise. In *The Spirit of Laws*, as in his *Considerations on the Causes of the Greatness of the Romans and their Decline* and his *Reflections on Universal Monarchy in Europe*, Montesquieu's aim is Machiavelli's defeat, and the critique that he directs at ancient republicanism is a crucial part of "the cure" that he has designed for the despotic temptations promoted by what he terms "Machiavellianism."[15]

In his moral and political outlook, Montesquieu has much less in common with the author of *The Prince* and the *Discourses on Livy* than with his fellow

Frenchman Michel de Montaigne.[16] Both men enjoy contemplating "rocks & mountains," but both would prefer to reside in "flower-strewn grasslands." The "beautiful system" admired by Montesquieu for taking political liberty as its "direct object" is not to be found among polities that are not in their nature free states. It must be sought among the forms of government that are intrinsically moderate.

MODERATION IN GOVERNMENT

When he first introduces the notion of "moderate government," Montesquieu insists that it "is able, as much as it wishes & without peril, to relax its springs [*ressorts*]. It maintains itself by its laws & even by its strength [*force*]." Such is not the case, he points out, with despotism, the quintessence of immoderate government—for if there were to appear in such a polity a "good citizen," and if, out of love of country, he were "tempted to relax the springs of the government" and then actually "succeeded" in doing so, "he would run the risk of losing himself, it, the prince, & the empire" as well. In fact, when "the spring [*ressort*]" of this species of government, "which is fear," is no longer present, "all is lost" and "the people no longer have a protector." For, in such a polity, "it is necessary that the people be judged by the laws & the great ones by the whimsy [*la fantaisie*] of the prince; that the head of the least subject be secure while that of the pasha is always exposed." If, when contemplating republics, Montesquieu at times betrays the same inclination "to shudder" that he ostentatiously displays when "speaking of these monstrous governments" (1.3.9, 4.3), it is because republics can only within limits approximate moderation: they cannot without danger relax their springs as much as they wish. Republics and despotic governments thus have this in common: they are fragile; they require apprehension; they must remain tense. "It is necessary," Montesquieu asserts, "that a republic dread something. The fear [*crainte*] of the Persians maintained the laws among the Greeks. Carthage & Rome threatened one another & rendered one another firm. It is a thing singular: the more these states have of security, the more, like waters excessively tranquil, they are subject to corruption" (1.8.5).

Moderate governments can profit from success and relax their springs because they encounter less friction than polities not in their nature moderate. Once set in motion, they possess a momentum all their own; like perpetual-motion machines, they do not run down. "To form a moderate government," Montesquieu tells us, "it is necessary to combine powers, to regulate them, to temper them, to make them act, to give, so to speak, a ballast to one in order to put it in a condition to resist another; this is a masterpiece of legislation, which chance rarely produces & prudence is rarely allowed to produce." It may be more difficult to sustain and stabilize the government of any given despot, but it is much easier to institute despotic government in the first place and to sustain it thereafter. Though it constitutes an assault on human nature (1.2.4, 8.8, 21), despotism is, in a sense, natural. It "jumps up, so to speak, before our eyes; it is uniform throughout: as the passions alone are necessary for its establishment, the whole world is good enough for that" (1.5.14, p. 297). Moreover, where the climate is exceedingly hot and self-discipline and courage are beyond the capacity of man, and where the terrain is unsuited to polities of a size middling or small, no other species of government is possible (3.14.1–3, 15.7, 16.2, 11–12, 17.1–18.5, 19).

In his initial discussion of moderate governments, Montesquieu is coy. For this, there is a reason. "I say it," he will later confess, "& it seems to me that I have composed this work solely to prove it: the spirit of moderation ought to be that of the legislator; the political good, like the moral good, is always to be found between two limits" (6.29.1). Political moderation is, in a sense, Montesquieu's cause. Already, in 1721, when he published his *Persian Letters*, he was prepared to float the notion that the government "most in conformity with Reason" and "most perfect" is "a Government gentle [*doux*]," free from unnecessary "severity," which "moves towards its end with minimal expense" by conducting "men in the manner that accords best with their propensities & inclinations" (*LP* 78.4–10/80).

In *The Spirit of Laws*, Montesquieu's purpose is not simply to describe the political phenomena: description is, in fact, subordinate to prescription throughout. Because Montesquieu is persuaded that "extreme laws," even when deployed "for the good," nearly always "give birth to extreme evil" and that "it is moderation which governs men & not excess" (*EL* 4.22.21 and 22, p. 682), he is eager to teach legislators just how the spirit of moderation can be encouraged within each form of government. Thus, when treating despotism, he is quick to remark that religion, which may be otherwise politically malign, is useful as a check on arbitrary power: "as despotism subjects human nature to frightful evils, the very evil that limits it is a good" (1.2.4).[17] And when speaking of moderate governments, he implies that various polities may qualify. Sometimes he even treats republics as moderate states (1.5.15, 6.9, 15, 8.8), for to suggest that this is so is to justify and encourage their evolution in this direction.

ARISTOCRATIC MODERATION

Where Montesquieu is direct and clear from the outset is in his contention that monarchy, as exemplified by his native France, is moderate. In fact, monarchy would appear to be moderate government par excellence. This polity's moderation is not, however, a consequence of the moderation of the monarch and his nobility. As a "principle," moderation is peculiar to aristocratic republics: it is "the soul of these governments," and it is "founded on virtue"; it does not "come from a cowardice & a laziness of soul." Virtue is required in an aristocracy for the same reasons that it is required in a democracy: "those who are charged with the execution of the laws against their colleagues will sense that they then act against themselves. . . . The nature of this constitution is such that it seems to place the same people under the power of the laws that it exempts from them" (1.3.4).

Virtue is, however, exceedingly difficult to achieve in an aristocracy, for this species of government is "ill-constituted" (1.7.3). In fact, as Montesquieu intimates, it is less a distinct form of government than a defective version of the democratic republic—one that has a certain, unfortunate "connection [*rapport*] with the government of one alone" (3.18.1). When Montesquieu first speaks of this polity, he insists that "the more an aristocracy approaches democracy, the more perfect it is," and that "it becomes less perfect insofar as it approaches monarchy" (1.2.3, p. 247). Later, he intimates that, to the degree that it approaches the government of one alone, aristocratic government exhibits a spirit more despotic than monarchical. Thus, like despotism, it is extremely intolerant of "the satirical writings" that flourish under democracy. "In consequence of the fact that they are ordinarily composed against powerful individuals," these "satirical works" are welcome "in democracy" since there "they flatter the malignity of the people who govern." Within an aristocracy, however, the opposite is the case, for "the magistrates there are little sovereigns who are not sufficiently grand to despise insults." When a barb is aimed at a monarch, it rarely reaches so high, and he can easily laugh it off. "An aristocratic lord is pierced by it through & through" (1.6.15, 2.12.13).

The problematic character of aristocracy is due to the fact that its nature or structure runs counter to the principle required for sustaining it. Put simply, the inequality fundamental to an aristocracy militates against the inculcation of a love of equality. This explains why Montesquieu has absolutely nothing to say concerning the education in virtue given the citizen in an aristocracy.[18] As he will later have occasion to observe, "silence sometimes expresses more than any discourse" can (2.12.12).

Within an aristocracy, because one cannot hope to educate the citizens in virtue, one must rely, instead, on laws with teeth in them, and these must themselves instill "a spirit of moderation" in its rulers and work to ensure that "everyone is as equal as the nature of the government permits." In an aristocratic republic, the nobles may have "riches," but they "are not supposed to spend them," and they become "so accustomed to miserliness that only courtesans can make them give money." As a consequence of the law, these nobles must display "modesty & simplicity of manners": they must "affect no distinction"; they must "confound themselves with the people"; they must "dress like them"; they must "partake of their pleasures"—and thereby make the people "forget their weakness."

Since all of this is contrary to the natural instincts of the well-born, there has to be within an aristocracy, "for a time or forever, a magistrate who makes the nobles tremble." Put bluntly, "this government has need of quite violent springs [*ressorts*]." One consequence, which would otherwise be counter-intuitive, is that there is "less liberty to be found in the republics of Italy" than in the "monarchies" of Montesquieu's Europe, for the former have to resort to "means as violent as the government of the Turks" if they are "to maintain themselves." If these aristocratic republics nonetheless fall short of corresponding "precisely with the despotism of Asia," it is only because "the multitude of the magistrates softens somewhat the magistracy." In Venice, Montesquieu tells us, it is a capital crime to bear arms, and it is necessary "that there be a hidden magistracy"—since the conspiracies "that it punishes, always profound, are formed in secrecy & in silence." For the letters of anonymous accusers, Montesquieu observes, there is "a mouth of stone open in Venice; you could say that it is the mouth of tyranny" (1.2.3, 5.8, 7.3; 2.11.6, pp. 397–98; 3.15.1; 5.26.24). In short, the state that inculcates and enforces the virtue of moderation is anything but moderate itself.

HONOR AS A PRINCIPLE

Although monarchy and aristocracy both embrace inequality, they are, in at least one crucial regard, diametrically opposed: monarchy can be moderate—precisely because within it no one need be such himself. "Monarchical government" can in fact "maintain & sustain itself" without "much in the way of probity," for "the force" possessed by its "laws" is sufficient. Severe self-discipline is not required where "he who causes the laws to be executed judges himself above the laws." If "bad counsel or negligence" prevents the monarch from "causing the laws to be executed, he can easily repair the evil: he need only change his counsel or correct the negligence itself" (1.3.3).

"In monarchies," Montesquieu explains, "policy makes great things happen with as little of virtue as it can, just as in the most beautiful machines, art also employs as little of movement, of forces, of wheels as is possible. The state subsists independently of love of the fatherland, of desire for true glory, of self-renunciation, of the sacrifice of one's dearest interests, & of all those heroic virtues which we find in the ancients & know only from hearing them spoken of." If virtue and moderation can be discarded, it is because in a monarchy "the laws take the place of all these virtues, for which there is no need; the state confers on you a dispensation from them." It is a good thing that monarchies have no need for the virtuous because therein "it is very difficult for the people to be so." Consider, Montesquieu urges, "the miserable character of courtiers. . . . Ambition in idleness, baseness in pride, a desire to enrich oneself without work, an aversion for truth, flattery, treason, perfidy, the abandonment of all one's engagements, contempt for the duties of the citizen, fear of the virtue of the prince, hope looking to his weaknesses, &, more than that, the perpetual ridicule cast on virtue form, I believe, the character of the greatest number of courtiers, as is remarked in all places & times" (1.3.5).

If monarchy can nonetheless produce good government, it is because in it honor "takes the place of the political virtue" found in republics (1.3.6). The honor that Montesquieu has in mind is an artifact: if it gives rise not to civic virtue but to the vices characteristic of courtiers, it is because it is a "false honor," more consonant with "vanity" than with "pride," which demands artificial "preferences & distinctions" and is grounded in "the prejudice of each person & condition" (1.3.6–7, 5.19, 2.19.9, 5.24.6). The consequences of this all-pervasive "prejudice" are paradoxical but undeniable. "In well-regulated monarchies," Montesquieu contends, "everyone will be something like a good citizen while one will rarely find someone who is a good man" (1.3.6). Monarchy he compares to Newton's "system of the universe, where there is a force which ceaselessly repels all bodies from the center & a force of gravity which draws them to it. Honor makes all the parts of the body politic move; it binds them by its own actions; & it happens that each pursues the common good while believing that he is pursuing his own particular interests" (1.3.7).[19] Monarchies are ruled by something like Adam Smith's "invisible hand."[20]

It is essential, Montesquieu emphasizes, that social distinctions be maintained, for these artificial preferences and distinctions, and they alone, can work a transformation in the paltry vanity, which all men possess, and turn it into the socially useful and far more formidable passion for honor, glory, and renown which serves as monarchy's *principe.* Those who urge that, in France, the nobles be allowed to engage in commerce know not what they recommend. "This would be the means for destroying the nobility," he insists, and it confers "no utility on commerce." It is the prospect of advancing from trade to nobility that is the chief motive for engaging in trade. In similar fashion, he adds, there is much to be said for maintaining the distinction between "the estate of the robe" and "the great nobility." The former may lack "the brilliance" of the latter, but it has "all the" requisite "privileges." It may leave individuals in a state of "mediocrity," but the "body" drawn from among its members which serves as a "depository of the laws" basks in "glory." It is an estate "in which one has the means to distinguish oneself only by the achievement of a competency [*suffisance*] & by virtue." It provides one with an "honorable profession, but always lets one see another more distinguished: that of the warrior nobility, who think that, however rich one may be, one's fortune is yet to be made, but that it is shameful to increase one's goods if one has not begun by dissipating them." This latter body is a part of the nation, Montesquieu remarks, "which serves always with the capital of its goods; which, when it is ruined, gives place to another which will serve with its capital in turn; which goes to war in order that no one dare say that it was not there; which, when it has no hope for riches, hopes for honors, & when it does not obtain them, consoles itself because it has acquired honor nonetheless: all these things contribute to the greatness of the realm." If, during the previous two or three centuries, France has steadily increased its power, Montesquieu concludes, it is due to "the goodness of the laws" (4.20.22).[21]

On the face of it, monarchical government would appear to be absolute and entirely unchecked: such was certainly the English view of France. But, according to Montesquieu, monarchical rule is far from arbitrary, and France is "the most beautiful monarchy in the world" (1.5.10). "In states monarchical & moderate," he explains, the logic of absolute sovereignty is frustrated, for "power is limited by that which is its spring or motive [*ressort*]; I mean to say honor, which reigns, like a monarch, over the prince & over the people." Honor reigns, "restrains [*arrête*] the monarch," and thereby limits the exercise of monarchical power — for "honor has its laws & regulations & knows not how to bend," and "it depends on its own caprice & not on that of another." Honor is an essential part of the "ballast" that puts the nobility "in a condition to resist" the court.

By this fact honor is linked with constitutional government: its rules and laws may be as irrational and capricious as honor is itself artificial and false, but, reinforced as they are by human vanity, they do persist; and honor, though it may be replete with "whimsicalities [*bizarreries*]," can therefore "be found only in states where the constitution is fixed & the laws are certain." This explains why a monarchy can relax its springs without danger as much as it wants: its nature or structure and its principle reinforce one another, for the love of honor is born of inequality. Relative to the "nobility," which is monarchy's distinguishing structural feature, "honor is, so to speak, both child & father." In consequence, as a form of government, monarchy is not fragile; it does not require apprehension; it need not remain tense; "it maintains itself by its laws"; and, like a well-made machine, it possesses a "strength [*force*]" all its own (1.2.3; 3.8–10; 5.9, 14, p. 297), for the longing for honor that sets it in motion is in no way painful: it "is favored by the passions & favors them in its turn" (1.4.5).

This false honor is taught "not in the public establishments where one instructs children," but in "the world," and it teaches "three things: 'that it is necessary to introduce into the virtues a certain nobility, into mores a certain frankness, & into manners a certain politeness.'" The pertinent virtues arise from honor itself: they are "always less what one owes others than what one owes oneself: they are not so much what summons us towards our fellow citizens as what distinguishes us from them." With regard to monarchical government, it can be said that "honor, mixing itself through everything, enters into all the modes of thinking & all the manners of feeling & directs even the principles" governing conduct. Under its influence, these become a matter of fashion: "this whimsical [*bizarre*] honor causes the virtues to be only what it wishes & to exist in the manner in which it wishes; on its authority, it sets down rules for everything that is prescribed for us; it extends or limits our duties in accord with its fancy—even though they have their origin in religion, in policy, or in morals." Laws, religion, and honor emphatically prescribe "obedience to the will of the prince," but this same honor restricts royal power, for it "dictates to us that the prince should never prescribe to us an action which dishonors us—since that would render us incapable of serving him" (1.4.2).

Monarchy is distinguished from despotism, Montesquieu insists, less by "the power" accorded the ruler than by "the manner" in which he is obeyed. "In despotic states," he tells us, "the nature of the government demands an extreme obedience." All that matters is "the will of the prince. There is no tempering, and there are no modifications, accommodations, terms, equivalents, negotiations, remonstrances: nothing can be proposed on the grounds that it is as good or better. Man is a creature who obeys a creature who wills." Montesquieu is nowhere so indelicate as to suggest that in a monarchy the prince may be disobeyed. In fact, he asserts the opposite. When he contends that "honor . . . reigns, like a monarch, over the prince & over the people" alike, he merely infers that "from this fact there results certain necessary modifications in the obedience" accorded the prince. It is this alteration in "the manner of obeying" that apparently gives rise to the tempering, the modifications, the accommodations, the terms, the equivalents, the negotiations, the remonstrances, and the propensity to propose alternative policies that typify monarchy, distinguishing it not only from the single-mindedness of despotism but from that of republicanism as well. Throughout, however, Montesquieu insists that, "to whichever side the monarch turns, he prevails, tips the balance, & is obeyed." In short, "the entire difference" distinguishing the two forms of one-man rule is "that, in monarchy, the prince possesses enlightenment [*des lumières*] & the ministers are infinitely more skillful & expert in public affairs than in the despotic state" (1.3.10, 6.4).

Later, Montesquieu indicates by example what he means by the "modifications in the obedience" accorded the prince that are somehow made "necessary" by honor's reign:

> Crillon refused to assassinate the duke of Guise, but he offered to Henry III to go into battle against him. After St. Bartholomew's day, when Charles IX wrote to all the governors to have the Huguenots massacred, the Viscount of Orte [Adrien d'Aspremont], who was commander in Bayonne, wrote back to his king, "Sire, I have found among the inhabitants & the men of war only good citizens, brave soldiers, & not one hangman; for this reason, they & I beg Your Majesty to employ our arms & our lives in things that can be done." This grand & generous courage regarded an act of cowardice as a thing impossible. (1.4.2)

From Montesquieu's perspective, neither refusal counts as disobedience properly understood—for neither was aimed at overthrowing the monarchy or even the prince, and neither posed a challenge to the authority of the French king. In fact, in the very act of refusal, Crillon and the Viscount of Orte gave vital support to all three.

One salutary consequence of the peculiar "manner of obeying" dictated by honor's reign is that in monarchies, as opposed to despotic states, "things are very rarely carried to excess." This arises from the fact that the leading men "fear for themselves; they fear being abandoned." In such a polity, "the intermediary, dependent powers" have almost as profound a stake in the existing constitution as the monarch himself and "consider it an honor to obey a king but regard it as sovereign infamy to share power with the people." Since the nobles "do not want the people to take too much," it is exceedingly "rare that the orders of the state are entirely corrupted. The prince depends on these orders: & the seditious, who have neither the will nor the expectation of overturning the state, neither can nor wish to overturn the prince." Instead, in times of disorder, when aristocratic resistance threatens to take a violent form, "the people who possess wisdom & authority intervene; temperings take place, arrangements are made, corrections are instituted; the laws regain their vigor & make themselves heard." Despotic states are characterized by "revolutions without civil wars," but the histories of the European monarchies are "filled with" the opposite. The histories of these "civil wars" and the conduct of those most responsible for fomenting them prove, as they did in the case of the Fronde, "just how little suspect ought to be the authority which the princes leave to certain orders in return for their service—for, even in their distractedness, the latter long for the laws & their duty, & they retard the ardor & impetuosity of the factious more than they can be of service to them" (1.5.11, 8.9).

A monarch who understands "the great art of ruling" will behave in such a manner as to take advantage of the proclivities of his subjects. Above all else, he will be accessible and easygoing, and he will never forget that, "in our monarchies, all felicity consists in the opinion that the people have of the gentleness [*la douceur*] of the government." "Towards his subjects," Montesquieu remarks, such a prince will "act with candor, frankness, & confidence," for "he who evidences a great deal of uneasiness [*inquiétudes*], suspicion, & fear [*craintes*] is an actor embarrassed & awkward in playing his role." In ordinary circumstances, he will refrain from employing domestic spies, and he will ignore anonymous accusations except where his own safety is at stake and in cases which "cannot suffer the tardiness of ordinary justice." Satirical writings he may prohibit, but he will not treat them as crimes, for "they can amuse the general malignity, console malcontents, diminish envy of those in public office, give to the people the patience to suffer, & make them laugh at their suffering." Such a prince will, however, be quite circumspect in resorting to raillery himself. In moderation, mockery may promote a pleasing familiarity. But when it is biting, it inflicts mortal wounds. A capable monarch will keep in mind the fact that he has it in his power "to make beasts of men & men of beasts" and that his "mode of conduct [*moeurs*] contributes as much to liberty as the laws" themselves. It is "an unskillful minister," Montesquieu remarks, who "always wants to inform you that you are slaves." The king who "loves free souls will have subjects" while he "who loves debased souls will have slaves." He should induce "honor & virtue" to draw near; he should "summon personal merit." At times, he may "even cast his eyes on talent." His task is to "win the heart" but "not imprison the spirit. Let him render himself popular." A wise prince will be "charmed to have subjects for whom honor is dearer than life & no less a motive for fidelity than for courage" (2.12.13, 23–28).

Above all else, Montesquieu insists, the false honor that sets monarchies in motion is significant because it contributes to the rule of law. As we have seen, monarchy is distinguished from despotism by the presence of "powers intermediary, subordinate, & dependent" constituted principally by the nobility. These sustain "the fundamental laws" of the kingdom "against the momentary & capricious will of one alone" by forming "intermediary channels through which power flows." The monarch creates the most important of these "intermediary channels" by delegating judicial responsibility: his "true function is to establish judges & not to judge himself." Were he or his ministers to act as judges them-

selves, Montesquieu observes, "the constitution would be destroyed, the intermediary dependent powers would be annihilated: one would see all the formalities associated with judgments cease; fear would seize all minds [*esprits*]; one
would see pallor on every visage; no longer would there be confidence, honor,
love, security," or even "monarchy" (1.2.4, 6.5–6, 2.11.11). Were he, instead, to
name commissioners to judge a particular case, the result would be no better, arguably worse, and "useless" to boot—for the subterfuge would be transparent,
and he would thereby "attack" and "weaken liberty" more effectively than if he
acted as a judge himself (2.12.22).

   In Montesquieu's France, the most essential of the intermediary dependent
powers are the parlements. These serve as a "depository for the laws," independent of the royal council and "the momentary will of the prince." They exercise
the right of remonstrance: they "announce the laws when they are made"; they
"recall them when they are forgotten"; and they "ceaselessly cause the laws to
come forth from the dust where they are buried" (1.2.4). These bodies, Montesquieu emphasizes, prevent the prince's salutary promptness in executing the
laws from degenerating into haste. They "never better obey than when they proceed tardily & carry into the affairs of the prince that reflection that one can
hardly expect from the lack of enlightenment [*des lumières*] in the court concerning the laws of the state & from the precipitancy of its councils" (1.5.10). It is
with the parlements in mind that Montesquieu writes, "Just as the sea, which
seems to wish to cover the entire earth is brought to a halt by the seaweed &
grasses [*herbes*] & the least bits of sand & gravel found on the shore, so monarchs
whose power seems without limits are brought to a halt by the smallest obstacles
& submit their natural haughtiness [*fierté*] to complaints & entreaty [*prière*]"
(1.2.4).

   The existence of a depository for the laws independent of the prince does
much more than encourage rational policy-making on his part. These bodies
serve as "tribunals." They "render decisions," and these decisions, Montesquieu
asserts, "ought to be preserved; they ought to be a subject for teaching & learning
in order that one may judge here today as one judged here yesterday & the property & the lives of citizens here may be as secure & fixed as the constitution of
the state itself." It is this that Montesquieu celebrates: the "fastidiousness [*déli-
catesse*]" of the judges, the manner in which jurisprudence becomes its own peculiar "art of reasoning," even the fact that confusion creeps in as different judges
rule and suits are ably or poorly defended. Montesquieu admits that in the end
there will be "an infinity of abuses," for these "creep into all that passes through
the hands of men." But he dismisses this as "a necessary evil that the legislator
will correct from time to time as contrary to the spirit of moderate government"

(1.6.1). The crucial fact is that "the formalities of justice" give rise to "the liberty & security of the citizens," for "the pains, the expenses, the delays, even the dangers attendant on justice are the price that each citizen pays for his liberty." In "moderate states," Montesquieu insists, "the head of the least citizen is accorded consideration [*est considérable*]," and "one does not relieve him of his honor & goods except after an extended examination: one does not deprive him of his life except when the fatherland itself attacks it; & it does not launch such an attack without leaving him every possible means for defending" that life (1.6.2). Montesquieu makes much of the fact that monarchy is distinguished from despotism by "the security" that it confers on "the great" (1.6.21). Where Machiavelli was concerned chiefly with the integrity of the state and its success in conquest and war, Montesquieu gives priority to "the security of individuals."[22] It is "in moderate governments," where the obstacles to the abuse of power are many, that "gentleness [*la douceur*] reigns" (1.6.9).

It would be tempting, then, to suppose that the government of England was conceived by Montesquieu as a variant form of monarchy. In more than one passage, he seems to take this for granted (2.9.9, 11.7), and the notion is by no means patently absurd. After all, in England there reigned a king whose ministers saw to the execution of the laws; and though Great Britain was obviously too large to sustain itself as a republic, it possessed a territory of middling size, well suited, so Montesquieu says (1.8.17), to monarchy. Moreover, Montesquieu associates monarchy not only with political moderation, but with liberty as well.

To this hypothesis, however, there are insuperable objections. Quite early on, Montesquieu remarks in passing that "the English, in order to favor liberty, have eliminated all the intermediary powers that formed their monarchy" (1.2.4), and soon thereafter he adds that "the English nobility were interred with Charles I under the debris of the throne" (1.8.9). Nowhere does he even intimate that love of honor is the passion that sets the English polity in motion.[23] England may be, as he puts it, monarchical in disguise—but it is monarchical neither in its nature and structure nor in its principle. It would appear, then, to be sui generis.

Here, we must pause and contemplate another approach, for by a process of elimination we have demonstrated that the English polity cannot be understood in terms of the political typology introduced by Montesquieu with such fanfare at the beginning of his book. Before starting over, before attempting once again to determine whether England's government has a "principle" and just what this "principle" might be, we must consider at length what is revealed by the fact that "political liberty" is this polity's particular "object."

Two

UNEASINESS

We never hold onto the present. We anticipate the future, as if it were too slow in coming, as if we could hasten its course, or we recall the past as if we could arrest its departure as too prompt. We are so imprudent that we wander in times which are not at all our own & think not at all of the only time which belongs to us, & we are so vain that we dream of times which do not exist & let escape without reflection the only time that really subsists. This is because ordinarily the present wounds us. We hide it from our view because it afflicts us, & if it is agreeable to us we regret seeing it escape. We attempt to shore it up with the future & think of arranging things which are not in our power for a time which we have no assurance of reaching.

— Blaise Pascal

In Part Two of *The Spirit of Laws*, Montesquieu makes freedom, rather than virtue, his focus;[1] and there he suggests that, while monarchies may give rise to political liberty, they do not do so in the course of pursuing it. Liberty is, as he demonstrates, an accidental by-product of their pursuit of that polity's "direct object," which is "the glory of the citizens, of the state, & of the prince" (*EL* 2.11.7). In similar fashion, monarchies may achieve moderation by combining, regulating, and tempering powers so that one power possesses the ballast to resist another—but moderation is not that at which they aim. Thus, if the government of France is, in this regard, "a masterpiece of legislation" (1.5.14, p. 297), as it surely is, this fact is largely a matter of chance. After confessing, "I do not believe that there has ever been on this earth a government as well-tempered as that which existed in each part of Europe during the [feudal] period in which" the Gothic monarchy "subsisted," Montesquieu adds that he finds it "a matter for wonder [*admirable*] that the corruption of the government of a conquering people has formed the best species of government that men have been able to imagine" (2.11.8).

One consequence of the fortuitous origin of Europe's monarchies is that they only "approach political liberty more or less." In this regard, England's government would appear to be quite different: if it actually provides for "political liberty"—as, Montesquieu insists, it does—it is because the form of government peculiar to England aims directly at it. English liberty is, at least in some measure, a product of "prudence" rather than "chance" (1.5.14, p. 297; 2.11.7).

Montesquieu prefaces his initial discussion of the English polity with an account of the nature of "liberty," which he carefully distinguishes from "independence" of the sort possessed by those in the state of nature. His point is that the former is much more valuable than the latter. He begins, however, with a puzzling claim—that "liberty," properly understood, consists in "being able to do what one ought to want & in not being constrained to do what one ought not to want." Then Montesquieu explains what this cryptic formula actually means: first, that "liberty is the right to do what the laws permit," and, then, that it is incompatible with genuine independence, for if a man is "able to do what the laws forbid, he no longer has liberty since the others would likewise possess this same power" and obstruct his freedom to do what the laws allow (2.11.3).[2]

To prevent those most likely to strive for this species of independence from being "able to abuse power," Montesquieu soon adds, "it is necessary that in the disposition of things power check power." It is his contention that "a constitution can be such that no one will be constrained to do things that the law does not require or prevented from doing those which the law permits him to do" (2.11.4). This would appear to be the object of the English polity, and it evidently constitutes what Montesquieu has in mind when he devotes the eleventh book of his tome to the laws which form "political liberty in its relation with the constitution" (2.11). The government of England pursues this end chiefly through what eventually came to be called the separation of powers. In its relation with the constitution, political liberty "is formed," we are told, "by a certain distribution of the three powers" (2.12.1). But, as one learns while reading the second part of *The Spirit of Laws*, political liberty can be conceived in two different ways, and the second of these is no less important for understanding the modern predicament than is the first.

TWO CONCEPTS OF POLITICAL LIBERTY

Montesquieu distinguishes "political liberty in its relation with the constitution" from "political liberty in its relation with the citizen." The latter is the sub-

ject of the twelfth book of *The Spirit of Laws*. But because it is the central focus
of Montesquieu's concern, it intrudes on that book's immediate predecessor as
well. "In a citizen," Montesquieu explains therein, "political liberty is that tranquillity of mind [*esprit*] which comes from the opinion that each has of his security." If he is to possess "this liberty, it is necessary that the government be such
that one citizen be unable to fear [*craindre*] another citizen" (2.11.6, p. 397). The
separation of powers is as essential to the elimination of this fear as it is to the
guarantee that "no one will be constrained to do things that the law does not require or prevented from doing those which the law permits him to do."

On the face of it, the two forms of liberty would appear to be inseparable.
Where the executive and the legislative power are united in the hands of a single
individual or corporate body, as they are in despotisms and tend to be in republics, one has reason "to fear [*craindre*]" that the individual or body that
"makes tyrannical laws" will "execute them in a tyrannical manner." In similar
fashion, if "the power of judging" is not somehow "kept separate from the legislative power & the executive power, there is no liberty." If it is united with the
legislative power, "the judge would be the legislator" and the citizen's life and
property would be subject to "arbitrary power." If it is united with the executive
power, "the judge would have the strength [*force*] of an oppressor." If the power
"of making the laws" were united with "that of executing public resolutions &
with that of judging crimes or the disputes of particular citizens," Montesquieu
exclaims, "all would be lost" (2.11.6, p. 397).

After having set up this standard, Montesquieu applies it to the polities he has
earlier described. If "the kingdoms of Europe" tend to be "moderate," we are
told, it is because the prince, who exercises the legislative and the executive
power, leaves the power of judging to his subjects. The unity of the three powers
in the Turkish Sultan produces "a frightful despotism." That same unity causes
there to be "less liberty in the republics of Italy" than in Europe's monarchies:
these governments can sustain themselves only with "means as violent" as those
used by the government of the Turks. As a "witness" Montesquieu summons the
example of Venice with its "state inquisitors & the lion's mouth into which every
informer can at any time throw his accusation by letter," and he mentions the
"tyrannical magistracy of the ephors" at Sparta in the same regard. It was generally true of "the ancient republics," he later notes, that "there was this abuse: that
the people were at the same time judge & accuser." It was generally true that in
these republics "one citizen" could "fear another." Republics can be "despotic"
in more than one way (2.11.6, pp. 397–99, 404). They "are not in their nature free
states" (2.11.4).

Montesquieu's account of the English constitution has an odd tone. Instead of describing, he resorts repeatedly to the language of prescription; and he underlines the point by issuing a disclaimer at the end: "It is not for me to examine whether the English actually enjoy this liberty or not." All that he will assert is that "it is established by their laws" (2.11.6, p. 407). One is left with the impression that his England is less a reality than an ideal type suggestive of the potential inherent in England's laws: one is given the same impression later by his persistent resort to the conditional in describing the contribution of England's laws in forming "the mores, the manners, & the character" of the nation (3.19.27). He is far more concerned with what is likely to happen than with what in fact does. "I will be," he warns, "more attentive to the order of things than to the things themselves" (3.19.1).

Moreover, Montesquieu seems to have his eye as much on the future as on the present or past, and though he betrays an enthusiasm for the political liberty embodied in England's laws, he qualifies this with a denial that it is his intention "to disparage the other governments or to say that this extreme political liberty should serve to mortify those who possess none but one that is moderate." "How could I say that," he exclaims, "I who believe that an excess even of reason is not always desirable & that men better accommodate themselves nearly always to middling things than to extremities?" (2.11.6, p. 407).

Montesquieu's refusal to issue a blanket endorsement of the English example should give us pause—for, however valuable political liberty may be, there may be something wrong with a polity that takes this liberty as its "direct object." In the chapter immediately following the one in which he celebrates the English constitution and then intimates that, for all its virtues, it somehow misses the mark, he adds to his readers' perplexity by singling out for praise "the monarchies which we know." Although, he explains (or perhaps because, we may add), these states "do not have liberty as their direct object," although or perhaps because they aim solely at "the glory of the citizens, the state, & the prince," they manage to instill in their citizens "a spirit of liberty"; and, in such states, this spirit is "able to accomplish things as great & to contribute perhaps as much to happiness as liberty itself" (2.11.7).

There is much in Montesquieu's description of the structure of the English polity which deserves discussion: his defense of the principle of representation, his endorsement of a bicameralism that leaves the initiative to the popularly elected branch and a veto to the hereditary nobility which stands in for the well-to-do, the case that he makes on behalf of a unitary executive armed with a veto and accountable to the legislature for his deeds solely through the principle of ministerial responsibility, the emphasis that he places on the linkage between taxation and representation, and the argument that he advances on behalf of an army of citizen soldiers commanded by the executive but ultimately dependent on the legislature (2.11.6). If our primary focus were "the laws that form political liberty in its relation with the constitution," this would be our principal subject, and we would no doubt have to consider at length Montesquieu's ostentatious silence concerning the polity's territorial constraints.

More revealing, however, of the source of Montesquieu's reservations concerning the English polity is the fact that, when he discusses the English constitution, he singles out for particular attention the power of judging and the criminal law. He argues for fixed judgments determined by statute, and he praises the practice by which defendants help select their panel of jurors.[3] Security and fairness are obviously a concern. But repeatedly another theme thrusts itself into the limelight: Montesquieu's interests seem to be largely psychological. Thus, in praising the jury system, he initially exclaims that "the power of judging" is "so terrible among men," and he then recommends that this power "be attached neither to a certain condition nor to a certain profession" and that it "become, so to speak, invisible & null." If this is the practice, "one does not continually have one's judges before one's eyes; & one fears [*craint*] the magistracy & not the magistrates." In much the same spirit, he adds that the jury should be made up of the peers of the accused so that "he cannot be of the mind that he has fallen into the hands of those inclined to do him violence" (2.11.6, pp. 398–99).

The emphasis placed on "fear" and on the defendant's state of mind is the feature of the argument that should catch and hold our attention. If Montesquieu can distinguish the liberty of the people from the power of the people, it is because he defines "political liberty in its relation with the citizen" in terms of "security, or, at least, the opinion that one has of one's security" (2.12.1–2). If anything, he seems more concerned with sustaining the citizen's "tranquillity of mind" than with sustaining his capacity "to do what the laws permit" him to do (2.11.3–4 and 6, p. 397). This explains why, in the end, he asks his readers to contemplate a paradoxical conclusion: that "it can happen that the constitution will be free & the citizen not" and that "the citizen will be free & the constitution not"; that while "only the disposition of the laws, & even the fundamental laws," can "form liberty in its relation with the constitution," liberty "in its relation with the citizen" can be made to arise "from the mores, from the manners, & from the received examples" prevalent within a political community and that it is less effectively promoted by political arrangements than by "certain civil laws" (2.12.1). It also clarifies why he can claim that "the knowledge which one has acquired in some countries and which one will acquire in others with regard to the surest regulations that one can hold to in criminal judgments interests human kind more than anything else that there is in the world" (2.12.2) and why he devotes so much attention to these regulations (2.12.3–30). And it makes sense of his other-wise inexplicable concern with the psychological impact of taxation and his as-sociation of "duties," such as those "on commodities," that "the people least feel" with both "moderate government" and "the spirit of liberty" (2.13.7–8, 14). If he claims that, "in our monarchies, all felicity consists in the opinion that the peo-ple have of the gentleness [*la douceur*] of the government" (2.12.25), it is because human happiness, and therefore "political liberty in its relation with the citi-zen," is a state of mind.

All of this suggests something about human nature and something about the "principle" of the "republic concealed under the form of a monarchy" that Mon-tesquieu investigated during his extended sojourn in England. If, in contrast with its ancient counterpart, this modern republic can be situated on a quite siz-able territory, as Great Britain is, it is because it requires on the part of its citizens little or no virtue. Nowhere does Montesquieu suggest that "self-renunciation" is required to sustain it. Nor does he even intimate that it demands anything "very painful." And nowhere does he speak of the need to deploy therein "the com-plete power of education." His silence in this regard is explained by the fact that what Montesquieu says of monarchy can be said of England's government as well: it "is favored by the passions & favors them in its turn" (1.4.5). But though the passion that it favors and is favored by is as solid and reliable as the "princi-ple" of monarchy, if not more so, this passion is not the longing for distinction. The "principle" of the modern republic is not honor; it is something very much like fear.[4] When, in 1753, the philosophe François Duverger Véron de Forbon-nais insisted that "the principle" of Montesquieu's England "is terror,"[5] he was not far off the mark.

ENGLISH INQUIÉTUDE

The government of England is not a despotism comparable to the Oriental states that Montesquieu so vehemently despised, but it has an undeniable kin-ship with despotism. It has as its object "political liberty," not "the delights of the prince." But it comprehends this political liberty in terms of the citizen's "opin-ion of his security." Whereas the "despotic state" in China takes as its object "public tranquillity" and other despotisms pursue "tranquillity" as their "aim [*but*]," if not their "object," England's government pursues the individual citi-zen's "tranquillity of mind."[6]

Despotisms sometimes attain their "object"; England's government generally fails to do so. If one were to examine the English constitution solely with regard to its "nature" or "structure," Montesquieu tells us, one would have to conclude that its three separated powers "form a condition of repose or inaction." But, of course, England's government is rarely, if ever, at rest (2.11.6, p. 405). In interpreting this fact, Montesquieu evidences something like an Epicurean understanding of the human condition,[7] comparable to that articulated by Machiavelli.[8] The foundation of the latter's teaching concerning politics is his claim that "all the things of men are in motion and cannot remain fixed." By this he meant to convey something closely akin to what Thomas Hobbes and David Hume had in mind when they subsequently asserted that reason is the slave of the passions. As Machiavelli put it by way of explanation, "the human appetites" are "insatiable"; "by nature" human beings "desire everything," while "by fortune they are allowed to secure little"; and since "nature has created men in such a fashion" that they are "able to desire everything" but not "to secure everything," their "desire is always greater than the power of acquisition [*la potenza dello acquistare*]."[9]

In writing of England, Montesquieu follows Machiavelli's lead—contending that "this nation" is "always inflamed" and that "it is more easily conducted by its passions than by reason, which never produces any great effects on the minds of men" (3.19.27, p. 577). And in speaking of "the three powers," he argues that when, "by the necessary motion of things, they are constrained to move [*aller*], they are forced to move in concert" (2.11.6, p. 405). One cannot say of the English constitution what Montesquieu says of despotism: that it "jumps up, so to speak, before our eyes"; that "it is uniform throughout"; that "the passions alone are necessary for its establishment." The modern republic is, after all, "a masterpiece of legislation," a product of chance and prudent artifice. One can say of it, instead, what, as we have seen (I.1, above), he says of monarchy: that in it, "policy makes great things happen with as little of virtue as it can" and that "just as in the most beautiful machines, art also employs as little of movement, of forces, of wheels as is possible. The state subsists independently of love of the fatherland, of desire for true glory, of self-renunciation, of the sacrifice of one's dearest interests, & of all those heroic virtues which we find in the ancients & know only from hearing them spoken of." Moreover, one can say that, once a modern republic is instituted, "the human passions that set it in motion" are "alone" necessary to sustain it (*EL* 1.3.5 and 5.14, p. 297)—and that the ruling passion that does so is closely akin to the very passion that is responsible for the "establishment" of despotism.

This helps explain, among other things, the tenor of Montesquieu's description of the contribution made by England's "laws" in forming "the mores, the manners, & the character" of the English "nation" (3.19.27). One consequence of the laws' provision of liberty is that "all the passions there are free: hatred, envy, jealousy, the ardor to enrich & distinguish oneself appear to their full extent; & if things were otherwise, the state would be like a man struck down by a malady who has no passions because he has no strength [*forces*]." In a sense, the English citizen is unaccommodated man: like the individual trapped within the state of nature, he is "always independent."[10] He therefore follows "his caprices & his fantasies"; he and his countrymen are inclined "not to care to please anyone," and so "they abandon themselves to their own humors." Frequently, they even switch parties and abandon one set of friends for another, having forgotten "the laws of love & those of hatred" (3.19.27, p. 575).

Precisely because the laws make no distinctions among men, each Englishman "regards himself as a monarch; & men, in that nation," are, in a sense, "confederates rather than fellow citizens." The fact that "no citizen ends up fearing [*craignant*] another" gives the Englishman a king-like "independence" that makes the English as a nation "proud." But, at the same time, "living," as they do, "much among themselves" in a state of "retirement" or "retreat [*retraite*]," they "often find themselves in the midst of those whom they do not know." This renders them "timid," like those men in the state of nature truly graced with independence, but the recognition of "reciprocal fright [*une crainte réciproque*]" does not have on them the effect that it has on men in their natural state: it does not cause them to draw near, to take "pleasure" in the approach of "an animal" of their "own sort," and to become sociable. They are similarly immune to "the charm" of sexual "difference" and to "the natural appeal" which draws women and men to one another even in that aboriginal state, and so, in England, "the women . . . hardly live among the men." By the same token, instead of friendliness and longing, "one sees in" the "eyes" of these Englishmen, "the better part of the time, a strange [*bizarre*] mixture of ill-mannered shame & pride." Their "character" as a "nation" most clearly appears in the products of their minds— which reveal them as "people collected within themselves" who are inclined to "think each entirely on his own" (compare 3.19.27, pp. 582–83, with 1.1.2, 2.11.3, 5.26.15).[11] In short, Montesquieu's Englishman is very much alone.

That so solitary a man should have an "uneasy spirit [*esprit inquiet*]" stands to reason (3.19.27, p. 582). Nor is it surprising that, unprompted by genuine peril or even by false alarm, he should nonetheless "fear [*craint*] the escape of a good" that he "feels," that he "hardly knows," and that "can be hidden from us," and that this "fear [*crainte*]" should "always magnify objects" and render him "uneasy [*inquiet*] in his situation" and inclined to "believe" that he is "in danger even in those moments when" he is "most secure" (3.19.27, pp. 575–76). The liberation of the passions does not give rise to joy. "Political liberty in its relation with the constitution" may well be "established" for the English "by their laws," but this does not mean that they "actually enjoy" what Montesquieu calls "political liberty in its relation with the citizen"—for the latter is constituted by "that tranquillity of mind which comes from the opinion that each has of his security" (2.11.1 and 6, pp. 397, 407), and the English are anything but tranquil of mind.

"Uneasiness [*inquiétude*]" without "a certain object" would appear to be the Englishman's normal state of mind. He is rarely given reason to fear another citizen: fear is not deployed to secure his obedience as it is in a despotism. But he is anxious and fearful nonetheless. Moreover, in such a country, "the majority of those who possess intelligence & wit [*esprit*] would be tormented by that very *esprit*: in the disdain or disgust" that they would feel with regard "to all things, they would be unhappy with so many reasons [*sujets*] not to be so" (3.19.27, pp. 576, 582).

PASCAL, NICOLE, LOCKE, AND MONTESQUIEU

In singling out *inquiétude* as the peculiar disposition of the English, Montesquieu is obliquely addressing an important contemporary debate, which was initiated in the previous century by certain Jansenists in France. The most important contributor to this debate was its instigator Blaise Pascal, the celebrated author of the *Pensées*, who noticed that, in passing, his chosen antagonist Michel de Montaigne had described "*inquiétude* and irresoluteness" as "our leading [*maistresses*] and predominant qualities," and who argued in turn that the only plausible way to make sense of human restlessness—of the profound disproportion between human longing and aspiration, on the one hand, and human grandeur and achievement, on the other—is to explain it, as Augustine had (*Conf.* 1.1), in terms of original sin, man's fallen nature, and his instinctive nostalgia for a repose in union with God that had evidently once been his.[12]

John Locke read the Port-Royal edition of the *Pensées*, and, in his *Essay concerning Human Understanding*, he described Pascal as a "prodigy of Parts."[13] There, he argued, as had Hobbes before him, "that the Philosophers of old did in vain enquire, whether *Summum bonum* consisted in Riches, or bodily Delights, or Virtue, or Contemplation," and in this context, he quipped that "they might have as reasonably disputed, whether the best Relish were to be found in Apples, Plumbs, or Nuts; and have divided themselves into Sects upon it." His point was that "Men may chuse different things, and yet all chuse right, supposing them only like a Company of poor Insects, whereof some are Bees, delighted with Flowers, and their sweetness; others, Beetles, delighted with other kind of Viands."[14] To clarify just why this should be the case, Locke recast Hobbes's conclusion by resorting to formulations introduced by Pascal, who had argued that, as a consequence of the Fall, man lacks tranquillity of soul and a capacity for dwelling in the present and that he is condemned to a life of boredom (*ennui*) and uneasiness (*inquiétude*) relieved only by senseless diversion (*divertissement*). What men have in common, Locke explained, is not an orientation toward the good defined in any concrete way, but "a constant succession of *uneasinesses*," such that "very little part of our life is so vacant from these *uneasinesses*, as to leave us free to the attraction of remoter absent good." Tellingly, Locke rips this characterization of the human condition from its theological context. With regard to the Fall, he is strikingly silent. For him, as for Montaigne, "*uneasiness*" and the irresoluteness attendant upon it are the distinguishing characteristics of mankind as such: for him, in fact, *uneasiness* is the motive for all human action.[15]

In the French translation of *An Essay concerning Human Understanding* that Pierre Coste produced in close collaboration with Locke, *uneasiness* was appropriately rendered by the term originally deployed by Montaigne and Pascal. "By *inquiétude*," Coste remarked, "the author means *the state of a man who is not at ease, the lack of ease & tranquillity in the soul*, which is in this regard purely passive." When he deployed *inquiétude* to translate *uneasiness*, Coste added, he had consistently italicized the French word. Unless one kept in mind precisely what Locke meant by the term, he explained, "it would not be possible to comprehend with exactitude the matters treated in" his crucial chapter "Of Power"—matters which Coste considered "the most important and troubling [*délicates*] in the entire work."[16]

Locke's forceful restatement of Montaigne's broad claims in this regard stirred up considerable discussion, especially among those who spoke French,[17] and Montesquieu was well positioned to contribute to the debate. As one would expect, he owned the French translation of Locke's *Essay*.[18] With the translator, he was personally acquainted (*MP* 1108, 1231, 1441), and he even had occasion to hear him speak concerning the author of that renowned work (1105). Montesquieu's strategic redeployment of the pertinent term in *The Spirit of Laws* is intended to suggest three conclusions: that, while Locke was right to follow Montaigne in wresting the notion from its Augustinian theological context, he had erred in presuming that his countrymen were representative of all mankind; that, while *inquiétude* may, indeed, be natural to man, as a settled disposition it is specific to the citizens who live under a particular form of government; and, most important of all, that the form of government "which has for the direct object of its constitution political liberty" characteristically fails to produce in its citizens the "tranquillity of mind" that constitutes "political liberty in its relation with the citizen."

Montesquieu's point becomes even more obvious when one reads his extended description of the character of the English nation in the context of what he has just written a few pages before concerning his native France. "If there were in the world," he observes, "a nation which had a sociable humor, an openness of heart, a joy in living, a taste, a facility for communicating its thoughts, which was lively, agreeable, playful, sometimes imprudent, often indiscreet; & which had along with this courage, generosity, frankness, a certain sensitivity to honor, it would be necessary not to upset [*gêner*], by the laws, its manners lest one upset its virtues" as well (*EL* 3.19.5). One could certainly not say of the French what Montesquieu says concerning the English: that they evidence so great "a disgust for all things" that "they kill themselves without one being able to imagine any reason that would cause them to do so, that they kill themselves when in the bosom of happiness" (3.14.12–13).

Just why the French should be exempt from *inquiétude* and from suicidal propensities required considerable rumination on Montesquieu's part. That he had closely examined and pondered the acute psychological analysis of human conduct hinted at by Pascal and developed in detail by the latter's friend and disciple Pierre Nicole in his *Essais de morale* there can hardly be doubt. In one passage in his notebooks (*MP* 2064), he cites Nicole's discussion of *amour propre*; in another (464), without mentioning his source, he restates the argument contained therein.

Above all else, Montesquieu was interested in the plasticity of human nature. In this connection, he seems to have paid especially close attention to Nicole's development of the implications of Pascal's description of the transformation worked by the Fall in man's "love for himself [*l'amour pour soi même*]." According to Pascal's account, after the Fall, this self-love, which had once been subordinated to the love of God, remained "alone" in what was a "great soul, capable of an infinite love"; and in the absence of a proper object for human longing, by "extending itself & boiling over into the void that the love of God had left behind," this self-love metamorphosed into the species of vainglory that Pascal, François, duc de La Rochefoucauld, and other French moralists in the seventeenth century called "*l'amour propre*." This had, Pascal contended, predictable consequences, for, in the process of becoming "infinite" in its scope, this self-love became both "criminal & immoderate" and gave rise to "the desire to dominate" others.[19] Then, after sketching what was a more or less conventional Christian account, Pascal went on—in a series of fragments omitted by Nicole and his coeditors from the Port-Royal edition of the *Pensées*—to suggest a paradox: that men in their "grandeur" had somehow learned to "make use of the concupiscence" spawned by *amour propre*; and that, despite the fact that it dictates

that "human beings hate one another," they had managed to deploy concupiscence in such a fashion as "to serve the public good." They had, in fact, "founded
upon & drawn from concupiscence admirable rules of public administration
[*police*], morality, & justice," and they had even succeeded in eliciting from "the
villainous depths" of the human soul, which are "only covered over, not rooted
up" by their efforts, a veritable "picture" and "false image of charity" itself.[20] To
this paradox, Nicole devoted a seminal essay suggesting that Christian charity is
politically and socially superfluous—that, in its absence, thanks to the particular
Providence of God, *l'amour propre* is perfectly capable of providing a foundation
for the proper ordering of civil society, of the political order, and of human life in
this world more generally.

Nicole's inspiration, and no doubt that of Pascal as well, was a passage in
which Saint Augustine dilated on the propensity for human pride (*superbia*) to
imitate the works inspired by Christian charity (*caritas*). It could, he claimed,
cause men to nourish the poor, to fast, and even to suffer martyrdom.[21] At the beginning of his essay, Nicole specifies that, when he speaks of "*l'amour-propre*,"
he has in mind the fact "that man, once corrupted, not only loves himself, but
that he loves himself without limit & without measure; that he loves himself
alone; that he relates everything to himself"; in short, that "he makes himself the
center of everything"; that "he wants to dominate over everything" and desires
"that all creatures occupy themselves with satisfying, praising, & admiring him."
This "disposition," which Nicole attributes to all men, he calls "tyrannical." He
acknowledges that it "renders human beings violent, unjust, cruel, ambitious,
fawning, envious, insolent, & quarrelsome," and he readily concedes that, in the
end, it gives rise to a war of all against all. He merely insists that, in the shocking
manner so famously described by Hobbes, to whom he with approval alludes, in-
strumental reason, animated by *amour-propre* and by nothing else, can provide
the polity with a firm foundation; and he contends that, by way of cupidity and
vanity, *amour-propre*, with its "marvelous dexterity," can promote commerce, encourage civility, and even elicit from men a simulacrum of virtue, as those who
desire security and prosperity are forced by the fear of death and the lust for gain
to embrace justice and "traffic in works, services, favors, civilities," and as those
who desperately crave admiration and love are driven to do admirable things. "In
this way," he writes, "by means of this commerce" among men, "all the needs of
life can in a certain fashion be met without charity being mixed up in it at all."
Indeed, "in States into which charity has made no entry because the true Religion is banned, one can live with as much peace, security, & convenience as if
one were in a Republic of Saints." Nicole is even willing to assert "that to reform
the world in its entirety—which is to say, to banish from it all the vices & every

coarse disorder, & to render man happy in this life here below—it would only be necessary, in the absence of charity, to confer on all an *amour-propre* that is enlightened [*éclairé*], so that they might know how to discern their real interests." If this were done, he concluded, "no matter how corrupt this society would be within, & in the eyes of God, there would be nothing in its outward demeanor that would be better regulated, more civil, more just, more pacific, more decent [*honnête*], & more generous. And what is even more admirable: although this society would be animated & agitated by *l'amour-propre* alone, *l'amour-propre* would not make a public appearance [*paraître*] there; &, although this society would be entirely devoid of charity, one would not see anything anywhere apart from the form & marks of charity."[22]

When he read Pascal and Nicole, Montesquieu appears to have paid little, if any, attention to what these two Jansenists had to say about Providence and the Fall. His concerns were, as Montaigne's and Locke's had been, political and psychological, not theological—and, like La Rochefoucauld, Pierre Bayle, and Bernard Mandeville, he found it easy to rip Nicole's discussion of the achievements of "*amour-propre éclairé*" from its theological context. It was from Nicole, La Rochefoucauld, Bayle, and Mandeville that he derived his remarkable analysis of the salutary role played in monarchies by the ethos of what he insists on calling "false honor."[23]

Nicole's analysis may also have prepared the way for Montesquieu's assimilation and appropriation of another exceedingly important passage in Pascal dealing with the effects on human conduct of *amour propre*, which can be seen to cast light on the psychological foundations of the "sociable humor" so evident among the French. "We are not content with the life that we have in ourselves & in our own being," Pascal observed. "We wish to live an imaginary life in the thinking of others. And to this end we endeavor to show ourselves to advantage [*de paraître*]. We labor incessantly to embellish & preserve this imaginary being & neglect the true one. And if we possess either tranquillity or generosity or loyalty, we hasten to make it known in order to attach these virtues to this being of the imagination; we detach them from ourselves in order to join them to it; & we would willingly be cowards [*poltrons*] in order to acquire the reputation for being valorous." It is, Pascal contended, "a great mark of the nothingness of our own being that we are not satisfied with the one without the other & often renounce the one for the other! For he who would not die to preserve his honor would be infamous."[24]

This discussion of the manner in which *amour propre*, with what Nicole had called its "marvelous dexterity," can produce a species of false consciousness and induce a thoroughgoing forgetfulness of self appears to have fascinated Montesquieu. In its light, at one point in his *Considerations on the Romans*, he paused to ponder the Roman propensity for suicide, which, tellingly, he did not trace to a disgust with life. Instead, he focused on the manner in which "the soul" of a human being can be so "totally preoccupied with the action that it is about to engage in, with the motive determining it, with the danger that it is going to evade that it does not properly see death—since passion makes us feel: it never makes us see." In this context, he remarks on the "many ways" in which "*l'amour propre*, the love of our own conservation, transforms itself," and he observes that it "acts by principles so much opposed to one another [*si contraires*] that it induces us to sacrifice our Being for the love of our Being." We take ourselves so seriously, he explains, "that we consent to cease living by an instinct natural & obscure that causes us to love ourselves more than we love even our lives" (*CR* 12.90–110).

This was not the first such discussion in Montesquieu. Earlier, in his *Persian Letters*, he had applied to his own countrymen this very analysis of the manner in which a capacity for self-forgetting is inherent in *l'amour propre*. There he had had Usbek remark that it is impossible to distinguish "the desire for glory" from "the instinct that all Creatures have for their own conservation."

> It seems that we expand our Being when we find it possible to convey [*porter*] it into the memory of others: it is a new life that we acquire, & for us it becomes as precious as the life that we have received from Heaven.
>
> But just as all men are not equally attached to life, so they are not equally sensitive to glory. This noble passion is always firmly engraved on the Heart: but imagination & education modify it in a thousand ways.
>
> This difference, which is found to distinguish one man from another [*se trouve d'homme à homme*] makes itself felt even more between Peoples [*de Peuple à Peuple*].
>
> One might even posit as a maxim that in each State the desire for glory grows in tandem with the liberty of the Subjects & diminishes with that: glory is never a companion of servitude.

Having made this observation, Usbek then quotes the opinion of "a man of good sense," who had traced the exaggerated French love of glory to the fact that "in France in many respects one is more free than in Persia." It is, he adds, "this fortunate fantasy" that "causes a Frenchman to do with pleasure & gusto [*goût*] what your Sultan is not able to obtain from his Subjects except by placing always before their eyes torments & rewards." This is especially evident in the conduct of French, as opposed to Persian, troops. The armies of the Sultan are "composed of slaves who, being cowardly by nature, do not surmount fear [*la crainte*] of death except in the face of Punishment [*Châtiment*], which produces in the soul a new species of terror & thereby renders it stupefied." French soldiers, in stark contrast, "present themselves for combat [*coups*] with delight & banish fear [*la crainte*] by means of their satisfaction in being superior" (*LP* 87.1–30/89).

In short, one could say of the French two things that Montesquieu never quite says himself in *The Spirit of Laws*: first, that in pursuing "glory" rather than "political liberty" as their "direct object," they become inattentive to their natural insecurity as men; and, second, that the forgetfulness rooted in the "fortunate fantasy" to which they fall prey enables them to cultivate in themselves "a spirit of liberty" (*EL* 2.11.7) and "a tranquillity of mind" which contribute far more to their happiness than the political liberty "established" by England's laws but not "enjoyed" by her citizens (2.11.6, pp. 397, 407). One could say this of the French because it is consistent with Montesquieu's overall argument in the book. One could say it as well because early on, in his notebooks, where he jotted down observations for future consideration, Montesquieu himself said the like.

"The sole advantage that a free people has over another," Montesquieu began, "is the security wherein each is in a position in which the caprice of one alone will not deprive him of his goods or his life." He then added that "a subject people, which has this security, well or badly founded, would be as happy as a free people, the mores otherwise being equal: for mores contribute still more to the happiness of a people than the laws." And in this context he concluded, "This security of one's condition [*état*] is not greater in England than in France" (*MP* 32). All of this helps explain why Montesquieu once remarked that France was made "to live in" and England "to think in."[25] It was his conviction that, as a settled disposition, *inquiétude* is the distinguishing feature of modern republican man.

PARTISANSHIP

Inquiétude is not, however, the principle of Montesquieu's modern republic, for in and of itself uneasiness can do little more than keep a polity on edge. It cannot animate it and give it a definite direction and orientation. Like *amour propre*, *inquiétude* is too shapeless: it is too plastic, too protean, too apt to succumb to whimsy and fashion, too much a creature of circumstance. If it is to assume the status of a political principle, *inquiétude* must undergo a metamorphosis—comparable to the one by which the presence of a nobility with all of its artificial ranks and distinctions transforms *amour propre* into the love of honor, giving to vanity a more precise and stable form. In Montesquieu's England, as we have seen, the laws are primary: they are themselves almost sufficient to give form to the nation's mores, manners, and character (*EL* 3.19.26 and 27, p. 574).

In practice, then, it must be the separation of powers itself, the fundamental law of the English constitution, that transforms the characteristic uneasiness of the English into a passion capable of setting their polity in motion.

England's constitution works this transformation by providing a focus for the *inquiétude* that makes modern republican man so inclined to "fear the escape of a good" that he "feels," that he "hardly knows," and that "can be hidden from us," and so prone to "believe" that he is "in danger even in those moments when" he is "most secure" (3.19.27, pp. 575–76). In the political realm, Montesquieu observes, the characteristic uneasiness of the English gives rise to occasional panic, and the separation of powers gives direction to these popular fears. It does so by way of the partisanship that it fosters.

Partisanship is, in Montesquieu's judgment, the fundamental fact of English life. In consequence, it is with this fact that he begins his analysis of the influence of the laws on English mores, manners, and character: partisanship is the premise from which his argument unfolds. "Given that in this state, there would be two visible powers, the legislative & the executive power," he observes at the outset, "& given that every citizen would have a will of his own & would value his independence according to his own pleasure, the majority of people would have more affection for one of these powers than for the other, since the great number is not ordinarily equitable or sensible enough to hold the two in equal affection." This propensity would only be exacerbated by the fact that the executive had offices in his gift, for his dispensing of patronage would alienate those denied favor as it turned those employed into adherents (3.19.27, p. 575).

"The hatred" existing between the two parties "would endure," Montesquieu tells us, "because it would always be powerless," and it would forever be powerless because "the parties" would be "composed of free men" who would be inclined to switch sides if one party or the other appeared to have "secured too much." The monarch would himself be caught in the toils of partisan strife: "contrary to the ordinary maxims of prudence, he would often be obliged to give his confidence to those who have most offended him & to disgrace those who have best served him, doing out of necessity what other princes do by choice." Not even the historians would escape with their judgment intact: "in states extremely free, they betray the truth on account of their liberty itself, which always produces divisions" such that "each becomes as much the slave of the prejudices of his faction as he would be of a despot" in an absolute monarchy (3.19.27, pp. 575, 583).

Montesquieu finds this spectacle droll but in no way distressing. In a polity so caught up in partisanship, he notes, "every man would, in his way, take part in the administration of the state," and "the constitution would give everyone . . .

political interests." One consequence of this widespread political participation would be that "this nation would love its liberty prodigiously since this liberty would be true." To "defend" its freedom, "it would sacrifice its well-being, its ease, its interests," subjecting itself to taxes that no prince, however absolute, would dare impose, and deploying against its enemies in the form of a national debt owed its own citizens "an immense fictional wealth that the confidence & nature of its government would render real." Another side effect of the party struggle would be that everyone "would speak much of politics," and some would "pass their lives calculating events which, given the nature of things & the caprice of fortune, . . . would hardly submit to calculation." It matters little, Montesquieu intimates, whether "particular individuals reason well or ill" concerning public affairs: in a nation that is free, "it suffices that they reason," for from their reasoning arises "the liberty" that provides them with protection against the unfortunate "effects of this same reasoning" (3.19.27, pp. 577, 582).

In a country governed in this manner, Montesquieu hastens to add, the charges lodged by the party inclined to oppose the executive "would augment even more" than usual "the terrors of the people, who would never know really whether they were in danger or not." The modern republic is, however, superior to its ancient predecessor in that "the legislative power," which is distinct from the people, "has the confidence of the people" and can, in times of crisis, render them calm. "In this fashion," Montesquieu observes, when "the terrors impressed" on the populace lack "a certain object, they would produce nothing but vain clamors & name-calling [*injures*]; & they would have this good effect: that they would stretch all the springs [*ressorts*] of government & render the citizens attentive" (3.19.27, p. 576).

In circumstances more dire, however, the English would comport themselves in a manner reminiscent of the various peoples of ancient Crete—who showed how "healthy principles" can cause even "bad laws" to have "the effect of good." In their zeal "to keep their magistrates in a state of dependence on the laws," the Cretans are said to have "employed a means quite singular: that of *insurrection*." In a procedure "supposed to be in conformity with the law," Montesquieu reports, "one part of the citizenry would rise up, put the magistrates to flight, & oblige them to re-enter private life." One would naturally presume that "such an institution, which established sedition for the purpose of preventing the abuse of power, would . . . overturn [*renverser*] any republic whatsoever," but Montesquieu insists that this was not the case in Crete because "the people possessed the greatest love for the fatherland" (1.8.11).

In England, where the citizens exhibit a love of liberty as prodigious as the patriotism of the citizens of Crete, something quite similar takes place. In his *Per-*

sian Letters, Montesquieu had had Rica observe that in England's historians "one sees liberty constantly spring forth from the fires of discord & of sedition" and that one finds "the Prince always tottering on a throne" which is itself "unshakeable." If the "Nation" is "impatient," this character remarks, it is nonetheless "wise in its very fury" (*LP* 130.30–33/136). In his *Spirit of Laws*, he returns to this theme. If the terrors fanned by the party opposed to the English executive were ever "to appear on the occasion of an overturning [*renversement*] of the fundamental laws," he observes, "they would be muted, lethal, excruciating & produce catastrophes: before long, one would see a frightful calm, during which the whole would unite itself against the power violating the laws." Moreover, if such "disputes took shape on the occasion of a violation of the fundamental laws, & if a foreign power appeared," as happened in 1688, "there would be a revolution, which would change neither the form of the government nor its constitution: for the revolutions to which liberty gives shape are nothing but a confirmation of liberty" (*EL* 3.19.27, p. 576). As Montesquieu remarks elsewhere, the "impatience" characteristic of a people such as the English, "when it is joined with courage," gives rise to an "obstinacy [*l'opiniâtreté*]" that makes a "free nation" well suited "to disconcert the projects of tyranny." If their characteristic restlessness renders the English incapable of taking repose, it renders them vigilant at the same time (3.14.13).

Paradoxically, then, the fact that Englishmen do not "actually enjoy" the sense of "security" and "tranquillity of mind" which Montesquieu describes as "political liberty in its relation with the citizen" helps account for the ethos of political distrust and the spirit of watchfulness and wariness which guarantee that "political liberty in its relation with the constitution" remains "established by their laws" (2.11.6, pp. 397, 407). The partisan conflict inspired by the separation of powers transforms the *inquiétude* characteristic of the English into a vigilance directed against all who might be tempted to encroach on their liberty. This vigilance is the passion that sets the English polity in motion, and it serves as a substitute for the republican virtue that the English need not and generally do not possess.

Here once again we must pause—for our analysis thus far leaves one crucial question unanswered and, in fact, as yet unposed: whether, to what extent, and under what circumstances the spirit of vigilance essential to the modern republic can be sustained.

CORRUPTION

Near the end of the long and elaborate chapter embodying Montesquieu's famous celebration of the virtues of England's constitution, in the paragraph immediately preceding the one in which he suddenly and unexpectedly intimates that the English may not actually "enjoy" the "liberty" that is "established by their laws," the author of *De l'Esprit des lois* advances yet another arresting claim, which attentive early readers found far more disturbing than the reservations suggested by the puzzling distinction that he had drawn between the establishment and the enjoyment of liberty. "Just as all human things come to an end," Montesquieu there observes, "the state of which we speak will lose its liberty; it will perish. Rome, Lacedaemon, & Carthage have in fact perished. This state will perish when the legislative will be more corrupt than the executive power" (2.11.6, p. 407).

The meaning of these cryptic remarks is by no means self-evident. Just as Montesquieu nowhere explicitly discussed "the human passions that set in motion" the English government, so nowhere in his great tome, apart from this one passage, did he explicitly address the question of this particular polity's "corruption." He did, however, devote considerable attention to the species of corruption to which the other forms of government are prone (1.8), and in each and every case, he insisted that what counts as corruption in political affairs is relative to the form of government. "The corruption of each government," he explained, "begins nearly always with that of its principles," and "once the principles of the government are corrupted, the best of its laws become the worst & turn against the state . . . for the strength of the principle drives everything" (1.8.1, 11–12). The source of the pertinent species of corruption need not be internal to each form of government as such, but quite frequently it is.

Monarchy is a case in point. Its principle—grounded, as it is, in vanity—may not seem especially fragile. But, in his *Persian Letters*, Montesquieu had nonetheless had Usbek openly lampoon as a would-be despot on the Oriental model no less an eminence than the late, great Sun King of France (*LP* 22/24, 35/37), and he had also had him describe monarchy more generally as "a violent state tending always to degenerate into a Despotism or a Republic" and then intimate that despotism is the more likely outcome (99.9–16/102). There is no reason to suppose that the future author of *The Spirit of Laws* ever changed his mind in this regard. In the latter work, he took it for granted that there would someday be a "dissolution of monarchies" (*EL* 1.5.11); he made it clear that Spain and Portugal had already suffered "a loss of their laws"; and he indicated that, thanks to Cardinal Richelieu and Louis XIV, France was not far behind (1.2.4). Wherever "the lucrative profession of tax-farmers" is in the process of becoming "an honored profession" (2.13.20), as was the case in France (*LP* 46.33–45/48, 95/98), monarchy is, he warned, in dire straits.

Monarchy's fragility is due in part, Montesquieu observed, to the fact that a polity that has "glory" as its "object" (*EL* 1.4.8) is apt to opt for "war & aggran-dizement," to outgrow its natural limits, and to descend into despotism—as "promptness in decision-making is required to compensate for the distance of the places to which orders are sent," as "fear is required to prevent negligence on the part of the governor or magistrate operating at a great distance," and as "law must be lodged in a single head and must change unceasingly" in response to "accidents," which "multiply in a state in proportion to its magnitude" (1.8.16–17, 19, 2.9.2). Monarchy's fragility is also due in part to the propensity of kings to encroach upon the intermediary powers, confine the authority of the par-lements, seize the judicial power, and gradually deprive "the corporations of their prerogatives" and "the towns of their privileges" (1.8.6). It also has some-thing to do with the fact that, in an age in which the projection of power to an ever increasing degree depends upon the wealth garnered by trade, mon-archies—which rely solely upon a "commerce of luxury" and cannot support the "commerce of economy" required for a vast expansion in trade—find it impossi-ble to compete with mercantile polities of the sort found in Holland and Britain (4.20.4–23, 21.7). But it may owe even more to the fact that, in an age of Enlight-enment, the ethos of "false honor" cannot long be sustained in the face of ridicule.[26]

Democracy is considerably more vulnerable to corruption than monarchy. The self-discipline that it demands is unnatural, and virtue is "always a very painful thing" (1.4.5). In the absence of "singular institutions" of a sort possible only within a small polity (1.4.7, 8.16)—where silver is not proscribed and travel abroad forbidden, where poverty is not the norm, where there is not an "equal di-vision of lands" and there are no sumptuary laws, where the elders are not en-trusted with the powers of censorship—all is soon lost (1.5.3–9, 14, 19; 7.2, 4, 5; 2.12.30, p. 458, n. a; 4.23.21, p. 697; 6.28.22). Moreover, in modern times, Chris-tianity, with its cosmopolitan, otherworldly orientation, rules out the ethos of particularism required to sustain the "love of the laws & the fatherland" in a re-public of virtue (1.4.4). Even, however, in antiquity, even when the proper insti-tutions have been established and the polity has not outgrown the territorial lim-its appropriate to it, democracy—governed as it is by a passion for equality—can easily succumb to "the spirit of extreme equality," and the magistrates, the old, husbands, and fathers can lose their authority and find it impossible to instill the "mores & love of order" requisite for sustaining virtue (1.8.2–3, 16, 3.15.18).

The Roman republic Montesquieu regarded as a special case. It succumbed, he made clear in his *Considerations on the Romans* (I.Pref., above), for all of the usual reasons. It outgrew the limits natural to a virtuous republic. When its Ital-ian allies demanded and eventually received citizenship, it lost its civic ethos;

and, as it grew into an imperial state, it found it necessary to admit into its armies propertyless men with no stake in the established order and to confer on its generals and the governors in its provinces despotic powers.[27] If the republic nonetheless managed to sustain itself in the face of all this for a considerable time, it was, he argued in *The Spirit of Laws*, because of the peculiar distribution of powers between the Senate and the Roman people (*EL* 2.11.12–18). This distribution had, however, one defect. At Rome, the legislative, executive, and judicial powers were "well distributed in relation to the liberty of the constitution" but "not so well distributed in relation to the liberty of the citizen"; and things went awry when the Gracchi successfully exploited the profound popular uneasiness occasioned by the constitution's failure to instill in the citizens that "tranquillity of mind [*esprit*] which comes from the opinion that each has of his security" and persuaded the Romans to deprive "the Senators of the power of judging." Thereafter, Montesquieu explains, "the Senate was no longer able to resist the people," and there resulted from this "ills infinite" in number. The Romans "changed the constitution in a time in which, in the fire of civil discords" occasioned by its expansion, "there was hardly a constitution." At the very moment when the Roman republic most needed the wisdom and resolve that the Senate had evidenced in earlier times—just before Marius first enrolled men lacking property in the Roman army and the Italians began demanding citizenship—the people gravely weakened that body. "At that time," according to Montesquieu, "they shocked the liberty of the constitution in order to favor the liberty of the citizen." What they did not expect is what then took place: "the latter" species of liberty "was lost with the former" (compare 2.11.18, pp. 425–26, with 2.11.6, p. 397). Something of the sort, Montesquieu implies, could happen to England as well.

ENGLAND'S ACHILLES HEEL

The only form of popular government to have survived classical antiquity is an anomaly, for there was a peculiar species of democracy "based" not on virtue instilled by "singular institutions" but "on commerce," instead. Inspired by the commercial ethos, Montesquieu tells us, citizens within this type of democracy quite often display "a spirit of frugality, economy, moderation, industry, wisdom, tranquillity, orderliness, & regularity [*règle*]" (1.5.6). In his judgment, the greatest of the republics to profit from the discipline supplied by the market was not ancient Tyre, Carthage, Corinth, Marseilles, or Rhodes. Nor was it modern Florence, Venice, or Holland. It was England, the only one in their number that was equipped with a fully articulated distribution and separation of powers;[28] and, as we have seen, England, too, was subject to a species of corruption.

Initially, at least, few appear to have taken notice of Montesquieu's acknowledgement of the fragility of England's government and of his puzzling suggestion that it would "perish" when "the legislative" power became "more corrupt than the executive power" (2.11.6, p. 407). But within a year of the book's publication, an Anglo-Irish acquaintance named William Domville, who was then busy on Montesquieu's behalf securing the publication of a corrected edition of *De l'Esprit des lois* in London and arranging for Thomas Nugent to translate the book into English,[29] did write to its author to express dismay at the licentiousness of his own compatriots and to ask whether Montesquieu thought that England was in any immediate danger of succumbing to corruption and thereby losing its liberty.[30]

Montesquieu was not immune to the fears voiced by Domville. As early as 1721, he had evidenced an interest in "the impatient humor" of the English, in the manner in which it underpinned their refusal to give allegiance to a despotic king (*LP* 101/104), and in the peculiar fashion in which "the Historians of England" depicted "liberty arising ceaselessly from the fires of discord & of sedition" in "a Nation" not only "impatient," but "wise in its very fury, which, Mistress of the Sea (a thing hitherto unheard of), mixes Commerce with Empire" (130.30–33/136). Moreover, in what survives from the journal that he kept during his sojourn in England from November 1729 to early 1731, Montesquieu exhibited a keen appreciation for the peculiar advantages of English liberty (*NA* 876, 884), an awareness of its dependence on the delicate balance achieved in the division and distribution of powers between Parliament and the King (884),[31] and genuine shock and dismay at the pervasiveness in England of political corruption. "Here," he wrote in one passage, "money is sovereignly esteemed and honor and virtue are little esteemed." "The English," he sputtered elsewhere, "are no longer worthy of their liberty. They sell it to the King; and if the King were to give it back to them, they would sell it to him again. A minister dreams only of triumphing over his adversary in the lower chamber; and to accomplish this, he would sell England and all the power in the world" (878, 880).

At some point during the same visit, however, Montesquieu appears to have shifted his ground, for there is a passage in his notebooks in which he puzzles over the mysterious process by which "the most corrupt of parliaments" was, nonetheless, the very one "that most assured the public liberty" by passing a bill severely punishing corruption, a bill that hardly anyone then holding public office actually wanted to see become the law of the land (881). Montesquieu appears to have been much impressed by what took place in Parliament on this particular occasion, and there is reason to think that he was no less surprised and delighted by the manner in which a vigilant public forced Sir Robert Walpole in 1733 to withdraw his proposal for an excise tax on wine and tobacco and threatened to drive the great man from office[32] — for it was in that very year, shortly after his return to Paris, that he first drafted the highly laudatory discussion of the English constitution that would appear fifteen years later, in revised form, in his *Spirit of Laws*. Moreover, a year later, when he first published his *Considerations on the Causes of the Greatness of the Romans and their Decline,* he buried within the book what were then two highly controversial claims — that "the Government of England is one of the wisest in Europe," and that its wisdom arises from two closely related circumstances: that "it has a Body which subjects it to continual examination, & which examines itself continually," and that the "errors" of this body "are such that they never last long & are often useful in giving to the Nation a spirit of attentiveness" (CR 8.101–6).

It was to the underpinnings of this argument that Montesquieu returned in the course of preparing a reply to Domville's query. First and foremost, he wanted to reassure his correspondent that "in Europe the last sigh of liberty will be heaved by an Englishman." He also wanted to suggest to him that England's peculiar position within the concert of Europe and the character of its foreign policy conferred on it a capacity and an inclination to conduct its affairs in such a fashion as to "slow down the velocity [*promptitude*]" with which "other nations" made their way to "total collapse [*chute entière*]." And, finally, he wished to draw Domville's attention to the intimate connection between English liberty and English commerce.[33] In pursuing the first and the last of these aims, Montesquieu sketched out in his notebooks in preliminary fashion a series of reflections elaborating what he had come to understand in pondering the political dynamic that had once guided "the most corrupt of parliaments" onto an unintended path (MP 1960).

In assessing the materials Montesquieu jotted down in what served him as a kind of a commonplace book, we must exercise considerable caution. At the head of the collection entitled *Mes pensées* in imitation of Pascal, he affixed a "warning [*avertissement*]" intended to alert future readers with access to his private papers to the fact that the numbered items contained therein were nothing more than "some detached reflections or thoughts that I did not place in my [published] works." "These are," he explained, "ideas which I have not plumbed to the depths [*approfondies*], and I keep them to think them through if and when the occasion presents itself. I carefully refrain from taking responsibility for all the thoughts that are here. I placed them here for the most part because I have not had the time to reflect on them, and I will think about them when I make use of them" (1–3).

This is a warning that we ignore at our own peril. To rely on the material in Montesquieu's notebooks to any great degree, to treat it as more than a supplement sometimes useful for fleshing out themes prominent already in his published works, is to court error—for except in those rare cases in which Montesquieu spells out in his notebooks an idea too controversial to be explicitly addressed and fully explored in his published works, such a procedure could easily result in our giving his passing impressions preference over his considered conclusions, and it invites on the part of his modern students indulgence in a vice to which scholars in all times are quite prone. Left to their own devices, freed from the discipline that Montesquieu as a writer imposes on readers of his published works, and inclined (as is only natural) to concentrate their attention on those of Montesquieu's passing comments which seem most attractive and penetrating, they are led by imperceptible steps to recast the great man's thinking along the lines of their own predilections.

On the face of it, the notes that Montesquieu penned in preparation for writing back to Domville would appear to be undigested or half-digested reflections of just the sort that he warns us against holding him responsible for. If they deserve respectful consideration, nonetheless, it is because we know in their regard what we almost never know with regard to any of the other entries in his *Pensées:* their precise provenance. To be specific, we know when they were written and why; we know that they were composed in the immediate aftermath of the publication of *The Spirit of Laws* and that they constitute an attempt on Montesquieu's part to flesh out and clarify for the purposes of his own understanding the thinking that lies behind an especially cryptic and important passage in his masterwork. As such, even in their half-digested form, they come as close as we are ever likely to get to Montesquieu's final judgment on a matter of considerable and continuing importance, and they can therefore serve as an appropriate occasion for rumination on our part.

Montesquieu begins this draft of his letter to Domville by remarking that it is "good" that England's monarch believes in the stability of the polity and "that the people believe that the foundations on which it is established are subject to disturbance [*peuvent être ébranlés*]": that it is "good" that "the prince renounces the idea of augmenting his authority" while "the people dream of preserving the laws." "I believe, sir," he then explains, "that what will conserve your government is the fact that the people basically have more of virtue than those who represent them." In England, he explains, "the soldier is worth more than his officers, and the people are worth more than their magistrates and those who govern them."

The pay given officers is so great that it seems as if the English wanted to corrupt them, and there are so many ways in which a man can make his fortune in and through government that it seems as if the English really wanted to corrupt their magistrates and representatives. "It is not the same with the whole body of the people," Montesquieu then adds, "and I believe that I have noticed a certain spirit of liberty that always flares up and is not readily extinguished."

Montesquieu acknowledges that corruption plays a role in parliamentary elections, but he denies that it affects the whole—for this species of corruption is limited to localities. Even more to the point: what Parliament lacks in probity, it possesses in what Montesquieu terms "enlightenment [*lumières*]." The attempts of the executive to corrupt individual members of Parliament cannot success-fully be covered up; and however much a given member may wish to be a rogue, he wishes as well to pass himself off as a good man. Indeed, even "those who be-tray their duty hope that the evil that they do will not extend as far as the mem-bers of the contrary party want to make men fear it will." In consequence, the evil that flows from the corruption that does exist is severely constrained.

From Montesquieu's perspective, the crucial fact is that within the populace there is a large and vigorous "middle class [*l'état moyen*]" which "still loves its laws and its liberty." As long as these "middling men [*gens médiocres*] preserve their principles," he avers, "it will be difficult" for England's "constitution to be overthrown." The steadfastness of these middling men is made possible by the fact that England is a mercantile society in which the chief "sources" of "wealth" lie in the private sphere: the ordinary Englishman, intent on making his fortune, looks not to high office, but to "commerce and industry," which are "of such a nature that he who draws on them is unable to enrich himself without enriching many others." Rome was more vulnerable to this species of corruption because it was a martial society and the principal "sources" of its wealth were public and political—"the profits from the levying of tribute and the profits from the pillag-ing of the subject nations." That which enriched an individual Roman impover-ished an infinite number of others. In consequence, Rome was distinguished by extreme wealth and extreme poverty, and whether one possessed the former or was subject to the latter was largely a consequence of the distribution of political power. Rome lacked not only "middling men" but "the spirit" of independence and "of liberty" that, characteristically, they and they alone display. In England, Montesquieu concludes, liberty will be secure as long as "great fortunes . . . are not drawn from military employment and as long as those drawn from civil em-ployment [*l'état civil*] remain moderate" (1960).

To begin to grasp the import of the observations that Montesquieu sketched out in preparation for writing back to his English correspondent, one must re-mind oneself that he is elaborating on his cryptic claim that England will con-tinue to exemplify "political liberty in its relation with the constitution" as long as its legislature is less corrupt than its executive—and that he is doing so in a manner intended to be easily understood by someone conversant, as both he and his correspondent were, with the principles espoused and the vocabulary cus-tomarily deployed by England's radical Whigs and their Country Tory imitators. In this context, therefore, Montesquieu does what he pointedly refrains from do-ing in his book: he attributes "virtue" to the English middle classes. Nowhere, however, does he specify what constitutes this virtue: nowhere does he attribute to these Englishmen a passion for equality or a spirit of self-renunciation; nowhere does he describe the "singular institutions" by which the English pro-vide for their education. Nor could he do so: for, as we have already noted, the "singular institutions" ordinarily necessary for the production of virtue of this sort are incompatible with the spirit of commerce and inconsistent with "the confusion, the negligence, the extended affairs of a great people" possessed of an extended territory. They can be found only in "petty" states, such as the cities of ancient Greece, where "one can provide a general education & rear a people as a family" (*EL* 1.4.6–7). The virtue that Montesquieu celebrates in his discussion of the English middle class amounts, then, to little more than the watchfulness typical of spirited men who are wary lest they be robbed of a prize possession. Di-minished though it may seem, this virtue deserves respect, for, as a political prin-ciple, vigilance is compatible with political moderation in a manner that repub-lican virtue is not, and this spirit is sufficient as a safeguard for sustaining in full vigor the distribution and separation of powers that guarantees the liberty estab-lished by England's laws.[34]

As Montesquieu and his English correspondent are both aware, the source of the pertinent corruption can be found in the military and civil offices and hon-ors that are in the gift of England's executive.[35] These are, as the former readily confesses, exceedingly lucrative, and they can be and frequently are used to in-fluence voting in Parliament. But this public largesse is nothing, he insists, in comparison with the money to be made by private initiative in industry and com-merce; and given the fact that this corruption extends to only a few members of Parliament, that the press and the Opposition are poised to expose and de-nounce it,[36] and that the multitude of those within the electorate who are of middling wealth are beyond corruption's reach, naturally fearful of executive en-croachment, and inclined to be vigilant in the constitution's defense,[37] there is no immediate danger that the legislature will fully succumb to executive influence and that there will for all practical purposes cease to be a separation of powers. Free enterprise provides the foundation for the peculiar species of virtue that sustains English liberty.

In reaching this conclusion, Montesquieu was guided by experience. While in England, as we have seen, he had watched with amazement from the sidelines as "the most corrupt of parliaments" passed a bill severely punishing corruption, and he had taken time to reflect on the political dynamics that had produced a result that virtually no one in Parliament at the time had genuinely desired. Then, from a greater distance, after his return to France, he had observed the excise crisis unfold in 1733, and he had recognized the decisive role played in Walpole's humiliating defeat by great merchants, tradesmen, and retailers aroused to great fury by what they took to be a tyrannical attack on their well-being. The answer to Domville that Montesquieu sketched out in his notebooks was an extended rumination on these two events.

A BRIBE OF SILVER

In Montesquieu's judgment, the legislature within a modern republic would be in serious danger of succumbing fully to executive influence only in the unlikely event that the management of commerce and industry within that republic were somehow, to a very considerable extent, entrusted to the executive. In such a polity, should the populace in general and the middle class in particular ever be beholden to government for their economic well-being, the situation of the citizens would indeed be grim—rather, we must suspect, like the circumstances confronted by their counterparts in a democratic republic in which "the people have been corrupted with a bribe of silver." Where this has taken place, we are told, partisan "intrigues come to an end," the people cease to be passionately involved in the rough and tumble of political life, and they "become cold-blooded" and completely indifferent with regard to public policy. "For silver, they display an affection, but they no longer have any affection for public affairs: without care for the government & concern regarding the proposals it entertains, in tranquillity [*tranquillement*] they await their pay" (1.2.2).

All of this helps explain why, on the very first occasion in which Montesquieu mentions England, he makes two surprising observations: that if you "abolish in a monarchy the prerogatives of the lords, the clergy, the nobility, & the towns," as England's Parliament did, "you will soon have a state popular—or, indeed, a state despotic"; and that the English who, "in order to favor liberty, have eliminated all the intermediary powers which formed their monarchy, . . . have good reason to conserve this liberty"—for, "if they should come to lose it, they would be one of the most fully enslaved peoples on the earth" (1.2.4).[38] In issuing this pointed warning, Montesquieu is doing more than merely reiterating the point that he had advanced earlier in his *Considerations on the Romans* that "there is no authority more absolute than that of the Prince who succeeds a Republic" because such a prince "finds himself in possession of all of the power of a People incapable of putting limits on itself" (CR 15.100–103). In the case of England, as we have seen, there is much more that needs to be said.

The principle of the English polity, the passion that sets it in motion, is by no means unnatural, and it is generally reliable. On more than one occasion in the centuries that followed the appearance of *The Spirit of Laws*, at the time of Napoleon Bonaparte and in the epoch of Adolf Hitler, Montesquieu's prediction that "in Europe the last sigh of liberty will be heaved by an Englishman" was proven apt. But the principle of the English polity is not utterly impervious to corruption. The uneasiness, the fear, the anxiety, the impatience, and the restlessness that contribute to the spirit of obstinacy and vigilance which enables the English to defend their liberty might take another, less salutary, and quite ominous form should they fail, by chance, to succeed in that defense and should their failure in this particular deprive them thereafter of the sense of sturdy independence that has hitherto sustained their courage. Because the modern republic and despotism are in the passions that set them in motion akin, the former can easily degenerate into the latter.

These observations should give us pause—for subsequent history suggests that Montesquieu was overly sanguine in supposing it highly unlikely that modern republics would be inclined to take over or regulate the management of commerce and industry. To understand fully the import of his analysis of the prospects for corruption in the modern republic, we will have to consider the ruminations he inspired on the part of Jean-Jacques Rousseau and Alexis de Tocqueville.

Book Two

THE MODERN REPUBLIC REVISITED

Of all the truths that I have proposed for consideration by the wise, here is the one that is most surprising and cruel. Our Writers all regard as the masterpiece of politics in our century the sciences, the arts, luxury, commerce, the laws, and the other bonds that draw tight among men the knots of society by way of personal interest, placing them in a position of mutual dependence, giving them reciprocal needs and common interests, and obliging each of them to contribute to the happiness of the others in order to provide for his own. These ideas are fine, without a doubt, and they have been presented in a favorable light. But, in examining them with attention and without partiality, one finds much in the advantages that seem at first on offer that is inflated and in need of correction.

— *Jean-Jacques Rousseau*

PREFACE

In 1720 or 1721, shortly before he dispatched his secretary, l'abbé Nicolas Bottereau-Duval, to Amsterdam to find a publisher for his *Lettres persanes*, Montesquieu is said to have approached his old friend Père Pierre-Nicolas Desmolets to ask whether he would be willing to look over the manuscript. Montesquieu's choice of a reader made excellent sense. Desmolets was a Jansenist, a learned man, and a literary critic of some note, who served as librarian for the priests of the Oratory in Paris, and he was known to be exceptionally astute. After complying with Montesquieu's request, he reportedly had three comments to make. He thought that, in publishing the work, his young friend would demonstrate that he had little regard for religion and for the demands of his social position. He feared that a scandal would ensue and would cause its author difficulty and distress, and he predicted that if Montesquieu ignored his advice and published the book, as he surely would, it would "sell like bread."[1]

All three comments were apt. The book's publication did confer upon its author a reputation for impiety; it stirred up a scandal that never fully went away; and it caught the fancy of the reading public. In what was, after all, a first book by an unidentified author initially intent on remaining nameless, there was sufficient interest to justify the publication of eight editions in 1721 and another seventeen before the appearance of Montesquieu's *Spirit of Laws* in October 1748. It was translated into English in 1722 and into Dutch in 1736, and, in English, it was published in three more editions before 1749. It would be fair to say that the *Lettres persanes* enjoyed a *succès de scandale*.

The same cannot be said for Montesquieu's *Considerations on the Causes of the Greatness of the Romans and their Decline*. Had it been published in a single volume alongside his *Reflections on Universal Monarchy in Europe* and a fully fleshed-out version of his little essay on England, it would no doubt have caused a ruckus, and it would quickly have acquired a broad audience thereby. Standing on its own, however, in less than splendid isolation, it seemed for the most part uncontroversial: one might even call it academic. Nonetheless, in 1734, four editions appeared, followed by another eight before 1749. It was translated into English and appeared in three separate editions in 1734, and it was published in Italian the following year. By any ordinary standard, it, too, was a publishing success.

Montesquieu's *Spirit of Laws* was something else again. The work was in a self-evident way serious, and enormous it was as well. One purchased it expecting instruction and not diversion — diverting though it might be. And yet, from the moment of publication, it, too, sold like bread. In the last three months of 1748, two editions were published; in 1749, there appeared eleven more. It was published in English and Italian in 1750, in German in 1752, in Latin in 1755, and in Danish, Dutch, Polish, and Russian not long thereafter. By the end of the century, the work had been published seven times in German, thirty-one times in English, and no less than eighty-four times in the original French. Moreover, in the period subsequent to its publication, *The Spirit of Laws* drove the sales of Montesquieu's other books. Before the century's end, the *Persian Letters* was republished fifty-two more times in French and eight more times in English, and it was translated into German, Polish, and Russian. In the same fifty-two-year period, the *Considerations on the Romans* was republished thirty-two more times in French, seven more times in English, and two more times in Italian, and it was translated into Dutch, Swedish, Polish, Russian, and Greek. To this one can add that, in this period, these two works appeared alongside *The Spirit of Laws* in editions of Montesquieu's complete works no fewer than thirty-six times.[2]

All in all, it would be fair to say that *De l'Esprit des lois* was a publishing phenomenon. It was that, and, of course, it was much, much more. For, as the eventful second half of the eighteenth century began, Montesquieu's great work became the political Bible of learned men and would-be statesmen everywhere in Europe, and beyond. In Britain, it shaped the thinking of Edmund Burke, Edward Gibbon, William Blackstone, Adam Smith, Adam Ferguson, John Robertson, John Millar, Lord Kames, and Dugald Stewart among others,[3] and in America, it inspired the Framers of the Constitution and their opponents, the Anti-Federalists, as well.[4] In Italy, it had a profound effect on Cesare Beccaria,[5] and in Germany, it was fundamental for Georg Wilhelm Friedrich Hegel.[6] In France, it was the starting point for all subsequent political thought.[7] Its influence can hardly be overestimated.[8]

In one particular, however — in a matter near and very dear to Montesquieu's heart — *The Spirit of Laws* was a failure. Initially, to be sure, it had a considerable influence on the thinking of the *parlementaires*, as Montesquieu had evidently hoped that it would.[9] But it did not succeed in making smooth the way for a grad-ual, unobtrusive transformation of the French monarchy in the direction taken by the English polity, as he had also hoped.[10] This was in part due to the folly of the *parlementaires*. Driven by the Jansenists within their midst—and by others of a radical disposition who later emerged, ready to take up and deploy the legal and constitutional arguments that the Jansenists had forged—the parlements consistently overreached, and they eventually persuaded the king and some of his ministers that they were simply obstructionists, intent on crippling the monarchy.[11] The failure of Montesquieu's project owed even more, however, to ineptitude, weakness, and inconsistency on the part of Louis XV; to the practice of intrigue by his mistress, Madame de Pompadour; and to the machinations of the king's ministers and their rivals at court—all of whom failed to recognize that the political order which they had inherited from Louis XIV was exceedingly fragile and that, with or without the cooperation of the parlements, monarchical absolutism could not long be sustained in France.[12]

To get a sense of the opportunity that was squandered in the crucial years sub-sequent to the publication of *The Spirit of Laws*, one need only consult the re-monstrances, which came to be called the *Grandes Remonstrances*, submitted to Louis XVI by the *Cour des aides* on the eve of his coronation in the spring of 1775. Drafted by one of Montesquieu's most outspoken admirers, the great liberal statesman Chrétien-Guillaume Lamoignon de Malesherbes, who had presided over that court for twenty-five years,[13] then approved by his fellow magistrates, it is a breathtaking indictment of the system of governance first articulated by Car-dinal Richelieu and brought to fruition by the Sun King, and it differs from Mon-tesquieu's critique only in its forthright tone and astonishing candor.[14] The ap-parent focus of the *Grandes Remonstrances* was the French system of taxation, which is precisely what one would expect in a document produced by a tax court, and it is with this subject that its authors, in fact, began. Their real focus was, however, the administrative state; and, in the course of a preliminary analy-sis of the various taxes imposed upon the French and of the abuses to which the system of taxation tended to give rise, Malesherbes and his colleagues managed to point to the price the French paid for the monarchy's obsession with military glory, to criticize the farming of taxes, and to attack the *lettres de cachet* as mani-festly unjust. This was, however, no more than a foretaste of what was to come—for the real charge that they wished to lodge was that the system of administration put in place by Richelieu and Louis XIV and further developed under Louis XV had made of the French monarchy an *"Oriental despotism"*; and, in making their case, they openly and bluntly said what Montesquieu had only implied in his *Persian Letters* and *Spirit of Laws* (I.2, above).[15] Because the courts are, in fact, fettered, they claimed, because there is no transparency and the royal administration operates in secrecy at all levels, because the ancient representative institutions of the realm and its provinces have been suppressed or reduced to ciphers, because the cities and the other corporations within France have largely been deprived of their traditional rights of self-governance, the king's ministers, their subordinates, and the tax farmers can operate unjustly without fear of punishment—confident that their master will never learn of their depredations.[16]

Such was their argument; and to clarify its significance, they insisted, as Montesquieu had, that there is more than one kind of one-man rule. When Malesherbes and his colleagues spoke of "*Oriental despotism*," they had in mind a government like the domestic tyranny depicted in the *Persian Letters*, in which Usbek and his eunuchs hold sway over the former's harem.[17] In such a polity, they observed, "absolute & unlimited power" is exercised not solely by "the Sovereign," as is only proper, but also by "every executor of his orders." This, they charged, produces "an intolerable tyranny," and they argued:

> There is an infinite difference between the power exercised by a master, whose real interest is that of his people, & that of a subject, who, made proud by a power for which he was not destined, takes pleasure in aggravating the burdens of his equals. This species of despotism, transmitted by gradation to Ministers of different orders, makes itself felt by every last citizen, so that there is not anyone in the great Empire who can protect himself from it.
>
> The vices of such a government derive both from the constitution & from mores; from the constitution, because the peoples who are subject to it have neither tribunals, nor bodies of law, nor popular representatives. There are no tribunals, for which reason authority is exercised by a single man. There are no fixed & positive laws, for which reason he who has authority in hand enacts laws according to his own lights, which is to say, ordinarily according to his likings. There are no representatives of the people, for which reason the despot of a Province may oppress it against the will & without the knowledge of the Sovereign with an assurance of impunity.

Where such a system of government is in place, they warned, not even "the most just Sovereign" can defend his subjects against abuse. "It would seem," they added, "that such a form of government could not exist in Nations possessing laws, mores, & enlightenment [*lumières*]." In "countries polished, polite, and well-policed [*pays policés*]," even where the power of the sovereign is in principle "absolute," all who are "entrusted with sovereign power [*tous les dépositaires de la puissance souveraine*] should be bridled in three ways: by the laws, by recourse to higher authority, & by public opinion." But "in France, some wish to establish the genuine despotism" typical solely "of countries not polished, polite, and well-policed"—so that "in a Nation exceedingly well instructed, in a century in which the mores are exceedingly gentle [*les plus douces*], we are menaced with that form of government in which the Sovereign cannot be enlightened [*éclairé*], however sincerely he may wish to be."

In keeping with the character of Montesquieu's project—after laying their indictment of a government but recently "introduced into France," which is "more fatal than despotism & worthy of Oriental barbarism, namely the clandestine administration, which, under the eyes of a just Sovereign & in the midst of an enlightened nation, permits injustice to show herself, nay more, to flaunt herself in notorious fashion"—Malesherbes and his colleagues proposed the abolition of what they termed "this despotism of Administrators," and in doing so they insisted that they were not proposing "innovations." They acknowledged, to be sure, that "a very old Monarchy," such as the one in France, was likely to have experienced "revolutions of many sorts," and they briefly surveyed the history of the administration of justice in France, acknowledging that with the spread of literacy within the ruling order certain adjustments had been required, and contending that in the age of print and widespread literacy even greater adjustments were in order. But their basic point was that the traditional resources of the French monarchy were sufficient to meet the challenge—that if venerable institutions, such as the Estates-General, the provincial estates, and government in the municipalities, were fully restored; if they were once more empowered to speak for the nation and its localities and to demand a redress of grievances; if the courts were once again allowed to perform their proper functions without interference; and if transparency were demanded of the royal administration as a whole, it would be possible to reconcile monarchy with justice and weather the storms that, everyone knew, were on the horizon. In effect, without ever deviating from a species of discourse proper to their function as a royal court, Malesherbes and his fellow magistrates argued that France had taken a wrong turn in the seventeenth century, that it could and should have followed a course akin to the one traversed by England, and that it was not too late to correct the grievous error that had been made.[18]

Whether in 1775 it was already too late is a question worth posing. The remonstrances sent to Louis XVI by the *Cour des aides* was by no means the only such document prepared for the king that year.[19] At about the same time, his *contrôleur general*, Anne-Robert-Jacques Turgot, baron of Aulne, had on his desk for review a *Mémoire sur les municipalités* intended for the king, which Turgot's young protégé Pierre Samuel du Pont de Nemours had drafted on his behalf and under his supervision. In it one can find an indictment of the system of administration in France strikingly similar to the one offered by Malesherbes and his colleagues. But to remedy the evils identified therein, Turgot did not call for a revivification of the ancient constitution of France.

Although he was a close friend of Malesherbes, the *contrôleur general* of France was a man of an entirely different disposition. Like Malesherbes, he was on very good terms with the philosophes. But born, as he was, the third son in a Norman family belonging from time immemorial to the nobility of the sword and that of the robe, Turgot had been, as was the custom, destined for the church; and the years that he had spent studying theology had given him an astonishing capacity for abstraction and had in other ways contributed to his peculiar turn of mind. His first intellectual contributions were two Latin discourses delivered at the Sorbonne in the course of performing his duties as prior over the assemblies of his fellow students of theology. In the first, which he delivered on 3 July 1750 at the age of twenty-three, he traced through history the advantages in this world conferred on the human race by the establishment of Christianity. In the second, delivered on 11 December of that same year, he reviewed the successive advances of the human mind — outlining a scheme of secular history closely akin to the account of salvation history developed by Jacques-Bénigne Bossuet some seventy years before in his *Discourse on Universal History*, arguing for the inevitability of human progress on the basis of an appropriation and redeployment of the four-stages theory of the development of civilization and of the history of commerce limned in *The Spirit of Laws* (EL 3.18.8–31, 4.20–21),[20] and describing the mechanism by which the inexhaustible neediness of man could be expected to assure his advancement.[21] What Montesquieu had treated as an adventitious unfolding, favorable to political liberty and to government and public policy on the English model, his rebellious young disciple considered, in effect, providential;[22] and, in later years, his firm faith in the processes that purportedly guarantee man's moral and intellectual progress rendered Turgot oblivious to the perils associated with a concentration of power that had haunted Montesquieu and that persistently worried Malesherbes.

For a time, after his father's death — when his inheritance of a competence allowed him to leave the Sorbonne, abandon the clerical calling, and remove the mask that he had been forced to don — Turgot was associated with the Parlement de Paris and with the administration of justice more generally. Subsequently, he did yeoman service as Intendant at Limoges for thirteen long years, and over the course of time — initially under the influence of Jacques Claude Marie Vincent, marquis de Gournay, and later under that of Physiocrats, such as François Quesnay — he became an economist of very great brilliance. He anticipated Adam Smith in his recognition that when left to its own devices, the market functions as a self-regulating mechanism, exploiting the local knowledge of those partici-pant in it to set prices and allocate resources in a manner far more intelligent and efficient than is possible for any central authority; and he actually surpassed the Scot and anticipated Joseph Schumpeter in his profound appreciation for the crucial role that entrepreneurship plays in organizing production and fostering transformative growth.[23]

In these years as well, Turgot became a devotee of rational administration, a friend to absolute popular sovereignty, and an advocate of undivided govern-ment. He was not a supporter of "legal despotism" in the manner of Victor de Ri-queti, marquis de Mirabeau, and the Physiocrats, as is generally supposed. In fact, he doubted whether despotism was in any way compatible with enlighten-ment, and there is good reason to believe that, privately, he thought republican-ism—with its propensity to promote a salutary exchange of information between the central authorities and the localities—far more favorable to rational admin-istration and popular enlightenment than monarchy in any form. Moreover, he did not share his friend Gournay's admiration for England. The form of govern-ment that Montesquieu most admired, Turgot despised. As he made clear in a fa-mous letter written to Richard Price, in which he heaped obloquy on the consti-tutions newly established in the fledgling American states, he had no patience at all with institutions—such as bicameralism, checks and balances, and the sepa-ration of powers—which were designed to divide and disperse power, to encour-age extended deliberation, to promote negotiation, and to safeguard the rule of law, for in these devices he discerned an insuperable obstacle to what, he thought, matters in politics most: the direct rule of unfettered reason in the mak-ing of policy.[24]

Not surprisingly, then, Turgot was perfectly comfortable in exercising the au-thority conferred on ministers by the monarchical absolutism championed by Cardinal Richelieu, Louis XIV, and their successors. To tempering, modifica-tions, accommodations, terms, equivalents, negotiations, and remonstrances, he was decidedly averse. In the short run, he hoped to put to good use what his friend Malesherbes had denounced as "this despotism of Administrators," and it is this intention which informed the document that he had Dupont de Nemours prepare for the king in 1775. "Give me five years of despotism," he is said to have prayed, "and France will be free."[25]

Like many another veteran of the royal administration—and in his family they were legion—Turgot was unfriendly to aristocratic privilege, utterly indifferent to corporate liberties, hostile to private foundations, impatient with tradition, and contemptuous of the conviction, articulated by Montesquieu and generally shared by the *parlementaires*,[26] that a sharp break with the past would thoroughly and perhaps permanently unsettle the realm.[27] In the *Mémoire sur les municipalités,* he not only denied that France had a proper constitution: he intimated that the existing representative institutions should be uprooted in their entirety; and, in their place, he advocated the establishment of a hierarchy of local, provincial, and national representative assemblies based solely on the distribution of property and designed not for the purpose of revitalizing local self-government but as an instrument of consultation in service to a system of rational administration and taxation desperately short on the local knowledge it required.[28] In his impatience, in his willingness to abandon tradition without a thought, and in his eagerness to cast aside and replace existing institutions, Turgot anticipated the posture that would later be adopted by his disciple Marie Jean Antoine Nicolas Caritat, marquis de Condorcet, and he laid the foundations for the criticism that the latter would eventually direct at Montesquieu.[29]

In favoring a profound rupture with the past, Turgot was not alone. By 1775, another, no less radical opinion of an altogether different sort was also in circulation. For, in that same year, Guillaume-Joseph Saige first published the *Catéchisme du citoyen,* in which he called for the institutionalization in France of a political regime, grounded solely on the principle of popular sovereignty, under which primacy would be accorded the Third Estate.[30]

The proposals advanced by Turgot and Saige were reflective of a sea change in public opinion that had quite recently occurred.[31] Four years before, in 1771, at the instigation of a chancellor, René-Nicolas-Charles-Augustin de Maupeou, who found it utterly impossible to manage the *parlementaires,* Louis XV had summarily abolished the various parlements, exiled the magistrates, deprived them of their offices, and replaced the old courts with new ones, more limited in their prerogatives and staffed by men known to be reliable who could easily be dismissed from office if they proved to be obstreperous.[32] In carrying out what can only be described as a coup d'état, the king undoubtedly acted within his rights. He was, after all, absolute. But, in cavalierly sweeping aside the intermediary powers that had for centuries been thought—in no way by Montesquieu alone—to distinguish a monarchy that abided by the law from a lawless despotism in which a single individual monopolized the legislative, executive, and judicial powers, Louis unwittingly crossed a line. Had he been alive, Montesquieu would have lamented that the king had "shocked" the "nation's way of thinking" thereby, and he would have warned that there was danger that this would instill in the governed "the opinion" that they lived under a "tyranny" (3.19.3). But, of course, Montesquieu was dead; and so, in his absence, his great admirer Malesherbes and the latter's colleagues on the *Cour des aides* took the occasion to make precisely the same point and to hint, as a number of the provincial parlements had already done,[33] that, under the circumstances, nothing short of a summoning of the Estates-General could dispel this damaging opinion. The remonstrance that they published at this time served, however, only to ensure the suppression of the *Cour des aides* and the exile of those who had issued it; and in the aftermath of Maupeou's ill-advised coup d'état, precisely as Malesherbes and his colleagues had warned, "first principles, which are the foundation of the authority of Sovereigns & of the obedience of Peoples,"[34] and other matters of state that had always seemed settled and beyond discussion, became for the first time the subject of a dangerous public debate.[35]

In a letter thought by some to be apocryphal,[36] which purports to have been written by Malesherbes' friend Louise Florence Pétronille Tardieu d'Esclavelles, marquise d'Épinay, in the immediate aftermath of what quickly came to be called the revolution of Maupeou, we encounter the following observation: "It is certain that, since the establishment of the French monarchy, this discussion of authority, or rather of power, has existed between the king and the Parlement. This very indecision forms part of the monarchical constitution—since, if one decides the question in favor of the king, all the consequences which result from this make him a despot in absolute terms [*absolument*]. If one decides in favor of the Parlement, the king in effect has no more authority than the king of England; and so, in one fashion or another, in deciding the question, one changes the constitution of the State." Moreover, the letter continues, the strident public debate that followed Maupeou's coup represents "an irreparable evil," opening up for examination and judgment the very foundations of "the constitution of the State" and calling into question what it pointedly refers to as "the theology of administration." Its author then goes on to express a fear that "the enlightenment [*les lumières*]" which the people of France would acquire in the course of this debate would give rise to "pity, terror, courage, and indignation"; that it would inspire in them a "taste for martyrdom"; and that it would "a little sooner, a little later, produce revolutions."[37] Even if not penned at the time by the marquise d'Épinay, even if forged decades thereafter by an author in a position to profit from hindsight, these reflections are nonetheless astute.

The philosophe Denis Diderot responded to the same event with a set of observations more striking yet. He was not an admirer of the parlements. He described them to Catherine the Great as "Gothic in their usages, opposed to every good reform, too much enslaved to forms, intolerant, bigoted, superstitious, jealous of the priest, and hostile to the philosopher," but he did not welcome their destruction. This was, he insisted, "a very great misfortune," which resulted in the substitution of a collection of malefactors, sycophants, wretches, and ignoramuses for men rendered "illustrious by the place they occupied, by their birth, their connections, their fortune, their importance, their great experience of affairs, if not their enlightenment." As a consequence, he added, the French nation had become "disconsolate—and with reason. There was," he explained, "a great spider's web between the head of the despot and our eyes, on which there appeared a great image of liberty adored by the multitude. Among us, those endowed with clear sight [*les clairvoyants*] had long before looked through the little holes in the web, and they knew perfectly well what there was behind. The web has now been torn away, and tyranny is on public display."[38] When they dismantled the parlements, Maupeou and Louis XV failed to grasp the import of Montesquieu's observation that "when power shocks" the *esprit général* of a people, "it shocks itself & brings itself of necessity to a halt" (CR 22.207–15); and as Malesherbes and his colleagues pointed out at the time, thereby they unthinkingly subverted the foundations in France of monarchical rule.

At the same time, by shunting aside the ancient depositories of the laws, the king and Maupeou dealt the authority of tradition itself a near-fatal blow; and by demonstrating that, in its central features, the ancestral constitution of France could simply be dispensed with if and when the king saw fit, they opened the floodgates for others, such as Turgot and Saige, to indulge in an abstract political speculation concerning the country's future that was fully capable of contemplating the wholesale elimination of Montesquieu's intermediary bodies and even a change of regime. Upon becoming king, Louis XVI could exile Maupeou and restore the old parlements, and this he promptly did. But he was not in a position to make ordinary Frenchmen forget what had taken place. The spell that had sustained the monarchy was broken: it could not be restored. In 1775, had he been exceptionally adept, Louis might have been able to carry out a reform, respectful of tradition, along the lines suggested by Malesherbes and his fellow magistrates, and such a reform might have provided a lasting framework for legitimate government and rational, efficient policy-making in France. But it is by no means certain that this was a viable option, even then.

In the event, for perfectly understandable reasons, this inexperienced, twenty-year-old king chose to follow what must have seemed at the time a far less risky course, and so he attempted, in vain, to prevent the publication of the remonstrances presented to him by Malesherbes and his colleagues, and he refrained from adopting the radical program recommended therein—until, to be sure, the year 1789, when he found himself forced by parlements once again grown recalcitrant and by a general collapse in public confidence to choose between declaring a state bankruptcy and summoning the Estates-General. And when, in due course, he did make a halting attempt to implement something like the program that the magistrates had suggested fourteen years before, he did so in circumstances far less propitious than those from which he might have profited at the very beginning of his reign.[39]

Of the regents, kings, and ministers who ruled France in the wake of Louis XIV's death in 1715, it could be said that they rarely, if ever, missed an opportunity to miss an opportunity. But they were hardly alone in bearing responsibility for the paralysis that afflicted the French monarchy. To the ultimate failure of the ingenious political strategy that he had devised, even Montesquieu can be seen to have contributed his mite. The picture that he drew of English society at the end of the third book of *De l'Esprit des lois* was certainly sober and arguably just, and it is a tribute to his integrity as a thinker (*EL* 3.19.27). But it was also uninspiring, to say the least; and given Montesquieu's political intentions, inspiring is precisely what it needed to be.[40] Moreover, despite Montesquieu's assiduous efforts to achieve the opposite effect, the account that he gave of early Rome in his *Considerations on the Romans* and that of the ancient Greek *pólis* that he proffered in Part One of his *Spirit of Laws* excited profound admiration on the part of many of his readers, and it intensified in France and elsewhere the already existing, nascent enthusiasm for classical antiquity that he had evidently hoped to dispel. It is not fortuitous that in the speeches they gave in defense of virtuous republicanism during the French Revolution, Maximilien François Marie Isidore de Robespierre and Louis Antoine Léon de Saint Just cited Montesquieu more often than any other political thinker.[41]

In looking to Montesquieu's description of the ancient republics for political inspiration, these two Jacobins were, in fact, following what was already then a well-worn path.[42] Among the very first to have exploited the *Considerations on the Romans* and *The Spirit of Laws* in this fashion was a music teacher and aspiring composer from Geneva, then as yet little known, who had been hired in or shortly before 1746 by Louise-Marie-Madeleine Dupin, the wealthy and spectacularly beautiful wife of the tax farmer Claude Dupin, to serve as her secretary. In this capacity, he had been made to read and abstract for his employer selections from the travel literature of the age as well as works by Plato, Jean Bodin, Hugo Grotius, Thomas Hobbes, John Locke, and the like; and in this capacity, he would also be made to work his way through Montesquieu's new book.

At the very end of 1748, or early in 1749, the two Dupins purchased and perused the first edition of *De l'Esprit des lois*. The work's author they knew well. From time to time, like Voltaire and the other luminaries of the day, Montesquieu had come to dine. What they found between the covers of the two volumes of his book, however, they did not much like. Claude Dupin was annoyed by the fierce criticism that Montesquieu had directed at tax farmers (I.2, above); Madame Dupin found his various discussions of female behavior—in classical antiquity, England, France, the tropics, and elsewhere (I.2, above; *EL* 3.16, 19.5–6, 8–9, 12, 14, 27; 6.28.22)—offensive in the extreme; and they were both outraged by what they rightly took to be an attack on the French monarchy. Without delay, Claude Dupin set out—with strong encouragement and aid from his wife, and with help from a number of their associates—to compose a reply; and to this end, he asked her secretary to read Montesquieu's magnum opus with care and to take detailed notes, which he dutifully did.

These notes—hundreds of pages as yet unpublished—languish in the Bibliothèque municipale in Bordeaux largely unremarked,[43] mainly because they are precisely what they purport to be: a more or less accurate abstract of large parts of Montesquieu's text taken down with an eye to the interests of others. Neither they nor the two books on the subject written by Dupin are generally thought to reflect the thinking of the note-taker.[44] But the existence of these notes in the handwriting of Jean-Jacques Rousseau does prove that in 1751, when he first caught the public eye and achieved a measure of notoriety with his *Discourse on the Sciences and the Arts*, and in 1755, when he brought forth his celebrated *Discourse on the Origin and Foundations of Inequality among Men*, this enfant terrible was as closely familiar with the elaborate argument presented in *De l'Esprit des lois* as was anyone in Europe, apart from its author.

The existence of these notes also suggests a possibility rarely even canvassed by scholars: that the abrupt and unanticipated, resolutely political turn taken in October 1749 by this ambitious thirty-seven-year-old was occasioned, above all else, by his *Auseinandersetzung* with Montesquieu's great book.[45] As we shall soon see, it is *The Spirit of Laws*, more than any other work, that provides the context within which one can best understand Rousseau's instigation of what turned out to be a profound and lasting revolution in political thought.

The Enlightenment Indicted

Every man who occupies himself in developing talents which are agreeable wants to please, to be admired, and he wishes to be admired more than anyone else. . . . From this is born, on the one side, refinements of taste and *politesse*; vile and base flattery; cares seductive, insidious, childish, which, in the long run, diminish the soul and corrupt the heart; and on the other side, jealousies, rivalries, the renowned hatreds of artists, perfidious calumny, duplicity, treachery, and every element in vice which is most cowardly and odious.

—*Jean-Jacques Rousseau*

At 7:30 A.M. on 24 July 1749, a young writer of great ambition and promise was arrested at his apartment in Paris. Subsequently, he was interrogated, and—after having perjured himself by denying under oath that he was the author of various incendiary works that, everyone knew, he had in fact composed—he was imprisoned in the dungeons at the château of Vincennes outside Paris. A month later, apparently at the instigation of Voltaire's mistress, who happened to be the sister of his jailer, he was released from his cell, given comfortable quarters in the château, and allowed to roam the park, receive visitors, and hold court. There, while under house arrest, he amused himself by translating Plato's *Apology of Socrates*. There he remained until the prospective publisher of the *Encyclopédie, ou Dictionnaire raisonné des sciences, des arts, et des métiers*, which this writer was about to launch in collaboration with Jean Le Rond d'Alembert, intervened on his behalf with the authorities. And there, until his final release on 3 November, Denis Diderot was visited with some frequency by his closest friend, the hard-working secretary of that transcendent beauty Madame Dupin.[1]

Jean-Jacques Rousseau was then, as always, impecunious, and it was his custom to make the six-mile journey to Vincennes on foot. Often, he brought some-thing with him to read on the road. "One day," he tells us in his *Confessions*, "I took the *Mercure de France*, and while walking and perusing it, I stumbled on the question proposed by the Academy of Dijon for the following year's prize competition: Whether the progress of the sciences and the arts has contributed to corrupting or purifying morals? At the instant that I read this, I saw another universe and became another man" (C 8.350–51).[2]

Elsewhere, Rousseau gave an even more arresting account of what happened that fateful October day:

> If ever anything resembled a sudden inspiration, it is the movement produced in me by reading this advertisement; at once I felt my mind dazzled by a thou-sand lights; crowds of lively ideas presented themselves to me at the same time with a force and confusion which hurled me into inexpressible turmoil.
>
> I feel my head seized by a dizziness similar to inebriation. A violent palpita-tion oppresses me, turns my stomach [*souleve ma poitrine*]. Not being able to breathe while walking, I let myself fall under the trees along the avenue, and there I passed a half hour in such an agitation that when I got up I perceived that the entire front of my shirt was damp with tears that I had not felt while I was shedding them. . . . Had I ever been able to write a quarter of that which I saw and felt under that tree, with what clarity would I have made visible all the contradictions of the social system, with what force would I have exposed all the abuses of our institutions, with what simplicity would I have demonstrated that man is naturally good and that it is by institutions alone that men have be-come wicked. All that I have been able to retain of the crowds of great truths which came to me as an illumination in a quarter-hour under that tree has been weakly scattered in my three chief works, which is to say, the first dis-course, that on inequality, and the treatise on education, which three works are inseparable and together form a single whole.

On the spot, Rousseau tells us, he wrote down the so-called prosopopeia of Fabri-cius;[3] and when he arrived at Vincennes, he not only showed his friend the ad-vertisement in the *Mercure de France*: he told him what had happened on the road to Vincennes and had him read what he had composed—and Diderot en-couraged him to expand upon the prosopopeia and to enter the competition for the prize offered by the Academy of Dijon (8.351).

How much of this is true is uncertain. That Rousseau came upon the perti-nent advertisement that day and that Diderot encouraged his candidacy for the prize is clear enough, as is the fact that the latter was genuinely amused at the prospect that, while he was himself busy composing the prospectus for a massive encyclopedia dedicated to promoting the sciences and the arts, his closest friend would be hard at work in a distant corner of Paris developing his argument that progress of this sort would serve only to corrupt morals and bring misery on men. We know as well that Rousseau submitted his entry to the academy at some point prior to 1 April 1750 and that his success in the competition was announced on 9 July 1750; that Diderot did what he could to help his friend to capitalize on his victory in the prize competition by arranging for the publication of his *Discourse on the Sciences and the Arts*; and that Rousseau's friend Guillaume-Thomas-François, abbé Raynal, who had become editor of the *Mercure de France* that very year, went to great lengths in 1751, after the little book had come out, to make its argument the talk of Paris. But the story that, like Paul on the road to Damascus, Rousseau experienced a revelation of sorts that October day may be a product of the latter's well-known propensity for self-dramatization. Years later, a number of those who knew both men reported that Diderot had told them that it was, in fact, he who first conceived of the notion that, in answering the question posed by the Academy of Dijon, Rousseau should take the part of a contrarian.[4]

To this brief account, one other fact can be added—that even if Rousseau told the truth in these accounts and nothing but the truth, he did not divulge the truth in its entirety. Among other things, in his various autobiographical writings, he deliberately concealed the fact that he had spent a great many hours in the months immediately preceding that October day reading Montesquieu's *De l'Esprit des lois*, taking copious notes, and helping Claude Dupin with the first of the two replies he penned.[5] At no time did he expressly acknowledge the full scope of his intellectual debt to the author of that great work—which was, as we shall soon see, profound.[6]

A SOURCE OF ILLUMINATION

It would be easy to prove that Montesquieu and Rousseau were opposed. The former was a proponent of enlightenment; the latter was its preeminent critic. The older man was friendly to commercial society; the younger man was hostile. The Frenchman was intent on dispelling the allure of classical republicanism; the Genevan did everything that he could to restore and enhance its allure. All of this is true, and it is exceedingly important, but it is also in one crucial particular misleading. For the arguments that Rousseau deployed against enlightenment and commercial society and those that he presented on behalf of ancient Sparta and early republican Rome were for the most part borrowed from Montesquieu's *Spirit of Laws*.

Rousseau was a polemicist; for the most part, in *De l'Esprit des lois*, Montesquieu was not. The latter's aim was objectivity and impartiality, and to this

end, in assessing the various forms of government and the divers modes of subsistence, he took great care to describe them in all their complexity and to de-
lineate the advantages and disadvantages attendant on each. Although he was
highly critical of the ancient city, as we have seen (I.Pref., 1, above), he was also
perfectly willing to acknowledge that, with its demise, something very impressive
of great value was forever lost. When the virtue of the ancients was "in full force,"
he concedes, "they did things that we no longer see & which astonish our little
souls" (*EL* 1.4.4). It is this which explains his passing reference to "the dregs &
the corruption" that typify what he calls "modern times" (1.4.6).

Montesquieu was a proponent of modern science, but he was prepared to concede that "the speculative sciences render men savage" (1.4.8). Similarly, though
he favored commerce, Montesquieu acknowledged that its advantages come at
a price. It may "cure destructive prejudices" and give rise to "gentle [*douces*]
mores." But, by the same token, it "corrupts pure mores" (4.20.1). He had visited
Holland, and at first he had been taken aback.[7] "In countries," he observed,

> where one is affected solely by the spirit of commerce, we see that one traffics
> in every human action and in all the moral virtues: the smallest things, those
> which humanity demands, are there done or given for money.
>
> The spirit of commerce produces in men a certain sentiment of exact jus-
> tice, opposed on one side to brigandage and on the other to those moral virtues
> that cause one not always to discuss one's interests with rigidity and that enable
> one to neglect them for those of others.

Commerce may render nations "reciprocally dependent" and thereby promote
peace. But, Montesquieu admits, if "the spirit of commerce unites nations, it
does not unite individuals at the same time." It makes of them rivals and sets
them at odds (4.20.2). It promotes a "communication between peoples" (4.21.5)
and causes "knowledge of the mores of all the nations to penetrate everywhere"
(4.20.1), but in the process it dissolves intimacy at the local level, and it produces
estrangement thereby (1.4.6).[8] And though he valued politeness and celebrated
it as a French achievement, Montesquieu nonetheless described it frankly, in
unfavorable terms, as an outward, artificial, insincere display of flattery suited to
promoting "the vices of others" (3.19.16).

In similar fashion, while Montesquieu marveled at the "commerce of luxury"
typical of monarchies and welcomed the great cities to which it and the "commerce of economy" typical of modern republics gave rise (4.20–21), he was perfectly willing to concede the drawbacks that city life brings with it. In Paris, his
Usbek reports, "liberty & equality reign." There, one may be distinguished by
"Birth, Virtue, even merit displayed in war," but, "however brilliant" one's ori-

gins and attainments "may be," these "do not save a man from the crowd, in which he is confounded. Jealousy of rank is there unknown. It is said that in Paris the man who holds first place is he who has the best horses for his Coach" (*LP* 86.1–4/88). In consequence, among the Parisians, there appears an "ardor for work" and a "passion for self-enrichment" that "passes from condition to condition, all the way from the Artisans to the Great," for "no one likes being poorer than the one he sees immediately below him." Paris presents itself as a city where "interest" is revealed as "the greatest Monarch on the earth." There, "you will see a man who has enough to live on until the day of judgment, who works without ceasing, & risks shortening his days, to amass, says he, enough on which to live" (103.45–60/106). There, in short, you will see none but the bourgeois.

Montesquieu was extremely sensitive to the consequences of this development. "The more there are of men together," he wrote, "the more vain they are and the more they sense the birth in themselves of the desire to draw attention to themselves in trivial ways [*par de petites choses*]. If they are so great in number that the majority are unknown to one another, the desire to distinguish oneself redoubles because there is more hope of success. Luxury gives this hope; each assumes the marks of the condition given precedence to his own. But as a consequence of the wish to distinguish themselves all become equal, and one distinguishes oneself no longer: where everyone wishes to make himself noticed, no one is noticed at all." And he did not conceal from his readers the fact that from all of this there comes "a general discomfort [*une incommodité générale*]" rooted in a mismatch "between needs and means," and thereby he allows his readers to discern that the ancient Greeks were, indeed, right to suspect that, if they failed to proscribe "silver" and to outlaw commerce, these would "multiply infinitely their desires and supplant [*suppléer*] nature, which has given us very limited means for irritating our passions and for corrupting one another." As a consequence of the vanity to which commerce gives rise, Montesquieu readily admits, men who live in towns and cities come to have "more desires, more needs, more fantasies." Commerce can never increase their means at a rate faster than vanity augments what they conceive of as needs. It is, as he puts it, in its "nature to render superfluous things useful and useful things necessary" (*EL* 1.4.6, 7.1, 4.20.23).

Finally, while Montesquieu describes "the constitution of England" as a "beautiful system" and analyzes in some detail the many advantages that it confers on the English (2.11.6, 3.19.27, 4.20.7, 21.7), he is nonetheless careful, as we have seen (I.2, above), to make it clear that the liberty that such a constitution actually would confer on its citizens (*EL* 2.11.2–5 and 6, p. 407; 3.19.27, pp. 574–77) is in no way conducive to the sense of security and the attendant tranquillity of soul that he describes as "political liberty in relation to the citizen" (2.11.1, 6, pp. 397, 407; 12.1–2). Instead, he tells us, the English form of government would leave "all the passions there . . . free" so that "hatred, envy, jealousy, the ardor to enrich & distinguish oneself would appear in their full extent," and the English would exhibit an *inquiétude* which would render them uneasy, restless, anxious, and, on occasion, irrationally afraid. Moreover, in such a polity, men "would abandon themselves to their own humors," and "the better part of those with intelligence & wit [*esprit*], would be tormented by that very *esprit*: out of a disdain or disgust for everything, they would be unhappy with so many reasons for not being so" (3.19.27, pp. 575, 582–83).

Montesquieu's account of the defects of commercial society and his poignant description of England's men of *esprit* and of the unhappiness that besets them should once again give us pause, for it has a double aspect. Although divorced from theology and resolutely political and historical in focus, his description of the psychology of Europe's city dwellers in general and of the English in particular owes a great deal, as we have seen (I.2, above), to the moving account that Blaise Pascal provided in his *Pensées* of the role played in human life by *ennui, inquiétude*, and *divertissement*.[9] At the same time, however, this description reads as if Montesquieu had set out to pen a discerning profile of Jean-Jacques Rousseau and of his life in Paris.

Rousseau was a watchmaker's son, reared on the fringes of a frugal, relatively egalitarian, self-consciously republican society.[10] In sophistication and urban polish, he was sadly deficient. He was, moreover, an exceedingly sensitive soul—an artist, deracinated both by temperament and by trade—and he shared many of the predilections that caused Voltaire to denounce Pascal as a "sublime misanthrope." Indeed, in Molière's portrait of Alceste in *The Misanthrope*, Rousseau recognized a cruel and misleading caricature of men possessed of a disposition and capacity for discrimination much like his own.[11]

Although, at first, he appears to have found life in the great metropolis thrilling, and although for an extended period he put up a good front, Rousseau soon became profoundly uncomfortable with the social whirl. He could not abide his status as a parasite of sorts, confined to the outskirts of high society, and he deeply resented the role played in that great capital by wealth, breeding, politeness, and the passing whimsies of fashion. Parisian society was, for all of its elegance, artificial and false. This he deeply felt. It was the offspring of vanity, as Montesquieu had readily acknowledged (*EL* 1.7.1, 8–9, 3.19.5–6, 8–9); and to Rousseau—given his personal awkwardness, his peculiar disposition and background, and the embarrassing urological malady that flared up with considerable frequency—all of this seemed a personal affront and a moral offense. For nearly everything he encountered in Paris, the man who sometimes called himself *le pauvre* Jean-Jacques really did come to feel disdain and disgust. Life in the great capital he eventually found an unending torment.[12]

Prior to his sojourn in Venice in 1744–45 as secretary to the French ambassador, there was nothing in Rousseau's experience or conduct to suggest a real interest on his part in great political questions.[13] And, before 1746, he may not have been fully in command of the intellectual tools requisite for addressing these. It was at Madame Dupin's behest, and not on his own hook, that he pored over Plato, Jean Bodin, Hugo Grotius, Thomas Hobbes, John Locke, and the like and dipped into the travel literature produced in the wake of the great voyages of discovery by missionaries, merchants, and the great venturers themselves. Thereafter, however, as he steadily worked his way through *De l'Esprit des lois*, we can be confident that the passages singled out above, and others of a similar sort, leapt out at him. It was only then, after he had devoted considerable energy under the direction of Madame Dupin and her husband to what he calls "the historical study of morality," that he came to see that "everything is radically related to politics [*tenoit radicalement à la politique*]" and that "no people will ever be anything except what the nature of its Government makes it" (*C* 9.404–5). If he experienced an epiphany on the road to Vincennes, if then and there Jean-Jacques Rousseau really did see "another universe" and become "another man," it was because, in the course of historicizing the Jansenist portrait of fallen man, Montesquieu had given him the intellectual framework within which to explain to himself in political terms the misery and discomfort that he so powerfully felt.[14]

THE INDICTMENT OF ENLIGHTENMENT

When Denis Diderot encouraged his friend Jean-Jacques Rousseau to compose his *Discourse on the Sciences and the Arts* and to submit it to the Academy of Dijon, he did not initially understand what he had unleashed. He knew that his friend was an odd duck, to be sure, and he recognized that the man had talent and even, perhaps, genius. But he thought Rousseau's initial venture a supremely clever joke nonetheless.

Looking back nearly a quarter of a century after the event, Diderot marveled at the trajectory taken by his erstwhile friend, and in response to the claim advanced by Claude Adrien Helvétius that the man's sudden achievement of fame proved "the power of accident," he wrote, "Rousseau was no more a masterpiece of chance than was chance the masterpiece of Rousseau." The author of the *Discourse on the Sciences and the Arts* he likened to "a barrel of gunpowder meant for a cannon." All that it took to produce an "explosion" was a "spark," and "if the impertinent question of Dijon had not been proposed," Rousseau would have been no "less capable of composing his discourse." Everything that had happened was a function of the man's peculiar character and temperament: "Rousseau did that which he had to do because he was Rousseau." Imagine, Diderot urged, that "I am no longer the one who is at Vincennes, that it is, instead, the citizen of Geneva. I arrive. The question that he then put to me I now put to him; he responds to me as I, in fact, responded to him. Would you believe that I would have devoted three or four months to propping up an ill-conceived [*mauvais*] paradox by means of sophisticated arguments, that I would have given this sophistry all the vividness [*couleur*] that he gave it, and that I would thereafter have constructed a philosophical system from what had then been only a *jeu d'esprit?*"[15] With these last words, Diderot did his former friend an injustice and demonstrated the limits of his own understanding. There is no reason to suppose that Rousseau ever regarded his argument as an intellectual game. But it is nonetheless easy to see why Diderot conceived of the matter as he did.

The work that Rousseau came to speak of as his *First Discourse* is, as the noun used to name it suggests, a highly rhetorical exercise. In accord with the terms of the contest, it was brief—fit to be read within a half hour—and the compression required was then and remains today an obstacle to clarity. Moreover, Rousseau wrote in circumstances which rendered complete candor exceedingly imprudent: if in public he were frankly to display the genuine hatred that he felt for monarchy,[16] if he were openly to attack every form of social and economic inequality, he would render untenable the precarious perch that he occupied within the Dupin household and in France more generally.[17] He could hint at what he thought. He could adopt more than one pose—as a humble citizen of Geneva, as an ordinary man of French nationality, as a genuinely civilized man condemned to live in Paris among the barbarians in the manner of a barbarian incapable of making himself understood. He could even present himself as a philosopher, distant from the fray and far above the madding crowd. And by oscillating between different identities, by speaking in different voices, and by other literary tricks, he could unobtrusively direct his argument to a number of different audiences at once. Than this he could do no more. He had to obfuscate, and obfuscate he did.[18] But what Rousseau's oration lacks, as a consequence, in obvious logical coherence and in lucidity, it makes up for in eloquence.

In the work, Rousseau makes two points which seem incompatible.[19] At the beginning and near the end, he celebrates the accomplishments of natural—and political—philosophy. "It is," he begins, "a grand & beautiful spectacle to see man somehow emerge from nothing by his own efforts; dissipate, by the light [*lumières*] of his own reason, the darkness with which nature has enveloped him; raise himself above himself; launch himself into the celestial regions; traverse, like the Sun, the vast extent of the Universe with the stride of a Giant; &, what is grander & more difficult still, return into himself, there to study man & to know his nature, his duties, & his end" (*DSA* 99.10–100.3). He follows this with a conventional Enlightenment depiction of Europe in its Christian centuries as having tumbled into a "Barbarism" like that of "the first ages" and as having entered into "a condition worse than ignorance" under the influence of scholasticism, and he celebrates the fall of Constantinople and the recovery of learning in the Christian West, which eventuated in a "commerce with the muses" that "renders men more sociable by inspiring in them the desire to please one another by works worthy of their mutual approbation" (100.6–101.13).

In this fashion, already by then conventional, Rousseau begins; and near the end of his discourse, he picks up the same thread, singling out "the Verulams, the Descartes, & the Newtons" as "the Preceptors of Humankind" (158.14–16). There, he raises the possibility that the first of these, the "Chancellor of England," the very man who had launched the Enlightenment project, was "the greatest of the Philosophers" (159.18–21); and with a discreet nod in the direction of Plato's suggestion that philosophers be made kings and that kings become philosophers (*Rep.* 5.473c11–e5), he calls on the world's monarchs to admit into their councils "learned men [*savants*] of the first rank." "Let them there obtain," he writes, "the only recompense worthy of them: that of contributing by the credit they possess to the happiness of the Peoples whom they will have instructed in wisdom. It is only then that one will see what virtue, science, & authority can do when animated by a noble emulation & when working in concert for the happiness of Humankind. But as long as power stands alone on one side, & enlightenment [*les lumières*] & wisdom in solitude on the other, learned men will rarely think of great things, Princes will even more rarely do fine things [*belles*], & Peoples will continue to be vile, corrupt, & unhappy" (*DSA* 160.3–161.7). One could hardly confer greater tribute on the Enlightenment project than Rousseau seems to confer in these passages, and it is easy to see that he regarded his own efforts as its culmination.[20] After all, as he would soon make clear,[21] he was the figure who had returned "into himself, there to study man & to know his nature, his duties, & his end."

In between these two passages, however, Rousseau takes what appears to be an entirely different tack, more consistent with the pose he assumes in his political works as "a Citizen of Geneva,"[22] arguing at length that, while the "progress" made in "the sciences & the arts" since the fall of Constantinople has been profound, it "has added nothing to our real happiness" and "has corrupted our morals" (157.12–15).[23] In doing so, he makes a direct but nonetheless circum-spect allusion to Montesquieu on one occasion (compare 134.15–21 with *EL* 4.23.17). But, in this work, he never mentions *The Spirit of Laws* or its author by name. What he does do, however, in the sentence immediately preceding this al-lusion is to paraphrase one of Montesquieu's more striking formulations, and it is on this observation that he grounds his argument. Where Montesquieu had re-marked that, while "the Greek statesmen & political writers [*les politiques grecs*] who lived under popular government knew of no force able to sustain them other than virtue," their counterparts in the republics of his own day "speak only of manufactures, of commerce, of finance, of wealth, & of luxury itself" (1.3.3), Rousseau writes, "The ancient *Politiques* spoke without cessation of morals & virtue; ours speak only of commerce & money" (*DSA* 134.12–15).[24]

Much of Rousseau's argument is devoted to a survey of classical antiquity, a period to which in later years he would frequently recur.[25] In conducting this survey, he repeatedly returns to Montesquieu's analysis of republics, of the virtue essential to their well-being, and of the role played by luxury and the arts in their corruption (110.16–112.2, 114.17–124.10, 133.12–135.8, 140.7–142.2, 142.18–145.3). This analysis he then applies, in a manner consistent with Montesquieu's overall discussion of corruption, to despotisms such as ancient Egypt (110.6–15), mod-ern China (112.18–113.18), and the Byzantine empire (112.3–17), and this he does for the purpose of laying the foundation for his critique of the emerging com-mercial and enlightened societies of his own time. He exhorts us never to forget ancient Sparta—"this City as celebrated for its happy ignorance as for the wis-dom of the Laws, this Republic of demi-Gods rather than of men, so much supe-rior to humanity did their virtues appear"—and precisely because the Spartans chased from their city "the Arts & Artists, the Sciences & Learned Men," he takes Lacedaemon as his cultural model (116.3–11). Rome, he observes, had once been "the Temple of Virtue." Later, however, at the time of the Enniuses and the Terences, it began its decline; and "after the Ovids, the Catulluses, the Martials, & that crowd of obscene Authors whose names alone suffice to alarm the sense of moral decency and shame [*pudeur*]," Rome "became a Theater of crime, the shame of Nations, & the plaything of barbarians" (111.9–112.2).

Nowhere does Rousseau's Jeremiad have greater force than in the proso-popeia of Fabricius. If that Roman patriot had been recalled to life, he wrote, ad-dressing him directly,

> "Gods," you would have said, what "has become of the roofs of thatch & the rustic hearths where moderation & virtue made their habitation? What lethal [*funeste*] splendor has succeeded Roman simplicity? What is this strange lan-guage? What are these effeminate morals? What mean these statues, these

Paintings, these buildings? Lunatics, what have you done? You, the Masters of Nations, have you made yourselves the slaves of the frivolous men you conquered? Are you governed by Teachers of Rhetoric? Is it to enrich the Architects, the Painters, the Sculptors, & the Actors that you shed your blood in Greece & Asia? The spoils of Carthage—have they become booty for a flute player? Romans, make haste to tear down these Amphitheaters; smash these marbles; burn these paintings; chase out these slaves who are subjugating you, & whose lethal arts are corrupting you. Let other hands become illustrious on the basis of vain talents; the only talent worthy of Rome is that of conquering the world & of making virtue there reign. When Cineas took our Senate for an Assembly of Kings, he was dazzled neither by vain pomp nor by a studied elegance. He did not there hear that frivolous eloquence, the study & charm of futile men. What did Cineas then see that was so majestic? O Citizens! He saw a spectacle which neither your wealth nor all your arts can produce: the most beautiful spectacle that has ever appeared under heaven, the Assembly of two hundred virtuous men, worthy of commanding at Rome & of governing the earth." (122.5–124.10)

Such is the standard by which Rousseau proposes to measure the polities of his own time, and he finds that they all fall short in much the same fashion as late republican Rome.

Here again, Rousseau looks to Montesquieu, pointing to the liberty that the latter had attributed to men in the savage state (*EL* 1.1.2, 2.11.5, 3.18.10–14, 18–19, 19.4), and emphasizing that the commercial and enlightened world in which man now lives is built upon flattery, vanity, and vice. He does not spell out his argument in full, as he will in his *Discourse on the Origin and Foundations of Inequality among Men*. He is not yet in a position to do so. But he does hint at the argument which will be presented in that work, which, he later says, is "of all my writings the one in which my principles are revealed with the greatest boldness, not to mention the greatest daring" (*C* 9.406–7). In this vein, he suggests that "the Sciences, Letters, & the Arts" serve despotism. He points to man's natural freedom, and he intimates that the emergence of civil society and of the political order is coeval with his subjugation. The arts, he contends, "spread garlands of flowers over the chains of iron with which men are burdened, stifle in them the sentiment of that original liberty for which they seem to have been born, make them love their slavery, & form from them that which one calls *Peuples policés*"—peoples polished, polite, and, of course, well policed (*DSA* 101.14–102.6).[26]

It was human need that "elevated thrones." This much Rousseau readily concedes, but he insists at the same time that it was "the Sciences and the Arts" that "made these thrones strong." The "Powers of the Earth" have ample reason to love "talents" and to "protect those who cultivate them," for their cultivation reduces men to "happy slaves." To talents, he writes, these slaves owe "the delicate and fine taste" in which they take such pride, "the gentleness [*douceur*] of character & the moral urbanity" that cause "the social interchange [*commerce*]" among them to be "so engaging & easy." To talents, "in a word," they owe "the appearance of all the virtues without the possession of a single one" (102.6–103.5).

Such, Rousseau implies, is what men of his own day, the French above all others, mean when they speak of politesse: "a philosophic tone without pedantry, manners natural yet engaging, equally removed from Teutonic rusticity & ultramontane Pantomime . . . the fruits of a taste acquired by way of a good education [*bonnes études*] & perfected by" the social interchange that he pointedly speaks of as "commerce in the World" (103.6–21). He admits that it would indeed "be sweet [*doux*] to live among us, if the exterior countenance were always an image of the dispositions of the heart, if decency were virtue, if our maxims served as rules for our conduct, if true Philosophy were inseparable from the title of Philosopher" (103.22–104.6). But, of course, all is false. Subtle research and refined taste "have reduced the Art of pleasing to principles," and there "reigns in our morals a vile & misleading uniformity" so that "all minds seem to have been cast in the same mold: unceasingly politeness demands, propriety ordains: unceasingly one follows the usages, never the genius that is one's own." In a world governed by politesse, no one ever dares to present himself as he is, one remains profoundly uncertain with regard to one's connections, and from "this incertitude" comes a veritable "procession [*cortège*] of vices." As Rousseau sadly puts it: "No more sincere friendships; no more real esteem; no more well-founded confidence. Suspicions, offenses, fears, coldness, reserve, hatred, treachery will conceal themselves unceasingly under the uniform & perfidious veil of politesse, under that urbanity so much vaunted, which we owe to the enlightenment [*aux lumières*] of our century" (104.6–107.3).

There is, as Rousseau sees it, one more dire consequence that flows from the spirit of commerce, politesse, and *lumières*, and it is political. "National hatreds will be extinguished, but the same will happen with love of the Fatherland. For an ignorance that is despised, one will substitute a Pyrrhonism that is dangerous" (107.12–16). The "idle Literati" who flourish in this atmosphere do much more with "their lethal paradoxes" than "sap the foundations of the faith." They "annihilate virtue. They smile with disdain at the old words Fatherland & Religion, & they consecrate their talents & their Philosophy to destroying & demeaning [*avilir*] all that is sacred among men" (132.5–133.4). With "the distinction of talents" promoted by commercial society comes not only a "lethal inequality," fatal to all fellow feeling, but a "demeaning [*avilissement*] of the virtues" (149.6–9). "We have Physicists, Geometricians, Chemists, Astronomers, Poets, Musicians, Painters," observes Rousseau. "We no longer have citizens; or if there still remain some among us, they are dispersed in country districts that have been abandoned; there they perish indigent & despised" (150.14–21).

All of this is implicit in the critical, muted remarks, quoted above, that Montesquieu makes in passing with regard to the peculiar species of sociability dominant within the emerging commercial society which he observed while in Paris, and it can be inferred as well from the penetrating account that he gives of the unsociable character of those then living across the water in enlightened, fully commercial England (I.2, above). As both Montesquieu and Rousseau recognize, the tinsel world produced by monarchy's "commerce of luxury" has more in common with the drab world produced by the republican "commerce of economy" than immediately meets the eye. If anything, despite appearances, Parisians are farther along the trajectory defined by commercial sociability than are Londoners, who are distracted in some measure from a total immersion in the social whirl by a genuine, if attenuated, participation in public affairs.

The chief difference between Montesquieu and Rousseau is that what the French aristocrat consciously embraces, albeit not without grave reservations, the self-styled citizen of Geneva in a great fury rejects. When Montesquieu contemplates the future, he is anything but complacent. But he does entertain the hope that, in France and in Europe more generally, something like commercial republicanism on the English model will become the norm, and he foresees the possibility that the various peoples of Europe will learn to live alongside one another for the most part in prosperity and peace. Rousseau is far less sanguine.[27] When he contemplates the sociopolitical logic unfolding before his eyes in Paris, he foresees the emergence of a Europe much more akin to the Byzantine empire, which had been "a place of asylum for the Sciences & the Arts proscribed from the rest of Europe—perhaps," he now says, reversing his rhetorical course, "more by wisdom than by barbarism." The "fabric" of the despotism that took hold in Constantinople was formed, he insists, by "everything that is most shameful in debauchery & corruption; everything that is darkest in treachery, assassinations, & poisonings; everything that is most dreadful [*atroce*] in the combination of all crimes." Such, he observes, is "the pure spring [*source*] from which emanates the Enlightenment [*les Lumières*] in which our century glories" (DSA 112.3–17).[28]

INTELLECTUAL CELEBRITY

There is one argument that Rousseau advances in his *First Discourse* that has no obvious analogue in the *Considerations on the Romans* or in *The Spirit of Laws*, and it deserves close attention for two reasons. To begin with, it helps explain how Rousseau can remain consistent while celebrating the sciences and the arts and while praising Bacon, Descartes, and Newton in a work so critical of the political and social consequences of progress in the sciences and the arts. At the same time, it points to the particular element within commercial society that he finds the most offensive and worrisome.

In *The Spirit of Laws*, Montesquieu had not only observed that "the speculative sciences render men savage" (*EL* 1.4.8): he had also laid considerable stress on the tension that exists between the contemplative impulse and the needs of civil society and the political order (2.14.7; 4.23.21, pp. 705–7; 5.24.10–11). Rousseau agreed, and in 1753, when he seized on the publication of his comedy *Narcissus* as an occasion in which to write a preface defending himself from the charge of hypocrisy and inconsistency, he wrote:

> The taste for philosophy relaxes all the ties of esteem and benevolence that attach men to society, and this is perhaps the most dangerous of the evils that it engenders. The charm of study soon renders insipid every other attachment. What is more, as a consequence of reflecting on humanity, as a consequence of observing men, the Philosopher learns to appreciate them at their value, and it is difficult to have much affection for that which one despises. Soon he brings together in his person all the interest that virtuous men share with those like them: his contempt for others is turned to the profit of his pride: his *amour propre* grows in the same proportion as his indifference regarding the rest of the universe. Family, fatherland become for him words void of sense: he is neither parent, nor citizen, nor man; he is a philosopher. (*PN* 967)

This was not a passing fancy on Rousseau's part. In his *Émile*, he returned to the same theme, observing that, "if atheism does not cause the spilling of human blood, it is less from a love for peace than from an indifference to the good. Nothing that takes place is of any great importance to the putative sage provided that he can remain in repose within his study." The "principles" of such a human being may not "cause men to be killed, but they do prevent them from being born by destroying the mores that cause them to multiply, by detaching them from their species, by reducing all of their affections to a secret egoism as fatal to the population as it is to virtue." The "indifference" of the philosopher he compares with "the tranquillity of the State under despotism. It is the tranquillity of death; it is more destructive than war itself" (*É* 4.632n–35n).

Of course, in the preface to *Narcissus*, Rousseau insisted that the true philosopher's detachment from his fellow man was not a judgment on him as such. Here, as in his *First Discourse*, he was perfectly prepared to praise as "sublime geniuses" and as "privileged souls" the handful "who know how to penetrate the veils with which the truth is enveloped." He even describes them as "the beacon [*lumière*] and the honor of human kind." And he insists that "it is fitting that they, and they alone, exercise themselves in study for the good of all," adding that "this exception itself confirms the rule—since if all men were Socrateses, science would not then be harmful to men, but they would have need of it" (*PN* 970–71).

What enables Rousseau to depict philosophers as unsociable while praising them as well is the razor-sharp distinction that he draws between philosophers and men of letters. "At the same time," he observes, "that the cultivation of the sciences withdraws, so to speak, the heart of the philosopher from the crowd, in another sense, it engages with the crowd that of the man of letters." The reason is easy to discern:

> Every man who occupies himself in developing talents which are agreeable wants to please, to be admired, and he wishes to be admired more than anyone else. Public applause belongs to him alone: I would say that he does everything to obtain it—if he did not do still more to deprive his rivals of it. From this is born, on the one side, refinements of taste and *politesse*; vile and base flattery; cares seductive, insidious, childish, which, in the long run, diminish the soul and corrupt the heart; and on the other side, jealousies, rivalries, the renowned hatreds of artists, perfidious calumny, duplicity, treachery, and every element in vice which is most cowardly and odious.

What distinguishes the philosophers from mere men of letters is that they are "capable of resisting the folly of vanity, the base jealousy, and the other passions that the taste for letters engenders" (967–68, 971). What distinguishes philosophers in Rousseau from the literati is the strength of soul and the profound desire for knowledge that had distinguished philosophers from sophists and poets in Plato's *Republic* (6.487b1–506d1).

This distinction is presupposed in the *First Discourse*. It explains why, in the preface to that work, Rousseau goes out of his way to explain that he does not "care to please the Wits [*Beaux-Esprits*] or the Fashionable [*Gens à la mode*]"; why he contends that "in all times there will be men made to be subjugated by the opinions of their age, of their Country, of their Society"; and why he then so ominously adds that "the sort who acts the part of the Freethinker [*l'Esprit fort*] & Philosopher today would have been for the very same reason nothing more than a fanatic" during the French wars of religion "at the time of the [Catholic] League" (*DSA* 94.3–14).[29]

Later in the same work, Rousseau asks what, precisely, is at stake in the "question of luxury"; and in answering his own query he not only abandons the concerns that had animated the prosopopeia of Fabricius: he raises a question that carries him beyond the analysis provided by Montesquieu. For, in his opinion, what is most at stake is the fact that "Minds [*Esprits*] degraded by a multitude of futile cares can never raise themselves to anything great." Even, he says, "when they have the strength for it, they lack the courage" (136.20–137.10).

After all, Rousseau explains, "every Artist desires applause. The praise of his contemporaries is the most precious part of his recompense." Then, he goes to the heart of the matter:

> What then will [such an artist] do to obtain [applause] if he has the misfortune to be born among a People & in times when Learned Men [*Savants*], having become fashionable [*à la mode*], have put frivolous youth in a state to set the tone; when such men have sacrificed their taste to the Tyrants of their liberty; when one of the sexes, daring to approve only that which is proportioned to the pusillanimity of the other, lets the chief works of dramatic Poetry fall by the wayside, & prodigies of harmony are dropped. What will he do, Gentlemen? He will lower his genius to the level of the age, &, by preference, he will compose vulgar [*communs*] works that will be admired during his lifetime, rather than marvels that will not be admired until long after his death. (137.11–138.11)[30]

Then, lest the full significance of his point be lost on his readers, Rousseau names as a malefactor along these lines no less a figure than the prince of the philosophes—the great Voltaire. "Tell us," he wrote, "renowned [*célébre*] Arouet, how many manly & powerful beauties you have sacrificed to our false delicacy, & how many grand things has the spirit of gallantry, so fertile in small things, cost you. It is in this fashion," he then remarks, "that the dissolution of morals, a necessary consequence of luxury, carries with it in turn the corruption of taste" (138.11–139.6).[31] Such is Rousseau's response to Montesquieu's mocking endorsement of a free, flirtatious, adulterous communicativeness between the two sexes and to his tongue-in-cheek celebration of the role women played within French society as the arbiters of morals and manners (*EL* 3.16.11, 19.5–6, 8–9, 14–15, 6.28.22).[32]

That Voltaire was henceforth Rousseau's enemy should come as no surprise. That for a time Rousseau retained the friendship and admiration of Diderot, d'Alembert, and others like them is a sign that the radicalism implicit in what the self-styled citizen of Geneva had to say simply lay at first beyond their ken. The most serious charge that he leveled against the project in which they were engaged was not that it subverted morality, friendship, and citizenship—though he certainly thought and claimed that it did just that. The most grievous charge was his flat denial that the Enlightenment project would result in a liberation of the human intellect.

It was Rousseau's claim that, since commercial society makes everything a matter of traffic, it will establish a tyranny of fashion in matters of the intellect just as it had in matters of dress. By way of transforming learned men, such as Voltaire, into what we now call celebrities, it will contribute mightily to the enslavement of the human mind. In Voltaire, Rousseau recognized the first and perhaps the most distinguished in what we can now see as an endless line of exceptionally talented artists and composers, novelists and journalists, poets and playwrights, filmmakers and actors, scientists, professors, and the like who take to the public stage to strut and fret; preen, pose, and pander; and condescend from a posture of pretended moral and intellectual superiority—and he regarded the example that this supremely capable man had set for men of letters not only as a disgrace but also as the harbinger of a profound threat to freedom of thought—not least, to his own.[33] It was with Voltaire in mind that he wrote, in the preface to the work, that "the sort who acts the part of the Freethinker [*l'Esprit fort*] & Philosopher today would have been for the very same reason nothing more than a fanatic at the time of the League" (DSA 94.3–14).

PRIESTCRAFT OLD AND NEW

As his sneering reference to the Catholic League may suggest, Rousseau was no friend to the Christian church, and he was especially hostile to Roman Catholicism, which was, he intimated, conducive to barbarism and to fanaticism as well. When he began drafting his *Discourse on the Origin and Foundations of Inequality*, he composed and polished a brief but trenchant passage analyzing the "proud curiosity" that causes man to suppose that he can "penetrate mysteries which are beyond his intelligence" and that engenders "follies and crimes" by erecting "idols" and inspiring "fanatics." To this propensity, Rousseau traced not just "astrology, the renown of the divinatory art, Magic, and the other pretended supernatural reveries that constitute the shame of reason, the recourse of malcontent imbeciles, and the triumph of con men," but "a novel sort of inequality," established neither by nature nor by convention, which rests solely on "chimerical opinions" and which enabled "a species of singular men," a congeries of "idolatrous and ambitious Priests," to raise themselves on high, "representing themselves as interpreters of things incomprehensible and as Ministers of the divinity" authorized "to subject the Human Race to their decisions."

> Adroitly substituting Gods of their own fashioning for the true God who did not suit their turn, and substituting their absurd and interested maxims for those of right reason, they redirected the Peoples insensibly away from the duties of humanity and the rules of morality that they did not dispose of at their whim—all for the purpose of subjecting them to practices indifferent or criminal and to arbitrary punishments and fines of which they were the sole dispensers and judges. Mortal enemies of the Laws and their ministers, always ready to authorize unjust usurpations on the part of the supreme magistrate for the purpose of usurping more easily themselves *his* legitimate authority, by always speaking of spiritual rights, they arranged affairs so that the goods, life, and liberty of the Citizen were secure only insofar as he placed himself at their discretion. Their power was all the more formidable because, establishing themselves without shame as sole judges in their own cause and suffering no common measure of the differences that they set up between themselves and other men, they overturned and annihilated all human rights without anyone ever being able to prove to them that they had exceeded their own.

If, in the end, Rousseau excised this passage from his discourse, it was not because he had in any substantive fashion changed his mind. It was rather because he realized that his attempt to couch it in such a manner as to slip it past the censor was bound to fail.[34] It was one thing to attack scholasticism and to pour scorn on the Catholic League; it was another to launch what everyone would recognize as a direct assault on Holy Mother Church, charging it with the terrible crime that the English republican James Harrington had dubbed "Priest-craft" a century before.[35] Even in the heyday when Rousseau's great patron and admirer the liberal statesman Chrétien Guillaume Lamoignon de Malesherbes served as *Directeur de la librairie* and made sure that the censors he employed gave *permission tacite* for the anonymous publication in France under a false imprint of many a scandalous tract,[36] a measure of authorial discretion was required. Malesherbes was a man of audacity and cunning, capable of astonishing feats. When forced by the Jesuits to issue an order providing not only for the suppression of the first two volumes of the *Encyclopédie, ou Dictionnaire raisonné des sciences, des arts, et des métiers* but also for a confiscation of all the articles written for subsequent volumes as yet unpublished, he was not only prepared to tip off Diderot and d'Alembert in advance: he offered and actually provided sanctuary for the outlawed manuscripts in his own house. But not even Malesherbes could protect an author who openly attacked the Christian religion and insisted that authorial integrity required that he forego anonymity.[37]

Rousseau would later take up the theme of priestcraft in *The Social Contract*, as in due course we shall see (II.3, below); and for his audacity in this work and in the *Profession of Faith of the Savoyard Vicar* that he buried in his pedagogical novel *Émile, or On Education*, he would soon thereafter pay a very high price.[38] Eventually, also, in an apologetic work entitled *Dialogues: Rousseau, Judge of Jean-Jacques*,[39] he would systematically apply his analysis of "priestcraft" to the philosophes as well, spelling out in detail the implications of his claim that "the sort who acts the part of the Freethinker [*l'Esprit fort*] & Philosopher today would have been for the very same reason nothing more than a fanatic at the time of the League" (DSA 94.3–14), and suggesting that Voltaire, Diderot, d'Alembert, and the like were in fact party to a conspiracy no less insidious than the one first mounted in the distant past by "idolatrous and ambitious Priests."[40]

The suspicions that Rousseau entertained in the 1770s may have been exaggerated, especially as they pertained to the conspiracy that, he believed, the philosophes had concocted against himself; and in expressing these suspicions, he had frequent recourse, as always, to hyperbole. But his fears, though blown out of proportion, were by no means utterly without foundation, for Rousseau's erstwhile friends among the philosophes really were party to a philosophical conspiracy, and they really did aim at dominating opinion and at giving direction to the larger society thereby. They were, moreover, in no way sorry to see this philosophical turncoat harried from refuge to refuge, and in modest ways they actively contributed to the difficulties he faced.[41] To this one can add that, when judged in light of the history of Europe and of the larger world after 1789, Rousseau's analysis of the role that intellectuals, loosely organized as a party, had come to play in the fabrication of public opinion seems remarkably prescient. Jean-Jacques Rousseau was the first to recognize that, within modern society, what we now call political ideology performs a function comparable to that served in earlier times by religious doctrine and that—as ideologues—scientists, men of letters, and artists now occupy a status once reserved for none but high priests.

Rousseau traced this remarkable revolution in human affairs back to the period in which Diderot and d'Alembert launched the *Encyclopédie*. Prior to the 1750s, he wrote, "opinions wandered in an incoherent fashion [*sans suite*] and without regulation at the whim of men's passions, and these passions, constantly banging into one another, caused the public to roam from one place to another in a direction inconstant." Thereafter, however, a profound change took place. A "spirit methodical and consistent" was applied for the purpose of guiding "public opinions," and "prejudices themselves" came to possess a "logic of progression [*marche*] and rules all their own." Rousseau had no doubt that he had been present at the creation of something entirely new. This trend, he argued, was "among the peculiarities [*singularités*] that distinguish the century in which we live from all others." It had its inception when "the philosophical sect" of which he had once been a member "united itself into a body under chiefs." It was under way the moment "these chiefs by the art of intrigue to which they applied themselves" made of themselves "the arbiters of public opinion," capable of determining "the reputation, even the destiny, of particular individuals and through them that of the State." And it reached its culmination when they made alliances with "powerful men" for the purpose of becoming "the arbiters of society" as well. These chiefs made their newfound allies "feèl," he wrote, "that, working in concert, they would be able to extend their roots under the feet of men in such a fashion that no one would any longer find solid footing [*assiete*], and no one would be able to march forward except on terrain that had been countermined."

Crucial to all of this was the fact that "the chiefs" of what Rousseau pointedly describes as "the philosophical league" possess a "doctrine" all their own and have mastered "the art of making their doctrine circulate . . . in the seminaries and colleges so that the newborn generation is devoted to them from birth." He acknowledges their animosity to the Jesuits, but he insists that this animosity is rooted solely in "professional jealousy [*jalousie de métier*]," and he contends that the philosophes are, in fact, "great imitators of the mode of proceeding [*marche*] followed by the Jesuits." They "govern minds with the same imperial control [*empire*], with the same dexterity that these others employ in governing consciences," and they are "shrewder" than these priests "in that they know better how to conceal themselves while acting": the Jesuits "rendered themselves all-powerful by exercising divine authority over consciences and by making themselves, in God's name, the arbiters of good and evil. The philosophes, not being able to usurp the same authority, applied themselves to its destruction; and then, in the course of appearing to explain nature to their docile sectaries and of making of themselves its supreme interpreters, they established, in its name, an authority no less absolute than that of their enemies—although it appears to be consistent with freedom [*libre*] and to rule over wills solely by way of reason."

The struggle between the two parties Rousseau compared with that between Carthage and Rome. "These two bodies," he wrote, "both imperious, both intolerant, were, in consequence, incompatible—since the fundamental system of both was to rule despotically. Each wishing to rule alone, they could not share the empire and rule together." Gradually, then, and inexorably, "the new" league, "following the erring ways of the other but with greater adroitness, supplanted it by way of debauching its supporters and through them brought about its destruction." Now, Rousseau adds, we can see this league "marching along" the tracks laid out for it "with as much audacity" as its predecessor "and with more success since the other always encountered resistance and this one no longer encounters any." In this fashion, moreover, the philosophes managed to "substitute little by little a philosophical intolerance" for the religious intolerance once propagated by the Jesuits; and "without anyone perceiving it, they became even more dangerous than their predecessors."

The danger posed by this new "philosophical league" Rousseau thought rooted in the fact that "the proud despotism of modern philosophy has carried the egotism" associated with the spirit of profound insecurity and fierce vainglory, which he calls *amour propre*, "to its ultimate extreme." It eventuates in a "taste for domination" that gives life to "all of the angry passions related to *amour propre*"; and from among "the apprentice philosophers," it produces "a generation of Despots" who, having "become slaves in order to be tyrants," exhibit "the liveliest intolerance." This intolerance may be "more hidden" than that once promoted by ambitious and idolatrous priests, but, Rousseau insists, it is "no less cruel." If the new conspiracy does not "appear to exercise the same rigor" as the old, it is only because "it no longer encounters rebels." If, however, there were a renaissance of religious belief, if "some genuine defenders of Theism, of tolerance and morality" were once again to present themselves on the public stage, "one would soon see raised up against them the most terrible persecutions," for quite "soon a philosophical inquisition, more cunning and no less sanguinary than the other, would burn without mercy anyone who dared to believe in God" (D 2.889–91, 3.964–68).

Such was the ultimate import of Rousseau's indictment of the Enlightenment. Such was the warning that he issued near the end of his life to all who were willing to pay attention. "The sort who acts the part of the Freethinker [*l'Esprit fort*] & Philosopher today would have been for the very same reason nothing more than a fanatic at the time of the League" (DSA 94.3–14). So he wrote in his first published work.

Chapter Two

SOCIABILITY AS A MALADY

The same causes which render us wicked make us also slaves and reduce us to servitude by depraving us; the sentiment of our weakness comes less from our nature than from our cupidity: our needs bring us together in the very measure in which our passions divide us, and the more we become enemies to our fellow men, the less are we able to do without them. Such are the first bonds of general society; such are the foundations of that universal benevolence, which appears to be stifled by the recognition of its necessity, from which each wishes to harvest the fruit without being obliged to cultivate it himself.

— Jean-Jacques Rousseau

Nowhere did Rousseau lodge a charge against Montesquieu similar to the one he leveled at Voltaire and the philosophes. Instead, in later years, he persistently expressed for the author of *De l'Esprit des lois* a profound, even exaggerated respect,[1] speaking of him as "an illustrious philosopher" (*DOI* 136), as "a celebrated author" and "noble genius [*beau génie*]" (*CS* 3.4), as a "great man," and even as an "immortal."[2] That he greatly admired Montesquieu there can be no doubt. In one passage, he treats him as a peer of Plato (*DEP* 273); in another, he implies that he is the equal of John Locke (*LM* 6.812). When reproached for something he has himself written or done, Rousseau repeatedly justifies himself by pointing to analogous conduct on the part of his illustrious predecessor (1.706–7, *C* 10.497, *RPS* 4.1029–30).[3] In responding to one correspondent, Rousseau recommends the *Lettres persanes* as a model for good writing;[4] in a missive to another, he mentions Montesquieu as a stylist alongside figures as distinguished as Tacitus and Pascal.[5] In *The Confessions*, he consciously writes at one point, as he readily admits, "in the manner of Montesquieu" (*C* 8.378). In

The Social Contract, he not only imitates the method of composition in short, pithy chapters that distinguishes *The Spirit of Laws*; he draws heavily on that work for his discussion of founding, for his analysis of political regimes and the psychology underpinning them, for his account of the effects of climate on mankind, and for his argument in defense of civil religion—and there, time and again, he paraphrases and cites as his authority the celebrated philosopher from Bordeaux (*CS* 2.7, 11, 3.4, 8, 4.3, 8).[6]

Rousseau published *The Social Contract* in 1762. Eleven years earlier, when d'Alembert, in the *Preliminary Discourse* written as a preface for the first volume of the *Encyclopédie*, suggested in passing that most of the ills that Rousseau in his *First Discourse* had blamed on the sciences and the arts were due, in fact, to entirely different causes of a highly complex sort, and when Stanislaus, the exiled king of Poland, made the same objection, pointing to the climate, to the nature of the government, to customs, to laws, and the like, Rousseau—presuming, no doubt correctly, that they both had in mind Montesquieu's elaborate scheme—alluded to d'Alembert's remarks, reiterated Stanislaus's list of possible causes, and conceded the import of "the relations quite hidden, but quite real, which are to be found between the nature of the government and the genius, the mores, and the knowledge of the citizens." With regard to "political establishments," he acknowledged, "time and place decide everything."[7] Four years later, in 1755, when he published his *Discourse on Political Economy* in the *Encyclopédie* edited by his friends Diderot and d'Alembert, Rousseau would insist that a lawgiver has to pay close attention to "everything demanded by the locale, the climate, the soil, the mores, the neighborhood, and all of the particular relations [*rapports*] of the people whom it is his intention to institute" (*DEP* 250); and three years thereafter, in the open letter he addressed to d'Alembert, criticizing the latter's suggestion that Geneva would profit from the establishment of a theater, he would marvel at the "prodigious diversity of mores, of temperaments, of characters" distinguishing the world's various peoples, adding that "man, modified by Religions, by Governments, by laws, by customs, by prejudices, by climates, becomes so different from himself that one ought not to search among us for what is good for men in general but for what is good for them in such a time or such a country" (*LS* 16).[8] From the outset, Rousseau was evidently in agreement with what the tutor in his pedagogical novel, *Émile, or On Education*, would later tell his charge: that "the necessary relations [*rapports nécessaires*] linking mores with government have been so well expounded in the book *De l'Esprit des loix* that one can do no better than to recur to this work to study these *rapports*" (*É* 5.850–51).[9] He must, therefore, have been gratified in the extreme when David Hume wrote to him in 1762, some weeks after the appearance of *The Social Contract* and *Émile*, to say, "I will use the Freedom of telling you bluntly, without affecting the Finesse of a well-turned Compliment, that, of all men of Letters in Europe, since the Death of President Montesquieu, you are the Person whom I most revere, both for the Force of your Genius and the Greatness of your Mind."[10]

ENGAGEMENT

All of this notwithstanding, Rousseau did level one serious charge against Montesquieu, and he did so initially by way of what appears to have been a deliberate misreading of the one passage in *The Spirit of Laws* to which he expressly refers in his *Discourse on the Sciences and the Arts*. Here is what Montesquieu actually wrote: "The knight [Sir William] Petty has supposed, in his calculations, that a man in England is worth what one would sell him for in Algiers. This [presumption] cannot hold good anywhere other than England: there are countries in which a man is worth nothing; there are those in which he is worth less than nothing" (*EL* 4.23.17). In paraphrasing this passage, Rousseau first alludes to the fact that the *politiques* of his own day speak of nothing but commerce and money. Then, he writes: "One such will tell you that a man in a particular country is worth the sum for which he would be sold in Algiers; another, in following up on this calculation, will find countries in which a man is worth nothing, & others in which he is worth less than nothing. They value men as they would herds of cattle. According to them, a man is worth nothing to the State, except in proportion to his performance as a consumer [*un homme ne vaut à l'État que la consommation qu'il y fait*]" (*DSA* 134.12–21).[11]

As a characterization of Petty's "Essay in Political Arithmetick," Rousseau's jibe is a cheap shot, but, in highlighting the manner in which the emerging administrative state and the new science of statistics on which it depends really do treat human beings as things, it does have a certain primitive rhetorical force. Had his attack been directed at Petty's mentor Thomas Hobbes, it might well have struck home.[12] As a representation of Montesquieu's point, however, it is plainly wrong, and it is hard to believe that, when Rousseau read *The Spirit of Laws*, he missed the note of irony, which is pervasive throughout and transparent. He was, after all, a composer and a musical theorist; and as he would soon thereafter demonstrate (*EOL* 373–429),[13] he had long pondered the close relationship between music and speech. As a writer and as a reader, he was not tone deaf in any way. If he misrepresented Montesquieu as valuing "men" as he would "herds of cattle," it was by way of implying that the relative serenity of the latter, the tone of detachment that runs through his great book, reflects a defect in the great man's character, which puts him in a class hard to distinguish from that of the pioneering statistician whose work he had pointedly cited and mocked. For Rousseau, when one is confronted with an equation of men with things, irony is evidently an insufficient response.

According to Rousseau, Voltaire was the very model of a modern charlatan: he was a literary whore—a man of letters caught up in a sad and degrading struggle for popular recognition and favor. Montesquieu was, he implies, the opposite: a philosopher in the fullest sense of the word, largely indifferent to the universe, and short on benevolence. Put simply, he lacked compassion.[14] He cared too little for his fellow men. Family and fatherland were for him words almost devoid of sense: in his outlook he was neither parent nor citizen, and he was hardly a man; in his cosmopolitanism, he was a philosopher and little more.[15] What bothered Rousseau as he read *The Spirit of* Laws was that conduct and conditions which evoked from the self-styled citizen of Geneva fierce indignation elicited from Montesquieu little more than distaste, a wrinkling of the brow, and a sharply disapproving glance. In the aristocrat from Bordeaux, the watchmaker's son found moral earnestness in short supply. In the face of the injustice constituted by social and economic inequality and the treatment of men as vendible items, Montesquieu was neither enraged nor fully engaged.

Of Montesquieu, from Rousseau's perspective, worse could be said; and at the very end of his life, Rousseau said it. The fourth of his *Reveries of the Solitary Stroller* he devoted to the question of lying. To frame his ruminations properly, he took as his working definition a philosopher's claim that "to lie is to hide a truth that one ought to make manifest." This definition he chose because it enabled him to distinguish noble or innocent fibbing, which serves a salutary purpose or, at least, does no one any appreciable harm, from lies and conceits that are instruments by which injustice is perpetrated. The principal example that he offered by way of clarifying what he meant by the second of these two categories was Montesquieu's false representation of his *Temple of Cnidus* as the translation of a newly discovered Greek manuscript. The charge that he lodged was that by means of this literary conceit the work's author sought to pass off pornographic "poison" as scholarship and to attract to it a greater audience than it would otherwise have secured. Although, in the original preface to the work, Montesquieu had claimed that its author's aim was evidently to demonstrate that our happiness stems from "the sentiments of the heart and not the pleasures of the senses," Rousseau doubted that Montesquieu had had any "moral object" in mind when he composed and published the book. If the author of *The Temple of Cnidus* had, in fact, entertained such an object, he remarks, "this object is very well obfuscated and spoiled by the voluptuous details and the lascivious images" on offer therein—which teach, he implies, what the book purports to deny: the primacy of sensual pleasure. It is Rousseau's contention that a literary conceit, such as Montesquieu's misrepresentation of this book's origin, is to be judged "a lie well worthy of punishment if the work" it recommends is, indeed, as "dangerous" as this one evidently was. What Montesquieu had apparently looked upon as an amusement was subversive of the only understanding of happiness consistent with the fellow feeling that underpins both public and private morality (*RPS* 4.1024–39, especially 1029–32).[16] In publishing the book, Montesquieu was acting in an irresponsible manner,[17] and he was undermining justice itself.

In *Émile*, Rousseau made the same point in an entirely different fashion. There he had his tutor observe that, as a field of study, "political right [*le droit politique*] has yet to be born, and it is to be presumed that it will never be born." Grotius he dismisses "as a child." Except in basing himself on the testimony of the poets, the Dutch jurist was hardly to be distinguished from the sophist Hobbes.

> The only modern in a condition to create this great and useless science was the illustrious Montesquieu. But he took care not to treat the principles of political right; he contented himself with treating positive right under established governments, and nothing in the world is more different than these two studies.
>
> Nonetheless, he who wishes to judge in a healthy manner concerning governments that exist is obliged to reunite the two; it is necessary to know what ought to be in order to judge well that which is. (*É* 5.836–37)[18]

The charge that Rousseau levels is that for all of his virtues, which are many, Montesquieu is, as a writer, insufficiently attentive to the demands of justice and the public good.

The accusation is, of course, grossly exaggerated, and Rousseau knew it. In responding to criticism leveled at the *First Discourse* by his old friend Charles Bordes, he described Montesquieu as a "celebrated philosopher" and specified that his great "work, always profound and sometimes sublime, everywhere breathes the love of humanity" (*DR* 72n). In a letter written in the wake of the great man's death, he traced his status as an "immortal" who ought "to remain alive through eternity" to the fact that he taught the various "Peoples their rights and their duties."[19] What Rousseau meant to convey when he resorted to hyperbole in the *First Discourse*, in his *Émile*, and in *The Reveries of the Solitary Stroller* was that Montesquieu had nonetheless fallen well short of what was required; and in his *Discourse on the Origin and Foundations of Inequality among Men* and in *The Social Contract*, which is pointedly subtitled *Principles of Political Right*, he sought to lay the foundations for a *droit politique* far more exacting than the flexible, prudential, latitudinarian doctrine taught in *The Spirit of Laws*.[20] What Montesquieu's teaching so "often lacked in aptness and accuracy [*justesse*]" and "sometimes in clarity" as well he would himself supply by the simple expedient of making manifest what, he claimed, that "noble genius" had "not seen—that the Sovereign authority is everywhere the same" (*CS* 3.4).

In this fashion, Rousseau aimed to provide what Montesquieu had, in fact, thought it inexpedient to supply—an uncompromising standard by which governments could and would in the future be judged—and he did so by reviving the doctrine of absolute sovereignty. The bulk of *The Spirit of Laws* is devoted to an examination of positive right and the myriad forms that it can and does assume. By spelling out the *rapports nécessaires* which explain the astonishing diversity of human laws, customs, mores, and manners, Montesquieu hoped to promote what he called "moderation." To this end, he sought to temper Hobbes's assertion that sovereignty must be absolute, which he judged favorable to despotic rule,[21] and he tried to blunt the impact of the doctrine of political legitimacy proposed by John Locke in his *Second Treatise of Government*, which he regarded as dangerously doctrinaire and as likely to inspire revolutions that would overturn imperfect polities and eventuate in their replacement with despotisms far worse.[22]

In pursuing this end, Rousseau was convinced, Montesquieu had gone much too far. Moderation in the pursuit of justice was, he thought, no virtue. As always, however, the Genevan's posture was complex. He took it for granted that a period of "crisis and a century of revolutions" was on the horizon. He thought "it impossible that the great monarchies of Europe would last a long time," and he did not restrain himself from openly announcing his opinion that they were doomed (É 3.468–69, *CP* 1.954). And yet he professed to share Montesquieu's conviction that, in most circumstances, revolution would do far more harm than good, and he thought piecemeal reform no less likely to wreak havoc—even within the great monarchies and commercial societies of Europe, where, in his view, corruption was already quite firmly ensconced (*DOI* 112–13, *CS* 2.8).[23] Moreover, Rousseau expressed great horror at the prospect that there might be a revolution in France;[24] and in the programs of reform that he drafted for countries such as Corsica and Poland, which he thought not beyond redemption, he displayed something very much like the legislative prudence and moderation that his great predecessor had preached (*PC* 899–950, *CP* 951–1041). In the former case, he even spoke of the necessity to attend to what he, like Montesquieu (*EL* 3.19), termed "the nation's *esprit général*" (*PC* 905).[25] Nonetheless, in his theoretical works, Rousseau aimed not just to restore Hobbes's account of absolute sovereignty and Locke's doctrine of political legitimacy, but to correct them both and to give the latter a polemical edge far keener than the one it had originally possessed.

Moreover, as we shall soon see, in depicting the large territorial states of eighteenth-century Europe, Rousseau went out of his way to describe in incendiary terms the plight of those who lived under their rule, deliberately fanning discontent and giving it a political focus. Men were, he insisted, by nature good. Freedom was their birthright. If everywhere they were in fact selfish and wicked, if they were miserable and unhappy, if psychologically they were slaves utterly dependent on the regard of others, if they were insincere and lived inauthentic and deceitful lives, it was not in any way their fault. It was solely because of the oppressive institutions under which they lived. Here, as in his *First Discourse*, Rousseau constructed his argument almost entirely from elements provided by the Frenchman whom he regarded as his most formidable and admirable antagonist.

MAN'S NATURAL STATE

Montesquieu's magnum opus was not devoted solely to the examination of positive right. In its first book, he dedicated the better part of three extremely dense and cryptic chapters to an examination of man's peculiar status as a being endowed with intelligence and freedom in a Newtonian universe governed by invariable laws (*EL* 1.1.1), to a discussion of man's natural condition (1.1.2), and to an account of the origins of positive law (1.1.3).[26] Montesquieu began with the fact that man is at the same time a physical being governed by invariable laws, a sentient creature subject to a thousand passions, and an intelligent being capable of choice and prone to error (1.1.1); and he ended by cataloguing both the physical and the moral causes that make up the *rapports nécessaires* which explain why it is that the laws of one people so rarely suit another (1.1.3). The presumption on which he operates throughout is that man's subjection to physical and moral causes makes of him an extremely "flexible being" more pliable and malleable, more plastic, than anyone had imagined hitherto (Préf.).[27]

Like Hobbes and Locke before him, Montesquieu argued that to understand "the constitution of our being," we must consider "man before the establishment of societies." When he speaks of "the laws of nature," he has in mind those which men would "receive in such a state." In contrast, however, with Hobbes in particular, he insists that "men, in the state of nature, would have the faculty of knowledge rather than knowledge" itself and that the "first ideas" entertained by a man "would not be speculative ideas." A man of this sort "would then feel only his weakness; his timidity would be extreme." The condition of such men would be like that of "the savage men" occasionally found "in the forests" in Europe. "Everything would make them tremble; everything would make them flee"; and "peace would be the first natural law." Hobbes's contention that they would desire "to subjugate one another" Montesquieu thought preposterous. "The idea of empire & that of domination are so complex [*composée*] & depend on so many other ideas" that primitive men could hardly have conceived of them. In effect, he argued, the English philosopher had ascribed to men "before the establishment of societies" notions antecedent to their establishment (1.1.2).

In the state of nature, Montesquieu went on, men would have a sense [*sentiment*] of their needs, and there would be another natural law which would inspire in them a search for nourishment. He also believed that "reciprocal fear" would eventually cause men to approach one another and that they would be drawn in by "the pleasure that one animal feels at the approach of another animal of the same species." Moreover, this pleasure would be increased by "the charm" associated with sexual difference so that "the natural appeal [*prière*] that they make to one another would be a third law." To this, Montesquieu added that in time men would succeed in gaining knowledge and that this would establish among them a "second tie that the other animals do not have" and give them "a new motive for joining together," and so he concluded that "the desire to live in society is a fourth natural law" (1.1.2).

It is, Montesquieu insists, only in society, only by rubbing up against one another and by acquiring knowledge, that men "lose the sense of their weakness"; it is only then that Hobbes's "state of war begins." Each of the particular societies "comes to feel its strength [*force*]," and this "produces a state of war between nation & nation," which then gives rise to the law of nations (*le droit des gens*) governing relations between peoples. In similar fashion, "individuals, in each society, begin to feel their strength; they seek to turn in their favor the principal advantages of the society; this makes among them a state of war"; and this in turn gives rise to political right (*le droit politique*) and civil right (*le droit civil*), which, when embodied in law, make it possible for individual human beings to live alongside one another in peace under a common government (1.1.3).[28]

The state is a necessity. This much Montesquieu concedes. But in asserting that men are naturally social, in denying that they are naturally wicked, and in intimating that there is in fact much good in man, he is preparing the ground for his rejection of Hobbes's contention that the sole passion to be reckoned on is fear,[29] and he is providing justification for the presumption that underpins his own political science. As we have had ample opportunity to observe (I, above), it is Montesquieu's contention that, in favorable circumstances, human beings can secure for themselves peace and prosperity without relying entirely on fear, without embracing absolute sovereignty, and without concentrating unchecked power in the hands of a single man.

In the first book of his *Spirit of Laws*, Montesquieu does not trace in fine detail man's emergence from the state of nature. In the eighth book, he indicates that this takes place in stages. But here, too, he is reticent. "In the state of nature," he writes, "men are, indeed, born in equality, but they know not how to remain in that condition. Society makes them lose their equality, & they become equal again by way of the laws" (*EL* 1.8.3). It is only much later, in that work's eighteenth book, where he distinguishes the four modes of subsistence—hunting, herding, farming, and commerce (3.18.8)—that Montesquieu reveals just how complex the process is. He has already remarked in passing that "natural liberty" is "the object" pursued by what little there is of "public administration [*la police*]" among "the savages" (2.11.5). Now he specifies that the savage peoples are distinguished as such by the fact that they depend on hunting for their livelihood, and he goes on to describe those who depend on herding as "barbarians." These peoples, we soon learn, are governed by mores rather than by laws. They are, in the strict sense, pre-political, and Montesquieu specifies that they "enjoy a great liberty." As he puts it, "among these peoples, the liberty of the man is so great that of necessity it carries with it the liberty of the citizen" (3.18.8–14, 30).

The establishment of laws is, Montesquieu asserts, coeval with agriculture, and this in turn depends upon the invention of money. Wherever one finds "a coin," there one will also find "a nation polished, polite and well-policed [*une nation policée*]." The cultivation of the earth "presupposes," he explains, "much in the way of arts & knowledge; and one sees always that arts, knowledge, & needs progress at an equal pace." Before there is agriculture and money, he adds, "each individual has little in the way of needs & satisfies them with ease and in an equal manner. Equality is then inevitable [*forcée*]; so their chiefs are emphatically not [*point*] despotic." Except when occasioned by superstition or by peculiarities in the terrain that obviate flight, the threat posed by despotism does not generally arise before the establishment of agriculture and the invention of money (3.18.15–19).

Despotism is, in fact, a latecomer. It presents itself as a serious danger after the arts have developed, after men have learned to farm and use money, after natural equality has disappeared, after man has lost his natural sense of weakness, after some have attempted to turn the advantages of society in their favor by trickery and violence, after the state of war has erupted within society—in short, when political and civil right emerge (compare 1.1.3 with 3.18.15–17). Moreover, as Montesquieu subsequently makes clear, the threat posed by despotism is not obviated, except under unusual circumstances (3.18.2, 5), until commerce, as a mode of subsistence, has achieved a modicum of autonomy that rulers have to reckon with (compare 3.18.1–2, 8, with 4.20–21). To drive despotism from a Europe of farmers subject to the yoke of imperial Rome, Montesquieu observes, it took a barbarian people—who "ventured forth" from the North "to destroy tyrants & slaves, and to teach men that, as nature has made them equal, so reason cannot render them dependent, except insofar as is requisite for their happiness" (3.17.5).[30]

REFLECTION AND DEPRAVITY

The account that Rousseau provides in what is customarily called his *Second Discourse* is almost identical to the one offered by Montesquieu in *The Spirit of Laws*.[31] Without doing any injustice to his own argument, Rousseau could have plagiarized his great predecessor's summary statement: "In the state of nature, men are, indeed, born in equality, but they know not how to remain there. Society makes them lose their equality, & they become equal again by way of the laws" (1.8.3). And in fact, in the *Discourse on Political Economy* that Rousseau composed for publication in the *Encyclopédie* of Diderot and d'Alembert, he paraphrased the passage, defining law as "that salutary organ of the will of all, which reestablishes in [the sphere of] right the natural equality among men" (*DEP* 248).

Between Montesquieu and Rousseau, there is, nonetheless, one great difference. In his *Discourse on the Origin and Foundations of Inequality among Men*, the latter does what the former deliberately chose not to do: he spells out the process of social and political evolution in fine detail, and he indicates how from this account one might derive clear principles of political right. In writing, this time he adopts a double pose—not as an ordinary Frenchman nor as a civilized man condemned, like Ovid, to live among barbarians, but as a citizen of Geneva, intent on public service, and as a philosopher prepared to be judged in Aristotle's Lyceum by the likes of Plato and Xenocrates (*DOI* 109, 121, 133).

Like Montesquieu, Rousseau argues that man is a physical being subject to physical causes and an intelligent being with a potential for free choice, and he, too, presumes that human nature is for this reason astonishingly plastic and open to a thousand influences (122–24, 131–32, 139–63, 193–94).[32] It is this that the two have in mind when Montesquieu calls man a "flexible being" (*EL* Préf.) and when Rousseau appropriates or coins the novel term *perfectibilité* and speaks of the quality that it denotes as the distinctive attribute of man (*DOI* 142, 162, 210–11).[33] Rousseau also joins Montesquieu in insisting that primitive man is distinguished from the other animals not by the possession of knowledge but by an as-yet-undeveloped capacity to obtain it, and he, too, expressly rejects Hobbes's description of the state of nature on the grounds that the Englishman attributes to man in that condition qualities that he could have acquired only within society (124–26, 132, 136, 145–46, 153–55). In the process, he openly asserts what Montesquieu only implies—that men are naturally good (156–57, 170); he echoes the Frenchman's contention that society predates government; and, in explaining the ultimate emergence of the latter from the former, he restates Montesquieu's account of the fateful shift from hunting and herding as modes of subsistence to the practice of agriculture (compare 164–78 with Montesquieu, *EL* 3.18.8–30).[34] Moreover, he agrees wholeheartedly with Montesquieu's claim that "nature" has made men "equal" and that "reason cannot render them dependent, except insofar as is requisite for their happiness" (3.17.5).[35] Rousseau is at odds with the author of *De l'Esprit des lois* in only two crucial particulars: he asserts that primeval man is given to pitying his fellows,[36] and he denies that dependence and human happiness are compatible at all.[37]

Jean-Jacques Rousseau was a dramatist. He wrote plays and composed operas; he had a gift for the histrionic and a love for hyperbole. Nowhere did he advocate on man's part a return to his original condition. But, in his *Discourse on the Origin and Foundations of Inequality among Men*, he did assert that the development of human society, the invention of agriculture, and the emergence of the state were accidents,[38] and he deliberately left his readers with the impression that these events were for mankind a catastrophe.[39] Moreover, he framed his narrative, which was evidently intended as an alternative to the story told in the early chapters of the Book of Genesis (*DOI* 132–33), as an account of man's fall from a state of secular grace.

That primitive man would have been especially timid Rousseau very much doubted, and with regard to human beings, at least in this work, he made no mention of the pleasure that, Montesquieu had claimed, one animal feels at the approach of another animal of the same species. Moreover, he denied that reciprocal fear, lust, and the acquisition of knowledge could render men sociable (126, 136–37, 151–52, 157–58, 164). As he represents it, solitude is man's natural state.[40] Moreover, there, before society emerged, in what is evidently intended as a secular substitute for the Garden of Eden, he insists, solitary man knew a species of bliss: there, we are told, "his soul, which nothing agitates, delivers itself to the sole sentiment of his actual existence, without any idea of the future" (144, 164).[41] There he could pursue his self-preservation on the basis of instinct, unworried by the prospect of death and untroubled by any lasting concern for the welfare or opinion of others.

Nor would there be frequent grounds for conflict. Man's genuine needs are modest. In the forests, there was plenty; and, as Rousseau points out, even Bernard Mandeville—who gained such notoriety by puckishly suggesting in his *Fable of the Bees* that private vices make for public virtues and that society profits greatly from vanity, luxury, and vice—acknowledged that human beings exhibit a natural propensity to pity those in distress who are of their own kind (154–55).[42] "Such," he contends, "is the pure movement of Nature, prior to all reflection" (155). Such is the character of primordial human instinct (125–26, 154–57, 170).[43]

It was Rousseau's conviction that man can never be fully at home with other men. To explain how men were forced to become social, he had recourse to the argument articulated in the fifth book of *De rerum natura*, where the Roman poet Lucretius denied the existence of Providence and traced the origins of human society to accidents bound to happen eventually in an infinite universe of atoms in motion through infinite time (compare 140, 162–63, with Lucr. 5.416–1457).[44] In effect, Rousseau suggested, it was the natural growth in population and a concomitant increase in the number of accidental encounters (*DOI* 221–22)—something which, he later admitted, was going to occur sooner or later in the course of time[45]—that occasioned the establishment of the family and taught man the advantages attendant on a measure of cooperation and a primitive division of labor (164–68), and it was society in turn that first prompted men to develop their capacity for speech and the attendant ability to reason and reflect (141–53, 165–73). It was society, in fact, that made of men something more than mere animals. This advance—and Rousseau did regard it as a profound advance—came at a price, however. For what man gained in dignity, he lost in bliss.

This conviction haunts Rousseau; and to describe the price that, he believed, human beings pay for the achievement of sociability, he appropriates language used by Blaise Pascal and Pierre Nicole to distinguish man in his fallen state. Because, however, his focus is neither sin, nor human nature in and of itself, nor even national character, but the artificial character of social relations as such, Rousseau has less to say about *ennui, inquiétude,* and *divertissement* than had Montaigne, Pascal, Nicole, John Locke, and Montesquieu (I.2, above). What concerns him most is the mixture of insecurity and vainglory that Pascal, Nicole, La Rochefoucauld, and other French moralists similarly influenced by Augustine had called *amour propre;* and, just as they tended to distinguish this defective self-love from the healthy prelapsarian love of self, so he juxtaposes the *Amour de soi-même* displayed by man in the solitude of the natural state with the *Amour propre* that emerges when human beings enter society and come to have need of one another.[46]

Like Locke, Bayle, Mandeville, and Montesquieu, in his maturity, Rousseau was drawn to these Augustinians by an appreciation for their psychological acuity, not by an admiration for the theological setting within which they framed their arguments. He was interested in Pascal's contention that, once *amour propre* is unleashed, it robs us of a capacity to live in the present and forces us to project ourselves into the future; that it prevents even the rich from simply enjoying the abundance that they possess; and that it inspires even in kings *ennui, inquiétude,* and a desperate desire for *divertissement*.[47] But he was even more interested in the fact that *amour propre* proves to be, in its very nature, "criminal & immoderate" and that it gives rise to "the desire to dominate" others. He attended as well to Nicole's recasting of Hobbes's account of the origins of the polity as a tale concerning the capacity of *amour propre* to become "enlightened" in such a fashion as to produce a community "in its outward demeanor . . . better regulated, more civil, more just, more pacific, more decent, and more generous" than any other, and he recognized the force of Nicole's argument. But he was struck most forcibly by Pascal's observation that, under the influence of *amour propre,* "we are not content with the life that we have in ourselves & in our own being"; that "we wish to live an imaginary life in the thinking of others"; that, "to this end, we endeavor to show ourselves to advantage"; and that "we labor incessantly to embellish & preserve this imaginary being & neglect the true one."[48] This was the phenomenon that he hated most, and it was to this propensity that he traced all of the other ills that Pascal, Nicole, and La Rochefoucauld had associated with *amour propre.*

Rousseau was at odds with Pascal, Nicole, and La Rochefoucauld in only one crucial particular. "I notice," he wrote at the beginning of an extended passage in which he anticipated the argument of his *Second Discourse,* "that in the world a multitude of petty maxims now hold sway which seduce the simple with a false air of philosophy, and which, beyond that, are very convenient for terminating disputes in a tone important and decisive—without there being any need to examine the question under consideration. Such a one is this: 'Men everywhere have the same passions; everywhere *l'amour-propre* and interest conduct them on their way; they are, then, everywhere the same.'" What Pascal and Nicole had said concerning all men in their fallen state and what La Rochefoucauld, Bayle, and Mandeville had said of men in general, Rousseau pointedly said of man only upon his entrance into society; and he did so, tellingly, in the preface to a play that he had written loosely based on the myth of Narcissus (PN 969n–70n). Moreover, he insisted, as we shall eventually see, that for the powerful human propensity to follow in the wake of Narcissus, there are remedies that can be applied—in this world.

Of course, in describing the emergence of the family, Rousseau is perfectly capable of celebrating what he calls "the first developments of the heart" and of suggesting that "the habit of living together occasioned the birth of the sweetest sentiments known to man: conjugal love, and Paternal love" (*DOI* 168). He is even willing to assert that the period of semi-settled life prior to the invention of agriculture was "the epoch" which was for man "the happiest and the most durable"; and, in depicting it, he pointedly corrects Lucretius' celebratory claim that the first stage in human development marked "the youth of the world" (Lucr. 5.780, 818, 943) by suggesting that this, the second stage, marked its "true youth" (*DOI* 171). But the whole time that he is describing primitive society there hovers in the background something ominous. To begin with, soon after men first settle down, frequency of contact changes the character of sexual encounter:

> They become accustomed to attend to different objects and to make comparisons; unawares [*insensiblement*], they acquire ideas of merit and beauty, which produce sentiments of preference. As a consequence of seeing one another, they are no longer able to do without seeing one another more. A tender and sweet sentiment insinuates itself in the soul, and at the least opposition it becomes an impetuous fury. Jealousy awakens with love; Discord triumphs; and the sweetest of passions receives in sacrifice human blood. (169)

Social practices grow up. In clearings, the villagers gather for singing and dancing. Thereafter, Rousseau observes, men developed a fatal capacity for reflection.

> Each began to look at the others and to want to be looked at [*regardé*] himself, and public esteem came to have a price. He who best sang or danced; the one most handsome, the one most strong, the most adroit or the most eloquent came to be the one most highly regarded [*le plus consideré*], and this was the first step towards inequality, and towards vice at the same time. From these first preferences were born on the one side vanity and contempt and, on the other, shame and envy; and the fermentation caused by these new leavens produced in the end compounds fatal [*funestes*] to happiness and to innocence.

First came "the idea of regard [*considération*]"; then came "the first duties of civility." Every "intentional wrong [*tort volontaire*]" was considered "an outrage" because the harm inflicted was accompanied by "contempt," which was "often more intolerable than the harm itself." In consequence, "acts of revenge became terrible, and men both sanguinary and cruel" (169–70).

Worse was yet to come—for what Rousseau is here describing is the primitive "epoch," which was for man "the happiest and the most durable." At this point, he insists, though "natural pity had already suffered a certain alteration," there was, nonetheless, "a proper balance [*un juste milieu*] between the indolence of the primitive state and the petulant activity" associated with the spirit of "*amour propre*" that he thinks dominant within modern life. As long as men's lives remained primitive, as long as they confined themselves to hunting animals and gathering fruit and nuts, this balance could be sustained. To be precise, "as long as men applied themselves only to tasks that one man alone could manage and to arts which have no need for cooperative effort on the part of a number of hands, they lived in as free, healthy, good, and happy a fashion as their Nature allowed, and they continued to enjoy among themselves the sweetness of a social interchange free from dependence [*un commerce independant*]."[49] But when this all changed, "the instant in which a man had need of another's help, when they perceived that it is useful for one to have provisions for two, equality disappeared, property was introduced, work became necessary, and the vast forests gave way to smiling Fields needing to be watered with the sweat of men—in which fields, slavery and misery were soon seen to germinate and grow with the crops intended for harvest" (171).

Like Montesquieu, and for similar reasons, Rousseau regarded the cultivation of the earth as a watershed in human history. Both recognized that agriculture presupposes a general progress in the arts; both recognized that it cannot be sustained without the establishment of private property in land; both emphasized that the shift from hunting and herding brings to an end the age of equality. Rousseau regarded farming as the fatal stroke: it required long-term planning; by putting an end to present-mindedness, it gave rise to anxiety. Even more to the point, it promoted the division of labor. In the process, it powerfully enhanced the significance of natural inequalities and guaranteed that rewards would be reserved for talent, skill, and strength—and in its wake came a division of the populace into poor and rich, slave and master, serf and lord (171–75). None of this greatly bothered Montesquieu. Rousseau regarded it with horror.

"Behold, then," he wrote, "our faculties developed, memory and imagination in play, *amour propre* interested, reason rendered active, and the mind arrived almost at the limit of the perfection to which it is susceptible."

> Behold all the natural qualities placed in action, the rank and fate of each man established, not only with regard to the quantity of goods and the power to help or to harm, but with regard to mind, beauty, strength or skill, with regard to merit or talents; and since these are the only qualities which are able to attract regard [*considération*], soon one had to possess them or affect them; soon it was necessary for one's advantage that one show oneself to be other than one, in

fact, was. To be and to seem became two things in every respect different, and from this distinction emerged impressive pomp, deceptive wiles [*ruse*], and all the vices in their train [*cortège*]. Behold, on the other hand, man, once free and independent, now by a multitude of new needs subjugated, as it were, to all of Nature—and above all to those who resemble him [*ses semblables*], whose slave he becomes in one sense, even in becoming their master; if rich, he has need of their services; if poor, he has need of their help, and being in between does not put him in a position to do without them. He must, then, seek incessantly to interest them in his fate and to make them find their profit, in fact or in appearance, in working for his.

All of this, Rousseau insisted, "makes him treacherous and artful with some, imperious and harsh with others, and it places him under the necessity of taking advantage of all those of whom he has need, when he is unable to make them fear him and does not have an interest in doing them a useful service." In the end, he adds, "devouring ambition, the ardor to raise one's relative fortune (less out of a true need than to get ahead of others) inspires in all men a dark inclination to harm one another and a secret jealousy all the more dangerous because often, for the purpose of striking a blow in greater safety, it dons the mask of benevolence." On the one hand, there is "competition and rivalry"; on the other, there is a profound "opposition of interest"; and "everywhere" there is "a hidden desire to profit at the expense of another." Such are "the evils" that follow on the establishment of private property, and they are "a procession inseparable from nascent inequality" (174–75).[50]

In this fashion, we are told, "the usurpations of the rich, the Brigandage of the Poor, the unbridled passions of all—stifling natural pity and the voice, still weak, of justice—rendered men avaricious, ambitious, and wicked," and "nascent Society gave way to the most horrible state of war," which was brought to an end only when a rich man, who had the most to lose and who sorely felt the pressure of necessity, "finally conceived the best-thought-out project ever to have entered the human mind." His design was simple. His aim was "to employ in his favor the very forces deployed by those who attacked him, to make defenders of his adversaries, to inspire them with other maxims, and to give them other institutions which would be as favorable to him as natural Right was adverse." To this end, he proposed a simple stratagem—that they all unite to defend the weak, fend off the oppressor, and secure to all the possessions that were theirs. In this fashion, Rousseau reports, the polity and law were first established, and their institution in one place forced their establishment elsewhere, as those outside the polity found it necessary to unite in self-defense. In consequence, natural liberty was abandoned once and for all; private property and inequality were reinforced;

"adroit usurpation became irrevocable right; and for the profit of a few ambitious men, henceforth the whole of Humankind was subjugated to labor, servitude, and misery" (175–78).

In the aftermath, "natural commiseration" lost its purchase except in the case of "certain great Cosmopolitan Souls," among whom we are no doubt meant to include Jean-Jacques Rousseau. Thereafter, none but these few "jumped over the imaginary barriers that separate Peoples," and only they, "on the example of the sovereign being who created them, embraced all of Humankind in their benevolence" (178). In general, Rousseau elsewhere observes, one must regard with suspicion those men of letters who represent themselves in public as friends to humanity. "All these grand words—society, justice, the laws, mutual defense, the assistance of the weak, philosophy, and reason's progress—are," he warns, "nothing but lures invented by adroit politicians and political writers [*politiques*] or by cowardly flatterers for the purposing of imposing themselves on the simple."[51]

POLITICAL SOCIETY

Although, according to Rousseau, men accepted the proposal of the rich that they band together for the protection of their goods, their freedom, and lives, they almost never achieved that at which they aimed. In part, this was due to their ineptitude. They had no experience to guide them in the framing of institutions. Mainly, however, it was due to their character, for "the very same vices which render social institutions necessary render their abuse inevitable; and with the exception of Sparta alone—where the Law attended principally to the education of Children, and where Lycurgus established mores which almost dispensed them from the need to add Laws—it is the case that the Laws, which are in general less powerful than the passions, contain men without changing them" at all (187–88).

First came law and the institution of private property; then came the magistracy; and, as a consequence of corruption, there ensued an inexorable drift from legitimate to arbitrary power (186–87). All of this reflected the unfolding logic of inequality. When Rousseau asserts that a magistrate cannot "usurp illegitimate power" and establish himself as a despot unless he has the aid of "creatures," and then adds that, to these, the despot "is forced to cede a certain part" of this power (188), he is merely reiterating a point dramatized in Montesquieu's elaborate depiction in his *Lettres persanes* of the eunuchs who guard and manage Usbek's seraglio.[52] "Citizens do not let themselves be oppressed," Rousseau insists, "except insofar as they are drawn on by a blind ambition and, regarding those below

them more than those above, come to hold Domination more dear than independence and consent to bear chains in order to be able to impose them on others in turn" (188).[53]

According to Rousseau, the explanation for all of this is *amour propre*—the
deep, insatiable longing for *considération*, identified by Pascal, Nicole, and La
Rochefoucauld, which is unleashed, however, not, as the first two of these three
contended, at the Fall, but when human beings in primitive society first begin to
compare themselves with one another (219–20). At each stage of the development of society, especially after the introduction of money, the invention of
agriculture, and the subsequent establishment of political order, their rivalry increases in intensity. "The universal desire for reputation, honors, and preferences, which devours us all, exercises and causes us to compare talents and
strength." At the same time, "it excites and multiplies the passions"; it renders
"all men competitors, rivals, or, rather, enemies"; and it gives rise to an "ardor to
get oneself talked about" and to a "fury to distinguish oneself which holds us almost always outside of ourselves." If, he adds, "one sees a handful of powerful
and wealthy men at the height of grandeur and fortune while those in the mob
grovel in obscurity and misery, it is because the former prize the things that they
enjoy solely to the degree that the others are deprived of them." In fact, he concludes, without any untoward "alteration in their own condition," the privileged
classes "would nonetheless cease to be happy if the People ceased to be miserable" (189).

It is easy to see why Rousseau should have spurned the Enlightenment. Like
Mandeville and Montesquieu, he was prepared to interpret the establishment
of political society and its refinement in the terms first set out by Hobbes and
so brilliantly developed by Pascal and Nicole. But where Mandeville, Montesquieu, and at times even Nicole were inclined to marvel at all that *amour propre* had wrought and to celebrate the contribution made by private vices to the
public good, Rousseau, like Pascal, recoiled in horror and disgust, seeing nothing but vanity, deceit, corruption, and rot. If successful, he believed, the program
of progress in the sciences and the arts proposed by Sir Francis Bacon and taken
up in France by the philosophes would serve only to intensify the ills coeval with
the establishment of society and the institution of government. In becoming a
"tyrant . . . over Nature," he intimates, man becomes a "tyrant over himself"
(142).[54]

The problem arises from sociable man's desperate need for regard. "The Savage," Rousseau observed, "lives within himself; sociable man, always outside of
himself, does not know how to live except in the opinion of others, and it is, so to
speak, from their judgment alone that he draws the sentiment of his own exis-

tence" (193).[55] Where, in the Garden of Eden constituted for Rousseau by the state of nature, there once had once been a "Celestial and majestic simplicity," all that remained was "the deformed contrast between passion that believes that it reasons and understanding caught up in delirium" (122). If Rousseau was not quite ready "to maintain that the state of reflection is a state contrary to Nature, and that the man who meditates is an animal depraved" (138), he came very, very close.

At the deepest level, as all of this suggests, the putative catastrophe identified by Rousseau has less to do with the distribution of property and progress in the sciences and the arts per se than with the impact on human psychology of the opportunities that social and economic dynamism afford for men of talent to excel and the social inequality produced thereby. In his *Émile*, the capstone of the triptych of works singled out in *The Confessions* for their central significance, Rousseau restates Montesquieu's contention (*EL* 1.4.4) that, in modern times, the education of man has three sources and that what he is deliberately taught by his preceptors in society is of necessity at odds with what he learns from nature and from experience in the world. Above all else, he emphasizes, we must attend to the "primordial dispositions" given by nature to man. If man were to be reared outside society solely for himself, these would be determinative. If, however, he is also to be reared for others, harmony (*le concert*) is unattainable. "One is forced to do battle," Rousseau concludes, "either against nature or against the social institutions: one must choose between making a man and making a citizen—since one cannot make the one and the other at the same time." After all, he explains, "natural man is for himself everything: he is a numerical unity, the absolute whole which has no relation [*rapport*] to anything but itself or that which resembles it [*son semblable*]. Civil man is nothing but a fractional unity which depends [*tient*] on the denominator, and his value lies in its relation with the whole, which is the body social." In consequence, "he who wishes within the civil order to preserve primacy for the sentiments of nature knows not what he wishes. Always in contradiction with himself, always floating between his inclinations and his duties, he will never be either man or citizen; he will be good neither for himself nor for others. He will be one of the men of our days: a Frenchman, an Englishman, a Bourgeois; he will be nothing."

For the moral instruction provided by the clergy in the *collèges*, Rousseau has no more regard than had Montesquieu, and he contends that the "education given by experience in the world [*l'éducation du monde*]" leads "to two contrary ends" and, in fact, "misses them both: it is proper only for making men double"— one might even say, duplicitous—"seeming always to relate [*rapporter*] everything to others, and never relating anything to anyone but themselves." It is, he concludes, "from these contradictions" that "the one which we experience un-ceasingly within ourselves is born. Drawn by nature and by men on contrary routes, forced to divide ourselves between these diverse impulses, we follow an impulse composed of the two which conducts us neither to the one nor to the other goal [*but*]. In this fashion, conflicted [*combatus*] and floating during the entire course of our lives, we reach the end without having been able to bring ourselves into accord with ourselves and without having been good either for ourselves or for others" (É 1.247–52).[56]

Such is the indictment that Rousseau levels at what he taught us to call with contempt and disdain bourgeois society. Such is his diagnosis of the ills that, he argues, the commerce and the technological dynamism espoused by the prophets of Enlightenment serve only to heighten and intensify.[57]

CITIZENSHIP AS A REMEDY

> But although there is no natural society general among men, although they be-
> come miserable and wicked in becoming sociable, although the laws of justice and
> of equality are nothing to those who live in the liberty of the state of nature and are
> subject at the same time to the needs of the social state, far from thinking that there
> is no virtue or happiness for us and that heaven has abandoned us without resource
> to the depravity of the species, let us bring our strength to bear on drawing from the
> ill itself the remedy which ought to be its cure.
>
> — *Jean-Jacques Rousseau*

It is, of course, one thing to diagnose and another to cure. The former Rousseau could, at least to his own satisfaction, claim to have accomplished in his first
two discourses; the latter, even by his own lights, he arguably never achieved (*D*
3.934–35).[1] To be sure, he tried. In *Julie, or The New Heloise,* he explored the
possibility that one could attain a measure of unity and happiness on the level of
political society by way of a withdrawal from the corruptions of the city into a rustic retreat and an immersion in a species of romantic and familial love closely
akin to the phenomenon which had evoked in savage men what he had celebrated in his *Second Discourse* as "the sweetest sentiments known to man" (*DOI*
168).[2] In his *Discourse on Political Economy* and, at greater length, in *The Social
Contract, or Principles of Political Right,* he sketched the conditions necessary
for a political cure that would in some measure liberate man from doubleness
and duplicity and confer on him a clear identity and a species of unity as part of
a larger whole.[3] In *Émile, or On Education,* he considered whether an omni-
scient, omnipotent tutor could by way of indirection prepare an ordinary young
man, destined to live in bourgeois society, to be good not just for himself but, in

the end, for others as well.[4] Had he judged any of these expedients fully viable, or even sufficient as a palliative, he would not at the end of his life have written his *Reveries of the Solitary Stroller* with its suggestion that in solitude, by way of what one might describe as an aesthetic loss of self, a civilized man of great refinement might for a time be able to recover something closely akin to the sense of wholeness and self-sufficiency, the capacity to live wholly in the present, and the expansive, blissful, full-blown sentiment of one's own existence that savage man had purportedly enjoyed in the natural state (*RPS* 5.993–1099, especially 1046–47).[5]

It would take a shelf of books to do justice to the works that Rousseau composed in the wake of publishing his *First Discourse* and his *Second Discourse*; and, in any case, a detailed discussion of *Julie*, *Émile*, and *The Reveries of the Solitary Stroller* would not be to the purpose here, for in these works Rousseau deliberately presents himself as something other than a citizen of Geneva. Rousseau's *Discourse on Political Economy* and *Social Contract* may not be works as central as *Émile*: after all, their author regarded the second and more important of the first two as "a species of appendix" to the third.[6] Even more to the point, neither the *Discourse on Political Economy* nor *The Social Contract* directly addresses in any obvious way the psychological issues raised in the *Discourse on the Sciences and the Arts* and the *Discourse on the Origin and Foundations of Inequality among Men*.[7] The focus of the *Discourse on Political Economy* is public administration, and that of *The Social Contract* is political legitimacy. In fact, the latter takes the form of a response to Hugo Grotius, Thomas Hobbes, Samuel Pufendorf, John Locke, and the like.[8] But these two works nonetheless deserve a glance, for in their pages, more clearly than anywhere else, Rousseau indicates what would be required were one intent on fashioning a political cure for man's woes; and, although the political remedy that he suggests therein stands in stark contrast to the course that Montesquieu seems to have preferred, the argument that Rousseau makes on its behalf presupposes that Montesquieu was in fact right when he corrected the accounts given of human psychology by Michel de Montaigne, Blaise Pascal, and John Locke by insisting on the plasticity of human nature and contending that within political society man's state of mind is decisively shaped neither by sin nor by nature as such—but by the form of government under which he lives.

PASSION AND POLITICS

In *Émile*, Rousseau indicates the most crucial element required. "Good social institutions," he writes, "are those which know best how to denature man, to remove from him his absolute existence in order to give him a relative existence, and to transport the *I* into a communal unity" (É 1.249). This explains why, in his *First Discourse*, he urged his readers never to forget Sparta, and it makes sense of the fact that, in his *Second Discourse*, he once again singled out Lacedaemon for extravagant praise. Sparta's very existence proved that things did not have to be as, in his day, they were: the Spartans were citizens in the fullest sense of the word; they were in no way bourgeois. "The embarrassment of my adversaries is visible every time that they find it necessary to speak of Sparta," chortles Rousseau. "What would they not give for that fatal Sparta never to have existed?" (*DR* 83).

In the end, however, it was not Sparta that served as his practical model—at least, not in the sphere of governance. In his *Second Discourse*, after presenting himself as a citizen of Geneva, Rousseau takes the epistle dedicatory, written in honor of that city, as an occasion for sketching briefly the institutional structure necessary to a good regime; and there, in the manner of Machiavelli, the figure whose vision of grandeur Montesquieu had so vigorously rejected, Rousseau looks to the early Romans, whom he describes in one passage as "the model for all free Peoples" (*DOI* 112–15), in another as "the freest and most powerful people on earth" (*CS* 4.4), and in a third as the people endowed with "the best Government that has ever existed" (*LM* 6.809).

Rousseau had a great deal in common with Machiavelli and with the Florentine's English republican admirer James Harrington. All three were persuaded that there is a considerable divide between what the author of the *Discourses on Livy* had called the *popolo* and the *grandi* and what the author of *Oceana* subsequently dubbed "the natural democracy" and "the natural aristocracy." All three were convinced that, while only the former can be relied upon to favor the common good, only the latter possess the prudence and cunning necessary to steer the ship of state.[9] With this in mind, in *The Social Contract*, Rousseau drew a sharp distinction between sovereignty and government (*CS* 1.2–2.6, 3.1–4.1), which earned him warm approbation and applause from that devotee of popular sovereignty and rational administration Anne-Robert-Jacques Turgot. If, in sharp contrast with that great modernizer, who had no sympathy at all for the critique of the Enlightenment and of commercial society laid out in the *Discourse on the Sciences and the Arts* and the *Discourse on the Origin and Foundations of Inequality among Men*,[10] the Genevan greatly admired ancient Rome, it was chiefly due to his conviction that, over a period of centuries, the Romans had managed to reconcile popular sovereignty with aristocratic governance in such a manner as to ensure not only justice but wisdom as well. About the character of these institutions, Rousseau had a great deal to say in *The Social Contract* (3.1–2, 4–7, 12–18, 4.2–7).

Rousseau's vision of the political good owes something to Plutarch's *Lives*, which he first read with great animation as a child.[11] It is indebted as well to Plato's *Republic, Statesman*, and *Laws*, which he studied with care at the insistence of Madame Dupin. But if, in the end, he came to think of the moderns as men possessed of "little souls,"[12] and if in the 1750s, when he first achieved fame, he became as "intoxicated with virtue" as he tells us he was (*C* 9.416), it was due chiefly to the impact on him of reading Montesquieu's dramatic depiction of the classical republic in his *Considerations on the Causes of the Greatness of the Romans and their Decline* and in *The Spirit of Laws*. After all, in his estimation of the roots of the human capacity for self-government, Rousseau sided with Machiavelli, Hobbes, Hume, and Montesquieu against Plato, Aristotle, and Plutarch on the question most crucial: he, too, insisted that reason is the slave of the passions. "Whatever the Moralists may say," he writes, "the human understanding [*l'entendement humain*] owes much to the Passions, which, as is commonly acknowledged, owe much to it as well." In fact, he insists, "it is as a consequence of their activity that our reason perfects itself. We seek to know only because we desire to enjoy, and it is not possible to conceive why he who has neither desire nor fear would go to the trouble of reasoning." Moreover, he adds, it is equally the case that "the Passions," which "derive their origin from our needs," derive "their progress from our knowledge," for desire, where not prompted by natural impulse, is grounded in "the ideas that one can conceive." The phenomenon that Rousseau calls *perfectibilité* arises from the dialogue that takes place between reason and passion as each spurs the other on (*DOI* 142–43). His outlook is emphatically modern.

As we have seen (I.1–2, above), Montesquieu grounded his political science on the same presumption, arguing that "reason never produces any great effects on the minds of men" (*EL* 3.19.27, p. 577). In consequence, he thought it better "to treat man as feeling [*sensible*] than to treat him as reasonable" (*LP* 31.22–34/33); and, with this proviso in mind, he distinguished forms of government not in the Aristotelian manner, with an eye to the rational principles of justice that each could claim to embody, but in terms of the diverse, unreasoning "human passions that set" each "in motion" (*EL* 1.3.1). In the case of despotism and monarchy, which depend on fear and honor, respectively, he thought it relatively easy to elicit the requisite passion. Democracy he took to be another matter. It depends, as we have also seen, on "political virtue," which demands "a continual preference for the public interest over one's own," and this in turn requires "a renunciation of self," which is "always a very painful thing." In effect, Montesquieu claims, republican virtue is artificial. It "restricts ambition to a single desire, to the sole happiness of rendering to the fatherland greater services than the other citizens," and it achieves this end only by inculcating in the citizens an irrational, unreasoning, unnatural passion for equality and a "love of the laws & the fatherland." To accomplish this, he tells us, one must deploy "the complete power of education" (1.4.5, 7, 5.2–7), and in practice this requires recourse to what Montesquieu calls "singular institutions," of the sort found in Sparta and in early Rome,[13] which "shock all the received usages by confounding" not just "all the virtues" but "things naturally separate" such as "laws, mores, & manners" (1.4.6, 3.19.21). "There is nothing," Montesquieu writes in his *Considerations on the Romans*, "so powerful as a Republic in which the Laws are observed not out of fear, not because of reason, but by way of passion, as was the case at Rome & Lacedaemon—since there to the wisdom of good Government was joined all the force that faction can possess" (CR 4.60–64).

Montesquieu's description of the ancient republics and his analysis of their character Rousseau thought entirely just, but he did not share the misgivings that had caused the French philosopher to devote so much effort to assessing the virtues and prospects of monarchy and the peculiar form of government found in England.[14] In fact, the very features of classical republicanism that had occasioned such misgivings on Montesquieu's part were the features that Rousseau found most attractive. If one's aim is "to denature man, to remove from him his absolute existence in order to give him a relative existence, and to transport the *I* into a communal unity," he believed that one must provide for the passions of men a focus entirely new, and this is precisely what the ancient republics, with what Montesquieu had referred to as their "singular institutions," had done. By turning things upside down, by confounding all of the received usages and by mixing up laws, mores, and manners, Lycurgus and the early Romans had suppressed the "private passions" of men and had left them with no other motive apart from that artificial, unnatural "passion for the rule" which Montesquieu had called "love of the laws & the fatherland."[15]

"If at times," wrote Rousseau in his *Letter to d'Alembert*, "the Laws exercise an influence on mores, it is when" the former "draw from" the latter "their strength [*force*]." To the mores, he explains, the laws thereby "return that very strength by a species of reaction well known among genuine statesmen and political writers [*des vrais politiques*]." This explains why, upon assuming office, the Spartan ephors took it as their first task to issue "a public proclamation by which they enjoined the citizens not to observe the laws, but to love them," for they were intent that "their observation not be hard." Indeed, he adds, "this proclamation, which was not a vain formula, shows perfectly the spirit of Sparta's institution, by which the laws and the mores, intimately united in the hearts of the citizens, made up, so to speak, one and the same body" (LS 61).

CIVIL LIBERTY

Rousseau begins *The Social Contract* by posing the question whether "in the civil order there is some rule of administration" that is both "legitimate and sure, taking men as they are, and the laws as they can be." Then, after reminding his readers that he writes in his guise as a citizen of Geneva, eager to reconcile "what right permits and interest prescribes" (*CS* 1.Préf.), he states with characteristic panache what he takes to be the fundamental problem. "Man is born free," he writes, "and everywhere he is in chains." Then, he specifies that he is not simply speaking of subjugation in the ordinary sense of the word. "He who believes himself the master of others is," he writes, "more a slave than they are" (1.1).

By means of this paradox, Rousseau does two things at once. He alludes to the harsh analysis of the human condition within political society that is spelled out in his two discourses, and he lays the foundation for a novel account of political liberty that will set him apart from and in opposition to Montesquieu. It will be his claim that none but republics, armed with absolute popular sovereignty, can be free states and that always and everywhere the liberty of the people depends upon the power of the people (1.6–8, 2.1–4, 6, 11, 3.1–7, 10–12, 14–18, 4.1–3). And though, in discussing the management of mores within monarchical France, he will prove to be perfectly capable of applying Montesquieu's analysis of the manner in which honor, as a political principle, sets the polity in motion and determines its direction (*LS* 61–68), he will nonetheless assert that virtue, as understood by that same author, is the sole foundation for liberty and legitimate government (*CS* 3.4).

There is, Rousseau insists, a radical divide between "citizen" and "bourgeois." When man leaves the state of nature and enters political society, he gives up his "natural liberty" and "natural equality" and agrees to a "total alienation" of "all his rights" to a "Sovereign" constituted by "the community" that becomes his "Fatherland" thereby. This he does not just in pursuit of protection against assault and theft, but also in the hope that he might secure for himself by artifice a series of goods analogous to those which he possessed in the state of nature: to wit, a "guarantee against all personal dependence," a species of "civil liberty," and "an equality moral and legitimate," providing that citizens "unequal in strength [*force*] or in genius" be treated as "equals by convention and of right." None of these aims can, Rousseau contends, be realized unless, under the influence of public-spiritedness, within a given community "the particular will" of the individual, rooted in "his absolute and naturally independent existence," gives way to a "general will" aimed solely at "the public utility" (1.6–7, 2.3).[16] The full meaning of this development Rousseau spells out in his *Émile*, observing:

There are two sorts of dependence: that on things, which is from nature; and that on men, which is from society. Dependence on things, which has no moral implications [*aucune moralité*], does no harm to liberty at all and engenders no vices. The dependence on men in disordered fashion [*desordonnés*] engenders them all, and it is by it that master and slave mutually render one another depraved. If there is any means for remedying this ill within society, it is to substitute law for man and to arm the general wills with a real strength superior to the action of every particular will. If the laws of nations could have, as those of nature do, an inflexibility that no human strength could ever vanquish, dependence on men would then become dependence on things once more, one would reunite in the Republic all of the advantages of the natural state with those of the civil state, and one would join with liberty, which maintains man exempt from vices, the morality which raises him to virtue. (É 2.311)

This is possible, Rousseau explains in *The Social Contract*, only if "justice" and "the voice of duty" come to hold sway where "appetite," "impulse," and the natural "instinct" for self-preservation and pity had once reigned. To this end, it is necessary that free-riders, inclined to ignore and disobey "the general will," come to know that, as Rousseau tellingly and provocatively puts it, they "will be forced to be free";[17] and, by the same token, it is essential that "partial societies" of interested individuals be suppressed or systematically thwarted. In the absence of these preconditions, Rousseau insists, there can be no "legitimate civil engagements." In the wake of their fulfillment, however, there arises "the moral liberty, which alone renders man the master of himself, for the impulse of mere appetite is slavery, and obedience to the law which one prescribes to oneself is liberty" itself (CS 1.7–2.3).

This is a tall order, and Rousseau knows it. Of all the requirements for sustaining such a polity, the most crucial in his estimation are two: that there be genuine social and economic equality, and that the laws and the fatherland be seen at all times by all the citizens to be their own. To sustain the former, Rousseau suggests in his *Discourse on Political Economy*, it may be necessary to establish a system of taxation that is not just steeply progressive but, in effect and in intention, punitive as well (*DEP* 269–78 with 258–59).[18] The latter can be achieved, he indicates in *The Social Contract*, if and only if the law that each citizen obeys is a law that, he knows and powerfully feels, he has in public assembly, in a manner consistent with all of the formalities associated with majority rule, deliberately and freely imposed upon himself (CS 1.5–8, 2.1–4, 6, 12, 3.1–2, 4–7, 10–18, 4.1–3).[19] Genuine self-government is therefore a central feature of Rousseau's political project, and this explains why he devotes close attention, as Montesquieu had done before him, to the preconditions for republican government and to the institutions conducive to its success, emphasizing that the climate must be favorable (3.8), the territory small, and the citizens intimately familiar with one another (2.9–10, 3.15); suggesting confederacy as an expedient favorable to the defense of the diminutive communities required (3.13, 15); and spelling out in considerable detail by way of a survey of Roman practices a set of institutional arrangements that would allow such a polity to reconcile democratic sovereignty with aristocratic government, and popular consent with political prudence and a reliable execution of the laws (3.1–2, 4–7, 12–18, 4.2–7).[20] The logic of this analysis and many of its details are entirely in accord with what one finds in the discussion that Montesquieu devotes to republics in general and to the distribution of powers at Rome in *The Spirit of Laws*.[21]

Even where Rousseau departs from the letter of Montesquieu's writ, he nonetheless observes its spirit. Montesquieu regards representation as a useful political device: in medieval Europe, it had been crucial for sustaining "a government" exceptionally "well-tempered" (*EL* 2.11.8), and in England, as he makes clear, it still serves in exemplary fashion as the foundation for self-government (2.11.6, pp. 399–400). Nowhere does he expressly argue that representation is incompatible with the virtuous republicanism found in classical antiquity, but it is easy to see just how alien it would be in that setting. It is on this last fact that Rousseau insists. "As soon as public service ceases to be the principal pursuit [*affaire*] of Citizens and they would rather serve by means of their purse than serve in person," he observes, "the State is already near its ruin." Deputies sent to serve in representative institutions he likens to mercenary soldiers hired from abroad, and he traces the desire to substitute a payment of taxes for service in person to "the worry and upset [*tracas*]" occasioned by "commerce and the arts," to "the avid interest in gain," to "softness and the love of comforts [*commodités*]." "One gives up a part of one's profit," he writes, "to augment one's ease." Then, he issues a warning: "Give money, and soon you will have chains. This word *finance* is a slave's word; it is unknown in the City. In a State genuinely free, the citizens do everything" on their own hook "and nothing with money." In general, he concludes, "the better constituted the State, the more, in the minds of the Citizens, public business [*affaires*] takes precedence over private." Where "domestic cares absorb everything," it is an infallible sign of "bad Government" (*CS* 3.15).

Rousseau charges that the principle of representation is inconsistent with popular sovereignty. "The instant that a People gives itself Representatives," he contends, "it is no longer free." In fact, "it is no longer" a people at all (3.15). Rousseau had a favorable opinion of England and the English. Like Montesquieu (*EL* 3.19.27), he recognized that there was a connection between the practices associated with self-government in England and the mores, manners, and character of the English people. In his *Letter to d'Alembert,* he touches briefly on the element of republican austerity evident in the distance maintained between the two sexes in England, and he does so, as one would expect, with considerably greater approbation than Montesquieu managed to muster (*LS* 74–84, especially 74–76, with 43–53).[22] In *Julie,* he depicts an English lord in a fashion suggesting an admiration on his part for the generosity, the pride, and the sturdy independence of the English.[23] And in the last of his *Letters Written from the Mountain,* he asserts that the laws and practices of the English are far more favorable to liberty than those currently in place under the narrow oligarchy that actually governed his native Geneva (*LM* 9.876–79). Moreover, in a footnote to *The Social Contract,* Rousseau is willing to concede that "in our days" the English come "nearer to liberty than all the others" (*CS* 1.6). But, in the body of the text, he nonetheless insists that "the English people" err in supposing that they are "free" in fact. "They greatly deceive themselves," he writes. "They are free only during the election of the members of Parliament; as soon as these are elected, this people is a slave, it is nothing." Moreover, he adds, "in the short moments of its liberty, the use that" the English people "make of this liberty fully warrants its loss" (3.15). Elsewhere he writes that it is "very easy to foresee that, twenty years from now, England, with all of its glory, will be ruined and, even more, that it will have lost the remnants of its liberty."[24] In contrast with Montesquieu (I.2, above), he appears to have thought the efforts made by the English court to influence and corrupt Parliament worrisome in the extreme (*CP* 7.975).

At a time of frustration and exceptional candor, Rousseau extended this critique to his beloved Geneva itself. "You are neither Romans nor Spartans," he wrote in a letter addressed to his compatriots. "You are not even Athenians. Leave aside these great names, which will not wash. You are Merchants, Artisans, Bourgeois, always preoccupied with their private interest, their work, their traffic, their gain: people for whom liberty itself is only a means — for acquisition without obstacle, and for possession in security" (*LM* 9.881). You like to think of yourselves as "Sovereign Lords," he wrote in another such letter, but that you are not. "Four hours a year you are subordinate Sovereigns; the rest of your lives you are subjects, delivered without reservation into the discretion of another" (7.814–15).

"Man is born free," observed Rousseau, "and everywhere he is in chains." In Europe, the only place where liberty seemed even possible, there was in Rousseau's day not a single polity that came even close to meeting the standard of le-

gitimacy he had laid out. Given the territorial constraints imposed by his requirement that the legislative power be exercised by a people assembled at frequent intervals en masse, there was little prospect that any polity—apart, perhaps, from
some backwater like Geneva, Venice, or Corsica—would ever become what he
called a free state. If Rousseau looked back with great nostalgia to Sparta and to
early republican Rome, it was because he had nowhere else to look.

FOUNDING

The greatest impediment to the achievement of Rousseau's political project
stemmed not, however, from the obstacles thus far identified: it arose, instead,
from the monumental difficulty posed by the establishment of such a polity in
the first instance. This challenge Rousseau regarded as doubly difficult because
he shared Montesquieu's conviction that human nature is exceedingly plastic
and that peculiar local circumstances, both physical and moral, rule out the possibility that laws devised for one people should be suitable for another (CS 2.11,
3.8). "To discover the best rules of society suited to Nations," Rousseau wrote,
"would require a superior intelligence who saw all the passions of men and experienced none of them; who had no relation with our nature but understood it
thoroughly; whose happiness was independent of us but who, nevertheless, was
quite willing to occupy himself with ours; finally, one who, for the purpose of
preparing for himself a distant glory in the progress of time, was able to work in
one century and enjoy his just deserts in another." In short, he observed, "it
would take Gods to give laws to men" (2.7).[25]

The difficulty is, in fact, considerably greater than this passage suggests. The
legislator that Rousseau has in mind would have to frame for a particular society
not only a code of political, civil, and criminal laws. He would also have to establish "a fourth" species of law, which Rousseau, like Montesquieu, regards as
"the most important of all." This is the kind "which is engraved neither in mar-
ble nor in bronze but in the hearts of the citizens." It is this species of law, which
never comes up for a vote on the part of the sovereign authority, that forms "the
true constitution of the State." Daily, it "takes on new strength," and "when the
other laws grow old or are extinguished," it "revives or supplants them, preserving a people in the spirit of its institution," and "substituting imperceptibly the
force of habit for that of authority." "I speak," writes Rousseau, "of mores, of customs and, above all else, of opinion—a part [of the law code], unknown to our
statesmen and political writers [*politiques*], upon which depends the success of
all the other parts, a part on which the great Lawgiver busies himself in secret,

while he seems to restrict himself to particular regulations which are but the ribs of the arch — of which mores, slower to be born, form in the end the unshakeable Keystone" (2.12).[26]

If Rousseau places great emphasis on the unwritten laws, it is because he is firmly convinced that well-framed institutions are useless in the absence of civic virtue. "When the social knot begins to relax and the State to weaken," he writes, "when particular interests begin to make themselves felt and the little societies begin to exercise an influence on the large one, the common interest undergoes an alteration and encounters opponents, unanimity no longer reigns in the voting, the general will is no longer the will of all, contradictions and debates arise, and the best advice does not pass without dispute." Eventually, as the process of moral corruption unfolds, the state comes to "exist only in a form illusory and vain," and "the social bond is broken in all hearts." Then, when "the vilest interest has the effrontery to assume the sacred name of the public good, the general will becomes mute," and "all, guided by secret motives, think no more as Citizens" and comport themselves "as if the State had never existed, causing to pass falsely under the name of Laws iniquitous decrees which have no end other than particular interest" (4.1).[27]

Even in his discussion of this fourth species of law, Rousseau understates the magnitude of the challenge facing the lawgiver, for the importance he attributes to mores, customs, and opinions derives from the fact that, like Machiavelli, Hobbes, Hume, and Montesquieu, he denies that man is by nature a political animal. In consequence, he observes, the polity depends on artifice, and a man

who dares to undertake the institution of a people must sense that he is in a condition to change, so to speak, human nature; to transform each individual, who by himself is a whole perfect and solitary, into part of a much greater whole from which each individual receives in a certain fashion his life and his being; to alter the constitution of man for the purpose of giving it added strength [*pour renforcer*]; to substitute an existence partial and moral for an existence physical and independent which we have all received from nature. In a word, it is necessary that he remove from man the strengths [*forces*] belonging to him in order to give him strengths which are foreign to him and which he cannot use without the help of others. The more these natural strengths are dead and annihilated, the more those acquired are great and durable, the more the institution is solid and perfect. Insofar as each Citizen is nothing, is able to do nothing except with all the others, and the strength acquired by the whole is equal or superior to the sum of the natural strength of all the individuals, one can say that the legislation is at the highest point of perfection that it can attain.

It is this task, which Lycurgus and the early Romans had once accomplished in the misty past, that, Rousseau insists, must now once again be carried out if men are ever to be free. "The great soul of the Lawgiver," he avers, "is the true miracle which must prove his mission" (2.7).

What makes such an undertaking theoretically possible is what makes it difficult beyond measure: the brute fact that reason is the slave of the passions and that man is, as Montesquieu claims (*EL* Préf.), a profoundly flexible being — endowed with the species of practical freedom and the capacity to reshape himself that Rousseau describes as *perfectibilité*.[28] What makes what is possible in theory conceivable also in practice is the remarkable human capacity for self-forgetting that Montesquieu identified (*CR* 12.90–110) when he reflected on the political role played by suicide in late republican and early imperial Rome and traced our propensity "to sacrifice our Being for the sake of our Being" to the capacity of *l'amour propre* to shift shape (I.2, above).

It is not important that Rousseau's legislator convince prospective citizens by rational argument that they are one. Nor is it really possible. After all, by nature, man is neither a rational nor a political animal. According to Rousseau, the ties that bind human beings to one another and make of them fellow citizens are entirely imaginary. They have no substantive existence. They are artificial and illusory; they have to be constructed in the mind. To make citizens of men, one must then lie and make them believe.[29] In consequence, if he is to be successful, the lawgiver has to be an artist of sorts, supremely capable of firing the imagination with arresting and seductive images. His task is rhetorical; his aim is persuasion.[30] Like a musician, he must address the passions and direct his appeal to the human heart.[31] By conjuring up a mesmerizing vision and by taking full command of the human imagination, he must redirect the *amour propre* that arises in man when he first enters society by giving it a new focus; in this fashion, he must politicize narcissism and transform the vanity responsible for the rivalry, the bitterness, the misery, and the unhappiness that beset bourgeois life into a passion corporate and communal — into what Montesquieu had called "a love of the laws & the fatherland."

As Rousseau puts it in his *Discourse on Political Economy*, it is "the love of the fatherland" that "joins the strength of *amour propre* with all the beauty of virtue, giving" democracy's political principle "an energy — which makes of it, without disfiguring it, the most heroic of all the passions." If young people, he adds, are trained from a very early stage in life "never to regard themselves except in relation with the body of the State, and not to perceive, so to speak, their own existence except as a part of the State, in the end they will come in a certain fashion to identify themselves with the whole, to feel themselves members of the father-land, [and] to love it with the exquisite sentiment that every isolated man feels only for himself." In this manner, he concludes, they will transform "into a virtue sublime that dangerous disposition from which all of our vices are born" (*DEP* 254–62, especially 255, 259–60).[32] In this manner, as Rousseau makes clear in his fragmentary *Constitutional Project for Corsica*, if properly directed, *amour propre* will eventuate—not in a vanity (*vanité*) that divides individuals, makes them rivals, and sets them at odds, but in a communal pride (*orgeuil*) that brings them together as citizens (*PC* 937–39).

In *Émile*, Rousseau describes in detail how such a reorientation of *amour propre* might be accomplished within an individual over whose formation one has unlimited control (*É* 4.523–48, especially 547–48), but he nowhere spells out how this might be done for the young people of an entire community. In his *Discourse on Political Economy*, he simply insists "that in the long run peoples are what the government makes them be," and he attributes to government an "authority most absolute," which "penetrates to the interior of man and exercises itself no less on the will than on the actions." To justify his claim, he points to the example set by governments in classical antiquity with their sumptuary laws, their multifarious regulations concerning morals, and the maxims they adopted, and he notes with evident admiration the care that the ancient Spartans took with regard to the education of the young (*DEP* 251–52, 259–62).

Elsewhere, in passing, Rousseau provides further information. In the open letter addressed to Jean Le Rond d'Alembert, which he published in 1758, he argued that the establishment of a theater at Geneva would do untold harm, subverting civic mores, promoting social competition, and encouraging inequality, and he suggested public festivals on the Spartan model as an alternative. In describing the influence of the theater in modern times, Rousseau rang changes on his critique of bourgeois society. "Men believe that they assemble at a *Spectacle*," but, he observes, "it is there that each isolates himself: it is there that one goes to forget one's friends, one's neighbors, one's relations; to interest oneself in fables; to cry over the misfortunes of the dead." Or, he adds ominously, it is to the theater that one goes "to laugh at the expense of the living." In modern times, theatrical heroism seems distant and false. It presents "virtue as a theatrical game [*un jeu de theatre*], good for amusing the public," but not suitable for introduction into society. In modern times, when men are pusillanimous, comedy is the more powerful art by far, and it wreaks moral havoc, for "the very pleasure" that it imparts is "founded on" envy, which is "a vice of the human heart." In the end, Rousseau argues, "satire [*charge*] does not render its objects hateful; it merely renders them ridiculous, and from this there arises a great inconvenience—that, out of a fear of ridicule, men are no longer frightened of vice." Virtue has its foundation in moral "indignation"; "ridicule is, by way of contrast, the weapon [*arme*] favored by vice." It is a means, Rousseau contends, for subjecting ordinary, relatively simple men to the opinions of clever, talented sophisticates—on whose corrupt judgment they will ultimately come to depend (*LS* 16, 24–25, 31, 61–62).[33]

Of course, in a place such as Paris, Rousseau sneers, drama may serve a genuine purpose. "In a big city," he writes, "full of intriguing do-nothings, without Religion, without principles, where men whose imaginations—depraved by idleness and laziness, by the love of pleasure, and by great needs—engender only monsters and inspire nothing but heinous crimes [*forfaits*]," there is something to be said for encouraging them to while away an evening at the theater. After all, plays attract foreigners, promote the circulation of coin, stimulate artists, encourage new fashions, distract the people from their misery, and, most important of all, they keep idlers off the streets and out of mischief. They serve not only "to cover the repulsive ugliness [*laideur*] of vice with a varnish of artifice [*procédés*]," but also "to prevent bad mores from degenerating into brigandage." In smaller communities, however, "in places less populated, where individuals, always under the eyes of the public, are born censors of one another, and where the public administration [*la police*] can easily oversee all, it is necessary to follow contrary maxims" (53–59).[34]

There, especially if the community is "a Republic," a different species of "*Spectacle*" is appropriate. There what is required are "public festivals" in the open air in which people "frequently assemble" and foster among themselves "sweet ties of pleasure and joy."

> Plant in the middle of a square a stake crowned with flowers, assemble the people, and you will have a festival. Better yet, do this: make a Spectacle of the Spectators; make of them actors themselves; cause each to see himself and love himself in the others so that all are better united. I have no need to turn to the games of the ancient Greeks; there are ones more modern, and they still exist, and I find them precisely among us. [In Geneva,] we have every year reviews, public prizes, Kings of the arquebus, of the canon, of the carrying trade [*navigation*]; one cannot too much multiply institutions so useful and so agreeable; there cannot be too many Kings of this sort.

To this end, Rousseau suggested military contests and contests in gymnastics, wrestling, running, discus-hurling, and the like, which would make of Geneva the veritable "image of Lacedaemon." To this end, he suggested balls in the winter. He favored anything that would render the citizens "lively, gay, affectionate"; anything that would cause them to display "their hearts" in "their eyes" and "on their lips"; anything that would induce them "to communicate their joy and their pleasures" so that "all of the societies become as one" and "everything becomes common to all." In short, he welcomed any pastime that would make of his fatherland "a great family" so that "from the bosom of joy and pleasures would be born the conservation, the concord, and the prosperity of the Republic." Such was the example set by Sparta, where "the citizens, continually assembled, consecrated life entire to amusements that were the great business of the state, and to games which they abandoned solely for war" (115–23).[35]

One seemingly insuperable problem remains. It is one thing to sustain such a regimen; it is another to put it in place. To sustain it, one must concentrate on the formation of the young and on their encouragement as they grow older; to establish it in the first place, one must reform those who have long before settled into another, contrary mold. In *The Social Contract*, Rousseau describes the problem in this fashion: "in order for a people in the process of being born to develop a taste for healthy political maxims and to follow the fundamental rules of reason of State, it would be necessary for the effect to be able to become the cause, for the social spirit that ought to be the work of the people's institution to preside at the institution itself, and for men to be before the provision of laws that which they ought to become as a consequence of the laws" (CS 2.7).

Later, Rousseau indicates just how this difficulty can be overcome. "Just as certain illnesses turn men's heads upside down and deprive them of the memory of the past," he writes, "so, in the duration of states, violent epochs sometimes take place in which revolutions do to peoples what crises do to individuals, where a horror of the past takes the place of forgetfulness, and where the State, set ablaze by civil wars, is reborn, so to speak, from the cinders and recovers the vigor of youth in emerging from the clutches of death." Such was the experience of Sparta in the age of Lycurgus, of Rome after the Tarquins; and in modern times, Rousseau claims, something quite similar took place in Holland and Switzerland "after the expulsion of the Tyrants" (2.8).[36]

SINGULAR INSTITUTIONS

In the course of surveying the obstacles to success, Rousseau adds an additional fact: that, to persuade the people, the ancient lawgivers always had recourse to the gods (2.7). He is, he confesses in *Émile*, in perfect agreement with Pierre Bayle in supposing that "fanaticism is more pernicious than atheism." He readily acknowledges that it is "bloody and cruel." But, in contrast with Bayle, he insists that "fanaticism is, for all of that, a passion great and strong, which elevates the heart of man, which makes him despise death, which gives him a prodigious motive for action [*ressort*], and which needs only to be better directed if it is to elicit from him virtues sublime." In Rousseau's judgment, "irreligion—and the *esprit* associated with reasoning and philosophy in general—attaches souls to [mere] life, renders them effeminate and vile, centers all the passions in the baseness of individual interest, in the abjectness of the human *I*, and thereby it saps with little fanfare [*bruit*] the true foundations of every society" (É 4.632n–35n).

In his *Considerations on the Government of Poland*, Rousseau spells out what is, in practice, required for the foundation of a well-ordered polity. There, with one eye on Machiavelli's account in *The Prince* of those "new princes" who introduced "new orders and modes,"[37] and with the other on Montesquieu's discussion of peoples with "singular institutions,"[38] he picks out three lawgivers for attention. First, he names Moses, who formed "a nation" and "a free people" from "a throng of unfortunate fugitives without arts, arms, talents, virtues, or courage" and did so by giving them "mores and usages incompatible with those of other nations" along with "rites" and "ceremonies peculiar" to them alone. "He embarrassed and inconvenienced [*gena*] them in a thousand ways in order to keep them on tenterhooks [*en haleine*] and to render them forever strangers among other men," Rousseau claims. Among "the members of his republic," he established "ties of fraternity" to serve as "barriers," which would "hold them separate from their neighbors and prevent them from mixing" with outsiders. These ties were so strong, Rousseau reports, that "this singular nation—so often subjugated, so often dispersed and apparently destroyed but always idolizing its rule—was nonetheless preserved until our days, dispersed among the others without being confounded with them in such a manner that its mores, its laws, and rites subsist and will endure as long as the world, despite the hatred and persecution" that this nation suffers at the hands of "the rest of the human race."

In this context, as one would expect, Rousseau also mentions Lycurgus, who "undertook the institution of a people," which was "already degraded by servitude and the vices which are its effect." On them, he imposed "a yoke of iron, such that no other people ever bore the like," attaching them "to this yoke," identifying them "with this yoke by occupying them with it all the time." Their "fatherland he kept constantly before their eyes in laws, games, homes, loves, and festivities that were their own." He did not "allow them an instant of relaxation" so that they could be alone, and "from this continual constraint, ennobled by its object, was born in this people that ardent love of the fatherland which was at all times the strongest or, rather, the unique passion of the Spartiates, and which made of them beings above humanity."

Most telling, however, is Rousseau's description of Numa, the third member of the trio. "Those," he observes, "who have seen in him nothing but an originator of rites and religious ceremonies have judged very badly regarding this great man." In his opinion, "Numa was the true founder of Rome." Romulus did nothing but "assemble brigands, whom a single reverse might have dispersed; his imperfect work did not have the ability to withstand time." It was, in fact, Numa "who rendered it solid and durable by uniting the brigands into a body indissoluble," and this he achieved by "transforming them into Citizens, less by laws," for which, in their rustic poverty, they had little need, "than by gentle institutions which attached them to one another and to the soil they shared" and by rendering "their city sacred by means of rites, frivolous and superstitious in appearance," which had a "strength and effect" that very few have properly appreciated.

According to Rousseau, these three statesmen were guided by "the same spirit." To "attach the Citizens to the fatherland and to one another," he tells us, they sought to deploy "peculiar usages" and "religious ceremonies," which were "always in their nature exclusive and national." These institutions they reinforced with public games and assemblies and with spectacles designed to remind the citizens of "the history of their ancestors, their misfortunes, their virtues, their victories." These spectacles were contrived in such a fashion as to "engage their hearts" and "to inflame them with a lively spirit of emulation," which would "attach them to that fatherland with which it was intended that they constantly occupy themselves" (*CP* 2.956–59).

It is the example set by Moses, Lycurgus, and Numa that Rousseau urges the Poles to emulate. What is required on their part is the establishment of singular, "national institutions," capable of forming "the character, the tastes, and the mores of a people"; of making that people "itself and not another"; of inspiring "in it an ardent love of the fatherland founded on habits impossible to uproot"; and of ensuring that, when abroad, its members will "die of boredom" even when "in the bosom of delights" denied them when at home. In short, what is required is that the Poles come to have a genuine homeland. "Today," Rousseau warns, "whatever people say, there are no longer Frenchmen, Germans, Spaniards, or even Englishmen: there are only Europeans." Everywhere, as a consequence of French influence, there is a drab uniformity. "All possess the same tastes, the same passions, the same mores, because no people has received a national form impressed upon it by an institution particular to it." This has untoward moral consequences:

> In the same circumstances, all will carry out the same undertakings; all will say that they are disinterested and behave as rogues [*fripons*]; all will speak of the public good and think only of themselves; all will boast of moderation and wish to be as rich as Croesus. They have ambition, but only for luxury; they

have passion, but only for gold. Confident that, with this last, they will be able to get everything that tempts them, they will sell themselves to the first bidder willing to pay. What matters it to them what master they obey, which State's laws guide their conduct? Provided that they find money to steal and women to corrupt, they are in their own country wherever they may be.

If the Poles are to avoid such a fate, the lawgiver must, Rousseau contends, "give to their passions another propensity [*pente*]" and "confer on their souls a national physiognomy distinguishing them from other peoples, preventing them from confounding themselves with other peoples, from being pleased with other peoples, from aligning themselves with other peoples." This lawgiver must make the Poles "do out of taste and passion that which is never well enough done when it is done out of duty or interest." He must instill in them "a grand opinion of themselves and their fatherland." He must prevent them from following "the tendency, general in Europe," to ape "the tastes and mores of the French." To this end, Rousseau encourages the lawgiver to revive "ancient practices," to "introduce others suited to the Poles," and to establish public games, exercises, festivals, and solemnities on the Spartan and Roman model—all with an eye to engaging their hearts (3.959–66).

In precisely the same spirit, Rousseau insists that "education" is the single most "important subject [*article*]" raised in his *Considérations*. It is, he contends, "education that ought to give to souls" what he calls *la force nationale*, directing "their opinions and their tastes in such a manner that they are patriotic by inclination, by passion, by necessity." From birth to death, he argues, a Pole should have nothing before his eyes apart from the fatherland. "Every true republican has drunk with his mother's milk a love of the fatherland, which is to say, a love of the laws and of liberty. This love makes up his entire existence; he sees only the fatherland; he lives for it alone. If he is alone, he is nothing; if he no longer has a fatherland, he is himself no longer; if he is not then dead, he is worse than dead." To achieve this, Rousseau urges the establishment of a system of public education under close supervision by the magistrates, which will promote the study of Polish history and encourage gymnastic exercise (4.966–70). It is telling and typical that to the discussion summarized here Rousseau gives precedence, turning only thereafter to the institutional reforms needed if Poland is to become a viable state (5.970–14.1056).

CIVIL RELIGION

In similar fashion, at the very end of *The Social Contract*, Rousseau devotes a chapter to what he terms "civil religion" (*CS* 4.8).[39] As he knew, Montesquieu had traced the disappearance of classical republicanism to the fact that, while the "education" given the ancients "never suffered contradiction, we receive three educations different" from and even "contrary" to one another—"that of our fathers, that of our schoolmasters, that of the world"—arguing that "what we are told in the last overthrows the ideas imparted by the first two." In modern times, because of Christianity, Montesquieu had insisted, there is "a contrast between the engagements" which arise "from religion" and those which arise "from the world" that "the ancients knew nothing of" (*EL* 1.4.4). It was this that rendered it impossible for the moderns to inculcate political virtue. So he believed.

With Montesquieu's judgment, Rousseau was in complete accord. In Roman Catholicism, he recognized the supreme obstacle to the political reform that he intended. Like Machiavelli and John Milton before him,[40] he regarded the church as a political conspiracy. The "communion of churches" was, he contended, the key to its power: "Communion and excommunication are the social pact of the clergy—with which it will be always the master of peoples and of Kings. All the priests who are in communion with one another [*qui communique ensemble*] are fellow citizens—be they at opposite ends of the world. This invention is a masterpiece in politics. There was nothing similar among the pagan Priests: so they never formed the Clergy into a body." In Rousseau's estimation, the only figure within Christendom "who saw the evil and the remedy with clarity, who dared to propose a reunification of the two heads of the eagle and a restoration of everything to the political unity without which no State or Government will ever be well constituted" was Thomas Hobbes. But even he underestimated "the domineering spirit of Christianity," and in consequence he failed to see "that the interest of the Priest will always be stronger than that of the State" (*CS* 4.8).

A few paragraphs thereafter, to be sure, Rousseau speaks with respect of "the Religion of man" as a religion "without Temples, without altars, without rites, limited to a worship [*culte*], purely interior, of the Supreme God and to the eternal duties of morality." This he calls "the pure and simple religion of the Gospel [*l'Evangile*]" and "the true Theism," but at the same time he remarks that it lends no support to the laws and that, "far from attaching the hearts of the Citizens to the State, it detaches them from it as it detaches them from all the things of the earth." And later in the chapter he asserts that a Christian republic is a contradiction in terms. "Christianity preaches nothing but servitude and dependence," he writes. "Its spirit is too favorable to tyranny not to profit from it. True Christians are made to be slaves; they know it and are hardly moved by the prospect;

this short life has too little worth in their eyes." Nothing, he contends, could be "more contrary to the social spirit" than is the Christian faith (4.8).

The alternative, which Rousseau speaks of as "the Religion . . . of the Citizen," can be found "inscribed in a single country," on which it confers "its Gods, its own tutelary Patrons: it has its dogmas, its rites, its public cult prescribed by the laws; outside the one Nation which follows it, everything is for it infidel, foreign, barbarous; it extends the duties and the rights of man only as far as its altars." It has this virtue. "It reunites the divine cult and the love of the laws, and it makes the Fatherland an object of adoration for the Citizens, teaching them that to serve the State is to serve the tutelary God." In such a polity, "to die for one's country is to become a martyr, to violate the laws is to be impious, and to submit a guilty man to public execration is an act of devotion delivering him to the wrath of the Gods" (4.8).[41]

The logic of Rousseau's argument suggests that a destruction of Christianity and something along the lines of a restoration of pagan religion must have been a central part of his aim, and it is certainly the case that he intended to displace organized Christianity.[42] But it is also true that he recoils in apparent horror at the prospect of embracing a religion, "based on error and on falsehood, that deceives men, renders them credulous, superstitious, and drowns the genuine cult of the divinity in vain ceremonial," and he condemns this species of civic religion for its propensity to become "exclusive and tyrannical" and to make "a people sanguinary and intolerant—so that it breathes nothing but murder and massacre, and believes that it commits a holy act in killing whoever does not admit its Gods." This religion, he quite rightly concludes, "places such a people in a natural state of war with all the other peoples," and he contends that this is "very harmful to its own security" (4.8).

Whether this last claim is always, in fact, just remains unclear. That Machiavelli thought otherwise is abundantly evident in his *Discourses on Livy*; and though Montesquieu sought to subvert the attractiveness of the Roman model in his *Considerations on the Romans*, he did not anticipate the indictment leveled at the ancient city by Rousseau in this particular passage. It is, in fact, highly revealing that, where Montesquieu had candidly identified "aggrandizement" as "the object of Rome" (*EL* 2.11.5), the citizen of Geneva balks and refuses to follow his lead. In his restatement of Montesquieu's argument, Rousseau alters his predecessor's analysis of the "principal object" to which each of the various states is devoted in only one crucial particular—by specifying that the object pursued by the Rome he takes as his model polity is "virtue" alone (*CS* 2.11). That he was preeminent among those who inspired the prophets of radical nationalism—

first, in France, and then elsewhere—there can hardly be doubt,[43] and he was perfectly prepared to acknowledge as a mere "inconvenience" the fact that "every patriot is harsh to strangers; they are only men; in his eyes, they are nothing" (É 1.248). But when faced with the full implications of the position he appeared to embrace, this great cosmopolitan soul pulled up short.

In any case, Rousseau insists, "there is now no longer an exclusive national Religion, and it is no longer possible for there to be one." In the end, then, he proposes, as an alternative to Christianity, a tepid, toothless Deism devoid of clergy—"a profession of faith purely civil" with a handful of articles set by the Sovereign "not precisely as dogmas of Religion but as sentiments of sociability without which it" would be "impossible to be a good Citizen and faithful subject" (CS 4.8).[44] Whether a civil religion of this sort could ever suffice to effect a transformation of human nature as radical as the one that Rousseau advocates elsewhere in *The Social Contract* and in his *Discourse on Political Economy* remains doubtful. There is an obvious discrepancy between the fierce, particularist "love of the laws & the fatherland" required to sustain a republic cast on the lines laid out by Montesquieu and Rousseau and the gentle, universalist religion that Rousseau describes here. As Machiavelli made clear,[45] and Montesquieu certainly understood, patriotism on the ancient model can hardly be sustained by a requirement that one merely affirm as a matter of public duty "the existence" of a single divinity—"powerful, intelligent, beneficent, clairvoyant, and provident"—and confess one's belief in "the life to come, the happiness of the just, the punishment of the wicked, and the sanctity of the social Contract and Laws" (4.8).

The "purely civil Religion" proposed by Rousseau in *The Social Contract* is an attempt to square the circle. As he put it not long after that work's publication, his aim therein was to "reaffirm all the dogmas of every good Religion, all the dogmas useful to society, whether universal or particular," and to "omit the others." In practice, however, such a compromise between universality and particularity is unworkable, and Rousseau knew it. His civil religion is what he calls "a universal Religion." As such, it is subject to certain of the objections that he leveled at Christianity. "In the eyes of the genuine Christian," he writes, "the citizen, the stranger, even the enemy—these men are equally his brothers; nothing is more contrary to the spirit of Christianity than exclusions and preferences. And what then is the love of the fatherland if not preference and exclusion?" (LM 1.704–6, with the variants found in JJR III 1592–95). In this passage, he could have been discussing his own civil religion and its adherents.

We are left to wonder whether for Rousseau classical antiquity is anything more than a stick with which to beat bourgeois modernity. After all, in one passage, he openly admits that "there is no longer a fatherland" and that "there can no longer be citizens" (É 1.250); and in another, he confesses that "the ancient Peoples are no longer a model for the moderns; to the latter, they are in all regards too alien" (*LM* 9.881). Moreover, by way of the critique that he levels at national religions with their warring gods, he betrays a distaste for the martial orientation of the ancient republics and for the fanatical patriotism that animated them, and he demonstrates once again just how much he owes to Montesquieu. Thus, when Rousseau proffers practical advice to his fellow Genevans, to the Corsicans, and the Poles, he has in mind a halfway house of sorts: a polity neither fully martial nor bourgeois, whose members occupy a position intermediate between that held by citizens in classical antiquity and that of the very first men, and who savor something approaching "the sweetness of a social interchange free from dependence [*un commerce independant*]" that had, he claims, typified early human society prior to the invention of agriculture (*DOI* 169–71).[46]

Moreover, when the tutor in Rousseau's *Émile* briefly outlines for his charge the argument of *The Social Contract,* he does not do so in order to instill in Émile a desire for revolution or even reform. He does so solely in order to equip his pupil with a standard by which to judge and assess the polities he observes on his grand tour. That none of these governments will measure up and that his charge will find the political arena a profound disappointment and direct his attention elsewhere the tutor takes for granted (É 5.826–68). It is evidently his intention that Émile come to recognize that man is not a political animal, that his life within the polity will never be fully satisfactory, and that the best life is a life of conjugal and paternal love, lived in a country retreat, outside the maelstrom, far from the madding crowd.[47] In such a setting, the civil religion proposed in *The Social Contract*; the profession of faith that the Savoyard vicar imparts to the tutor in *Émile*; and the reasonable Christianity, almost bereft of dogma and reduced to a religion of sincerity, that Rousseau attributes to Julie all seem appropriate. By promising men judgment after death at the hands of a just and providential God, each of these bolsters in a politically and socially salutary fashion the confidence, otherwise untenable, that there is a moral order in which moral virtue and self-interest are fully reconciled.[48]

ROUSSEAU'S LEGACY

Montesquieu died in February 1755, some months before the publication of the *Discourse on the Origin and Foundations of Inequality among Men.* There is little likelihood that he had an opportunity to read that work in manuscript, and concerning Rousseau's later works—*Julie, Émile, The Social Contract,* and *The*

Reveries of the Solitary Stroller—he can have known nothing at all. He may, however, have been tolerably well informed concerning the future author of these works. He had probably met Madame Dupin's secretary on the occasion of one of the visits he made to the Dupin household in the last few years before the publication of his magnum opus,[49] and in mid-February 1752 he was told by a correspondent that a certain Rousseau from Geneva was among those aiding Claude Dupin in his attempt at a refutation of *The Spirit of Laws*.[50] Whether by this time he had bothered to read the *Discourse on the Sciences and the Arts* we do not know, but he can hardly have missed learning about its contents. After all, thanks to the abbé Raynal, it was the talk of the town, and by early 1752 it had been so for nine months or more.

Montesquieu's only recorded comment regarding Rousseau is cryptic in the extreme. Years later, Rousseau's compatriot Jean-Vincent Capperonnier de Gauffecourt wrote to him that Montesquieu "told me on a number of occasions that there was no one but you who was capable of working on *The Spirit of Laws*."[51] Whether Rousseau's correspondent was correct in supposing the remark a compliment, we cannot tell. It might have been an oblique reference to the *First Discourse*, which rehearsed certain themes from Montesquieu's great book and did so in a fashion suggesting to the discerning reader a keen understanding. But, given Montesquieu's awareness of Rousseau's labors alongside Dupin, we should not rule out the possibility that the remark was barbed. We know that the author of *The Spirit of Laws* found Dupin's efforts at articulating a critique of that work highly disagreeable (*MP* 2239), and there is an utterly plausible report that Dupin's decision to withdraw and suppress the printed version of the first of his two efforts came at the behest of the king's mistress, Madame de Pompadour, who had been prompted to intervene by Montesquieu himself.[52] That the latter should have been annoyed at Rousseau as well makes perfect sense. More we will probably never know.

What should by now be clear, however, is that Jean-Jacques Rousseau constructed his system within the framework of Montesquieu's political science. It is also evident that the critique of bourgeois society that he shouted from the rooftops was a restatement of themes presented in a highly muted fashion in *The Spirit of Laws*. Rousseau was an archaeologist of sorts. He unearthed and displayed to startling effect certain quite serious defects in commercial society that Montesquieu had clearly wished to indicate but without highlighting them or conferring on them undue stress.

In the process, Rousseau struck an exposed nerve. With rare exceptions, every one of his books was a best seller. In the last half of the eighteenth century, in sales and in influence, no other contemporary author came even close. In

France especially, with its tinsel culture—but also in England and elsewhere in Europe—there evidently existed, as he was convinced, a powerful strain of discontent, a profound and pervasive *inquiétude*, a sense of displacement and alienation that had not yet found its voice. Rousseau persistently argued, as we have seen, that—within the large, territorial states of Europe and within societies already thoroughly bourgeois—nothing good could come from either revolution or reform, and therein he appears to have counseled political resignation and a species of withdrawal. But his rhetoric was incendiary nonetheless, and he persistently led his readers to the edge of the precipice before shying away. It is hard to believe that as a writer he did not know what he was about. After all, with consummate skill, he laid hold of the inchoate uneasiness afflicting his contemporaries and gave it both substance and form. In doing so, he fomented the revolutionary and the nationalist impulses and the democratic envy that he so frequently professed to abhor; and by insisting that men are naturally good and that all of the wickedness they display and all of the misery they suffer can be traced to the political institutions under which they live, he fostered within what was in origin a secular impulse an almost messianic hope, and he inspired in many a reader a profound longing to establish new institutions capable of transforming the human condition and of reworking thereby the very nature of man.[53]

It was the titanic ambition of Jean-Jacques Rousseau that determined the shape that moral, political, and aesthetic speculation would take for decades and even centuries to come. He was, in fact, a legislator of sorts—supremely capable of fabricating mesmerizing images of the miseries and bitterness spawned by bourgeois society, of the simple pleasures that purportedly sufficed for primitive man, of the joys attendant on romantic and paternal love, of the potential inherent in an education of the sentiments, of the glories inspired by the intense patriotism that characterized the ancient republics, and of the satisfactions associated with an aesthetic loss of self. In crafting and projecting these arresting images, he fired the imaginations of subsequent artists and thinkers; and, with their assistance, he worked profound and lasting changes in the mores, the manners, and the opinions of future generations.[54]

In every generation since, commercial society has had as its Doppelgänger a powerful, bohemian counter-culture grounded in a vulgarization of one or more aspects of the thinking of Rousseau. Every radical movement of both left and right, from Jacobinism at the time of the French Revolution through communism and fascism in the twentieth century to the anti-globalization movement, the environmental movement, and the Islamist jihad characteristic of our own time, has wittingly or unwittingly taken as its starting point one or another variation on the powerful critique of bourgeois society first suggested in the *Discourse on the Sciences and the Arts,* first fully fleshed out in the *Discourse on the Origin and Foundations of Inequality among Men,* and then summarized again and again in Rousseau's subsequent works; and every such movement has served up as a remedy a program inspired in one fashion or another by the vision of revolutionary transformation and integral community that Rousseau intimated in those works and projected most fully in the *Discourse on Political Economy* and *The Social Contract.*[55]

The arguments that the citizen of Geneva disinterred from *The Spirit of Laws* and distilled, extended, refined, and supplemented are very much with us even today.[56] Within our world, wars and revolutions come and go. They sometimes seem almost epiphenomenal; they appear to be utterly superfluous. They occupy us for a time, and when they are over, we find ourselves back in the same place, right where we began. From a cultural perspective, events seem hardly to matter at all. Through thick and thin, Rousseau's diagnosis of our plight and the various palliatives he suggested somehow retain their purchase. If at times they appear to be the ravings of a profoundly tortured soul, they cannot simply be dismissed as such. Rousseau's panoramic vision may seem preposterous and outlandish, but it cannot be ignored. It speaks to the felt needs of untold millions, many of whom have never even read a line of Rousseau. It exercises a profound and largely uncharted influence within the culture at large, shaping attitudes toward religion, the environment, the family, child rearing, education, gardening, music, art, literature, romantic love, politics, and the good life more generally. As a brute fact, it must be taken into account.

We live, even now, in the new world that Voltaire and Montesquieu discovered when, separately, they crossed the English Channel in the late 1720s. We profit in astonishing ways from the advantages that these two Frenchmen discerned within the peculiar society that took shape in England after the Glorious Revolution, and we suffer from the defects characteristic of that society, which Montesquieu identified in *The Spirit of Laws* and Rousseau took as his principal theme. Fortunately for us, Montesquieu's muted misgivings and Rousseau's deepest concerns were not ignored: they were thoughtfully considered, assessed, and in a certain fashion assimilated by the most careful student that liberal democracy has thus far known. It is a matter of poetic justice that this student should turn out to be who he in fact was—great-grandson of the liberal statesman Chrétien-Guillaume Lamoignon de Malesherbes: the passionate admirer of Montesquieu and the patron and friend of Rousseau, who, in his capacity as *Directeur de la librairie* from 1750 to 1763, had connived in the publication or circulation in France of the *Encyclopédie* and of every one of Rousseau's most important works.

Book Three

The Democratic Republic Considered

Today, whatever people say, there are no longer Frenchmen, Germans, Spaniards, or even Englishmen: there are only Europeans. All possess the same tastes, the same passions, the same mores, because no people has received a national form impressed upon it by an institution particular to it. In the same circumstances, all will carry out the same undertakings; all will say that they are disinterested and behave as rogues; all will speak of the public good and think only of themselves; all will boast of moderation and wish to be as rich as Croesus. They have ambition, but only for luxury; they have passion, but only for gold. Confident that, with this last, they will be able to get everything that tempts them, they will sell themselves to the first bidder willing to pay. What matters it to them what master they obey, which State's laws guide their conduct? Provided that they find money to steal and women to corrupt, they are in their own country wherever they may be.

— *Jean-Jacques Rousseau*

PREFACE

On 2 April 1831, two well-dressed Frenchmen boarded a ship in Le Havre bound for New York. Like Voltaire and Montesquieu, who had journeyed to unknown shores barely more than a century before, these two young men were intent on making a political pilgrimage—one which, they, too, hoped, would enable them to discern the shape of things to come. Like Montesquieu, both were trained in the law. Both were also magistrates. But neither seriously expected to eke out a life as a functionary deep in the bowels of the administrative state. Like their two predecessors, they had literary—and political—ambitions. Like them as well, these two had grown up in the shadow of a profound, epoch-making event in the history of France and that of the larger world,[1] and they had chosen to go abroad for the purpose of attempting to come to grips with the world-historical significance of that transformative event.

The younger and more precocious of the two had been obsessed with the French Revolution for at least six years. With it in mind, he had read widely. He had reviewed the great debate that had taken place between the liberal monarchists and the ultra-royalists in the wake of the second Bourbon Restoration, perusing books and speeches by Madame de Staël, Benjamin Constant, Pierre-Paul Royer-Collard, Amable-Guillaume-Prosper Brugière de Barante, François Guizot, and their opponents.[2] For just over two years, from 9 April 1828 to 29 May 1830, with considerable fidelity, he had attended and taken detailed notes on the celebrated lectures on the history of civilization in Europe and in France delivered by Guizot,[3] who was the leading theorist among those in France labeled by their opponents the *Doctrinaires*; and, when these lectures were published, he had read them, and other works by their author, with very great care. In consequence, by the time he and his companion had left France, he had made his own what he called "the *esprit analytique* of Guizot," with its insistence on the existence of a correlation between the evolution in man's social condition and the changes that take place in his outlook, sentiments, and mores. In the process, he had also located and identified defects of profound importance in Guizot's overly confident and complacent account of the progress of European civilization;[4] and with these defects in mind, he had developed a conceptual scheme enabling him to frame the questions that he wanted to ask when he reached America.[5]

Guizot, who greatly admired Anne-Robert-Jacques Turgot, was persuaded that the history of the Christian West would soon eventuate in the establishment of a representative government dominated by the bourgeoisie, which would in turn consent to governance by a cadre of men, such as himself, distinguished by their natural superiority.[6] It was this prospect, that politics really would be reduced to rational administration by a class claiming expertise, that haunted the younger of the two travelers. By April 1830, he had come to the conclusion that if Guizot's understanding of the historical evolution of Europe was more or less correct, as he assumed it was, what was most likely in store was the establishment of a "social body" that would be intent on exercising foresight with regard to everything; that would act as a "second providence," nourishing men from birth and protecting them from "perils"; and that would function as a "tutelary power" capable of rendering men "gentle [*doux*]" and "sociable" in such a manner that "crimes" would become "rare"—and, he ominously added, so would "virtues as well." For, under the rule of this "tutelary power," he foresaw that the human "soul" would enter into a "long repose." In the process, "individual energy" would be "almost extinguished," and, when action was required, men would "rely on others." In effect, a peculiar brand of "egoism" would reign, for everyone would "withdraw into himself." If "fanaticism" disappeared, as he suspected it would, so would "convictions" and "beliefs" and action itself.[7] Such was his reading of Guizot's prognosis for France and for Europe more generally; and, with it in mind, he set off for the United States, hoping that there he would find an alternative.

The reasons that these two young men had for undertaking the journey were personal as well as political. Both were scions of the legitimist aristocracy. Both came from families that looked back to the *ancien régime* with nostalgia and deep regret. To chart for themselves a future in nineteenth-century France, they had to come to terms with the rupture that had taken place in that country during the period stretching from 1789 to 1815. However reluctant they may have been personally, this necessity they understood perfectly well. The simple fact that, after his escape from the island of Elba, Napoleon Bonaparte had merely had to present himself in order to seize control in France was sufficient proof of the permanence of the rupture and of its profound significance for all concerned. Moreover, at the end of July 1830, the two young men were forced to abandon any lingering doubts that they may have entertained in this regard, for at that time an insurrection brought the Restoration monarchy to an abrupt end, and Louis-Philippe, duc d'Orléans, found his way to the throne. From the legitimist perspective, this self-styled "king of the French" was a usurper—a schemer and a traitor well worthy of his father, the infamous duc d'Orléans, who in the course of the Revolution had first renamed himself Philippe Égalité and then voted in the National Convention to send his unfortunate cousin Louis XVI to an ignominious death.

Among the relatives of Gustave-Auguste de Beaumont de la Bonnière, the elder of the two travelers, there were those who had served Napoleon, but his more immediate family had remained doggedly loyal to the House of Bourbon. In consequence, under the restored monarchy, his father, Jules, had been named a departmental councilor, and his uncle Armand had served as a prefect. In August 1830, when, in his capacity as a magistrate, Beaumont was asked to take an oath of loyalty to the new regime and did so, it marked a public acknowledgement on his part that the *ancien régime* was forever gone and a sharp break with the policy adopted by stalwart aristocrats in his parents' generation.

For his traveling companion, Alexis-Charles-Henri Clérel de Tocqueville, taking this oath was arguably more difficult still—for, on him, family tradition weighed even more heavily. On 12 March 1793, some seven weeks after the execution of Louis XVI, Tocqueville's father, Hervé, then but twenty years in age, had married Louise Le Peletier de Rosanbo in the presence of her maternal grandfather, Chrétien-Guillaume Lamoignon de Malesherbes, at the latter's family seat.[8] Apart, perhaps, from Jacques Necker, there was no statesman in France who commanded greater respect at the end of the *ancien régime* than did Malesherbes. Under Louis XV, as we have seen, he had served as *Directeur de la librairie* for thirteen years. In this capacity, he had licensed for publication the first two volumes of the *Encyclopédie, ou Dictionnaire raisonné des sciences, des arts, et des métiers* edited by Denis Diderot and Jean Le Rond d'Alembert, and he had given tacit permission for the initial publications of Jean-Jacques Rousseau. Later, in 1771, as president of the *Cour des aides*, he had distinguished himself by drafting the remonstrance in which that court had vigorously protested against the judicial revolution effected by Maupeou;[9] and in the aftermath, when Louis XVI recalled the exiled magistrates and reestablished the courts, he had authored the famous *Grandes Remonstrances* attacking the administrative state as an Oriental despotism and demanding that the Estates-General be summoned, that the parlements be allowed to play their traditional role, and that the administration of the state be made transparent to all. Thereafter, Malesherbes had twice served this same king as a minister, and in 1788 this erstwhile friend and admirer of Rousseau had advised Louis against summoning the Estates-General in its traditional form as three separate assemblies, arguing that the old distinction between nobles, churchmen, and bourgeois had become an anachronism, and urging him to anticipate the coming storm by arranging from the outset for the Estates-General to sit, instead, as a single, national assembly reflecting the will of the nation as such. Finally, and most important of all, in December 1792, at his own insistence, Malesherbes had come out of retirement at the ripe old age of seventy-one to help defend that ill-fated monarch in his trial before the National Convention. In doing so, he knew at the time precisely what he was about; and when called upon by a deputy at the Convention to explain what had occasioned the audacity that he had just displayed in his stirring defense of the king as king, Tocqueville's great-grandfather had simply replied, in a fashion calculated to remind one and all just what it was that had once made the French nobility so impressive, "Contempt of death!"[10]

This proved to be all too prescient a response—for the grim reaper soon paid him a visit. On 17 December 1793, two functionaries arrived at the Chateau de Malesherbes to arrest the great man's son-in-law, Louis Le Peletier de Rosanbo, who, in his capacity as presiding officer of the Chambre des Vacations of the Parlement of Paris in 1790, had drafted a formal remonstrance protesting the Constituent Assembly's decree abolishing the parlements. After searching the chateau for incriminating evidence suggestive of communication with the emigrés, they took into custody as well the king's erstwhile attorney and the entire family there gathered and carted them off to Paris, where, after being scattered among divers prisons, they were reunited in a facility once renowned as the Convent of Port-Royal. On 20 April 1794, Alexis de Tocqueville's maternal grandfather was executed. Malesherbes confronted the guillotine a day later, and his daughter, Tocqueville's maternal grandmother, soon met the same fate. Had it not been for the fall of Robespierre on 9 Thermidor that same year, Tocqueville's parents, who had remained at the chateau with his mother's family after their wedding, would no doubt have been executed as well, for they were scheduled to appear before the tribunal just three days thereafter.[11]

Tocqueville's mother never fully recovered from the shock. His father, who emerged from prison a young man in his twenties whose hair had gone white, was made of sterner stuff, and he persevered and led an exceedingly active life after the Restoration, serving as a prefect in various venues, being named a count, and ultimately being elevated to the Chamber of Peers.[12] If we are to fathom what it was that explained the remarkable intensity of Hervé de Tocqueville's third son, his cautious but firm embrace of liberal modernity, and the titanic ambition that induced him to write *Democracy in America* and *The Ancien Régime and the Revolution*, we must recall to mind, as in his youth he undoubtedly was often made to do, the glorious example set by the ancestor whom he revered as the man who had defended the people against the king and the king against the people, the ancestor whose bust he tellingly elected to place upon his desk, and on whose example he modeled his own words and deeds—the great Malesherbes.[13]

The journey that Beaumont and Tocqueville undertook in 1831–32 was exciting, there can be no doubt. But it was in no way a lark. The Atlantic passage took thirty-eight days. On shipboard, the two Frenchmen spent time with the other passengers, especially those in first class, but they did so to purpose, closely questioning the Americans in their number and others familiar with the United States about the new nation on the other side of the Atlantic, and making contacts that would serve them well on the great tour that they were about to begin. Most of their time awake, however, seven-and-a-half hours a day and more, they spent in solitude, reading and taking notes both on their reading and on what their fellow passengers had told them.

Neither of the two young magistrates had had to resign his post in France. Both had managed to secure a leave of eighteen months. In applying to the interior minister for a leave of absence, they had proposed to undertake a study of the penitentiary systems established in the various American states, and to this task they devoted considerable time both during and after the Atlantic passage. But, of course, from the outset they had another goal as well. Tocqueville had for years dreamed of making just such a journey, and he had long contemplated writing a book on the democratic polity in North America. Beaumont came to share his aspirations, and for a time, the two planned on writing such a book in tandem. They had before them, they both knew, the opportunity of a lifetime, and they had no intention of squandering it. Their time was short. They had not a moment to lose.

Beaumont and Tocqueville were by no means the first in Europe to have taken America as a subject. The British had never entirely lost interest in their former colonies; and, as recently as 1829, Captain Basil Hall had published a volume, highly critical of the Americans and their ways, entitled *Travels in North America in the Years 1827 and 1828*. Frenchmen who had fought in the Revolutionary War were more than willing to write on the subject, as were those who had visited the country thereafter, and those of all political stripes tended to look with favor on the new regime. To begin with, one could read Hector St. John Crèvecoeur; François Jean de Beauvoir, marquis de Chastellux; and Louis

Philippe, comte de Ségur. Then, one could turn to those who had addressed the subject in later years—among them, Jacques-Pierre Brissot; Constantin-François de Chasseboeuf, comte de Volney; Marie Jean Antoine Nicolas Caritat, marquis de Condorcet; Antoine Louis Claude Destutt, comte de Tracy; François Alexandre Frédéric, duc de La Rochefoucauld-Liancourt; and Charles Maurice de Talleyrand-Périgord, prince de Benevente, just to mention a few. Our information is, of course, incomplete. But we know that Beaumont and Tocqueville read some of these authors, and the odds are good that before leaving France, during their trip, or after their return, one or the other consulted each and every one.

On this subject, however, no writer exercised greater influence in France than François-René, vicomte de Chateaubriand, who had journeyed to the nascent United States in 1792 with encouragement and support from Malesherbes and who, in novels, such as *Atala* and *René*, and in various works of nonfiction, had returned to the subject repeatedly—most recently in 1827 in his *Voyage d'Amérique*. Chateaubriand, who is generally regarded as the progenitor of French romanticism, wrote with breathtaking verve and imagination not only concerning the physical setting, the lives of those of European stock who made their way to the frontier, and the native peoples, but also concerning the democratic prospects of the new republic.[14] No one in France who contemplated addressing this subject could afford to ignore him—least of all, Alexis de Tocqueville, who was by marriage a relative. An elder brother of Chateaubriand had wed Tocqueville's mother's eldest sister; and in 1794, when Chateaubriand's brother and Tocqueville's aunt had been executed along with her parents and Malesherbes, the care of their two sons and the management of their inheritance had fallen to none other than Hervé de Tocqueville.[15]

The *Le Havre*, the American brig on which Beaumont and Tocqueville made their passage and conducted their studies, reached New York on 11 May 1831, and in that city and its environs, where they were welcomed with open arms by the mayor and other dignitaries, the duo settled down for seven weeks devoted to further study and to the valuable conversations that took place when they dined out. On study, the two never stinted, and their purview was by no means restricted to North America. A week after their arrival in New York, Tocqueville wrote to a friend in France to ask that his copy of Guizot's *Histoire de la civilisation en Europe* be sent to him in the New World.[16]

The two were more than merely studious. They were good listeners as well. They were also, as highly intelligent young people so often are, exceedingly energetic and astonishingly alert, and they took detailed notes, summarizing what they had been told. Just under half their time they spent in the great cities. They remained in New York until 30 June 1831. They visited Boston, Philadelphia, and Baltimore in the period stretching from 9 September to 22 November, and they stayed in Washington and, once again, New York from 18 January to 20 February 1832. In these cities, they could find libraries, such as New York's Atheneum, in which to work. There they would encounter well-informed notables with whom to speak, and nearby they could generally find prisons to visit, such as Sing Sing up the Hudson from New York, the Wethersfield Prison in Hartford, and the Cherry Hill Prison in Philadelphia.

The remainder of their time Beaumont and Tocqueville dedicated to two lengthy forays into the hinterland. From New York, in the late spring and summer of 1831, they journeyed into the Northwest as far as Detroit, Saginaw, Green Bay, and Sault Ste. Marie, and on this trip they paid a brief visit to Montreal to learn about the fate accorded the French living in Canada under British dominion. Later, after their sojourn in Baltimore, in the late fall and early winter of 1831–32, they journeyed West to Cincinnati, then down the Mississippi to New Orleans, and finally, by stages, through the South to Nashville and on to Washington, D.C. They had hoped to spend considerably more time in the South, to sojourn in Charleston for an extended period, and then to visit James Madison in Montpelier in the mountains above Charlottesville, Virginia, while in transit to the nation's capital. But the prospect that their leave of absence would be curtailed caused them to cut this part of their trip short.

Like Voltaire and Montesquieu in England, Beaumont and Tocqueville managed in the course of their travels to meet a great many of those who were important and influential in the new republic. In New York, they were befriended by the Livingston clan, one of the oldest and most distinguished families in the state, and there they met and conversed at length with James Kent, former chief justice and chancellor of the state of New York, and with Albert Gallatin, who had been secretary of the treasury in the federal government, then ambassador to France and to Great Britain. In or near Albany, they met Elam Lynds, the creator of the Auburn prison system so much admired in Europe, as well as John Canfield Spencer, a man who had served as a congressman and who had helped draft the revised statutes of the state of New York, who would go on to serve as secretary of war and secretary of the treasury, and who would produce the first American translation of *Democracy in America*. In Boston, the intellectual capital of the new republic, they became acquainted with a host of luminaries — including Daniel Webster and John Quincy Adams, as well as the Unitarian leader William Ellery Channing; the historian Jared Sparks; Josiah Quincy, president of Harvard University; Alexander Everett, former ambassador to Spain and editor of *The North American Review*; and his younger brother Edward, then a U. S.

senator. There they also met Joseph Coolidge, who had married Thomas Jefferson's granddaughter; Nathan Hale, editor of the *Boston Daily Advertiser*; and Franz Lieber, who had fought in the battle of Waterloo and in the Greek War of Independence, who had published the *Encyclopedia Americana*, and who would later take it upon himself to translate into English the little book on the American prison system that Beaumont and Tocqueville were soon to produce.

In Philadelphia, where they were feted by the American Philosophical Society, the two would spend time with Benjamin W. Richards, the mayor; with George Howard, the governor; and with Andrew Jackson's nemesis Nicholas Biddle, president of the Second Bank of the United States. Outside Baltimore, they met with the ninety-five-year-old Charles Carroll, the last living signer of the Declaration of Independence. While en route to New Orleans, they encountered Sam Houston, former governor of Tennessee, Indian chief by marriage, and future president of the Republic of Texas. On their return to Washington, D.C., they met Joel Roberts Poinsett, whom President Jackson had sent to South Carolina to organize opposition to nullification; and in the nation's capital, they saw John Quincy Adams once again, they were presented to President Andrew Jackson, and they spent time with Edward Livingston, once senator from Louisiana and then secretary of state; with Louis McLane, Jackson's secretary of the treasury; and with Roger B. Taney, who just recently had been named attorney general and who would ultimately achieve notoriety as chief justice of the U.S. Supreme Court. The fact that their visit coincided with the Nullification Crisis, with Nat Turner's Rebellion in Virginia, and with the forced removal of the Five Civilized Tribes to Oklahoma (part of which they witnessed) meant that there was a great deal to discuss.[17]

From time to time, in turns, the two young men drafted interim reports concerning the American prisons and dispatched them from the United States to the authorities in France. When they got home, Beaumont produced a draft of their final report, *Du système pénitentiaire aux États-Unis et de son application en France*; Tocqueville helped him recast it and provided the notes; and the work was published in early January 1833 to considerable acclaim. That August, shortly after Tocqueville's twenty-eighth birthday, the two were awarded the Montyon Prize by the Académie française, along with the sum of six thousand francs, which helped offset the expense of their journey. Their little book, which would inform Tocqueville's ruminations on despotism,[18] was reissued in 1836 and once more in 1844, and they had the satisfaction of having achieved renown for their expertise.[19]

By this time, however, neither was a magistrate. There had been a scandal touching on an inheritance awarded a son of the Orléanist king, and the authorities had seized on this as an opportunity to force Beaumont, who was a deputy public prosecutor in the superior court of the department of the Seine, to take sides against his fellow legitimists. When he demurred, pleading that he was still on leave and hard at work on the duo's final report, he had been summarily dismissed from his post, and Tocqueville had resigned in sympathy.[20]

When the Montyon Prize was awarded, only Beaumont was present. Tocqueville was once again abroad—this time in England, whither, not long after the passage of the first Reform Bill, he had gone to get a preliminary feel for developments in what was for Americans the mother country. Well before this time, the two travelers appear to have agreed on what must have seemed at the time like a sensible division of labor. Tocqueville was to write on American institutions; Beaumont was to tackle American mores. Whether either recognized in mid-September 1833, when the younger of the two settled down in Paris to write what would become the first great section of *Democracy in America*, that the elder would produce a novel dealing with racial relations in America rather than a treatise on morals and manners we do not know.[21]

It took Tocqueville roughly a year of steady work in a solitary setting to knock out his study of American institutions. It was published to great acclaim on 23 January 1835, when its author was not yet thirty years of age. He was hailed in the press as "the Blackstone of America," and it was suggested that he might actually merit comparison with "an even greater name"—Charles-Louis de Secondat, baron de La Brède et de Montesquieu. In due course, Tocqueville was once again awarded the Montyon Prize by the Académie française. On this occasion, he took home no less than twelve thousand francs.

Beaumont prospered as well. His novel, which was entitled *Marie, ou l'esclavage aux États-Unis*, was an immediate hit. In part, no doubt, to celebrate their good fortune, and in part to deepen their understanding of history's tides, the two young men embarked on a second voyage. This time, they went to England, where the Reform Bill of 1832 was beginning to bear fruit, and on to Ireland. They left Paris together on 21 April 1835. Four months later, Tocqueville returned alone from Ireland via England to France, where he landed on 23 August, while Beaumont journeyed on to Scotland. On 26 October, the former would marry an English woman named Mary Mottley, with whom he had been involved for some time; and, within a month of their nuptials, he would begin work on the second great section of *Democracy in America*.[22]

Well before their second journey together, Beaumont had ceded America to his friend in its entirety,[23] and on the trip Tocqueville agreed in recompense to leave England to Beaumont[24]—who would, in fact, go on to write and publish a distinguished study of Ireland.[25] In the event, the second great section of

Tocqueville's magnum opus was to have as its focus the very topic once allocated to his traveling companion: the mores and manners of the Americans. Its composition he found an ordeal.

A year after starting work on what scholars now call the second *Democracy*, Tocqueville wrote to his oldest friend, Louis de Kergorlay, to report that he labored on the project seven hours a day but made hardly any progress at all. He recognized that the sequel would lack one advantage possessed by its predecessor: it would not catch the public by surprise. He foresaw as well that it would be subject to criticism far more severe than that directed at his initial effort. The work that scholars now call the first *Democracy* had set an exceedingly high standard. With it Tocqueville had made his name, and he had raised expectations. Its sequel was quite likely to be seen as a letdown. Such, he knew, was a punishment frequently meted out to authors once they had secured a measure of fame.[26]

There were also distractions. Tocqueville's wife was in less than perfect health, and, in 1836, the two spent four months in Baden in Switzerland, where she took the waters. In 1837, he sought a seat in the Chamber, ran a full-scale electoral campaign in Valognes, and lost. Two years later, he ran again in Valognes, and this time he was returned and took up a seat. In 1839, during the session, in his capacity as a deputy, he drafted a report calling for the abolition of slavery. All of this took time.[27]

There were literary distractions as well. Tocqueville was now well-known, and as a commentator he was in demand. In 1835, he published his *Mémoire sur le paupérisme*, and we know that after February 1837, he spent some time working on the promised sequel.[28] In February 1836, he dispatched an essay entitled *L'État social et politique de la France avant et après 1789* to his friend and admirer John Stuart Mill for translation and publication in the *London and Westminster Review*.[29] And in June and August 1837, he published *Deux lettres sur l'Algérie* in a short-lived Versailles newspaper called *La Presse de Seine-et-Oise*, in which he owned stock.[30] In each case, the research and the writing took time; and although the reading and research that he did informed his larger project, it was not directly relevant to it.[31]

It was also the case that the second *Democracy* was a more difficult undertaking than the first. In both sections of his great work, Tocqueville took as his subject democracy, a term which he consciously used in an equivocal sense to specify, at times, a social condition and, at other times, a form of government.[32] He was interested in America only to the extent that it exemplified the phenomenon that he wanted to study. Inevitably, the section dedicated to institutions and political mores was the more empirical of the two. To clarify for a French audience the character of the American democracy in its political aspect, Tocqueville had to discuss the geography of North America, the history of the British settlements there, local self-government during the colonial period, and the institutions at both the state and the federal levels that the Americans had framed for themselves after their revolution. Serious thinking was required, to be sure. Tocqueville had to decide what was truly important and what was not, but in *The Federalist* he had an invaluable aid,[33] and he had gleaned a great deal from the conversations that he and Beaumont had had with a considerable array of luminaries in the United States. By the time that they returned to France, he had a pretty good idea of what he wanted to say and of how he needed to marshal the evidence.[34]

Tocqueville's second *Democracy* was of a different character. To begin with, the subject of mores and manners was, by its very nature, less easy to define and confine. Moreover, it was here that Tocqueville's concern with democracy as a way of life came to the fore, and in it he was far less interested in providing his readers with a factually accurate description of the United States and its citizens than with sketching the direction in which he thought habits, practices, sentiments, customs, opinions, and manners were likely to evolve as the logic implicit within the new political and social order gradually worked its way out. Of himself at this point, he could have said what Montesquieu had written with regard to his treatment of the *esprit général*: "I will be more attentive to the order of things than to the things themselves" (*EL* 3.19.1).[35]

The same point can be made in another way. In the second *Democracy*, Tocqueville's task was much more theoretical in character than it had been in the first. He had less occasion to fall back on empirical description; and when he touched on matters American, as of necessity he frequently did, he had to rely to a much greater degree on his own fleeting impressions and on those of others who had visited and written about the United States. If he often allowed himself to be distracted in the years in which he was working on it, it must at least in part have been due to the fact that he found the enterprise that he had undertaken daunting in the extreme.[36]

One

DEMOCRATIC DESPOTISM

That which I would like to paint is less the events themselves, however surprising or great they may be, than the spirit informing events, less the different acts in Napoleon's life than Napoleon himself. . . . I would desire to make visible how and why at that moment this recalcitrant [*indocile*] nation ran of its own volition to meet servitude [and] with what incomparable art he discovered in the most demagogic works of the Revolution everything that is appropriate to despotism and caused it to emerge from them. . . . I would like to contemplate society, crushed and suffocated under the weight of this wondrous machine, becoming sterile, with the motion of intelligence slowing down, the human spirit growing listless, souls contracting, great men ceasing to appear, an horizon immense and flat, in which to whatever side one turns there appears nothing but the colossal figure of the Emperor himself.

—Alexis de Tocqueville

In early November 1836, when Tocqueville wrote to Louis de Kergorlay to voice his frustration and his worries, he complained that "a multitude of ideas remains obscure in my mind," and he lamented that, in the absence of his childhood friend, he had no one residing nearby suitable for serving as a touchstone on which to test the validity of his intuitions. He was not, however, entirely bereft of intellectual companionship. He did have company of a sort, and it was, he confessed, very valuable company indeed. "There are," he remarked, "three men with whom I live a little bit each day." His friend, were he present, would make a welcome fourth. The three men—whom he named—were "Pascal, Montesquieu, and Rousseau."[1]

Although Tocqueville penned this striking line late in 1836, he almost certainly could have written it late in 1833 or in 1834—for the three great writers with whom he would later "live a little bit each day" are as much a presence in the first *Democracy* as they are in the second. Throughout the 1830s, and in subsequent years as well, these three men were for Tocqueville something akin to what his great-grandfather Malesherbes had always been: tutelary deities and household gods.

In the case of Montesquieu, Tocqueville's debt is especially obvious.[2] It would in no way be misleading to describe *De la Démocratie en Amérique* as a sequel to *De l'Esprit des lois*.[3] It was, in fact, universally regarded as such from the very outset—and by figures as perspicacious as the great liberal monarchist Pierre-Paul Royer-Collard, the English philosopher John Stuart Mill, and the intellectual journalist Henry Reeve.[4] Moreover, the starting point for Tocqueville's ruminations appears to have been Montesquieu's striking depiction of England as "a republic concealed under the form of a monarchy" (*EL* 1.5.19, p. 304). In *Democracy in America*, he echoed this description (*DA* I.i.8, p. 97), and in *The Ancien Régime and the Revolution*, he restated the argument underpinning his predecessor's claim, observing that, although one might be tempted to suppose that "in England the ancient constitution of Europe is still vigorous," this would be a grave blunder.

> If one is willing to forget the old names and to avert one's gaze from the old forms, one will find there, from the seventeenth century on, the feudal system abolished in substance, the classes mixed up with one another, a nobility blotted out, an open aristocracy, wealth become power, equality before the law, equality in taxation, freedom of the press, public debate—all new principles that the society of the Middle Ages did not know. But these are precisely the new things which, introduced little by little and with art into the old body, reanimated it without risking its dissolution and filled it with a fresh vigor while leaving intact the ancient forms. In the seventeenth century, England is already a nation entirely modern, which has preserved within its bosom, as if embalmed, some debris from the Middle Ages.[5]

To this insight, at the outset, Tocqueville joined his predecessor's observation that a nation so constituted is apt to be quite generous with its colonies, conferring on them "its own form of government," along with Montesquieu's prescient claim that this form of government is likely to bring "with it prosperity" so that, if it were to be conferred by a polity on certain of its colonies, there "one would see great peoples take shape in the forests which they were sent to inhabit" (*EL* 3.19.27, p. 578).[6]

MONTESQUIEU'S HEIR

In fact, the argument that Tocqueville advances in *Democracy in America* is to a very considerable degree set within the frame of Montesquieu's political science. He begins the first *Democracy* with a brief discussion of "the external configuration" of the United States (*DA* I.i.1), and he then turns to the Anglo-Americans' "point of departure," tracing to it their "prejudices, habits, dominant passions—all that in the end composes the national character" (I.i.2, especially pp. 24–25).[7] Like Montesquieu,[8] he is clearly interested in charting the role played by both physical and moral causes, and he has evidently paid close attention to the significance accorded France's point of departure in his predecessor's celebrated account of the evolution of French law (*EL* 6.27–28, 30–31), as well as to Rousseau's assertion that, "in general, the most instructive part of the annals of peoples" is constituted by "the history of their establishment" (*CS* 4.4, p. 444).

In no way, however, is Tocqueville slavish in his imitation of *The Spirit of Laws*. He makes use of Montesquieu's interpretive framework but he does not adopt the technical language that the latter had deployed. Although he is no less focused on institutions and political psychology, Tocqueville does not speak of the "structure" of the American polity as its "nature"; and though he regards "equality" as its "principle," he only sparingly employs the latter term. Moreover, though his aim is evidently to discover with regard to the American people what Montesquieu had called the *esprit général*, for the most part he avoids this locution as well.

For Tocqueville's decision in this regard, there is a reason. He shares Montesquieu's propensity to give great weight to what they both call "general causes" and to suppose that if, on any given occasion, "chance [*le hazard*]" has a great influence on developments, it is because general causes have paved the way.[9] Like David Hume,[10] however, he is far less prone than were Montesquieu, and, for that matter, Rousseau, to suppose that climate and terrain decisively shape national character, and he accuses "Europeans" in general of exaggerating their significance. Throughout, in fact, he gives a decided priority to what Montesquieu had dubbed "moral causes," arguing that, in the United States, "the laws contribute more to the maintenance of the democratic republic . . . than do physical causes," and contending that "mores contribute more than the laws." The primacy of moral causes he illustrates by pointing to the quite different uses to which the Indians, the French, and the Anglo-Americans have put the territory that they hold in common, and he demonstrates the manner in which mores trump laws by citing the failure of republican institutions in the former colonies of Spain (*DA* I.ii.9, pp. 220–22, 236–41).[11] Even Mexico, he observes, although it had closely modeled its constitution and laws on those of the United States, was prone to despotism—when it was not bedeviled by anarchy (I.i.8, p. 127; ii.9, p. 238).

Moreover, in the case of the United States, Tocqueville treats mores largely as a product of what he terms the "social condition [*état social*] of the Anglo-Americans."[12] In all important respects, he claims, this *état social* was "democratic" at their "point of departure," and it remained so thereafter. The most important feature of the Americans' social condition was not, however, at least strictly speaking, social at all: it was their political heritage as Englishmen.[13] The colonists sent to North America profited from the outcome of the extended struggle between Crown and Parliament that took place in seventeenth-century England, and they were heirs to the English tradition of local self-government, which took a radically egalitarian form when transplanted to a continent in which there was ample land for all to clear and farm and no aristocracy of any kind to take the lead and set the tone (I.i.3; II.iv.4, p. 246).

If, when they meet, Tocqueville subsequently remarks, Americans are free and easy, "frank, natural, and open," in their relations with one another, while their English cousins display a "singular unsociability" and "a humor reserved and taciturn," it is not due to "causes purely physical." After all, both peoples are of the same "blood." If, he explains, they differ markedly in mores and manners, it is because of the *état social*. In America, "privileges of birth have never existed," and "wealth confers on the possessor no special privilege or right [*droit particulier*]." Strangers who meet by chance "entertain hardly any hopes or fears with regard to one another," and they can therefore converse in a manner relaxed. In England, where there once was a genuine nobility of blood and where there is now an aristocracy of wealth which all can aspire to enter, no one ever quite knows where he stands in the social pecking order, and everyone fears that, if a certain "familiarity" were to grow up between men otherwise unacquainted, it might give rise to "a friendship *mal assortie*"—unsuitable and awkward, between individuals quite poorly matched (II.iii.2, pp. 148–50).[14]

Montesquieu had distanced himself from the presumption, voiced by Aristotle and accepted by political scientists in antiquity generally, that in virtually all situations the political regime (*politeía*), with its distinctive distribution and disposition of offices and honors (*táxis tōn archōn*), is not just politically but also, in the long run, culturally and socially determinative as well.[15] But he had done so while acknowledging that there are, nonetheless, cases where this may indeed be so (for example, *EL* 3.19.26–27).[16] When, in turn, Tocqueville distanced himself from Montesquieu, eschewing the emphasis that his predecessor had placed on physical causes, he did so by tentatively, and perhaps inadvertently, making his way back in the direction of something like the outlook of the ancients.[17] In matters metaphysical and moral, he may well have been much closer to Pascal than he was to Aristotle.[18] But, in his appreciation for the dignity of political life, he had considerably more in common with the peripatetic than with the Jansenist sympathizer.[19] If he interested himself in "civil society" as it had come to be distinguished from its more narrowly political counterpart,[20] if he paid more attention to man's *état social* than to political institutions as such,[21] it was neither because he was disdainful of statesmanship in the manner of Pascal,[22] nor because he thought the political a product of anything subpolitical.[23] If he contended that "in the long run political society cannot escape becoming the expression and image of civil society," it was only because, like Aristotle and the other practitioners of political science in classical antiquity, he recognized that there is more to the distribution and disposition of offices and honors within a *politeía* than the mere working of constitutional mechanisms.[24] "There is," he tellingly wrote, "nothing more political about a people than its civil legislation" (DA II.iii.8, p. 165, n. 1).[25]

If anything, Tocqueville went beyond Aristotle in his estimation of the practical importance of what he calls "the political sciences." Here, he may in fact have been inspired by Montesquieu's depiction of Plato, Aristotle, Machiavelli, Thomas More, James Harrington, and the like as preeminent among legislators (*EL* 6.29.19). In an address that he delivered in April 1852 in his capacity as presiding officer of the Academy of Moral and Political Sciences, Tocqueville conceded that there was a point to the criticism leveled at political speculation by practitioners of politics. He was perfectly prepared to draw a sharp line between political science and what he called "the art of government"; and though he made no mention of François Guizot and Adolphe Thiers and of the inauspicious role that these great penmen had played under the July Monarchy,[26] everyone in his audience must have known that he had these luminaries in mind—and perhaps also, by that time, himself—when he acknowledged that those expert in political science and gifted in writing were more often than not inept at practical politics. Others, he remarked, might regret that Montesquieu had never had the opportunity "to try out politics," but he was not among these. Perhaps as a consequence of his brief stint as foreign minister under the Second Republic, he was sensitive to the possibility that "the delicacy and flair [*la finesse*]" of the great man's "mind" might have been a bit too "subtle" for the cut and thrust of politics. From painful personal experience as a member of the drafting committee appointed by the Constituent Assembly to draw up a constitution for the Second Republic, Tocqueville had learned just how easy it is "to miss in practice the precise point on which success in politics" turns, and he suspected that Montesquieu's refinement might "often have caused him" to do so as well. Had he entered the political arena, Tocqueville observed, "instead of becoming the rarest of those who specialize in public law [*publicistes*]," Montesquieu might have turned out to be "nothing but a rather bad minister."[27]

All of this Tocqueville acknowledged in his address. But he then went on to suggest that *publicistes*, such as Plato, Aristotle, Machiavelli, Montesquieu, and Rousseau; students of international law, such as Grotius and Pufendorf; specialists in criminal justice and economics, such as Cesare Beccaria and Adam Smith; and the great jurisconsults of the past had had a considerably greater influence on politics than its actual practitioners. If the grandfathers of those in his audience would have found the world in which their grandchildren lived unrecognizable and incomprehensible, he observed, it was because the political scientists of the eighteenth century, the "great artisans" of the French Revolution, by instigating "the greatest event in history," had "changed the face of the world." This, he explained, they had done by depositing "in the minds of our fathers all the seeds [*germes*] of the novel notions [*nouveautés*] from which were suddenly hatched so many political institutions and civil laws unknown to their forerunners." This particular event was not, he concluded, in this regard an aberration. "That which the political sciences achieved" in France at that time, "with a power so irresistible and a radiance [*éclat*] so marvelous, they achieve everywhere and at all times—although with greater secrecy and less speed." Among civilized peoples, he observed, "the political sciences give birth or at least form to the general ideas from which emerge in turn both the particular facts in the midst of which the politicians operate [*s'agitent*] and the laws that they believe they have invented. Around each society, these ideas form an intellectual atmosphere of sorts—from which the minds of the governed and the governors draw breath, whence the one and the other, often without knowing it, sometimes without wishing it, derive their principles of conduct." In Tocqueville's judgment, none but barbarians can hope to escape the architectonic influence exercised by the political science regnant in their time.[28]

Here a word of caution is in order. Tocqueville considered himself a political scientist, and he prided himself on his "impartiality" (*DA* II.*Avertissement*, p. 8). But he did not succumb to the myopia dominant within the profession of political science in and after the twentieth century. He did not pretend to the attainment of some sort of value-free, pseudo-scientific neutrality, and it was not his aim to uncover universal laws of historical causation. He was perfectly aware that there were those among his contemporaries who thought "that here below peoples are never their own masters and that, of necessity, they obey" some sort of "insurmountable and unintelligent force born from prior events, the race, soil, or climate." These presumptions he regarded as "false and cowardly doctrines, which will never produce anything but weak men and pusillanimous nations." Around each individual, he acknowledged, there is "a fatal circle from which he cannot depart." But "within its vast limits," he insisted, "man is powerful and free," as are "peoples" as well. The nations of his time might not be able to escape the democratic *état social*, but it was up to them to determine whether "equality is to lead them to servitude or liberty, to enlightenment [*lumières*] or barbarism, to prosperity or misery" (II.iv.8, pp. 281–82).[29]

Tocqueville's political science was addressed to this great question. Statesmanship of the highest order was his primary concern. He was in no respect apolitical, and it never even crossed his mind that, as a political scientist, he should cease to be engaged. He knew better than to suppose that, in the sphere of morality and politics, detachment and objectivity should or even can be grounded in indifference and neutrality. Like Montesquieu, he regarded the composition and publication of his magnum opus as an act of philosophical statesmanship. Three years before his death, he wrote to a friend, "The unity of my life and thought is the thing in the world that I most wish to maintain before the public eye; in this, the man has as great an interest as the writer."[30]

At times, as Royer-Collard appears to have recognized,[31] Tocqueville's actual mode of proceeding was more like the one followed by Aristotle in *The Politics* than it was like the one adopted by Montesquieu in *The Spirit of Laws*. In *Democracy in America*, he did not ignore political opinion or give it short shrift; he did not treat it as secondary or epiphenomenal. He certainly did not suppose that by applying scientific method one might be able to bypass its substance altogether. Instead, he took it for granted that there was a great deal to be learned from attending to the arguments concerning justice and the common good advanced by partisans of every sort, and he treated what Aristotle called "reputable opinions [*tà éndoxa*]" with consideration and a measure of respect. If partisans were partial to one view or another, as they always were, he suspected that it was not simply and solely because they were wrong-headed, self-seeking, and malevolent: it was due, at least as much to the natural human propensity to mistake the part that they think they understand for the whole.[32] "In writing," he remarked in good Aristotelian fashion, "I have not had it in mind to serve or battle against any party; I have attempted to see, *not in another fashion, but further* than the parties; and, whilst they occupy themselves with the morrow, it has been my wish to ruminate concerning the future" more generally (I.Intr., p. 16, emphasis added).[33]

Although he evidenced powerful Aristotelian proclivities, Tocqueville's debt to the author of *The Spirit of Laws* was nonetheless profound. He wrote *Democ-*

racy in America with legislation in mind and sought with his new political science to determine the intellectual atmosphere within which, in the future, statesmen would operate and laws would be framed.[34] But like Montesquieu, who had done the same, he took great care to play down the notion that a visionary lawgiver might recast a polity in its entirety. He was aware that "sometimes a legislator succeeds, after a thousand efforts, in exercising an indirect influence over the destiny of nations, and [that] one then celebrates his genius." But he immediately added that it is all too often the case that "the geographical position of the country, with regard to which he can do nothing; an *état social*, which was created without his cooperation; mores and ideas, of whose origin he has no knowledge; a point of departure with which he is unfamiliar—all impress on the society movements irresistible, against which he struggles in vain, and which sweep him along in turn." Tocqueville likened the lawgiver to a "man who plots his route in the midst of the seas." Such a man, he observed, "may be able to direct the vessel which bears him, but he knows not how to alter its structure, to create the winds, to prevent the Ocean from rising beneath his feet" (I.i.8, p. 125). Though profoundly ambitious, his political science partakes of the species of moderation and prudence that Montesquieu practiced and preached.

In other respects as well, Tocqueville followed the path his predecessor took. The first *Democracy* deals with the themes announced by Montesquieu in his famous chapter "The Constitution of England" (*EL* 2.11.6). Tocqueville's second *Democracy*, which he insists on describing as a completion of the enterprise projected in the first (*DA* II.*Avertissement*, p. 8), takes up the questions raised in the chapter that Montesquieu had entitled "How the Laws Can Contribute to the Formation of the Mores, Manners, & Character of a Nation" (*EL* 3.19.27). Like Montesquieu, and in much the same fashion, Tocqueville is intent on exploring the theme, first sounded by Plato in *The Republic*, of the correspondence between the political regime and the citizen's soul.[35]

To this observation, one can add another. Tocqueville's first and his second *Democracy* both have as their focus Montesquieu's haunting observation that if you "abolish in a monarchy the prerogatives of the lords, the clergy, the nobility, & the towns," as England's parliament had done, "you will soon have a state popular—or, indeed, a state despotic." In both, Tocqueville attempts to tease out the implications for his own time of his predecessor's further remark that the English who, "in order to favor liberty, have eliminated all the intermediary powers which formed their monarchy, . . . have good reason to conserve this liberty"—for, "if they should come to lose it, they would be one of the most fully enslaved peoples on the earth" (1.2.4).

FROM ROBESPIERRE TO BONAPARTE

These last two claims need to be underlined. In France, Tocqueville's father had witnessed a democratic revolution that had swept away "the prerogatives of the lords, the clergy, the nobility, & the towns"; that had abolished the monarchy and established "a state popular"; and that had eventuated in a reign of terror and ultimately in "a state despotic." Tocqueville had spent the first decade of his life in a country governed by a tyrant who commanded overwhelming, even fanatical popular support. What he did not himself discern in his childhood about what it meant to be a member of "one of the most fully enslaved peoples on the earth" and how his compatriots had found their way into such a condition, he had learned from innumerable conversations with his parents and their contemporaries among the legitimists, who paid close heed to Montesquieu's analysis;[36] and he refined his understanding by reading works written by Madame de Staël, Benjamin Constant, Royer-Collard, Amable-Guillaume-Prosper Brugière de Barante, François Guizot, and the like.[37]

Late in his life, when he made preparations for writing about French "society" in the first fifteen years of the nineteenth century, Tocqueville gave vent to the powerful feelings that its memory evoked, describing that society as having been "crushed and suffocated under the weight" of a "wondrous machine" fashioned by "the almost divine intelligence" of Napoleon Bonaparte, which was "rudely employed to suppress human liberty." He wrote of society "becoming sterile" with "the motion of intelligence slowing down, the human spirit growing listless, souls contracting, great men ceasing to appear." In France, he remarked, there was "an horizon immense and flat, in which, to whatever side one" turned, absolutely "nothing" appeared—apart, that is, from "the colossal figure of the emperor himself." Of this new species of despotism, he added, no one beforehand "was able to form a notion"—no one, that is, with the single exception of Montesquieu, whose stature was so self-evident that there was no need even to name the man. It was sufficient—or so Tocqueville thought—that one simply refer to "the greatest genius" to have arisen "in the middle of the most enlightened and civilized century" known to man, and everyone would know precisely whom he had in mind.[38]

Tocqueville was born under the First Empire; he died under the Second. For understandable reasons, Bonapartism was for him an abiding concern.[39] But he lived also in an age in which the memory of the Terror was likewise fresh; and, as he well knew, the Jacobin impulse was by no means dead. Many of his fellow citizens were persuaded that the distinguishing feature of republican government is not "the rule of the majority, as was believed until now." In their view, it is "the rule of those who are strong in their feelings [*se portent fort*] for the majority." It is the rule of those who are most firmly persuaded that they and they alone "know the people's greatest good." This Tocqueville wryly terms a "fortunate distinction," for it permits this self-styled elite "to act in the name of nations without consulting them and to demand their gratitude while trampling upon them." Once one accepts this distinction, one will come to think of "republican government" as a polity possessed of "the right to do all," and eventually one will even come to suppose that, as such, it is authorized to "express contempt for that which men have respected up to the present time, from the highest laws of morality to the vulgar rules of common sense." There was a time, Tocqueville added, when "despotism was odious, whatever form it took. But in our day, it has been discovered that in the world there are legitimate tyrannies and holy injustices, provided that one acts in the name of the people" (*DA* I.ii.10, pp. 301–2).

By the time in which he came to compose *Democracy in America*, it had become Tocqueville's firm conviction that "a great democratic revolution" was "working its way out [*s'opère*] among us." In contrast to many of the legitimists, he had also come to believe that what was happening in this regard was not "an accident" capable of being checked and easily reversed. In the introduction to the first great section of his magnum opus, he spoke of this democratic revolution in the manner of the *Doctrinaires*: as something "irresistible." He described it as "the most continuous, the most ancient, and the most permanent fact known to history." And in a fashion owing a great deal to Guizot's sweeping histories of civilization in Europe and France,[40] he suggested that virtually every major development in medieval and early modern European history—the growth in the power and influence of a Christian clergy drawn promiscuously from every rank, the emergence of the legal profession as a source of authority, the increase in trade that took hold during the later Middle Ages, the struggles that had occurred between the kings and their vassals, the Crusades and the wars between France and England, the establishment of self-governing municipalities, the invention of firearms, the establishment of the postal system, the emergence of Protestantism, the growth in technological dynamism, the spread of literacy, and the discovery of America—had contributed to "a double revolution" within Western Christendom, reducing the noble in stature and raising the commoner until it was hard to distinguish the one from the other. This "gradual development of the equality of conditions" Tocqueville represented as "a Providential fact," exhibiting all of the "principal characteristics" of such a phenomenon. This trend "is universal," he explained. "It is durable. Each day it escapes human power. All events contribute to its development, as do all men." As a consequence, "conditions are more equal in our day among Christians than they ever have been at any time and in any place in the world." So he wrote; and, in a passage reminiscent of his kinsman Chateaubriand, he warned his readers that *Democracy in America* was composed "under the impression of a species of religious terror produced in the soul of the author by the sight of this irresistible revolution, which has marched on for so many centuries over all obstacles, and which one still sees today advancing in the midst of the ruins it has made." It was in this context that he penned the famous line: "A new political science is required for a world entirely new" (I.Intr., pp. 3–9).

Tocqueville was concerned because, although he really did suspect that the tendency toward equality was for all practical purposes irresistible, he did not harbor the same opinion at all concerning liberty.[41] To be sure, he could conceive of his compatriots settling into a posture of love for the law, which they had come to regard as "their own work." He could imagine the government's authority being "respected as necessary," though not divine, and he could foresee the possibility that its chief magistrates would attract an affection in no way passionate but grounded, instead, in "a tranquil sentiment rooted in reason." In such a situation, where all could take it for granted that their rights would be respected, there might be "established between all the classes a manly confidence and a species of reciprocal condescension" neither haughty nor base. Men might come to understand the relationship between social benefit and obligation, "the free association of citizens might be able to replace the individual power of the nobles, and the State would be sheltered from tyranny and from license" as well. In a democracy of this sort, glory would play less of a role than in an aristocracy, but "there one would find less misery; enjoyments would be less extreme and well-being more general; knowledge less grand and ignorance more rare; the sentiments less energetic and habits gentler; there one would notice more in the way of vice and less in the way of crime" (I.Intr., p. 11).

Tocqueville could imagine such a France because he had witnessed something of the sort in America. But when he closely examined his native land, this was not the pattern he discerned. In France, he remarked, "the people despise authority but fear it." Class hatreds are there intense. The poor harbor "the prejudices" of their ancestors but not "their beliefs" and "their ignorance but not their virtues." Above all, if "society is tranquil," it is "not at all because it possesses a consciousness of its strength and of its well-being, but on the contrary because it believes itself weak and infirm; it fears dying if it makes an effort: each senses the evil, but none has the courage and energy necessary to search for that which is better; one has desires, regrets, sorrows, and joys, but these — like the passions of old men, which eventuate only in impotence — produce nothing visible or durable" (I.Intr., pp. 11–12).[42]

IN THE ABSENCE OF INTERMEDIARY POWERS

It was in this context that Tocqueville restated Montesquieu's blunt warning. In his judgment, as in that voiced under the Restoration regime by Royer-Collard, Constant, Guizot, Prosper de Barante, and many a diehard royalist as well,[43] France's malaise was rooted in two facts: his compatriots had "destroyed the individual entities which separately were able to struggle against tyranny," and they had then made government the sole heir of "all the prerogatives wrenched from families, from corporations, or from [individual] men." In consequence, he contended, "to a strength [*force*] sometimes oppressive but often protective, belonging to a small number of citizens, there had succeeded the weakness of all" (I.Intr., p. 12).

For Tocqueville, in contrast with Guizot and the *Doctrinaires*, this was by no means a passing concern. He touched on the dangers attendant on this development again and again. In concluding the argument of the first *Democracy*, for example, in the very last section of a chapter exploring "The Principal Causes Tending to Maintain the Democratic Republic in the United States," he issued a warning to those among his compatriots, drawn largely from his own class, who, "having tired of liberty, desired to find repose at a distance from its storms." The monarchy of Henry IV and of Louis XIV was forever gone, he frankly told them; "absolute power" was no longer what it had once been. "If absolute power were to establish itself anew among the democratic peoples of Europe," he wrote, "I do not doubt that it would take a new form there and that it would reveal itself by way of traits unknown to our fathers."

> There was a time in Europe in which the law, as well as the consent of the people, clothed kings with a power almost without limits. But almost never did it happen that they made use of it.
>
> I shall not speak of the prerogatives of the nobility, the authority of the sovereign courts, the rights of corporations, the privileges of provinces, which, while cushioning the blows of authority, maintained in the nation a spirit of resistance.
>
> Independent of these political institutions—which, though often contrary to the liberty of individuals, served nonetheless to sustain in souls the love of liberty, and whose utility in this regard one can without difficulty imagine—opinions and mores raised barriers about the royal power less well-known but no less powerful.
>
> Religion, love on the part of the subjects, the goodness of the prince, honor, family spirit, provincial prejudices, custom, and public opinion limited the power of kings and confined their authority within an invisible circle.

At that time, the constitution of the peoples was despotic, and their mores free. The princes had the right but neither the capacity nor the desire to do all.

But, Tocqueville then asks, "of the barriers, which in earlier times put a stop to tyranny, what remains today?" And in answer to this question, he points to the undeniable fact that the French Revolution swept away more than "the prerogatives of the nobility, the authority of the sovereign courts, the rights of corporations, the privileges of provinces."

When these institutions were swept away, salutary mores and opinions — which they had fostered, reinforced, and relied on in turn — disappeared as well. In part as a consequence of the assault directed at the Church as a corporation, Tocqueville implies, religion has "lost its empire over souls," and now it sets no limits on the conduct of a prince. But, by the same token, kings are no longer an object of veneration and profound public esteem. Precisely, then, because he is despised, feared, and hated, the prince "sees himself as a foreigner in his country, and he treats his subjects as men vanquished" in the field. The towns and provinces of France are no longer "different nations in the midst of a common fatherland," capable of opposing "a particular *esprit* to the *esprit général* of servitude." Instead, they are "all parts of the same empire, having lost their franchises, their usages, their prejudices, and even their memories and names," and over time they "have become habituated to an obedience to the same laws." When the nobility lost all power, "aristocratic honor" died as well, and now no one stands out: everyone is equally submerged in the crowd. For similar reasons, family spirit is dying out; and as a consequence of the great upheaval that has occurred, customs, mores, and opinions are in constant flux. What can be done to bolster liberty, he asks, when "each citizen, being equally powerless, equally poor, equally isolated, can oppose to the organized force of government nothing but his individual weakness?"

In short, it is Tocqueville's contention that the world described by Montesquieu in the chapters within *The Spirit of Laws* that he devotes to monarchy is forever lost. "In our annals," he claims, nothing "analogous to that which might now come to pass among us" can be found. To find a proper analogue, one must look further afield. One must "inquire into the monuments of antiquity." One must "recur to the frightful centuries of Roman tyranny, in which mores were corrupted, memories effaced, habits destroyed." These were centuries in which "opinions became unsteady, and liberty, chased out of the laws, knew no longer where to seek refuge in order to find an asylum; in which nothing any longer provided protection for the citizens, and the citizens no longer provided protection for themselves; in which one sees men make sport with human nature and princes tire out the mercy of heaven rather than the patience of their subjects" alone. In his view, the only alternatives left to mankind are "democratic liberty" on something like the American model and "the tyranny of the Caesars" (I.ii.9, pp. 241–45).[44]

Tocqueville was not, however, fully satisfied with Montesquieu's depiction of despotism, and he specified the reason. When he contemplated Ottoman Turkey and the Russia that had contributed so much to the defeat of Napoleon, he traced the astonishing vigor and the strength that these two polities had on occasion displayed not to fear (*la crainte*), as Montesquieu had (*EL* 1.3.9–10), but to the force of religion, which transformed their subjects into "citizens" participant in what was for them a "holy city," and which produced thereby "a free concurrence of wills." In his judgment, the combination of religious enthusiasm and unitary direction made the attacks mounted by such polities almost irresistible. In the absence of religion, however, should belief fade, should the subjects within such polities become passive, utterly indifferent, and incapable of taking the initiative, even with regard to objects near and dear, such as the state of the local roads and the fate of their own children, "absolute governments" of this sort could not sustain themselves for long. Such, he could see, was the fate reserved for the Ottoman polity, and he evidently wondered whether the same could be said for Russia under the czars (*DA* I.i.5, pp. 76–77, with the attendant notes).[45]

Tocqueville was perfectly ready to acknowledge the capacity of such a polity to elicit from men "a certain uniformity" in their public conduct, and he acknowledged that this uniformity might end up "being loved for its own sake," without regard to its purpose, in something like the fashion in which "the devout" come to "offer adoration to a statue while forgetting the divinity that it represents." The central authority "succeeds without difficulty in imposing an appearance of regularity [*une allure régulière*] on day-to-day business; in adroitly regulating the details of social order [*la police sociale*]; in repressing mild disorders and petty offenses; in maintaining society in a status quo, which cannot properly be called either decline [*décadence*] or progress; in sustaining in the social body a species of administrative somnolence which the administrators are accustomed to call good order and public tranquillity. In a word, it succeeds in preventing, not in doing." When, however, circumstances present themselves in which the central authority is called upon to stir up the society and to force it to move "at a rapid pace, its strength abandons it. Once its initiatives require the concurrence of individuals, one is entirely surprised at the weakness of this immense machine; all of a sudden it finds itself reduced to powerlessness" (I.i.5, pp. 74–75).

Here, the example that Tocqueville has chiefly in mind is China, which exemplifies the "species of social well-being that a highly centralized administration is able to furnish to the peoples who submit to it." Like Montesquieu, he had read the travel literature on the subject, and in that literature he had found reports suggesting that "the Chinese possess tranquillity without happiness, industry without progress, stability without strength, and material order without public morality." In their case, he adds, "society works well enough at all times, never very well" (I.i.5, p. 75, n. 50). That this description owes something to the ruminations of Montesquieu is abundantly clear,[46] but Tocqueville does not trace Chinese orderliness to imperatives derivative from the climate and terrain. In keeping with the primacy that he accords moral causes, he treats China as symptomatic of a potential possessed by despotism more generally.

These reflections were by no means Tocqueville's last word on this subject. Near the end of the first *Democracy*, in the penultimate section of the chapter devoted to "Some Considerations Regarding the Actual Condition and the Probable Future of the Three Races That Inhabit the Territory of the United States" which serves as its appendix, he pauses once more, briefly to assess the prospects for survival of the republican government established in North America. Although with regard to the United States he tends to be sanguine, he issues an admonition nonetheless—observing that if, for one reason or another, the Americans were to abandon republican government, they "would pass rapidly to despotism without stopping very long at monarchy"—and to reinforce his point, he cites Montesquieu (*DA* I.ii.10, p. 304) and paraphrases the passage from the *Considerations on the Causes of the Greatness of the Romans and their Decline* in which the latter had observed that "there is no authority more absolute than that of the Prince who succeeds a Republic" (*CR* 15.100–103).[47] Then he restates a point that he had made earlier (*DA* I.ii.5, pp. 158–59), warning that "the undefined powers" ordinarily granted "without fear to an elective magistrate" within a republic would in these circumstances find their way "into the hands of an hereditary chief." While "generally true," he continues, Montesquieu's observation is "particularly applicable to a democratic republic" such as the one established in the United States. "The American magistrate would hold onto his undefined power while ceasing to be responsible," he remarks, "and it is impossible to say where the tyranny would then stop." That here in particular he once again has Napoleon in mind is clear from passages in the surviving manuscripts that he excised from the copy that he dispatched to the printer in the end (I.ii.10, p. 304).

ROUSSEAU'S SECRET ADMIRER

Nowhere in *Democracy in America* does Tocqueville even mention Jean-Jacques Rousseau. Had he openly treated him as an authority, he would no doubt have risked alienating the legitimists and the churchmen whom he hoped to reconcile, if not also rally, to the democratic cause by way of depicting its victory as the work of Providence.[48] Tocqueville's silence with regard to the self-styled Citizen of Geneva—who even passes unmentioned in his unpublished notes—should not, however, be taken as evidence that his thinking was in no way indebted to that of the man.[49]

When Montesquieu warned that, if the English were to lose their liberty, they would be "one of the most fully enslaved peoples on earth," he made it clear that their vulnerability was a consequence of their having dispensed with "the prerogatives of the lords, the clergy, the nobility, & the towns." He did not say more. In keeping with his overall practice, he was reticent. He left it to his readers to fill in the details. He left it to them to imagine the character of absolute power unchecked; and by holding out on them, he encouraged them to reflect on their own with regard to the subversive effect that the abolition of these intermediary bodies would be likely to have on the mores which they had inspired or merely reinforced—and this, of course, is precisely what Alexis de Tocqueville did. In doing so, however, he did more than simply follow Montesquieu's lead. With consummate discretion, he turned as well to Montesquieu's wayward disciple—Jean-Jacques Rousseau.

The latter's influence is especially evident in Tocqueville's famous discussion of "the tyranny of the majority." The theme is, of course, nothing new. It was central to the critique of democracy developed in classical antiquity.[50] In his *Notes on the State of Virginia*, which was published in French before it appeared in English, Thomas Jefferson—no enemy to democracy—had railed against legislative despotism,[51] and James Madison had made the need to counter majority tyranny the centerpiece of the argument that he had advanced on behalf of the new federal constitution in the tenth and fifty-first numbers of *The Federalist*.[52] Tocqueville, who had studied both books with care,[53] had both authors in mind when he penned the pertinent chapter of *Democracy in America*, and in due course he quoted pertinent passages from each (I.ii.7, pp. 203–4). His concerns were far broader, however, than those which the two Virginians had voiced. Above all else, he was interested in the influence of democracy on the human soul.

Tocqueville owned an early eighteenth-century reprint of the Port-Royal edition of Pascal's *Pensées*.[54] He read the book with attention, and, at some point, when he found himself in a position to do so, he took notes on material by Pascal not published therein.[55] All of this struck a nerve exposed. Tocqueville was not himself blessed with serenity and a tranquillity of mind; he recognized that *amour propre* was prominent among his own attributes; and he knew only too well what it meant to be condemned to a life of *ennui* and *inquiétude* relieved only by senseless *divertissement*.[56] He had pored over Montesquieu as well, and from him he had learned to attend closely to the manner in which the egalitarian ethos fostered within a commercial republic differed from the aristocratic ethos nourished within a monarchy. In the process, he had also come to appreciate the degree to which monarchies rely on and foster a false and unjustifiable sense of honor, rooted in vanity and inconsistent with what philosophy has to teach concerning the natural equality of man. The great-grandson of Malesherbes could quite easily see how a passion, in itself unjust, which demands artificial preferences and distinctions and is grounded in prejudice, might nonetheless be politically salutary. But he recognized, as had Montesquieu and Malesherbes before him, that illusions of this sort cannot survive the ridicule that they are likely to attract in an age of enlightenment (I.2, above).[57]

Tocqueville had lived in Paris, and this had brought home to him the force of Montesquieu's depiction of the dialectic between commerce and vanity. He recognized the degree to which the universal quest for distinction inadvertently gives rise to a no less universal equality; the manner in which it multiplies desires, needs, and fantasies; and the fashion in which it promotes a profound and inescapable discontent rooted in a disproportion between felt needs and the available means (II.1, above).

Moreover, before going to America, Tocqueville had devoted considerable time to the study of English history, he had attended the celebrated cycle of lectures delivered over the course of twenty-five months by Guizot in which England's trajectory loomed large, and he had reached an assessment at odds with that of his instructor.[58] Upon his return from that extended journey, before starting the first great section of his magnum opus, Tocqueville had paid a brief visit to England, and he went there again in Beaumont's company for a lengthier visit after that work's appearance, then married an English woman before starting work on its sequel. To one correspondent, he would later remark that he shared "so many sentiments and ideas . . . with the English that England has become for me a second intellectual fatherland."[59] To another, he would subsequently write, "I am, above all, and will be to the end of my life a soldier of *the good old cause*."[60] As his appropriation of a slogan devised by the republican opponents of Oliver Cromwell's Protectorate suggests,[61] Tocqueville had devoted considerable thought to the course taken by English history and to its pertinence to that of France.[62] In the course of his ruminations, he had certainly had ample occasion to assess the truth of Montesquieu's denial of the contention—advanced from different perspectives by Montaigne, Pascal, and Locke—that, as a settled disposition, *inquiétude* is a universal attribute of man, and he was exceedingly well situated for weighing the validity of the French philosopher's contention that this disposition is, instead, the defining characteristic of those who reside in liberal, commercial polities.[63]

Perhaps even more to the point, Tocqueville had studied Rousseau in tandem with Pascal and Montesquieu, and from the first of the three he had learned to appreciate the force of the argument that the only legitimate form of government is democratic republicanism.[64] Under the influence of the Jansenist fellow traveler and his Genevan disciple, he had also come to recognize just how vulnerable the human spirit is to corruption, psychological enslavement, and a despair born of *inquiétude*, and by them he had been induced to ponder whether this vulnerability is especially pronounced within enlightened, technologically dynamic, commercial societies that systematically promote and depend upon *amour propre*—and if so, why.[65]

Tocqueville's subsequent restatement of the argument originally framed by Rousseau was at the same time an appropriation and a critique. The savage assault that the Citizen of Geneva had launched against civil society in general, and against bourgeois society in particular, his French admirer thought exceedingly apt—but only when applied to the democratic social condition as such. In his judgment, equality gives rise to the problem. In no way does it constitute the solution. Like men in earlier times, those who live in the modern democratic age are born free—but to a degree unprecedented, as he saw it, they are everywhere intent on putting on chains.[66]

Of course, institutional mechanisms might be established to counter majority tyranny, at least as this phenomenon was understood by Jefferson and Madison. Tocqueville granted as much, and on the subject he had a great deal of interest to say. He had read *The Federalist* with care. He could imagine "a legislative body composed in such a manner that it represents the majority without being necessarily the slave of its passions, an executive power which has a strength all its own, and a judicial power independent of the other two powers"—in sum, "a democratic government" in which it is almost the case that "there is no longer any chance for tyranny." On the federal level, he may have supposed, the Framers of the Constitution had put something of the kind in place. But, at least within the American states, if not also in Jacksonian America as a whole, it was his impression that there was "little to be found in the way of a guarantee against tyranny" of the species that he most feared (*DA* I.ii.7, p. 198).

In any case, Tocqueville seriously doubted whether there could be any effective checks on the influence that the majority in a strictly egalitarian polity exercises over the human mind. As he knew all too well, majority rule is based on the utterly preposterous presumption that with numbers come "enlightenment and

wisdom." He saw as well that this doctrine — "the theory of equality applied to intelligence" — constitutes an attack "on human pride in its last asylum," and he
recognized that it confers on public opinion a species of "moral imperium [*empire*]" (I.ii.7, p. 193).[67] It is, he supposed, here that the greatest danger lies.
"Thought," he wrote, "is a power invisible." It is "almost *insaisissable*" — almost
impossible for the authorities to lay hold of — and as such, in the past, it made
"sport of every tyranny." Even in our own times, he remarked:

> the most absolute sovereigns in Europe know not how to prevent certain
> thoughts hostile to their authority from circulating within their States and even
> within the bosom of their courts in a manner muted, muffled, and well-con-
> cealed [*sourdement*]. It is not the same in America, however: there, as long as
> the majority is in doubt, one speaks; but as soon is it has issued an irrevocable
> pronouncement, everyone falls silent, and friends and enemies alike seem
> then to hitch themselves in concert to its wagon. The reason for this is simple:
> there is no monarch so absolute that he is able to unite in his hand all of the
> strength of the society and to vanquish resistance — but this a majority is able to
> do, vested, as it is, with the right to make the laws and to execute them as well.

The key to understanding this is simple. The "power" that a king possesses is
merely "material." It effects "actions" but "knows not how to touch the will." The
"strength" with which the majority in a democracy is "clothed" is "at all times
both material and moral." It "acts as much upon the will as upon actions," and it
"prevents at the same time the deed and the desire to do it." The results are quite
striking. "I know no country," Tocqueville observes, "where, in general, independence of mind and true liberty of discussion are less the rule than in America" (I.ii.7, pp. 199–200).

In "the constitutional States" within Europe, Tocqueville contends, there is
"no religious or political theory that one cannot freely preach," and these theories penetrate with ease into states lacking constitutional government, "for there
is no country within Europe so thoroughly subject to a single power that he who
wishes to speak the truth finds there no support capable of ensuring him against
the consequences of his independence" of mind. In absolute monarchies, he
can look to the people for support. If he resides where the government is free, he
can seek shelter behind the royal authority. Within democratic countries, the
remnants of the old aristocracy provide him with sustenance; elsewhere, he can
look to the democracy. "But," he adds, "in the bosom of a democracy organized
along the lines of the one in the United States, one encounters only a single
power, a single element of strength and success, and nothing outside that."

In America, the majority draws a formidable circle around thought. Within its limits, a writer is free, but misfortune awaits the man who dares to go beyond these. It is not that he has to fear an *auto-da-fé*, but he is an object of aversion [*dégoûts*] in every form and the butt of everyday persecution. A political career is closed to him: he has offended the only power which has the capacity to open such a career to him. He is refused everything, even glory. Before publishing his opinions, he believed that he had partisans; it seems to him that he has them no longer now that he has been made manifest to all—for those who hold him at fault express themselves volubly, while those who think as he does, without having his courage, remain silent and distance themselves from him. He gives way; in the end, he bends under the strain [*effort*] of each day and reenters the realm of silence as if he felt remorse for having spoken the truth.

In effect, Tocqueville concludes, "the clumsy instruments" once employed by tyranny have been perfected under democratic rule. Violence has ceased to be "material." It has been transformed into something "as intellectual as the human will that it wishes to constrain." When, "under the absolute government of one alone, despotism struck crudely at the body in order to reach the soul," the soul quite often evaded "these blows" and "elevated itself in glory above" the despotic impulse. Now, however, "in democratic republics, this is not the way in which tyranny proceeds: it leaves aside the body and goes straight for the soul." The despotic spirit threatens man with death no more. It leaves him free to think as he wishes—without fear of losing his life and goods. "But," it tells him, "from this day you are a stranger among us." You retain your citizenship but lose its advantages. "You will remain among men but you will lose for yourself the rights of humanity. When you approach those who resemble you [*vos semblables*], they will flee you as a being impure, and those who believe in your innocence, these very ones will abandon you, for one would flee them in turn. Go in peace, I leave you life, but I leave you a life worse than death." If in America there is a dearth of literary genius, if since the American Revolution great men have disappeared from the scene, it is, Tocqueville suggests, a consequence of the lack of intellectual freedom (I.ii.7, pp. 200–201).

Montesquieu had once lamented "the miserable character of courtiers," writing, as we have seen (I.1, above), "Ambition in idleness, baseness in pride, a desire to enrich oneself without work, an aversion for truth, flattery, treason, perfidy, the abandonment of all one's engagements, contempt for the duties of the citizen, fear of the virtue of the prince, hope looking to his weaknesses, &, more than that, the perpetual ridicule cast on virtue form, I believe, the character of the greatest number of courtiers, as is remarked in all places and times" (*EL*

1.3.5). In much the same spirit, as we have also had occasion to note (II.1, above), Rousseau depicted the modern phenomenon of literary and intellectual celebrity so brilliantly exemplified by Voltaire.

In Tocqueville's opinion, "democratic republics" follow a similar path, taking "the spirit of the court" and placing it "within reach of the multitude," so that it "penetrates into all of the classes at once." This he considers a grave reproach:

> Among the immense crowd, which in the United States thrusts its way into a political career, I have seen very few men who demonstrate that virile candor, that manly independence of thought which often distinguished Americans in earlier times, and which, everywhere where it is found, forms the salient trait of greatness in character. At one's first approach, one would say that in America minds [*esprits*] have all been formed on the same model, so much do they follow exactly the same tracks. Sometimes, it is true, the foreigner meets Americans who stray from a rigorous adherence to slogans [*de la rigueur des formules*]; it can happen that these men deplore the viciousness of the laws, the fickleness of the democracy, and its lack of enlightenment. Often they even go so far as to remark on the defects that are altering the national character, and they indicate the means that one might be able to take for their correction. But no one, apart from you, listens to them; and you, to whom they confide these secret thoughts, you are but a foreigner, and you will pass on. They willingly deliver to you truths that are of no use to you, and, when they make their way down into the public square, they stick to another mode of speech [*langage*].

Americans tend to discourse in a patriotic vein, Tocqueville observes, and he does not doubt the sincerity of ordinary folk. But he is less sanguine with regard to their rulers. "Despotism," he explains, "depraves the man who submits to it much more than the one who imposes it. In absolute monarchies, the king often has great virtues, but the courtiers are always vile." Of course, he adds, in America the forms are quite different. There, "the courtiers" do not address the people as "Sire" or "Your Majesty." But they do "speak incessantly of the natural brilliance [*lumières*] of their master," and if they fail to debate which of the virtues of their prince deserves to be admired the most, they nonetheless "assure him that he possesses all the virtues, without having acquired them, and so to speak without even wishing to do so." Moreover, if they do not hand over to their new sovereign their wives and daughters in the hope that he will make of them his mistresses, "they do sacrifice to him their opinions," and in this fashion "they prostitute themselves" instead. In all governments, Tocqueville concludes, "baseness will attach itself to strength and flattery to power. I know only one means for preventing men from degrading themselves—and that is to accord to no one, along with total power, the sovereign capacity to make men vile" (*DA* I.ii.7, p. 202).

STAGNATION

In the second *Democracy*, Tocqueville frequently returns to the theme of majority tyranny—but without ever using the phrase.[68] Here, to be sure, his primary focus is not on institutions and political mores as such: it is not on what he calls "the physiognomy of the political world." It is on mores and manners more generally. His subject is what he pointedly calls "civil society" (II.*Avertissement*, p. 8). He begins by tracing the influence of democracy on the characteristic turn taken by the intellect within the United States (II.i); he then turns to the question of its influence on sentiments (II.ii); and he subsequently examines its influence on mores narrowly defined (II.iii). Only after completing this survey does he return to the question of the prospects for democratic political society and lay out his conclusions (II.iv). It would, nonetheless, be fair to say that his worries concerning the future of democratic political society drive his inquiry throughout.[69]

In pursuing this important question, Tocqueville follows the lead of Montesquieu by devoting himself above all else to the study of political psychology;[70] and as one would expect, in surveying "civil society" in America, he gives central place, as Montesquieu had in his discussion of England (*EL* 3.19.27), to the problem posed by *inquiétude* (*DA* II.ii.13).[71] He begins, however, by charting the influence of the democratic *état social* on the American mind, attributing to the Americans in particular and to democratic peoples more generally a species of unconscious Cartesianism.[72] During his visit, he found a people free "from the *esprit de système*, from the yoke of habits, from family maxims, from class opinions, and, up to a certain point, from national prejudices" as well. They regarded "tradition solely as a source of information"; they considered the existing situation merely "as a useful object of study for the purpose of doing otherwise and better." They were inclined "to seek" by themselves and in themselves alone for the reason why things are as they are, "to attend to the result without allowing themselves to be bound up with the means, and to look beyond the form to the foundation." None of this was due to their study of philosophy, for, of all the civilized nations in the world, the Americans were the people least inclined to spend their time in this fashion. Their adherence to the approach pioneered within one sphere by Martin Luther and John Calvin and extended to all subjects by Sir Francis Bacon, René Descartes, and their successors is due entirely to their *état social*, which relaxes the links between generations, abolishes class distinctions, and leaves those in its possession with no authority to rely on but the judgment that is their own (II.i.1).

In practice, however, men are incapable of sorting out everything for themselves. They have, Tocqueville tells us, neither the time nor the capacity. Even the great philosophers must take "a million things on faith." In consequence, a great deal must be and always is accepted on trust; and though this constitutes a species of servitude, it can be "a salutary servitude which permits men a good use of liberty." Within democratic societies, however, this independence of mind throws men back on the one authority left intact—that of public opinion—and in this species of servitude Tocqueville discerns nothing salutary at all. "Not only is common opinion the only guide which remains available to individual reason among democratic peoples," he writes, "but it is a power infinitely greater among these peoples than among any other. In times of equality, because of their similarity, men have no faith in one another, but this same similarity gives them a confidence almost unlimited in the judgment of the public, for it does not seem to them reasonable that, if they are all alike in enlightenment, truth will not be found on the side of the greatest number." In short, "the same equality that renders" a man "independent of each of his fellow citizens in particular delivers him up, isolated and without defense, to the influence exercised on him [*l'action*] by the greatest number," and the public, without even attempting to persuade men of the truth of its beliefs, "imposes them and makes them penetrate into souls by a species of immense pressure exercised by the mind of all on the intellect of each."

All of this is reinforced where popular sovereignty holds sway. But in fact, wherever equality defines the *état social*, "one can foresee that faith in common opinion will become a species of religion in which the majority will be the prophet." Tocqueville fears that, in the end, public opinion will become powerful enough to "confine the action of individual reason within limits narrower than are suited to the grandeur and happiness of the human race." He worries that, "after having broken all the fetters that classes or men formerly imposed on it, the human mind" will come to be "tightly shackled to" what he ominously speaks of, with Rousseau in mind, as "the general will of the greatest number" (II.i.2).

Tocqueville's worries in this regard were exacerbated by his awareness of a phenomenon that he denominated *"individualisme."* The word itself was new.[73] It is, he acknowledged, "an expression recently coined for the purpose of giving birth to a new idea." Where others employed it to refer to a new set of political principles, however, he used it to point to a tendency encouraged by the democratic *état social*. "Individualism," he wrote, "is a sentiment, well thought out [*réfléchi*] and conducive to peace [*paisible*], which disposes each citizen to isolate himself from the mass of those who resemble him [*ses semblables*] and to retire apart with his family and his friends in such a fashion that, after having created a little society for his own use, he willingly abandons society at large to its own devices." Put in this fashion, individualism would, at least at first glance, appear to be innocuous and unobjectionable, and Tocqueville concedes that it is rooted in "a judgment gone astray rather than in a sentiment depraved." It finds "its source," he writes, "in the defects of the mind as much as in the vices of the heart." Nonetheless, he regards it as an extremely dangerous propensity. It arises from the fact that men in a state of equality are left almost entirely to their own devices—with next to nothing on which to fall back. In the absence of the intermediary institutions identified by Montesquieu, especially when aristocratic privileges have been abolished, municipal institutions have been demolished, and the spirit of family and locality has waned, men are connected to their neighbors and others farther afield only by ties, obviously artificial, which they have consciously crafted for themselves. It is only natural that they should decide whether to fashion such ties on the basis of a calculation of self-interest alone, and it is not immediately evident to most men that the effort is worth the bother. "In this fashion, not only does democracy make each man forget his ancestors, but it also hides from him his descendants and separates him from his contemporaries; it constantly throws him back on himself alone; and, in the end, it threatens to close him up entirely within the solitude of his own heart" (II.ii.2). Finally, and most important of all, Tocqueville intimates, a man isolated in this fashion is in no condition to resist the pressure of public opinion and put up a fight.[74]

The psychological tyranny of the majority is one problem. There is another, and it is arguably no less severe. The absence of social distinctions within democracies militates against discrimination in matters of judgment and taste. In egalitarian societies, high-mindedness of every sort tends to be in short supply. But, of course, in such societies, everyone can easily agree on the value of material well-being, for the desire for comfort is universal. Everything else comes to seem superfluous, if not, in fact, pretentious as well. The useful is preferred to the beautiful; the practical, to the theoretical; the mundane, to the metaphysical—and so the horizon within which democratic men exercise their imaginations and form their aspirations becomes constricted (II.i.10–11, ii.10).

Tocqueville is not fearful that "the love of material enjoyments" will produce moral disorder. That such a passion would pose such a danger within an aristocratic society, he readily concedes. But within democratic peoples, "the love of well-being reveals itself as a passion tenacious, exclusive, universal, but constrained. There is no question of building vast palaces, of conquering or tricking nature, of exhausting the universe to better quench the passions of a single man. It is all about adding a few acres to one's fields, planting an orchard, enlarging an abode, rendering life easier at every instant and more comfortable, preventing trouble, and satisfying the least needs without effort and almost without expense." The "objects" pursued by democratic man are, as this list is intended to suggest, "petty." Within democratic societies, "public sensuality has taken on a certain shape [*allure*], moderate and tranquil, to which all souls are made to conform. It is as difficult to escape the common rule in one's vices as it is in one's virtues," and "softness" is far more likely to be the result than "debauchery." In short, within democracies, the taste for physical pleasures is "not naturally opposed to order; on the contrary, it often has need of order if it is to satisfy itself." Nor is it an enemy to "regularity in mores, for good mores are useful to public tranquillity and favor industry." Tocqueville's objection is that democratic man "delivers his heart, his imagination, his life without reserve" to the pursuit of material goods which are legally sanctioned and unobjectionable as such. "In attempting to lay hold of these," such a man "loses sight of the more precious goods which constitute the glory and grandeur of the human race." In this fashion, Tocqueville laments, "a species of respectable, decent [*honnête*] materialism is able to establish itself in the world"; and though it will certainly "not corrupt souls" in the ordinary sense of the phrase, it will nonetheless "soften them, and it will finish up by noiselessly loosening all the springs [*ressorts*] of theirs" that induce them to act (II.ii.11).[75]

This propensity is further exacerbated by the fact that equality of social condition begets the love of equality. In arguing that this is so (II.ii.1), Tocqueville might seem to be aping Montesquieu's description of the "principle" or "passion that sets in motion" democratic republics (*EL* 1.3.1–3). In fact, however, he is correcting what he took to be an error on the part of his compatriot. The ancient republics that Montesquieu had found so enticing—and that Rousseau had eulogized—were not, in Tocqueville's estimation, egalitarian societies. Athens, Sparta, and Rome were, he claims, founded on slavery. They were, in short, "aristocracies of masters" (*DA* II.i.3, p. 28), and they evidently did not encounter the peculiar difficulties peoples face in modern times where, to a degree hitherto hardly imaginable, an ethos of genuine, universal equality defines the *état social*.

Modern democracy is characterized by a conjunction between the taste for material well-being, democratic envy (the true spur to the love of equality, as Tocqueville clearly was aware [I.ii.5, p. 152]), and a third propensity, which is of profound political and social significance: democratic man believes instinctively and passionately in what Tocqueville, tacitly following Rousseau,[76] calls "the indefinite *perfectibilité* of man." The basic idea itself is, he acknowledges, self-evident, and it is as old as the world. Man "perfects himself"; animals do not; and "the human race could hardly fail" to notice. In aristocratic societies, however, where human beings are "classified according to rank, profession, and birth, and all are constrained to follow the path on which chance has placed them," men tend to presume that human perfectibility is limited and to accept their lot. In democratic societies, to the contrary,

> insofar as castes disappear; classes converge; human beings are jumbled together tumultuously; usages, customs, and laws undergo change; new facts crop up; new truths are brought to light; ancient opinions disappear; and others take their place—there the image of a perfection that is ideal and forever fugitive presents itself to the human mind.
>
> Continual changes take place at every instant under the eyes of each man. . . . His setbacks make him see that no one can flatter himself with having discovered the absolute good; his successes inflame him in pursuing it without respite. In this fashion, always searching, falling, picking himself up, often disappointed, never discouraged, he tends incessantly towards this immense grandeur which he discerns confusedly at the end of a long path that humanity is obligated to follow still. (II.i.8)

When combined with democratic envy and a taste for material well-being, this conviction can be, as Tocqueville makes clear, a source of real trouble.

During his tour through America, Tocqueville was powerfully struck by the manner in which the wilderness, which existed nearby and beckoned the settlers on, had shaped the American character; and in the first *Democracy*, he had commented on "the avidity" with which "the American hurls himself on the immense prey that fortune offers him." In pursuing this prey, he remarked, "he braves without fear the arrow of the Indian and the maladies of the wilderness [*du désert*]; the silence of the forests offers him no surprises, the approach of savage beasts moves him not: a passion stronger than the love of life unceasingly spurs him on. Before him there extends a continent almost without limits, and one would say that, fearing that he has already lost his place within it, he hastens in fear of arriving too late." Almost everywhere, he wrote, those who had left one fatherland in search of well-being, only to move on again from their second fatherland in the hope of being better off, "encounter fortune but not happiness. Among them, the desire for well-being has become a passion, uneasy [*inquiet*] and ardent, which grows in satisfying itself." In Europe, he was well aware, it was customary to regard "uneasiness of mind [*inquiétude de l'esprit*], the immoder-

ate desire for wealth, the extreme love of independence" as "a great social danger." But in America, he was convinced, the *passions inquiètes* evoked by the opportunities afforded by an empty continent were, in fact, favorable to orderly government. Were it not for these "uneasy passions," he wrote, "the population
would concentrate itself about certain places and soon experience, as among us,
needs difficult to satisfy." Because of these passions, the Americans are a profoundly commercial people, and they "carry over into the political realm the
habits of trade [*negoce*]. They love order, without which business knows not how
to prosper, and they prize in particular regularity of mores, which provides the
foundation for successful trading houses [*les bonnes maisons*]; they prefer the
good sense which creates large fortunes to the genius which often dissipates
them. . . . Among them, practice is accorded more honor than theory" (I.ii.9,
pp. 220–22).

In this propensity, Tocqueville discerned danger as well; and in the second
Democracy, he addressed this theme in a manner strikingly reminiscent of
Rousseau's depiction, in the *Discourse on the Origin and Foundations of Inequality among Men*, of the most important stages in the evolution of human sociability.[77] In the Old World, Tocqueville tells us, he had come across backwa-
ters in which the inhabitants were ignorant, worthy of pity, politically isolated,
and oppressed but nonetheless displayed a species of serenity and even a jovial
humor. In America, by way of contrast, he observed: "I have seen the freest and
most enlightened men placed in the happiest condition that there is in the
world. It seemed to me that a cloud of sorts habitually covered their features; they
seemed to me grave and almost sad in the midst of their pleasures." The difference he traced to their outlook: the men he had encountered in Europe's back-
waters "think not at all concerning the evils that they endure," he reports, while
the Americans "dream constantly of the goods that they do not have." The "fever-
ish ardor" that the latter display in their pursuit of "well-being" he found utterly
bewildering, especially since "they showed themselves to be tormented constantly by a vague fear [*crainte*] of not having chosen the shortest route leading to
it." An American, he wrote, "lays hold of everything but without getting a grip on
it, and he soon lets it escape from his hands in order to run after enjoyments that
are new." He will build a house for his old age and sell it while the roof is being
built; he will plant a garden, then rent it out just as it is coming to harvest. He set-
tles in one place, then another. If he is successful in business, he will plunge into
politics. If he has finished the year's work, an "uneasy [*inquiète*] curiosity" will
take hold of him and hurry him off on a trip—as if his sole purpose were to "distract himself from the happiness that is his" (II.ii.13, pp. 123–24).

Tocqueville would not have found this spectacle arresting had it not been true of an entire people, and to describe it, as should by now be evident, he borrows language that Montesquieu had appropriated from Montaigne, Pascal, and Locke.[78] The "secret *inquiétude*" and the "inconstancy" that the Americans display are largely due, he says, to their "taste for material enjoyments." If, moreover, "to the taste for material well-being," one were to join "a social condition in which neither law nor custom holds anyone any longer in his place," this would be a great additional stimulus for the "*inquiétude d'esprit*" that is their defining quality (II.ii.13, p. 124). The Americans described by Tocqueville bear a striking resemblance to the Parisians and to those resident in the other great cities of Europe whom Montesquieu depicts in his *Persian Letters* and in *The Spirit of Laws* (II.1, above). "When all the prerogatives of birth and of fortune are destroyed," Tocqueville observes,

> when all the professions are open to all, and one is able to succeed on one's own to the summit of each of them, an immense and easy course seems to open itself up for the ambition of men, and they willingly imagine that they are called to great destinies. But this is an erroneous view that experience will correct all the days of their lives. This same equality, which permits each citizen to conceive vast hopes, renders all of the citizens individually weak. It limits on all sides their strength at the same time that it permits their desires to extend themselves.
>
> Not only are they powerless by themselves, but they find at each step immense obstacles that they had not at all perceived before.
>
> They have destroyed the troublesome privileges possessed by some of those who resemble them [*leurs semblables*]; they encounter the competition of all. The barrier has changed form rather than place. When men are more or less similar [*semblables*] and follow the same route, it is very difficult for any of them to walk faster and break through the uniform crowd that surrounds and presses on him.

No matter how "democratic the *état social* and the political constitution of a people may be," Tocqueville concludes, it will not be satisfactory, for it will not eliminate the last bastion of privilege — "the inequality of intellect." The equality for which democratic peoples have contracted so powerful a taste "retreats before them every day without ever concealing itself from view; and in withdrawing, it draws them on in pursuit. Unceasingly, they believe that they are going to lay hold of it, and it escapes unceasingly from their grasp. They see it close enough to know its charms, they do not approach it close enough to enjoy it, and they die before having fully savored its sweetness." It is this that accounts for "the singular melancholy" displayed by the inhabitants of democratic countries "in the bosom of their abundance," and it explains as well "the disgust with life that comes at times to lay hold of them in the midst of an easy and tranquil existence" (*DA* II.ii.13, p. 125).

In describing England, Montesquieu had remarked that, because of the laws' provision of liberty, "all the passions there are free: hatred, envy, jealousy, the ardor to enrich & distinguish oneself appear to their full extent" (*EL* 3.19.27, p. 575). In describing the Americans, Tocqueville makes the same point, then draws out the consequences that Montesquieu had only implied. One might suppose, he begins, that the aspect presented by American society would be highly likely "to excite and nourish curiosity." After all, "fortunes, ideas, laws vary constantly there. One would say that unmovable nature is itself mobile, so thoroughly does it undergo transformation each day at the hands of man." But he found that, in the long run, "the sight of a society so agitated can seem monotonous, and the spectator, who for a time contemplates this pageant, so much in motion, becomes bored." To explain why this should be the case, Tocqueville tacitly resorts, as he often does, to the language of Rousseau. In aristocratic societies, "men are prodigiously dissimilar [*dissemblables*]: they have passions, ideas, habits, and tastes that are in their essence diverse. Nothing is in motion; everything is different." In democracies, on the other hand, "all the men are alike [*semblables*] and do things more or less alike [*semblables*]." To be sure, individuals suffer dramatic ups and downs, but their resemblance—that which makes them *semblables*—is nonetheless profound: "the same successes and the same reverses continually recur; the name of the actors alone is different, the play is the same." In America, therefore, society is "agitated because men and things undergo constant change; and it is monotonous because all of the changes are similar." To understand this, one need only attend to the fact that, while "men who live in democratic times have a multitude of passions," these passions for the most part eventuate in or emerge from "the love of wealth." After all, Tocqueville observes, "prestige" is no longer attached to "birth, status [*état*], or profession." The only thing left, which gives rise to "exceedingly visible differences" between men, is "money"; and since "one cannot enrich oneself by war, by public employment, or by political confiscations, the love of wealth directs men chiefly to industry," which promotes in turn "exceedingly regular habits" and "a long succession of exceedingly uniform little acts." In effect, "habits grow more regular and conduct more uniform as the passions grow more lively. One could say that it is the violence itself of their desires that renders the Americans so methodical," and, he adds, what has been said regarding America now applies to nearly all of mankind. As a consequence of the drift toward equality, diversity is disappearing as everyone inadvertently comes to pursue the same goal (*DA* II.iii.17).

One consequence is that the Americans have little use for the aristocratic code of honor. They call "noble and estimable ambition that which our fathers in the Middle Ages denominated servile cupidity," and they speak of "the conquering ardor and warlike humor" of medieval combatants as "blind and barbarous fury" (II.iii.18, p. 197). Another consequence is that, although nearly everyone in the United States is ambitious, almost no one entertains ambitions that are lofty and grand (II.iii.19). A third is that, within democratic societies such as the one Tocqueville visited in America, great revolutions will become rare.[79] Within egalitarian polities, he tells us, men are always contracting "new and uneasy [*inquiets*] desires." But, as he has indicated elsewhere as well, the commercial character of these societies elicits from these same men a species of orderliness. When faced with the call to revolution, men of this sort may applaud, but they are not likely to follow. To the "ardor [*fouge*]" of the agitator, "they oppose in secret their inertia; to his revolutionary instincts, they oppose their conservative interests; to his adventurous passions, they oppose their stay-at-home tastes; to the peculiarities [*écarts*] of his genius, they oppose their good sense; and to his poetry, they oppose their prose" (II.iii.21).

Tocqueville was no friend to revolution[80]—although in 1848, when he actually got caught up in one, it gave him a great thrill.[81] In general, his outlook was cautious and prudential. After 1830, he actually persuaded himself that the revolution of 1789 had run its course, that France for the first time since that upheaval lacked "great parties" radically opposed, and that this situation would continue for a considerable stretch of time.[82] During this period, he worried, instead, that in his compatriots the Revolution had instilled a "contempt for forms" and a "taste" for rapid and violent change; he feared that "revolutionary instincts would become soft, gentle, and regular without being extinguished" and that they "would transform themselves gradually into mores of government and habits of administration" (II.iv.7, p. 276). He was aware, to be sure, of the socialist undercurrents in France. He suspected that someday the question of property would give rise to "great parties" there.[83] But it was not until three weeks before the revolution of 1848 that he recognized that this day had already arrived.[84] In the aftermath of that cataclysmic event, he came to the conclusion that the issues raised in 1789 had not been settled after all, and he then began to worry that France had entered an unending cycle in which it was destined to oscillate between arbitrary government and anarchy.[85]

Even then, however, when he turned his mind from the present and contemplated the future more generally, Tocqueville remained, in fact, far less worried about "the audacity of desires" that men would display than about their "mediocrity." That which should most be feared, he wrote, was "that in the centuries to come, in the midst of the petty, incessant, and tumultuous occupations of life, ambition will lose its *élan* and its grandeur; the human passions will exhaust themselves and become debased; and the disposition [*allure*] of humanity will become quieter [*paisible*] and less exalted with each passing day" (II.iii.19, p. 208).[86]

When Tocqueville suggested that great revolutions would become rare, he had in mind intellectual as well as political revolutions. In America, he was struck by the immobility of opinion, which he traced to what he had called in the first *Democracy* "the tyranny of the majority." In democracies, he observed, "public favor seems as necessary as the air that one breathes, and to be in disagreement with the mass is, so to speak, not to live. The mass has no need to employ the laws for the purpose of causing those who do not think as it does to bend" to its will. "It suffices that it disapprove. The sense of their isolation and powerlessness overwhelms them immediately and causes them to despair." One consequence of these reflections is that Tocqueville finds it easy to foresee the emergence of a "political condition," which, "when it comes to be combined with equality, will render society more stationary than it ever has been in the Occident." When he considers the speed at which wealth changes hands and when he reflects on "the love of property, so uneasy [*inquiet*] and so ardent," he cannot restrain himself from entertaining the suspicion "that men will reach a point in which they regard every new theory as a danger, every innovation as trouble worthy of regret, every instance of social progress as the first step towards a revolution, and that they will refuse altogether to make any move for fear that they will be swept away. I tremble, I confess, in fear that, in the end, they will allow themselves to become so fully possessed by a cowardly [*lache*] love of present enjoyments that their interest in their own future and in that of their descendants will disappear and they will come to prefer listlessly [*mollement*] following the course of their destiny to making a sudden and energetic effort at redress in time of need" (II.iii.21, pp. 215–20). In short, what Tocqueville feared most was an acquiescence and a passivity that he associated with the Orient. It is with an eye to the larger threat of intellectual and cultural stagnation that in the second *Democracy* he once again raised the specter of China.

Ancient Rome had eventually succumbed to barbarian invasions, he readily admitted. But this, he insisted, did not mean that there was only one way for civilization to die, for there was much to be feared from the democratic distaste for metaphysics and theoretical science. "If the lights [*les lumières*] that are the source of our enlightenment [*qui nous éclairent*] were ever to be extinguished," he warned, "they would go dark little by little as if by themselves." This, he suspected, is precisely what had happened in the Orient.

When the Europeans made their landing in China three hundred years ago, they found there nearly all the arts developed to a certain degree of perfection, and they were surprised that, having arrived at this point, the Chinese had not gone further. Later, they discovered the vestiges of profound knowledge [*hautes connaissances*] that had been lost. The nation was industrial; for the most part, the methods derived from science had been preserved within it, but science itself no longer existed. This explained to them the singular species of immobility that characterized the popular mind. The Chinese, in following the path taken by their fathers, had forgotten the reasoning which had guided them. They still made use of the formula without inquiring into its sense; they retained the instrument and no longer possessed the art of modifying it and of reproducing it. They were then incapable of changing anything. They had to renounce improvement. Always and in everything, they were forced to imitate their fathers lest they hurl themselves into impenetrable darkness if they strayed for an instant from the trail which the latter had traced. The spring from which human knowledge flowed had almost dried up, and though the stream still flowed, it could no longer increase its rate of flow [*ses ondes*] nor change its course.

Of course, this did not prevent the Chinese from subsisting "peaceably for centuries." Those who had conquered China had, in fact, always succumbed to the mores of the Chinese. A species of "material well-being" remained in evidence. "Revolutions were very rare, and war was, so to speak, unknown." We should not "reassure ourselves," Tocqueville wrote, "on the supposition that the barbarians are still far from us, for there are peoples who allow the light [*la lumière*] to be snatched from their hands, and there are other peoples who stifle it under their own feet" (II.i.10, p. 52).[87]

SOFT DESPOTISM

It is not fortuitous that, in the second *Democracy*, Tocqueville dwells on the example set by China. Nor should it seem odd that he is silent in the first three parts contained therein concerning the species of despotism found in imperial Rome. It took him four years to pen the second *Democracy*. In the interim, he read widely and, for a time, with great intensity. As is only natural, he had ample occasion in which to rethink, and this induced him to do a great deal of writing and rewriting. In this case, as he thought through more fully than before the implications for mores and manners of the doctrine of universal equality and of the emergent democratic *état social*, he came to the conclusion that what American propensities portended fit imperial China, with its docile population and its vast, intrusive bureaucracy, well-practiced in the science of administration, far better than it fit the loose suzerainty of imperial Rome.[88] As he put it in the fourth and last part of the second *Democracy,* "One sees that at the time of the greatest power of the Caesars, the different peoples who inhabited the Roman world had still preserved diverse customs and mores: although subjected to the same monarch, the better part of the provinces were administered separately; they were filled with powerful and active municipalities; and, although the entire government of the empire was concentrated in the hands of the emperor alone, and although he remained, in time of need, the arbiter of all things, the details of social life and of individual existence ordinarily escaped his control." In principle, of course, "the emperors possessed a power immense without counterweight," and this allowed Caligula, Nero, Domitian, Caracalla, and the like to indulge themselves in a most capricious fashion and to "employ the entire strength of the State in satisfying themselves." But the tyranny of these monsters touched only a handful and left everyone else to their own devices (II.iv.6, pp. 263–64).

If despotism were to establish itself among the democratic nations of his own time, Tocqueville had come to think, "it would have a different character: it would be more extensive and gentler or softer [*plus doux*], and it would degrade men without tormenting them." In the past, it may not have been possible for a sovereign to attempt "to administer on his own and without the help of secondary powers all the parts of a great empire," but times have changed. In the past, no one had even attempted "to subject all of his subjects to the details of a uniform set of regulations [*régle*]." Nor did any prince seek to lord it over and guide each and every one of his subjects. No one had ever even thought of such a thing: "the want of enlightenment [*lumières*], the imperfection of administrative procedures, and, most important of all, the natural obstacles that the inequality of conditions had thrown up would soon have put a stop to the execution of so vast a design." Now, however, in the epoch "of enlightenment [*lumières*] and equality," sovereigns are better placed for uniting "all of the public powers into their hands alone," as Napoleon had proven, and they are also better situated for "penetrating more habitually and more deeply into the circle of private interests" than was ever possible in antiquity. But, of course, "the very same equality, which eases the way for despotism, tempers it." To the very degree that "men have become *semblables* and equals, public mores have become more humane and gentler [*plus douces*]. When no citizen has great power or great wealth, in a certain way tyranny lacks occasion and stage [*théatre*]. All fortunes are mediocre, the passions are naturally constrained, the imagination limited, pleasures simple. This universal moderation moderates the sovereign himself and stops within certain limits the disordered impulse of his desires." The danger that men face is less a matter of tyranny than of tutelage (II.iv.6, pp. 263–65).[89]

As should be evident, Tocqueville did not foresee the totalitarianism of the twentieth century in all of its horror.[90] He was thoroughly familiar with the course taken by the French Revolution, however, and no one in his family could ever forget the Terror. That, "at certain moments of great effervescence and great peril, democratic governments can become violent and cruel," he was perfectly prepared to concede, but he expected such crises to be "rare and transient" (II.iv.6, p. 265), and he was arguably right. As the last two centuries of French history demonstrate, it is exceedingly difficult for radical movements to sustain the requisite revolutionary élan,[91] and, as developments within the last two decades make abundantly clear, this propensity to lassitude pertains even within totalitarian regimes. When the generation that made the revolution finally passes from the scene, the regime that its members established tends to go slack, to soften, and even to dissolve.

For the peculiar "species of oppression" that he thought most "threatening to democratic peoples," Tocqueville lacked a proper vocabulary. The old terms, tyranny and despotism, he thought inadequate, and so he resorted to description, outlining the "novel features" of this new species of despotism in such a way as to lay an indictment against the emerging welfare state.[92] On the one hand, he wrote, one had to imagine

> an innumerable multitude of men, alike [*semblables*] and equal, who turn about without repose in order to procure for themselves petty and vulgar pleasures with which they fill their souls. Each of them, withdrawn apart, is a virtual stranger, unaware of the fate of the others: his children and his particular friends form for him the entirety of the human race; as for his fellow citizens, he is beside them but he sees them not; he touches them and senses them not; he exists only in himself and for himself alone, and, if he still has a family, one could say at least that he no longer has a fatherland.
>
> Over these is elevated an immense, tutelary power, which takes sole charge of assuring their enjoyment and of watching over their fate. It is absolute, attentive to detail, regular, provident, and gentle. It would resemble the paternal power if, like that power, it had as its object to prepare men for manhood [*l'âge viril*], but it seeks, to the contrary, to keep them irrevocably fixed in childhood; it loves the fact that the citizens enjoy themselves provided that they dream solely of their own enjoyment. It works willingly for their happiness, but it wishes to be the only agent and the sole arbiter of that happiness. It provides for their security, foresees and supplies their needs, guides them in the principal affairs, directs their industry, regulates their testaments, divides their inheri-

tances. Can it not relieve them entirely of the trouble of thinking and of the effort associated with living?

In this fashion, every day, it renders the employment of free will less useful and more rare; it confines the action of the will within a smaller space, and bit by bit it steals from each citizen the use of that which is his own. Equality has prepared men for all of these things: it has disposed them to put up with them and often even to regard them as a benefit.

First, Tocqueville continues, the government gets the individual into its hands and molds him as it likes. Then, "the sovereign extends its arms about the society as a whole; it covers its surface with a network of petty regulations—complicated, minute, and uniform—through which even the most original minds and the most vigorous souls know not how to make their way past the crowd and emerge into the light of day." The sovereign power has no need to break wills. It simply "softens them, bends them, and directs them; rarely does it force one to act, but it constantly opposes itself to one's acting on one's own; it does not destroy; it prevents things from being born; it does not tyrannize, it gets in the way [*gêne*], it curtails [*comprime*], it enervates, it extinguishes, it stupefies [*hébète*]." By such methods, in the end, the sovereign power achieves its final goal: "it reduces every nation to nothing but a herd of timid and industrious animals, of which the government is the shepherd" (II.iv.6, pp. 265–66).[93]

The new and unprecedented "species of servitude" that Tocqueville had in mind was "regulated, gentle or soft [*douce*], and favorable to peace," and he suspected that it could be "combined more easily" than men were inclined to imagine "with some of the external forms of liberty." He even suggests "that it would be possible for it to be established in the very shadow of the sovereignty of the people." In this fashion—with the institution of a "unitary, tutelary, all-powerful" government "elected by the citizens" at regular intervals—one might actually satisfy the two contradictory impulses found among his contemporaries: the felt "need for guidance, and the longing to remain free." What this would involve, Tocqueville explains, is a "species of compromise between administrative despotism and the sovereignty of the people" (II.iv.6, pp. 267–68), a corrupt bargain between the ghost of Jean-Jacques Rousseau and that of his erstwhile admirer Anne-Robert-Jacques Turgot, in which the political doctrine of the former is deployed rhetorically for the purpose of legitimizing a law-abiding, steady, reliable despotism on the Chinese model—of the sort that was espoused in full knowledge of what they were embracing by Turgot's mentors among the Physiocrats.[94] Under such an arrangement, Tocqueville remarked, cannily redeploying against the heirs of the Physiocrats a trope favored by Rousseau (CS 3.15), "the citizens emerge for a moment from dependence for the purpose of indicating their masters and then re-enter," without further ado, "their former state. They console themselves for being in tutelage with the thought that they have chosen the tutors themselves," and "they think that they have sufficiently guaranteed the liberty of the individual when they have delivered it to the national power" (*DA* II.iv.6, p. 268).

However undesirable such a settlement might be, Tocqueville nonetheless considers it "infinitely preferable" to an arrangement in which, "after having concentrated all the powers, the constitution would deposit them into the hand of an irresponsible man or body." He had lived most of his childhood in the shadow of one Napoleon; he quite rightly feared that he would live out his days in the shadow of another; and on this subject he was prepared to be categorical: "Of all the different forms that democratic despotism can take," he writes, "this would assuredly be the worst" (II.iv.6, p. 268).

Two

AMERICAN EXCEPTIONALISM

One of the happiest consequences of the absence of government (when a people is fortunate enough to be able to do without it, which is rare) is the development of individual strength that inevitably follows from it. Each man learns to think, to act by himself, without counting on the support of an outside force—which, however vigilant one supposes it to be, can never answer all social needs. Man, thus accustomed to seek his well-being solely through his own efforts, raises himself in his opinion as he does in the opinion of others; his soul becomes larger and stronger at the same time.

—Alexis de Tocqueville

In the letter of admonition (*avertissement*) that he placed at the head of the second great section of *Democracy in America* published in 1840, Tocqueville warned his readers that they might find what he had to say in his new book surprising. He was firmly of the opinion "that the democratic revolution, of which we are the witnesses, is an irresistible fact—against which it would be neither desirable nor wise to struggle." This those who had perused the first *Democracy* no doubt knew. But in the second *Democracy*, which they were about to read, he had often addressed "to the democratic societies that this revolution had created words so severe" that, he feared, his readers would find them strange, if not, in fact, off-putting in the extreme. Tocqueville's response was straightforward: "it is because I was not an adversary of democracy that I have wanted to be sincere in her regard. From their enemies, men do not receive the truth, and their friends hardly ever offer it to them: it is for this purpose that I have spoken." Tocqueville took it for granted that there would be many who would "announce to men the novel goods that equality promises them." He knew that there would be only a few who "would dare to indicate the dangers with which it threatens them." It is, he wrote, "chiefly with regard to these dangers that I have directed my attention"; and having come to the conclusion that he had discovered these, he explained, "I have not had the cowardice to remain silent in their respect" (*DA* II.*Avertisse-ment*).

In issuing this warning, Tocqueville was no more than prudent. By and large, as he was aware, the first *Democracy* is upbeat and encouraging.[1] Though largely descriptive, its sequel is at times quite dark. The discrepancy is not due to a profound change in attitude on Tocqueville's part. As we have already had occasion to note, by the spring of 1830, before he had even left for America, he had already formulated his gloomy analysis of man's future prospects.[2] There is, moreover, as Tocqueville insisted (II.*Avertissement*, p. 8), remarkable consistency between the first and the second *Democracy*.[3] If the shift in tone is reflective of anything, it is a function of a change in the subject discussed. When focusing on what he later referred to as "the physiognomy of the political world" in America, Tocqueville was bound to express admiration—for, as every impartial observer before and since has recognized, the American founding was the handiwork of truly great men. When, however, he turned to "civil society" and to the mores and manners to which the "democratic social condition" gives rise, Tocqueville found that there was considerably less to admire (II.*Avertissement*). This social condition might well be more just, and he conceded as much. But he was enough of an aristocrat to realize that democratic justice can be achieved only by way of a sacrifice of other, arguably less significant goods.[4] On this point, he was surely right. No one has ever seriously suggested the superiority of American high culture in the nineteenth century, and there is, by the same token, even less to be said in frank praise of European culture in the fully democratic age that finally dawned on that continent in 1945. Democratic societies tend to think push-pin as good as poetry, and the novels, plays, music, and art which they celebrate and embrace are for the most part dreck. The museum, founded as a memorial for the greatness of a past forever gone, is the only genuine cultural monument of the fully democratic *état social*.

Tocqueville's interest in America was twofold. On the one hand, by closely observing a purely democratic society largely unaffected by an aristocratic past, he hoped to be able to isolate, study, and reflect on the tendencies peculiar to the democratic social condition. On the other hand, he wanted to know whether democratic government in America really was the success it seemed to be and, if so, why.

Tocqueville did not suppose that one could simply transplant American institutions. If he had ever been naive in this fashion, living a little each day in the company of Pascal, Montesquieu, and Rousseau had cured him of such foolishness. But he did think that what the Americans had accomplished by one means, the French might be able to achieve by another; and he hoped that, by describing accurately and analyzing intelligently what the Americans had managed to achieve, he might be able to inspire the leading men among his compatriots to join with him in working out a political settlement for their troubled country that, by means appropriate to their peculiar situation and history, might serve as well.[5]

DEMOCRATIC *INDOCILITÉ*

When Tocqueville warned of the danger that liberal democratic man might succumb to what he called "democratic despotism," it was France—and not the United States—that he chiefly had in mind. In his day, the tendencies fostered by the democratic social condition were no doubt more evident in the latter than in the former, but the American Revolution had eventuated in an orderly, democratic republican government while the French Revolution had produced chaos, disorder, revolutionary war, and judicial murder on a grand scale—all before its descent into a populist tyranny under Napoleon Bonaparte. The American example was, to say the least, encouraging. It confirmed Tocqueville's conviction that there is a foundation within human nature for self-government, and it suggested that there is something about the democratic social condition that is, in fact, conducive to it.

Human beings are subject, Tocqueville remarks, to "two passions to one another inimical [*enemies*]: they feel the need to be guided and the yearning to remain free." This can quite easily be observed in young children, as he undoubtedly knew. They wish to be looked after, coddled, cosseted, and catered to, and with no less passion they wish to do everything themselves—and between these "contrary instincts," they oscillate in a fashion hard to predict. Among adults, if Tocqueville is to believed, no one feels these two opposed impulses as powerfully as do those whom he terms "our contemporaries," who are, he says, "unceasingly worked over by" both (II.iv.6, p. 268). On the one hand, Tocqueville tells us:

> equality, which renders men independent of one another, causes them to contract the habit and taste for following none but their own wills with regard to activities particularly their own. This thoroughgoing independence, which they continually enjoy vis-à-vis their equals and in the usages of private life, disposes them to look on all authority with an eye discontent, and it soon suggests to them the idea of political liberty and a love for it. Men who live in our time proceed, then, down a natural incline which directs them towards free institu-

tions. Pick any one of these men at random: if possible, work your way back to his primitive instincts: you will discover that, among the different governments, the one he would first conceive of and prize the most is the government whose chief he has elected and the one over whose acts he exercises control.

On the other hand, he adds, this same equality gives rise to a second, no less powerful impulse, one which "conducts men by a path longer, more secret, but more certain—in the direction of servitude." The first impulse men can hardly fail to notice; by the second, they "allow themselves to be swept along without seeing it" at all (II.iv.1).[6] In Tocqueville's estimation, soft despotism really is democracy's drift.

Tocqueville's self-imposed task was to expose and exhibit to mankind the second tendency so that men would be alert to the danger it poses. If, in contrast to most propertied Frenchmen, he was less afraid of anarchy than of tyranny; if he was not put off by the "recalcitrance [*indocilité*]" that equality inspires; if, in fact, he was inclined to praise liberal democratic man chiefly for his lack of docility, it is because he had a more than sneaking admiration for the stubbornness that causes human beings to resent and resist tutelage and to want to act entirely on their own. He found it heartening to see equality "deposit at the bottom of the mind and heart of each man the obscure notion of political independence and an instinctive penchant for it." It is "in this fashion," he explains, that equality prepares a "remedy for the evil to which it gives birth" (II.iv.1).

If Tocqueville admired the United States of America, it was because that country exhibited in an admirable fashion the particular "remedy" that he had in mind. It was, he believed, as egalitarian a society as any rational human being could hope for or expect, and yet it did little or nothing to encourage tutelage. Instead, to his delight, it fed and encouraged the longing for freedom, and it starved, insofar as this was possible, man's instinctive desire for guidance. It was as if American institutions and mores had been carefully designed to prepare men for manhood, where other polities sought to confine them in perpetuity within limits appropriate to a child. The political institutions of the United States were built on and even encouraged the *indocilité* that equality inspires. They sought to lay hold of this unreasoning, irrational, instinctive resistance to taking direction and to being taught what to think and how to live. Their aim was to invigorate this impulse and to transform it into something consistent with the dictates of reason and perhaps even conducive to reasoning itself.

In England, as we have seen (I.2, above), Montesquieu had encountered a people, rather like Tocqueville's Americans, who, although they were citizens in a free state, displayed a species of individual "independence" reminiscent of that which was thought to typify man in the state of nature. In *The Spirit of Laws*, he had explored the manner in which the constitution of England—embodying, as it does, a distribution and separation of powers—takes advantage of the uneasiness (*inquiétude*) that emerges as the dominant disposition of men possessed of such an "independence," who live within a polity that leaves all the passions free; then turns this disposition into a settled propensity for jealousy and wariness by giving it a focus; and ultimately deploys this unreasoning passion as a political principle, capable of animating free institutions and conducive as well to sustaining them. In *Democracy in America*, Tocqueville followed his mentor's lead but gave to his argument an unexpected turn. As he appears to have noticed, the authors of *The Federalist* had appropriated Montesquieu's analysis (I.1, above) of the manner in which the love of honor, the passion that sets monarchy in motion, elicits what can only be described as virtuous conduct from men who are in no evident and obvious way virtuous themselves; and this analysis they had applied to the separation of powers embedded within the American Constitution, arguing that the heightened vanity natural to men constantly in the public eye would elicit from the chief federal officeholders in whom trust had been placed—from presidents, senators, and judges, and even, on occasion, from congressmen as well—a genuine virtue, which these writers were among the first to denominate *responsibility*.[7] It was Tocqueville's contention that precisely the same process was at work throughout the American union at a level far more mundane. It was his conviction that American institutions worked a no less impressive transformation in the *indocilité* to which the democratic social condition naturally gives rise, turning stubborn recalcitrance into a fierce and unbending passion for political liberty; and he believed that, at the same time, these institutions elicited from *indocilité*, combined with a narrow and uninspiring concern for self-interest, a genuine public-spiritedness and an elevated sense of responsibility akin to the popular virtue that was said by Montesquieu to have animated and sustained republics in classical antiquity.[8]

THE TOWNSHIP

From Tocqueville's perspective, the single most crucial fact about the United States was that the Anglo-Americans had retained one of the intermediary institutions typical of the *ancien régime* in Europe at its height.[9] In his day, they knew nothing of the prerogatives of the lords, the clergy, and the nobility, and these they had, in fact, never known at any time. But, from the outset, they had been thoroughly familiar with the prerogatives of the towns—for throughout the colonial period, much in the manner of the bourgeois of medieval Europe, the Anglo-Americans had enjoyed municipal liberties specified in charters that they regarded with something like the awe and reverence reserved for Holy Writ. This was their heritage as Englishmen. As Tocqueville put it, "communal government, that fertile seed [*germe*] of free institutions, had already entered deeply into English habits, and with it the dogma of the sovereignty of the people had been introduced into the very heart of the Tudor monarchy" (*DA* I.i.2, p. 26).[10] Moreover, in America, where land was plentiful and almost anyone could meet the minimum property standard for exercising the franchise, liberties that had been the privileges of oligarchies in Europe became, in practice, the rights of nearly every free man. In America, Tocqueville says, "the communal independence" that developed early on formed and "in our day still forms the principle [*principe*] and lifeblood [*vie*] of American liberty" (I.i.2, pp. 26–36).

Tocqueville was well aware of the fact that the American Revolution had grounded itself in a set of controversial claims concerning the rights of man as man. When he visited Albany, New York, in the summer of 1831, he witnessed and even participated in a Fourth of July celebration in which the Declaration of Independence was publicly read. "This really was a fine spectacle," he wrote two weeks thereafter in a letter dispatched to a friend.

> A profound silence reigned in the assembly. When in its eloquent plea Congress retraced the injustices and the tyranny of England one heard a murmur of indignation and anger circulate about us in the auditorium. When it appealed to the justice of its cause and expressed the generous resolution to succumb or liberate America, it seemed that an electric current made the hearts vibrate.
>
> This was not, I assure you, a theatrical performance. There was in the reading of these promises of independence so well kept, in this return of an entire people towards the memories of its birth, in this union of the present generation with that which is no longer, all of whose generous passions it shared for a moment—there was in all of this something deeply felt and truly great.[11]

Subsequently, however, in *Democracy in America*, Tocqueville emphasized that the great upheaval celebrated on that day had, in fact, had its origins in a struggle on the part of the Anglo-Americans to preserve their rights as Englishmen under the various charters issued England's North American colonies (I.i.4). From this historical accident derived a single, crucial consequence. In rethinking the foundations of freedom, in abandoning their status as Englishmen abroad, and in turning from particularism to abstract, universal principles, the Americans never contemplated giving up their heritage of municipal liberty. Local self-government embodied what they had fought to defend, and the political regime that they fashioned on the national level in fits and starts in the years stretching from

1776 to 1788 was intended chiefly, if not solely, as a guarantor for what they had once regarded as their chartered liberties. In effect, as the most astute of the Americans realized,[12] the United States had originated as a collection of small republics bound together in a federation like the one envisaged by Montesquieu in *The Spirit of Laws.* As Tocqueville pointed out, paraphrasing both Montesquieu (*EL* 2.19.1) and Rousseau (*CP* 5.970–71; *CS* 3.15, p. 431), the new republic on the other side of the Atlantic sought to combine the defensive capacity of a medium-sized state, such as monarchy, with the liberty and public-spiritedness typical of small republics, and it managed to achieve this by way of a division of powers between the federal and the state governments (*DA* I.i.8, pp. 121–25). There was, of course, a great deal more to the story than this,[13] and Tocqueville, who was exceedingly alert, realized as much (I.i.3–8). But the fact that the Constitutional Convention of 1787 had produced what many regarded as a chimera—a government partly national and partly federal of a sort that not even Montesquieu had imagined—merely confirmed what Tocqueville regarded as the most salient fact of American political life: the presence of a centralization of government with regard to matters unavoidably federal in the absence of a general centralization of public administration (I.i.5, pp. 69–80).[14]

In practice, this meant that on the local level Americans were more or less autonomous. They were not alone and defenseless in the face of a mass society; they lived in small communities. With the state government, they had limited contact; with the national government, they had almost none. In New England, their world was the township; in the South, it was the county; and elsewhere it was one or the other or both. Within this restricted municipal sphere, they could be almost as active in governing themselves as had been the citizens of the Greek *pólis* and the Roman *civitas* (I.i.5, pp. 49–66). Self-government was the liberty that they had fought the War for Independence to retain, and this was a liberty that in considerable measure Americans in the age of Andrew Jackson still enjoyed.[15] In Tocqueville's estimation, citizenship is as much a remedy for the evils to which equality gives rise as, in Rousseau's estimation, it is for the evils attendant on political society itself.[16]

Here again Tocqueville merits comparison with Aristotle.[17] He asserts that "a new political science is required for a world entirely new" (I.Intr., p. 9), and he remarks, "When I compare the Greek and Roman republics to the republics of America, the manuscript libraries of the former and their coarse populace with the thousands of newspapers that criss-cross the latter and the enlightened people who inhabit them; when I muse thereafter over all the efforts still made to judge the one with the aid of the others and to foresee on the basis of what happened two thousand years ago what will happen in our time, I am tempted to burn my books in order to apply only new ideas to an *état social* so new" (I.ii.9, p. 235). But, of course, Tocqueville did not burn his books. He read them—with care and consideration. And though he drew a sharp distinction between antiquity and modernity and quite rightly insisted that the ancient republics were "aristocracies of masters" unfamiliar with the democratic *état social* (II.i.3, p. 28), he was perfectly prepared to draw on classical examples for comparative purposes, and he made considerable use of the various species of political science that he had inherited.

Nowhere, to be sure, did Tocqueville identify rational speech (*lógos*) as the capacity that distinguishes man from the animals; nowhere did he explicitly endorse Aristotle's claim that man is a political animal; nowhere did he expressly assert that human beings forced or induced to conduct their lives outside the political arena are rendered servile and virtually subhuman thereby; and he certainly owed a great deal to Pascal, Montesquieu, and Rousseau, who deliberately stopped well short of suggesting, as Aristotle had, that political association has the capacity to complete and perfect human nature.[18] All of this is true, but it is nonetheless the case that Tocqueville appears to have taken for granted something of the sort—for, like Aristotle, he seems to have supposed that there is a doubleness to politics. He clearly recognized that the polity has its origins in man's most basic material needs, in a craving for the advantages attendant on arrangements for collective security and economic cooperation. But he did not restrict himself, in the manner of Pierre Nicole, to celebrating the "marvelous dexterity" of "*amour-propre éclairé.*" Nor did he puckishly suggest, as had Bernard Mandeville, that private vices, properly managed, can make for public virtues.[19] He was not in their sense a mere exponent of asocial *sociability.* Nor did he follow Rousseau in asserting the need "to change, so to speak, human nature; to transform each individual, who by himself is a whole perfect and solitary, into part of a much greater whole from which each individual receives in a certain fashion his life and his being; to alter the constitution of man for the purpose of giving it added strength; to substitute an existence partial and moral for an existence physical and independent which we have all received from nature" (CS 2.7).[20] He was not an advocate of suppressing human individuality.[21] In any case, nothing quite so dramatic was required. Instead, as we have already observed, Tocqueville appears to have followed the authors of *The Federalist* where they drew on and broke ranks with Montesquieu and to have extended the argument that they had advanced with regard to the new virtue of responsibility. Once established, he believed, the political association has the precise capacity attributed to it by Aristotle: without doing violence to human nature in any fashion, it elicits from ordinary human beings a genuine and abiding concern for justice and the common good. First, he intimates, come interests, then the passions inspired by vanity, and finally an ennobling and rational appreciation for one's duties and rights.

In describing the "point of departure" of the Anglo-Americans, for example, Tocqueville emphasizes that, from the very beginning, the English colonists were familiar with "the general principles on which modern constitutions rest—principles that the majority of Europeans in the seventeenth century hardly comprehended, and that had at that time achieved in Great Britain a triumph incomplete." They migrated from "a country that the struggle of parties had agitated for centuries," in which, one by one, "the factions had been obliged, each in turn, to place themselves under the protection of the laws." The "political education" of their English compatriots had taken place in a "rough school," which taught them "more notions of rights, more principles of true liberty" than were generally recognized among "the majority of the peoples of Europe." In fact, Tocqueville contends, "by the laws of New England, these principles were already recognized and given fixed form [*fixé*]" quite early on. In the New England colonies, "the involvement [*intervention*] of the people in public affairs, the free voting of taxes, the practice of holding agents of power responsible for their conduct in office [*la responsabilité des agents du pouvoir*], individual liberty, and the giving of judgment by jury were established beyond question [*sans discussion*] and in fact" (*DA* I.i.2, pp. 26, 33).

By 1650, Tocqueville insists, everything crucial was already in place, and then, around an "individuality" that was nonetheless profoundly "communal" in character, "interests, passions, duties, and rights began to group themselves," and to this "communal individuality," they "began to be strongly attached." "In the very bosom of the township," for which Tocqueville uses the evocative French word *commune,*

> one sees reign a form of political life that is active, entirely democratic, and republican. The colonies still recognize the supremacy of the mother country [*la métropole*]; monarchy is the law of the State, but the republic is already very much alive within the township.
>
> The township names its own magistrates of every sort; it taxes itself; it assesses and levies imposts on itself. Within the township in New England, the law of representation is not admitted. As in Athens, it is in the public square and within the bosom of the general assembly of citizens that matters which touch the interest of all are dealt with [*que se traitent . . . les affaires qui touchent à l'intérêt de tous*].

It is revealing and highly appropriate that, in a sentence in which he is comparing the New England township with ancient Athens (I.i.2, p. 33), Tocqueville should paraphrase the fundamental principle—imported initially into canon law and, then, into the various law codes of medieval Europe from the Roman law of private corporations as applied to the management of waterways—that had in the past been so frequently cited in Europe in defense of communal liberty: "that which touches all should be dealt with by all [*quod omnes tangit ab omnibus tractari debeat*]."[22] It was, after all, the medieval *commune*—along with the church, the guild, and the other corporate bodies graced by charter with the privilege of self-government—that provided the bridge between the republics of classical antiquity and those of modern times,[23] as Tocqueville, who was trained in the old law of France and in the new, here intimates.

Of course, Tocqueville was not an unabashed admirer of every aspect of Anglo-American colonial legislation: in New England especially, that legislation smacked too much of religious intolerance for the Frenchman's tastes. But he did admire the effects of self-government on the American character, and in thinking along pedagogical lines, he was at one with Aristotle and with ancient political science more generally.

Tocqueville insisted that "the dogma of the sovereignty of the people," which was first publicly preached at the time of the American Revolution, "emerged" at that time "from the township and laid hold of the government" (I.i.4, p. 46); and, when he came to describe the government that subsequently took shape, he insisted on beginning with the township, which he depicted in terms suggesting that it comes into being without human artifice and is even more deeply rooted in nature than Aristotle supposed was the case with the ancient Greek *pólis*.[24] It is, he writes, "the only association which is so much in accord with nature [*si bien dans la nature*] that everywhere where men are gathered, the township takes form by itself." This fact notwithstanding, he asserts that "communal liberty is a thing rare and fragile." The township is composed of comparatively coarse elements ill-suited to the conduct of affairs, and the prospects for the survival of communal liberty actually diminish as nations become enlightened: for "a highly civilized society" is not likely to be tolerant of the township's propensity to blunder, and "the liberties" possessed by the townships are of all the species of liberty known to man those that are "the most exposed to the invasions of power." Among "the nations on the continent of Europe," Tocqueville observes, "one could say that there is not a single one that knows" communal liberty (I.i.5, pp. 49–50).

This fact Tocqueville greatly regretted—for, while there is no absolutely dispositive evidence that he read and fully appreciated the letters in which Thomas Jefferson articulated his enthusiasm for what he termed "ward republics,"[25] it was his conviction, as it had been Jefferson's before him,[26] that "it is in the township that the strength of free peoples resides." As he puts it: "Communal institutions are for liberty what primary schools are for science; they place it within reach of the people; they make the people taste its peaceful employ and habituate them to its use. Without communal institutions a nation is able to give itself a free government, but it lacks the spirit of liberty. Passing passions, the interests of a moment, the hazard of circumstances can give a nation the external forms of independence, but despotism, pressed back into the interior of the social body, sooner or later reappears on the surface" (I.i.5, p. 50). In New England, he adds, one can easily see just how beneficial are the results, for there "communal institutions" are sustained and given life by "a communal spirit."

This spirit develops because the New England township possesses "two advantages, which, everywhere where they are found, excite lively interest on the part of man"—which is to say, it possesses "independence and power." The township operates, to be sure, within a narrow "circle from which it cannot emerge, but within this circle its movements are free," and "this independence alone" would be sufficient "to confer on it a real importance even if its population and extent did not assure" its importance as well. The township the inhabitant of New England perceives as "a corporation free and strong of which he makes up a part and which it is worth the trouble to attempt to direct." It is "the home of lively affections," for there is no rival capable of "strongly attracting the ambitious passions of the human heart." In New England, county leaders are not elected; the state has "only a secondary importance"; and, for all but the most exceptional of men, the federal government is not only far away: it is genuinely out of reach. It is, therefore, "in the township, at the center of the ordinary relations of life, that one finds concentrated the desire for esteem, the needs associated with real interests, the taste for power and acclaim [*bruit*]." If their focus were elsewhere, "these passions" might upend society, but "they change character when they can be exercised so near the domestic hearth and, in a sense, within the bosom of the family" itself.

Consider, Tocqueville writes, "with what art, in the American township, care is taken, if I may express myself in this fashion, *to scatter* power in order to interest more people in public affairs. Independently of the electors summoned from time to time to carry out acts of governance, how many diverse offices there are, how many different magistrates, who, within the circle of their prerogatives, represent the powerful corporation in whose name they act! How many men exploit in this fashion to their profit the communal power and take interest in it on their own behalf!" In the end, then, the inhabitant of New England treasures his township as a consequence of its strength and independence. "He interests himself in it because he joins in directing it." It is the focus of his ambition and of his dreams with regard to the future; he involves himself in "every one of the incidents of communal life: in this restricted sphere, which lies within his reach, he attempts to govern society; he habituates himself to the forms without which liberty proceeds only by revolutions, he is penetrated by their spirit, he gets a taste for order, he comprehends the harmony of powers, and in the end he gathers together clear and practical ideas with regard to the nature of his duties as well as the extent of his rights" (I.i.5, pp. 54–55).

One consequence of the vigor of civic life within New England is that there is no need for administrative centralization: the local citizens are perfectly capable of managing their own affairs; they can provide for the local enforcement of state and national laws; and all of this they do. Moreover, any dereliction of duty can be corrected by the courts (I.i.5, pp. 56–63), and much the same story can be told about other parts of the country as well (I.i.5, pp. 63–66). Another consequence of the vigor of local government is that the Americans are patriotic: as Jefferson had emphasized in his discussion of the "ward republics,"[27] they love their country and take an interest in its welfare because they know from concrete experience in local administration that it really is theirs. In America, thanks to the division of responsibilities between the federal, the state, and the local governments, democracy is in no way a phantom: to a very considerable degree, it is something close and personal (I.i.5, pp. 77–78; I.i.8, pp. 121–25; I.ii.6, pp. 184–86). Moreover, in a manner that Rousseau might have found gratifying (CS 1.6–8), Tocqueville claims that, when Americans look on public officials, they think not of "force," as Europeans so often do, but of "right," so that one could say "that in America never does man obey man; instead, he obeys justice or the law" (*DA* I.i.5, p. 78).

Even more important, Tocqueville contends that "provincial institutions" are in fact crucial for the maintenance of liberty, especially within the democratic *état social.* In aristocratic societies, as Montesquieu and Malesherbes had pointed out, the people can find "shelter from the excesses of despotism because organized forces ready to resist the despot are always to be found." Unless, however, there are "provincial institutions," within an egalitarian society there exists no such "guarantee against similar ills." It is not likely, Tocqueville intimates, that liberty can find support in great affairs from a multitude "which has not learned to make use of it in small matters." Nor is it likely that men will be able "to resist tyranny in a country where each individual is weak and where the individuals are not united by any common interest." It is in this context that Tocqueville first discusses the propensity for administrative centralization to emerge where the social condition is democratic (I.i.5, pp. 78–80). Later, when he turns from the discussion of majority tyranny to consider how it is tempered in America, he once again emphasizes the significance of local self-government—observing that, if "the power which directs American societies" were to combine "the right to command in all matters" with "the faculty and habit of executing everything itself, . . . liberty would soon be banished from the New World"; and then describing "the municipal bodies and county administrations" that the central authority depends upon "for the execution of its commands" with a hydraulic metaphor quite similar to the one which Montesquieu had deployed to describe the influence exercised by the intermediary bodies that distinguish monarchy from despotism. Where the latter had compared the *corps* of the *ancien régime* with "the seaweed & grasses & the least bits of sand & gravel found on the shore" that arrest the sea (*EL* 1.2.4), Tocqueville observes that, in the United States, the municipalities and counties form "so many hidden shoals, which slow down or divide the flood" constituted by "the popular will" (*DA* I.ii.8, pp. 204–5). Moreover, "if the law were to be oppressive," Tocqueville adds, "liberty would find shelter, nonetheless, in the manner in which the law was executed," for "the majority would not know how to descend into the details and, if I dare say, into the puerilities of administrative tyranny" (I.ii.8, p. 205).

THE JUDICIAL POWER

In defending liberty against the tyranny of the majority, Tocqueville adds, local administration finds assistance from another quarter. One of the distinctive features of American constitutionalism that a nineteenth-century French admirer of Montesquieu, who happened as well to be the great-grandson of Malesherbes, could hardly fail to notice was the set of provisions and practices specifying the nature and scope of the judicial power—for, when called upon to apply a law to a particular case, an American judge was in a position not unlike that of a French *parlement* asked under the *ancien régime* to register a new law. Just as the latter was expected to refuse registration and to remonstrate if the new law was inconsistent with existing law, so the American judge was expected to declare unconstitutional and void a state or federal statute that contravened the Constitution. Moreover, just as there was always the possibility that the French king would register the law himself through a *lit de justice*, so it was also conceivable that the American people would alter the Constitution to accommodate legislation of the sort previously declared void—though in neither case was it easy to reverse the jurisprudential conclusions of a common-law court.[28] All of this Tocqueville recognized—he was, after all, a student of French law—and he was all the more struck by the American arrangement in light of the severe constraints imposed on the judiciary in France under the constitutions drawn up during and after the French Revolution (I.i.6, pp. 81–84).

In their antipathy to Montesquieu's beloved judicial power, the framers of Article III, Chapter 5 of the French constitution promulgated on 3 September 1791 could not have been clearer, stipulating, as they did therein, that "the tribunals [of justice] cannot interfere with the exercise of the legislative power, nor suspend the execution of the laws, nor encroach upon administrative functions, nor cite any administrators to appear before them on account of their functions."[29] Six years later, as Tocqueville pointed out (I.i.6, pp. 85–86), the framers of Article LXXV of the French constitution adopted in year VIII would specify that "the agents of the government, other than ministers, cannot be prosecuted for acts relating to their functions except by virtue of a decision of the Council of State, in which case the prosecution will take place before the ordinary courts." The antipathy to judicial intervention of any sort displayed by these particular revolutionaries would not have much mattered had they not set a precedent in their treatment of the courts of justice that would govern French constitutional procedures from their day on.[30] There is, then, a polemical edge to Tocqueville's suggestion that the mode of proceeding evidenced by judicial tribunals in America may be "at the same time . . . most favorable to public order" and "most favorable to liberty," and the same can be said regarding his contention that the judicial power as constituted in the United States "forms one of the most powerful barriers ever erected against the tyranny of political assemblies" (I.i.6, p. 84).

This edge is no less evident in Tocqueville's subsequent discussion of the manner in which majority tyranny is tempered by the prestige accorded the legal profession in America, the influence that it is allowed to have within a democracy, and the practice of trial by jury in civil as well as criminal cases. Here his contention is threefold. To begin with, he argues that where lawyers are accorded great respect and are given political responsibilities, as tends to happen within democracies, they will form a "privileged class within the intelligentsia [*parmi les intelligences*]" and come to exhibit some of "the tastes and habits of an aristocracy: like aristocrats, they have an instinctive penchant for order and a natural love for forms; like them as well, they conceive a great disgust for the actions of the multitude and secretly scorn the government of the people." Instinctively, they are "strongly opposed to the revolutionary spirit and to the unreflective passions of the democracy."

To this observation, Tocqueville then adds another. Like the English, the Americans operate within a common-law system akin in certain respects to the legal system that existed in France in the day of Montesquieu and Malesherbes—before the adoption of the Napoleonic Code. They have, as he puts it, "conserved the law of precedents": they "continue to draw from the opinions and legal decisions of their fathers the opinions that they are obligated to hold in matters of law and the decisions that they are obligated to render." This makes the American lawyer, Tocqueville observes, something like a priest of ancient Egypt: "the unique interpreter of an occult science." And, of course, it reinforces his conservative instincts and his love of formalities. In consequence, "when the American people let themselves be intoxicated by their passions or deliver themselves up to be swept away by their ideas, the lawyers make them feel an almost invisible bridle that moderates and brings them to a halt. To the democratic instincts of the former, they secretly oppose their aristocratic propensities; to their love of novelty, they oppose their superstitious respect for that which is old; to the immensity of their designs, they oppose their narrow views; to their contempt for rules, they oppose their taste for forms; and to their impulsiveness [*fougue*], they oppose their habit of proceeding slowly." Tocqueville was not oblivious to the vices of lawyers—he knew them for what they are—and he could easily imagine circumstances in which their contempt for ordinary human beings would induce them to collaborate with the enemies of freedom, as they had at the time of the French Revolution. He acknowledged that they tend to prefer legality to liberty and that they are far less fearful of tyranny than of arbitrary rule, and he did not doubt that, "provided that it is the legislator who takes responsibility for snatching away from men their independence, they would be more or less content." He merely asserted that, in the United States of his own day, their prejudices and tastes were salutary (I.ii.8, pp. 205–11), and he praised trial by jury because it tended to instruct ordinary citizens in a respect for the forms and formalities that serve to restrain, check, channel, and keep within bounds the violent populist instincts of the rising democratic tide (I.ii.8, pp. 211–15).[31]

SELF-INTEREST RIGHTLY UNDERSTOOD

In the first *Democracy*, Tocqueville touches only briefly and in passing on what will prove in the second *Democracy* to be the most salient aspect of the tyranny of the majority: its unwitting propensity to effect a subjugation of the human mind (I.ii.7, pp. 199–201). In similar fashion, in the first, he carefully prepares the grounds for his subsequent discussion of the resources that the American democracy affords its citizens for resisting psychological subjugation.

Toward the end of his discussion of the New England township, Tocqueville remarks on the manner in which experience in local self-government affects national character, alluding to the manner in which in America municipal liberty contributes to the citizen's confidence in his own capacities, and noting that the ordinary citizen of the country tends, therefore, to "conceive of himself an opinion that is often exaggerated but nearly always salutary."

Without fear, he trusts in his own strength, which to him appears sufficient for all. An individual conceives the thought of some enterprise; this enterprise has in itself a relation with the well-being of society; the idea that he should address himself to the public authority for the purpose of obtaining its help does not even occur to him. He makes his plan known; he offers to execute it; he summons the strength of other individuals [*les forces individuelles*] to the aid of his own strength; and he engages in hand-to-hand combat against all the obstacles. Often, without a doubt, he succeeds less well than if the State were to take his place. But, in the long run, the general result of all these individual enterprises greatly exceeds that which the government would be able to accomplish. (I.i.5, p. 78)

In a later chapter, Tocqueville traced to this disposition the remarkable facility that Americans display for forming political associations. Apart from the "permanent associations" that dot the land, such as the townships, cities, and counties "created under the law," there are, he observes, "a multitude of others which owe their birth and their development solely to individual will."

In fact, from birth, Tocqueville reports, "the inhabitant of the United States recognizes that he must rely upon himself in the struggle against the evils and obstacles of life; on the authority of society [*l'autorité sociale*], he casts a defiant and uneasy [*inquiet*] regard, and he makes appeal to its power only when he cannot do without it." Instead of turning to the government, he forms associations. This disposition is evident in the propensity for children at school to invent new games, to "submit to rules that they have established" themselves, and to "punish offenses that they have themselves defined," and it extends into every corner of life. Americans associate not only to promote pastimes, but also for the encouragement of temperance, public security, commerce, industry, morality, and religion. They are sociable, and this is no doubt essential. But, according to Tocqueville, society is not their only—nor even their primary—aim. For the most part, their purposes are not simply social: they are public. More often than not, they associate with an eye to civic agency. They take for granted "the right of association," which is for all practical purposes "unlimited." In exercising this right, they are free "to assemble," and this they do. Within the political sphere, "men who profess the same opinion establish among themselves a tie purely intellectual"; then, "they come together in small assemblies which represent only a fraction of the party"; and, in the end, "they form something like a separate nation within the nation, a government within the government" organized for the purpose of attacking existing law (I.ii.4, pp. 146–47).

That such a development might pose a threat to public order Tocqueville readily acknowledges. He is inclined to regard "the independence of the press" as a necessary evil (I.ii.3). It is, he says, "the capital element and, so to speak, the constitutive element of liberty." But "the *unlimited* liberty of association"—the very idea makes him nervous; and yet he finds himself forced to admit that in America, where there are no restrictions placed on the freedom to associate for political ends, this unlimited freedom "has not, up to the present, produced the fatal results that would perhaps be attendant on it elsewhere." For this, Tocqueville surmises, there may be a reason: "in countries where associations are left free, secret societies are unknown. In America, there are factions, but no conspirators" (I.ii.4, pp. 147–49).

With this observation in mind, Tocqueville hazards another. "In our time," he writes, "freedom of association has become necessary as a guarantee against" a very great evil—to which he gives a name here for the first time: "the tyranny of the majority." In the United States, he explains,

> once a party becomes dominant, all public power passes into its hands; its particular friends occupy all the posts and dispose of all the organized forces. The most distinguished men of the contrary party, not being able to cross the barrier that separates them from power, find it necessary to establish themselves outside it; the minority finds it necessary to oppose all of its moral strength in its entirety to the material power that oppresses it. It then constitutes a danger opposed to another danger more to be feared.
>
> The omnipotence of the majority seems to me to be a threat to the American republics so great that the dangerous means that one makes use of to restrict it to me seems even a good.

"Here," Tocqueville then adds, "I will express a thought which will recall what I said elsewhere with regard to communal liberty: there is no country in which associations are more necessary to prevent the despotism of parties or the arbitrary rule of the prince than those where the social condition is democratic." And here he once again restates what Montesquieu had said long before concerning the role played within monarchies by intermediary powers, and he adds that where these do not exist, "if individuals are unable by artifice [*artificiellement*] and on the spur of the moment to create something which resembles them, I no longer perceive a dike of any sort against tyranny, and a great people may be oppressed with impunity by a handful of the factious or by a single man" (I.ii.4, pp. 148–49).

In this discussion, Tocqueville deliberately restricts his purview to political associations, but he already has in mind something more to say, for he promises that he will find "occasion, later, to speak of the effects produced by the association in civil life" (I.ii.4, p. 146). This subject he dutifully takes up in the crucial chapters within the second *Democracy* in which he considers the manner in which the Americans deploy "free institutions" in "combat" against the debilitating effects of the propensity he calls "individualism" (II.ii.2–8).[32]

Before embarking on this discussion, Tocqueville pauses briefly to observe that "individualism" is especially pronounced in the immediate aftermath of "a democratic revolution," such as the one that had occurred in France not so long before. On the one hand, he explains, such a social upheaval isolates the old adherents of the aristocracy, turning them into "strangers within the bosom of the new society"; on the other, he adds, although it empowers and elevates those "formerly placed at the bottom of the social scale," it leaves them profoundly uncomfortable, incapable of fully enjoying "the independence that they have newly acquired," subject to "a species of uneasiness [*inquiétude*] secreted within." This malady the Americans, who are "born equal," have largely been spared (II.ii.3), and this is for them highly beneficial, for "despotism, which is in its very nature fearful, sees in the isolation of men the most certain guarantee of its own duration, and it ordinarily puts all its care into isolating them." Those who propose "to unite their efforts to give rise to a shared prosperity" it denounces as "spirits turbulent and uneasy [*inquiets*]," whom it must keep apart (II.ii.4, pp. 99–100).

If the Americans do not succumb to what Tocqueville calls "individualism," if they do not withdraw from public life into a circle of family and intimate friends, it is first and foremost because of the formative influence on them of the municipal institutions that he had singled out for close attention and praise in the first *Democracy*. As he puts it, "when citizens are forced to occupy themselves with public affairs, they are drawn of necessity out of the milieu of individual interests and, from time to time, they are wrenched away from looking at themselves." In the midst of their discussion of communal affairs, each gradually comes to see "that he is not as independent of those whom he resembles [*ses semblables*] as he at first imagined," and he comes to recognize that he cannot secure their help without offering his own. In this fashion, he comes to appreciate "the value of public good will," and he attempts to secure it "by attracting the esteem and affection of those within the milieu within which he has to live." In the process, "many of the passions that chill hearts and divide them are then obliged to retire into the depths of the soul and to hide themselves there. Pride practices dissimulation; contempt dares not see the light of day. Egoism fears itself." Moreover, where the government is free and public offices are filled by election, "men who feel constrained in private life on account of the elevation of their souls or the uneasiness [*inquiétude*] of their desires sense every day that they cannot do without the population that surrounds them," and "it then comes to pass that by ambition one is made to reflect on those whom one resembles [*ses semblables*], and in a sense one finds it in one's interest to forget oneself" (II.ii.4, p. 100).

The Americans, Tocqueville claims, "have deployed liberty in combat against the individualism born of equality, and they have vanquished it." This they have accomplished, and something more. "I should say," Tocqueville adds, "that I have often seen Americans make great and genuine sacrifices on the public's behalf, and I have noted a hundred times that, in time of need, they almost never fail to lend one another faithful support" (II.ii.4, pp. 101–2). Later, to be sure, he will acknowledge that the Americans he met were not especially high-minded. In the past, he concedes, within aristocratic societies, those possessed of wealth and power "were enamored of forming for themselves a sublime idea of the duties of man." At that time, "they took pleasure in professing that it is glorious to forget oneself and that it is fitting that, like God, one do good in the absence of interest." This is not, he found, a posture that the Americans are likely to adopt, but he doubts "whether men were more virtuous in aristocratic centuries than they are in ours, though it was certainly the case that they constantly talked of the beauties of virtue" and "studied only in secret the manner in which it was useful." Now, however, he observes:

> Insofar as the imagination takes a flight less lofty and each concentrates upon himself, moralists take fright at this idea of sacrifice and no longer dare offer it to the human mind; they are reduced then to inquiring whether it is not to the individual advantage of the citizens to work for the good of all; and when they have discovered one of the points in which particular interest comes to coincide with the general interest and to be confounded with it, they hasten to place it in the light; little by little these similar observations multiply. That which was but one isolated observation becomes a general doctrine, and finally one believes one perceives that, in serving those who resemble him [*ses semblables*], man serves himself and that his particular interest is to do good.

The Americans may not say that "virtue is beautiful"; they contend instead "that it is useful, and this they prove every day"; and in the mundane manner exemplified in the *Essays* of Michel de Montaigne,[33] they embrace as a principle what Tocqueville calls "the doctrine of self-interest rightly understood." If thereby "they often do not do themselves justice," if they systematically overlook the fact that in America, "as elsewhere, the citizens abandon themselves under the influence of impulses [*élans*] disinterested and unreflective," it is because they prefer "honoring their philosophy to honoring themselves" (II.ii.8).

This strange phenomenon is, in Tocqueville's opinion, easily explained. The existence of "free institutions" in America and of "political rights," of which the citizens regularly "make use," reminds "each citizen in a thousand ways that he lives in society." In the beginning, such men "occupy themselves with the general interest out of necessity." Then, they do so "by choice: that which was calculation becomes instinct; and by dint of working for the good of one's fellow citizens, in the end one acquires the habit of and a taste for serving them." In Tocqueville's estimation, the qualities that local self-government elicits from men are indistinguishable in their effects from the virtue that Montesquieu and Rousseau had attributed to the citizens of the ancient republics. In his judgment, moreover, "political liberty" is "the only effective remedy" for "the evils that equality" is apt to "produce" (II.ii.4, p. 103).

The public-spirited dispositions that municipal institutions foster Tocqueville found at work in every corner of American life. The Americans were, he knew, inclined to form associations to campaign for or against particular laws, but this was only the beginning. He discovered that they formed associations "of a thousand sorts: religious, moral, grave, futile, exceedingly general and very particular, immense and exceedingly small." They did so "to put on festivals, to found seminaries, to build inns, to raise churches, to distribute books, to send missionaries to the Antipodes." In this fashion, he reported, "they create hospitals, prisons, schools." This he found heartening. If the government were "generally to take the place of associations," he wrote, "the morals and intelligence of a democratic people would run dangers" as great as those incurred in such a situation by "its business and its industry." Where such associations are abundant, however, "sentiments and ideas renew themselves, the heart expands and the human mind [*esprit*] develops for no other reason than because of the reciprocal action of men upon one another." In the absence of such associations, were the government "to emerge from the political sphere" in a vain attempt "to renew the circulation of sentiments and ideas among a great people," it would "exercise, even without wanting to, an insupportable tyranny." For men "to remain or become civilized," he concludes, "it is necessary that among them the art of association develop and perfect itself in the same measure [*rapport*] in which the equality of conditions grows" (II.ii.5).

Elsewhere, Tocqueville explores the relations (*rapports*) between civil and political associations and the manner in which they inspire, foster, and even blur into one another (II.ii.7). There, he also examines the intimate relationship (*rapport*) that exists between associations and newspapers. These two institutions are, he argues, mutually supportive: newspapers are essential for the establishment of extensive associations, and for this reason, to this very day, associations tend to establish journals of one sort or another. If in America one finds a vast number of newspapers, it is a function of the existence of vigorous local self-government.

"Among a democratic people," he therefore warns, "the number of newspapers can be expected to diminish or increase in proportion to whether there is a greater or lesser centralization of administration." Also, he adds, "the more that conditions become equal, the less that men are as individuals strong, the easier that it is for them to allow themselves to be swept along in the current of the crowd." In such circumstances, men have "trouble holding themselves aloof [*seuls*] in an opinion abandoned by the crowd." In democratic societies, there is rarely strength in anything but numbers (II.ii.6).

THE SPIRIT OF RELIGION

There was one other aspect of American life that Tocqueville thought especially conducive to the maintenance of liberty: the Americans were religious. He was even willing to argue that among the Americans, although religion "never directly involved itself in the government of society," it was nonetheless "the first of their political institutions"—for, "if it did not give them a taste for liberty, it singularly facilitated their use of it" (I.ii.9, p. 227).[34]

It stands to reason that something of the sort should be the case. For it is by no means an accident that, in describing the purportedly providential process by which the democratic *état social* emerged within Europe (I.Intr., pp. 3–9), Tocqueville mentions first of all the growth in influence and power of a clerical order that opened "its ranks to poor and rich, to commoner and seigneur" alike. Nor is it fortuitous that he then specifies that "equality" first began "to penetrate into the heart of the government by way of the Church," explaining that, because of its influence, a man who might have vegetated "as a serf in an eternal slavery" would "take his place as a priest in the midst of the nobles and frequently go on to sit above kings" (I.Intr., pp. 4–5). For Tocqueville shares the conviction, voiced by both Montesquieu and Rousseau (I, II.3, above), that Christianity had profoundly altered the human prospect.

The great democratic transformation that Tocqueville has in mind was in fact far less "universal" than at first he claims. It occurred, as he acknowledges from the outset, "among Christians" alone; it was restricted to "Christian peoples," to "the Christian universe" (*DA* I.Intr., pp. 6–8). Later, Tocqueville will assert that "the most profound geniuses of Rome and of Greece," those with "the greatest [*les plus vastes*]" scope, "were never able to arrive at the idea, so general, but at the same time so simple, of the similarity of men and of the equal right to liberty that each possesses at birth," and he will suggest that "it was requisite that Jesus Christ come to earth to make men comprehend that all members of the human species" are, in fact, "naturally similar [*semblables*] and equal" (II.i.3, p. 28). One can make sense of the "double revolution" that took place in Europe "over seven centuries," lowering the noble in stature and raising the commoner until it was virtually impossible to distinguish the former from the latter; one can explain why every new development and every accident somehow conspired to advance this revolution without reference to Providence. Everything within Europe took place in this fashion because of the instinctive human propensity for regulating "political society and the divine city in a uniform manner," for attempting "to *harmonize* earth with heaven" (I.ii.9, p. 223).[35] If Providence played any role, it was in the coming of Christ.[36]

But, of course, it was by no means inevitable that the emergence of the democratic *état social* eventuate in the establishment of self-government as opposed to despotic rule, and Tocqueville, who had read Machiavelli, Montesquieu, and Rousseau with care, was sensitive to the tension between the otherworldly orientation of Christianity and the demands of patriotism.[37] In these regards, there really was something special about America. From the outset, Tocqueville emphasized, the English colonists in North America had managed in a most remarkable way to combine *"the spirit of religion"* with *"the spirit of liberty."* On the eve of the great migration, England was caught up in "the religious quarrels that agitated the Christian world," and these took a people who "had always been grave and reflective" and made them "austere and argumentative" as well. Their participation in "the intellectual struggles" of the day contributed to their "instruction," and these debates encouraged in the English and in the Anglo-Americans alike "a more profound cultivation" of "the mind" than hitherto, while the fervor and enthusiasm that accompanied the ongoing disputes fostered "mores" that were "purer" than they had previously been (I.i.6, pp. 26, 35).

The New England colonies had been founded by Puritans of various sorts. These were not like the aimless adventurers and ne'er-do-wells found elsewhere in the colonial world. Frequently, they were prosperous and well-educated, and they "wrenched themselves from the sweetness of their fatherland" and migrated to the New World less for the purpose of enriching themselves than "in obedience to a need purely intellectual." Put simply, "in exposing themselves to the inevitable miseries of exile, they sought the triumph of *an idea*," which was, as it happens, perfectly consonant "with the most absolute democratic and republican theories" of government. The royal government in England was content and even eager to set at a distance from itself "the seeds of trouble and the elements of new revolutions," and it seemed "to look on New England as a region delivered up to the dreams of the imagination" and as a place "which one should abandon to the free experiments [*essais*] of innovators." The colonists, for their part, were delighted to be able to escape persecution and to separate themselves from those who conducted themselves in a fashion they found morally repulsive, and they made provisions for "public education" wherever they settled, persuaded, as they were, that the Bible should be read by everyone. "In America," Tocqueville wrote with puckish delight, "it is religion that leads to enlightenment [*lumières*]; it is the observance of divine law that guides men to liberty" (I.i.2, pp. 28–30, 34).

The coincidence of the spirit of religion and the spirit of liberty had consequences that Tocqueville thought favorable to both, and to bring this home to his readers, he asks them to imagine the situation of the colonists: "Before them fall the barriers that had imprisoned the society in the bosom of which they were born; the old opinions, which for centuries had directed the world, vanish; a course almost without limits, a field without horizon is exposed: the human spirit hurls itself forward; it runs through it in every direction; but, having arrived at the limits of the political world, it stops on its own hook [*de lui-même*]; trembling, it sets aside the use of its most formidable faculties; it abjures doubt; it renounces the need to innovate; it abstains even from lifting the sanctuary veil; it bows down with respect before truths that without discussion it admits." In this fashion, Tocqueville then adds, "everything in the moral world is classified, coordinated, foreseen, decided in advance," while "in the political world everything is agitated, contested, uncertain. In the one, obedience passive though voluntary; in the other, independence, contempt of experience, and jealousy of every authority." And though these "two tendencies" might seem opposed, they lend one another "mutual support." Religion regards "civil liberty" as "a noble exercise of the faculties of man"; in "the political world," it sees "a field delivered up by the Creator for the efforts of intelligence"—while liberty regards religion as "the companion of its struggles and triumphs, the cradle of its infancy, the divine source of its rights," and it considers it "the safeguard of mores," which are, in turn, "the guarantee of the laws and the pledge of its own duration" (I.i.2, pp. 35–36).

DOMESTIC TRANQUILLITY

Later in the first *Democracy*, when Tocqueville turns from America's past to its prospects, he pays particular attention to the "indirect influence" of religious belief on politics, which he regards as salutary. "It is," he writes, when religion "does not speak of liberty at all that it best instructs Americans in the art of being free." Tocqueville's point is simple and straightforward. The Americans are Christian; and though the Christian sects quarrel vociferously over doctrine, they all teach the same morality. Religion may not exercise great influence over the law, and it may have little effect on the details of political opinion, "but it does give direction to mores, and it is in regulating the family that it works to regulate the state." Not for an instant does Tocqueville doubt "that the great severity of mores that one observes in the United States has its primary source in belief. Religion there is often powerless to restrain man in the midst of the temptations without number that fortune presents him with. It knows not how to moderate in him the ardor to enrich himself that everything contributes to spurring, but it reigns in sovereign fashion over the soul of woman, and it is woman who makes the mores. America is assuredly the country in the world in which the bond of marriage is the most respected, and in which men have conceived the most elevated and most just idea of conjugal happiness." In Tocqueville's opinion, libertinism is a great enemy to liberty, for the social disorders that characterize Europe have their origin "about the domestic hearth, not far distant from the nuptial bed. It is there that men conceive a contempt for natural bonds and licit pleasures, a taste for disorder, an uneasiness [*inquiétude*] of heart, an instability of desire." If the European finds it difficult to submit to the legislative powers accorded the state, it is because he is "agitated by tumultuous passions which have often troubled his own home" (I.ii.9, pp. 226–27).

At the end of the day, an American will "emerge from the agitations of the political world" and return "to the bosom of his own family," where he will "immediately meet up with an image of order and peace." In this place, "all of his pleasures are simple and natural, his joys innocent and tranquil; and as he arrives at happiness by means of a regularity in life, so will he habituate himself without pain to impose regularity [*régler*] on his opinions and tastes." Thus, "while the European seeks to escape his domestic sorrows by troubling society, the American derives from his home the love of order that he carries over afterwards into affairs of State" (I.ii.9, p. 227).

Domestic tranquillity was not for Tocqueville a matter of passing concern. In the second great section of his magnum opus, he returns to the theme, arguing initially that the loosening of paternal authority and the abolition of primogeniture within democratic societies strengthens familial ties by reducing the resentment that ambitious young men in aristocratic societies so frequently direct at their fathers, by eliminating envy between brothers, and by encouraging on the part of all an informality conducive to intimacy and affection (II.iii.8). Then, he devotes a series of chapters to the peculiar status accorded women in the United States (II.iii.9–12). In the very first paragraph of the first of these chapters, Tocqueville alludes to his earlier discussion, reiterates his claim that "the woman makes the mores," and restates his conviction that "everything that influences the condition of women, their habits and their opinions" is of "political interest" (II.iii.9,

p. 169). In the last paragraph of the last such chapter, he traces "the singular prosperity and the growing strength" of the Americans to "the superiority of their
women" (II.iii.12, pp. 180–81).

In keeping with his overall outlook, Tocqueville gives short shrift to Montesquieu's contention that climate decisively shapes sexual mores (*EL* 3.16).[38]
That the climate may render "the reciprocal attraction of the sexes . . . particularly ardent," like David Hume,[39] he readily admits. But he is convinced that
"the *état social* and political institutions" have a far greater impact on what he
calls "this natural ardor" (*DA* II.iii.11, p. 174). What interests him most is the astonishing "independence" that American women evidence before marriage and
their submissiveness thereafter.

The "independence" exhibited by young women in America Tocqueville
traces to three sources: to Protestantism, which teaches its adherents to judge for
themselves; to self-government, which teaches its practitioners self-reliance; and
to the democratic *état social*, which powerfully reinforces both propensities. In
America, he explains, girls are neither tied to their mothers' apron strings nor
sent off to convent schools. Instead, each is shown the world, which she is taught
to "look on with an eye firm and tranquil." Early on, she becomes aware of "the
vices and perils that society presents." These "she sees with clarity, these she
judges without illusion, and these she confronts without fear, for she is full of
confidence in her strength, and her confidence seems to be shared by all of those
who surround her." Like her counterpart in Europe, she may "wish to please, but
she knows with precision the price." Her "mores" may be "pure," but her "mind"
is not "chaste" (II.iii.9, pp. 169–70).

In observing "the singular dexterity and happy audacity with which young
women in America know how to conduct their thoughts and words in the midst
of the hazards of a playful conversation," Tocqueville admits that he was not only
"surprised" but "almost afraid." It amazed him that, even when quite young, an
American girl "never entirely ceases to be mistress of herself: she enjoys all of the
pleasures permitted without abandoning herself to any of them, and her reason
does not let go of the reins, although she often seems to let them hang loose." In
the end, upon reflection, he came to admire what the Americans had done.
They had recognized "that, in the bosom of a democracy, individual independence could not fail to be very great, that the young will be hasty, tastes ill-con-
fined, custom changeable, public opinion frequently uncertain or powerless,
paternal authority weak, and marital power contested." Judging it virtually impossible "to repress in women the most tyrannical passions of the human heart,"
they teach her instead "the art of battling against them herself" by arming "her

reason" and revealing to her from the outset "the corruptions of the world" (II.iii.9, p. 170).

It helps a great deal, Tocqueville acknowledges, that the Americans are a people both religious and commercial, for both qualities give them an appreciation for "regularity in the life of a woman," and both demand of her "a self-abnegation and a continual sacrifice of her pleasures" that is "in Europe rare." In the United States, he explains, "there reigns an inexorable public opinion that carefully restrains woman within the circle of her domestic interests and duties and that prohibits her from departing from it." When she first enters the larger world, the young American woman "finds these notions firmly established; she sees the rules that flow from them"; and she quickly realizes that "she cannot for a moment escape from the usages of her contemporaries without immediately placing in peril her tranquillity, her honor, and even her social existence, and she finds, in the firmness of her reason and in the virile habits that her education has given her, the vigor [*énergie*] to submit." What reconciles her to her confinement is the fact that the choice of a husband is hers and hers alone, and "the strength of will" that she displays in weighing her options and making her choice sustains her through "all the great trials of their life" together (II.iii.10). American women may seem cold and calculating, and in some measure, Tocqueville reports, this they are (II.iii.9, p. 171; II.iii.10, p. 173). But they do not display the weakness and inconstancy and suffer the misery that so often are the lot of women in Europe for whom marriages have been arranged (II.iii.11).

To those who, in his day, argued for the absolute equality of man and woman, Tocqueville issued a stern word of warning. That the two are "equal," he readily acknowledges. But he denies that they are fully "similar [*semblables*]." Those who give to both "the same functions, impose on them the same duties, and accord them the same rights," and those who "mix them together in everything—work, pleasure, business"—risk "degrading them both." From "so coarse a mix of nature's works," he insists, can come only "men weak and women indecent [*déshonnêtes*]" (II.iii.12, pp. 178–79). Of course, the Americans do believe that there is a "species of democratic equality" that can and should be "established between woman and man." They accord "the same esteem to the role of each and consider them as beings of equal value." But they are cognizant that "nature has established a very great difference [*variété*] between the physical and moral constitution of man and that of woman," and from this they have concluded that "its aim, clearly indicated, was to give to their differing faculties a diverse employment." In their judgment, "progress did not consist in causing the same things to be done by beings dissimilar [*dissemblables*] but in getting each of them to accomplish his task in the best manner possible." In effect, the Americans have applied the "great principle" of the division of labor to "the functions of man and woman." Equality comes into play when American men display, as they customarily do, "full confidence in the reason of their mate and a profound respect for her liberty. They judge that her mind is as capable as that of a man in discovering the naked truth and her heart as firm in pursuing it, and they have never sought to place the virtue of the one, any more than that of the other, under the protection of prejudices, ignorance, or fear" (II.iii.12, pp. 179–80). It is this set of attitudes that provides the foundations in America for the democratic household.

AN EMPIRE OVER THE INTELLECT

Domestic tranquillity is one blessing that Americans owe in part to religion; there is another as well—for, in America, religion "extends its empire over the intellect" as well, rendering "everything certain and settled [*arrêté*] in the moral world," while leaving "the political world" open for "discussion and experiment [*essais*]." In this fashion,

> the human mind never perceives in front of it a field without limit: whatever its audacity, it senses from time to time that it must come to a halt before barriers which are insurmountable. Before innovating, it is forced to accept certain first principles as given and to submit the boldest of its conceptions to certain formalities that slow it down and bring it to a halt.
>
> The imagination of Americans, in its greatest aberrations, moves forward, then, in a manner circumspect and uncertain; its pace is interrupted and its work incomplete. These habits of restraint are found again within the political society and favor in a singular manner the tranquillity of the people and, in this fashion, the duration of the institutions that have been conferred on them.

If in the United States, some things remain sacred, if to date no one has dared to advance the "impious maxim, which seems to have been invented in an age of liberty to legitimate all the tyrants to come," that "everything is permitted in the interests of society," it is, Tocqueville asserts, because of the Christian religion. It is in this context that he tells us that religion is for the Americans "the first of their political institutions" and adds that even "if it does not give to them a taste for liberty, it facilitates in a singular manner their use of it." Tocqueville is aware that there are those among his fellow Europeans who believe that in America "the liberty and happiness of the human race fall short in nothing" apart from the fact that the Americans do not "believe with Spinoza in the eternity of the world and assert with Cabanis that the brain secretes thought," and to them he poses a question: "How can society fail to perish if, while the political bond is relaxed, the moral bond is not drawn tight? And what can one do with a people fully master of itself, if it is not" at the same time "subject to God?" (I.ii.9, pp. 227–29).[40]

Tocqueville had studied with great care Rousseau's *Discourse on the Origin and Foundations of Inequality among Men,* and he had apparently read *The Reveries of the Solitary Stroller* as well. He had considerable personal experience with *inquiétude* and *ennui,* and he understood why a dissolution of the self of the sort described by Rousseau in the latter work should be attractive to human beings living in a democratic age.[41] For this reason, he was sensitive also to the manner in which his contemporaries were drawn to Spinoza's doctrine. Thanks to the emergence of the democratic *état social,* to the disappearance of all distinctions and ranks, and to the new taste for general ideas, he tells us, "the idea of unity" now "obsesses" the human mind (II.i.7, p. 39). Thus, just as there are no more intermediary powers in this world, so there will be an aversion to the "cult, almost idolatrous," of "secondary beings" and "secondary agents" such as "the angels and saints," which was so popular in the preceding aristocratic age (II.i.5, pp. 35–36; II.i.17, p. 74). In such a setting, the human mind seeks unity "on all sides; and, when it believes that it has found it, it willingly takes it to heart and there it finds repose."

> Not only does it come to discover in the world but one creation and one creator; this first division of things bothers it still, and it seeks willingly to expand and simplify its thought by enclosing God and the universe in a single whole. If I meet up with a philosophical system according to which the things material and immaterial, visible and invisible that the world contains are no longer considered anything other than the diverse parts of an immense being which alone remains eternal in the midst of the continual change and incessant transformation of everything that composes it, I would have no trouble in concluding that such a system, although it destroys human individuality, or rather because it destroys it, has secret charms for men who live in democracy. All their intellectual habits prepare them for its conception and place them on the road to its adoption. It naturally attracts their imagination and holds it fixed; it nourishes the pride and flatters the laziness of their minds.

When confronted with the popularity of this doctrine among German philosophers and French novelists and the prospect that it will become dominant everywhere, Tocqueville shudders. "Against it," he writes, "all those who remain enamored of the true greatness of man should unite and fight" (II.i.7).

In the face of all of this, Tocqueville's discussion of the role played by the Christian religion in the United States is reassuring, and it would be heartening in the extreme were it not for one discomforting fact. In America, he intimates, under the influence of the democratic *état social*, religion appears gradually to have ceased to be a focus of deep faith, and it seems to have become more and more a function of public opinion. The Americans whom Tocqueville met were far more likely to praise Christianity for its utility than to testify to revelation's truth (I.ii.9, pp. 227–28; II.i.2, pp. 22–23), and the clergymen he encountered were inclined to recognize and respect "the intellectual empire exercised by the majority," to "adopt willingly the general opinions of their country and time, and to let themselves go, without resistance, into the current of sentiments and ideas that carries all things about them" (II.i.5, pp. 37–38). We are left to wonder whether this great edifice—and the ethos of moral severity that it supports—is not, in fact, a house of cards, as unstable as the *état social* in which it is rooted, and subject to collapse should the winds of public opinion really begin to blow.[42]

Tocqueville leaves this unspoken question open. But he does offer an observation suggesting that the Americans with whom he spoke may not have done themselves full justice in what they had to say about religion, just as, in his estimation, they did not do themselves justice when they attempted to make sense of their own public-spirited acts solely in terms of self-interest. Like Rousseau, Tocqueville was convinced that religious longing has a firm foundation in human nature itself.[43] Of its power he had personal experience. Although he regularly attended mass, there is reason to believe that in his youth Tocqueville had lost his faith.[44] But he was apparently never thereafter content, and, like many another lapsed Christian, he found the *Pensées* of Pascal hard to ignore.[45] In an especially poignant passage in the first *Democracy*, he wrote:

> Never will the short space of sixty years coop up the whole imagination of man; the incomplete joys of this world will never be sufficient for his heart. Alone among all the beings, man displays a natural disgust with existence and an immense desire to exist; he despises life and fears nothingness. These different instincts drive his heart constantly towards the contemplation of another world, and it is religion that guides it there. Religion is, then, nothing but a particular form of hope, and it is as natural to the human heart as is hope itself. It is by a kind of aberration of the intellect and with the aid of a sort of moral violence exercised on their own nature that men distance themselves from religious belief: an invincible inclination draws them back to it. Incredulity is an accident. Faith alone is the permanent condition of humanity.

Tocqueville was by no means averse to what he called "the desire for immortality that torments the heart of every man equally" (I.i.9, pp. 230–31). He, in fact, thought such longings essential to human dignity; and in the second *Democracy*, when he returned to the question of religion, he expressed the fear that the quest for well-being so natural to the democratic *état social*, legitimate and decent though it might be, would result not only in making "life comfortable, easier, sweeter" for men but that it would also eventuate in the degradation of man (II.ii.15).

When, in a free country, Tocqueville observes, "religion is destroyed, doubt lays hold of the highest portions of the intellect, and it half paralyzes all the others." In matters of the greatest importance to men, they have nothing but "notions confused and changing." Opinions are poorly defended or simply dropped; men give way to despair, doubting their capacity "to resolve the greatest problems that human destiny presents"; and they are reduced "in a cowardly manner to not thinking about them at all." The result is an enervation of soul, for the plight in which they find themselves "relaxes the springs [*ressorts*] of the will and prepares citizens for servitude. Not only does it happen that they let their liberty be taken; often they hand it over." The reason for this is straightforward: "When, in religious and political matters, there no longer exists authority, men soon take fright at the prospect of an independence without limits. The perpetual agitation of all things makes them uneasy [*les inquiète*] and tires them out. As everything within the world of the intellect is in motion, they want at least that everything be firm and stable within the material order, and, no longer being able to take up their ancient beliefs, they give themselves a master" (II.i.5, pp. 33–34). "It is to be feared," Tocqueville subsequently added, that in the end democratic man "will lose the use of his most sublime faculties"; and with this possibility in mind, he argued that "it is incumbent on the lawgivers of democracies and on all upright and enlightened men who live therein to apply themselves without respite to elevating souls and to holding them erect pointed towards heaven." It is necessary, he added, that those "interested in the future of democratic societies unite and that all, in concert, make continual efforts to spread within the bosom of these societies a taste for the infinite, a sentiment of grandeur, and a love of immaterial pleasures" (II.ii.15, p. 130).

Tocqueville was convinced that, in centuries of faith, men learn "to repress a thousand passing, petty desires in order better to succeed in satisfying the grand and permanent desire that torments them," and this, he believed, explains "why religious peoples have often accomplished things so durable." In "occupying themselves with the other world, they have met up with the great secret of success in this one." The reason is simple: religions confer on their adherents "a general habit of conduct with a view to the future. In this they are no less useful to happiness in this life than to felicity in the next." If religion is politically important, this is one of the reasons why.

But, Tocqueville argued, "insofar as the light [*lumières*] of faith is obscured, the vision of men narrows." In fact, when men cease "to occupy themselves with that which one can expect to happen after their lives, one sees them fall back easily into a complete and brutish indifference with regard to the future." One sees them focus their attention on the immediate satisfaction of their least desires, and "it seems as if, at the moment in which they despair of eternal life, they are disposed to act as if they expect to live no more than one day." In Tocqueville's time, "when everyone seeks constantly to change position, when an immense competition is open to all, when riches are accumulated and dissipated in a few instants in the midst of the democratic tumult, the idea of a sudden and easy fortune, of great goods easily acquired and lost, the image of chance in all its forms presents itself to the human mind. The instability of the *état social* comes to favor the natural instability of desire. In the midst of the perpetual fluctuations of fate, the present grows large; it hides the future, which fades away, and men do not want to reflect on anything beyond tomorrow." All of this, Tocqueville observes, is exacerbated by religious skepticism; and for this reason, if for no other, statesmen should do what they can by indirect means to promote the Christian faith and to encourage the citizens to set for themselves distant aims (II.ii.17). He regards it as "the most precious heritage" left to man from "the aristocratic centuries (II.ii.15, p. 130), and he worries that conflict over the religious question will do great harm to the cause of Christianity and, then, to that of democracy in his native France.[46]

Three

THE FRENCH DISEASE

Although I very rarely spoke of France in the book, I wrote not one page of it without thinking of her and without having her, so to speak, before my eyes. And that which I above all sought to place in relief with regard to the United States and to make properly understood was less a complete picture of that foreign society than the contrasts and resemblances between it and our own. It was always either by way of opposition or by way of analogy with the one that I set out to give a just and, above all, an interesting idea of the other.

—Alexis de Tocqueville

Tocqueville's account of democracy as a way of life in the United States needs to be put in the proper perspective, and, to do so, one must attend to two crucial facts. The first is that as a writer Tocqueville preferred indirection. At the time that he composed *Democracy in America*, it was his conviction, as it had been Montesquieu's, that "the books that have occasioned the most reflection on the part of men and that have had on their opinions and acts the greatest influence are those in which the author has not sought to tell them dogmatically that which it is suitable that they think, but in which he has placed their minds on the path that leads to the truth and in which he has caused them to find it for themselves."[1]

The second crucial fact is that the primary audience that Tocqueville had in mind when he composed *Democracy in America* was not American at all. From the outset, as he explained in a letter written to his father prior to his return from the United States, it was his plan "to present only subjects that have relations [*rapports*] more or less direct with our own *état social et politique*."[2] To Henry Reeve, who translated the work into English, he wrote, when he had finished the second *Democracy*, that he had composed *Democracy in America* "principally for France" and "from a French point of view."[3] What he meant by these remarks Tocqueville did not make fully evident until years later when he penned a response to a letter from his friend Louis de Kergorlay in which the latter indicated that he was thinking about writing a book on German affairs.

If his friend really were to undertake the project that had struck his fancy, Tocqueville told him, the primary difficulty that he would face would be that of rendering the "truth" that he wished to convey "perceptible to the French reader." It would not be easy to paint for this reader "a picture *saisissable*—one which he could comprehend—of a condition of society and of minds so different not only from that which we imagine but above all from that which our sense [*sentiment*] of ourselves inclines us to imagine." The real difficulty stems, he explained, less from "our ignorance" than from a "natural prejudice born from contemplation of our own country and from recollections of its history." If Kergorlay were to persist, there was a question that he would have to come to grips with: "Is it necessary to explain the differences and the resemblances that the two countries present? Or should one speak solely with an eye to making them understood?" Tocqueville was not sure. "In my own work on America," he observed, "I nearly always followed the second method. Although I very rarely spoke of France in the book, I wrote not one page of it without thinking of her and without having her, so to speak, before my eyes. And that which I above all sought to place in relief with regard to the United States and to make properly understood was less a complete picture of that foreign society than the contrasts and resemblances between it and our own. It was always either by way of opposition or by way of analogy with the one that I set out to give a just and, above all, an interesting idea of the other." It was his considered judgment that "the perpetual return" that he made in this oblique fashion "to France was one of the primary causes of the book's success."[4]

A MUTED POLEMIC

Tocqueville might have said a great deal more, for, in fact, *Democracy in America* constitutes a muted polemic—designed first and foremost for consideration by his contemporaries. The warnings that he issued with regard to the propensities inherent in the democratic social condition were directed to them; and when he singled out various aspects of American life as portents of doom or as harbingers of hope, he nearly always did so with an eye to the presence of the former and the absence of the latter in his native France. When he spoke of democracy as such, it was the present condition or the likely future prospects of his own country that he chiefly had in mind; and when he discussed the manner in which the Americans tempered majority tyranny and resisted individualism, his aim was to draw the attention of his compatriots to the absence of the pertinent institutions and practices in France.

If Tocqueville highlighted the New England township; insisted that the American Revolution was fought in defense of local, municipal, and provincial liberty; and ignored the manner in which the American colonists, during the period stretching from 1765 to 1776, gradually abandoned their appeal to charters guaranteeing their rights as Englishmen and came to ground their defense of their traditional liberties solely on their rights as men,[5] it was not because he was oblivious to or disdainful of the principles ultimately enshrined in the Declaration of Independence.[6] He was, after all, a Frenchman, fully aware of the Declaration of the Rights of Man and of the Citizen adopted by his compatriots in 1789, and he was no less hostile to the institution of slavery in the American South than Abraham Lincoln would later be and on the same grounds, for he did not think that any human being has the right to rule over another without the latter's consent. In *Democracy in America*, however, his purpose was not to celebrate abstract principles or even to do full justice to the American regime. His aim was to instruct his compatriots in what they most needed to know, and, in this particular context, his goal was to remind them of something quite concrete that they had lost soon after they had adopted their own declaration. Put simply, Tocqueville's purpose was to inculcate in his countrymen an appreciation for the fact that the municipal liberties still treasured by the Americans were liberties that they had themselves once enjoyed; liberties that Richelieu, Louis XIV, and their successors had sought to eliminate; liberties that Malesherbes had defended in the *Grandes Remonstrances* (DA I.i.5, n. K, pp. 324–25); liberties that the French Revolution had impaired and that Napoleon had swept away; liberties that had not been restored at all by Louis XVIII or Charles X and that Louis-Philippe had only in the most minimal fashion reestablished; liberties that were, he argued, far more precious in the age of democracy than they had ever been under the *ancien régime*.[7]

In similar fashion, if, in contemplating the political institutions of the United States, Malesherbes' great-grandson paid particular attention to the judicial power, it was because something of the sort had once existed in France, because the parlements had been a bastion of liberty under the absolute monarchy, and because the judicial power—which had repeatedly come under attack in the age of Louis XIV and Louis XV, which had lost all of its political functions in the course of the Revolution, and which had regained none of them under Louis XVIII, Charles X, and Louis-Philippe—was, in his opinion, even more essential to the maintenance of liberty in a democratic age than it had been in the time of absolute monarchy.[8] If he drew attention to the Americans' mastery of the art of association, it was not solely as a corrective to Rousseau's diatribe against "partial societies" (CS 2.3). It was, above all, because the French, though highly sociable and apt to form clubs,[9] had never fully mastered the *political* art that he had in mind,[10] and it was because successive French governments of every sort, with the July Monarchy being the most extreme, had proved to be obsessed with the need for national unity, fearful of conspiracy, and hostile to the very notion of corporate civic agency and had, in consequence, outlawed both civil and political associations — except, of course, those formed or co-opted as instruments of consultation and rational administration with the express sanction of the State.[11] If Tocqueville contended that, in America, the spirit of religion and the spirit of liberty were mutually supportive, it was because, in France, those who thought of themselves as the friends of religion and those who supposed themselves the friends of liberty were at daggers drawn (*DA* I.Intr., p. 13; I.ii.9, p. 229).[12]

Furthermore, if Tocqueville had nothing but praise for the severity of sexual mores in the United States, if he evidenced for the prudent, chaste women of Jacksonian America an admiration that may seem to many today extravagant, if not in fact offensive as well,[13] it was because — in reading Montesquieu's ostentatiously disingenuous celebration of a free, flirtatious, adulterous communicativeness between the two sexes (II.1, above) and the fiercely critical response that Rousseau had elaborated in *Émile* and *Julie* — he had become profoundly sensitive to the psychological and political consequences of the rampant sexual promiscuity for which his aristocratic compatriots had been notorious in and for some time after Montesquieu's day. Even more to the point, he had thereby been made aware that radically abstracting from natural differences in "the physical and moral constitution" of the two sexes and treating women and men in public as if they are indistinguishable (*semblables*) is destructive of marital harmony, which presupposes a genuine appreciation for and an enthusiastic affirmation of sexual difference and complementarity. From men made weak and women indecent, he thought, there can come nothing good, nothing good at all (*DA* II.iii.11–12).[14]

FRANCE'S TRAJECTORY

Tocqueville was not sanguine about the immediate future of his country, and he was as prescient as he was gloomy in foretelling what was soon to come. In the period stretching from August 1829 to May 1830, as it gradually became evident that Charles X and the ultra-royalists would no longer abide by the Charter, he wrote a series of letters to his brother Édouard, who was abroad on his honeymoon, describing developments as they took place and predicting, in the end, that the Bourbon monarch would lose his throne.[15] In November 1836, when Louis Napoleon made an abortive attempt at a coup d'état, he remarked that, in a matter of time, he or someone like him would succeed;[16] and, with this likelihood in mind, he composed for the second *Democracy* a series of chapters contrasting the pacific propensity of democratic peoples and the longing for war that tends to grip the ambitious minority who in a democratic age make a profession of arms (II.iii.22–23). On 27 January 1848, less than a month before the uprising that would bring the reign of Louis-Philippe to an abrupt and ignominious end, Tocqueville gave a speech in the Chamber warning that revolution was nigh.[17] Four years later, in his correspondence, he predicted that the imperial polity of Louis Napoleon, which had in fact begun with a coup d'état and owed its popularity to the memory of military glory, would survive for a considerable time and end in a clash of arms disastrous for France.[18] And, in a memorandum he sent at this time to Henri, comte de Chambord and duc de Bordeaux, the grandson and heir of Charles X, Tocqueville—who had long supposed France best suited to hereditary, constitutional monarchy[19]—correctly forecast as well that when the Second Empire collapsed, as it eventually would, there would once again be an opening for the legitimists, and in vain he urged the Bourbon pretender to distance himself from the absolutist propensities of his grandfather and to declare himself a champion of liberty.[20]

Tocqueville was even less sanguine about the long-term future. He was by no means a fatalist, but he had a keen appreciation for the direction of democracy's drift; and in the last few chapters of the second *Democracy*, he specified what it was that so worried him. To be sure, he began its fourth part, which he regarded as "the most difficult and delicate spot in the entire work,"[21] with a chapter asserting that "equality naturally gives to men a taste for free institutions" and praising *indocilité* (II.iv.1), as we have seen; and it is evident that it was this propensity that gave him hope. Immediately thereafter, however, he changed his tune; and, in the remaining chapters of the fourth part, he pulled together the various threads of his argument concerning the political psychology of liberal democratic man in such a way as to demonstrate that the democratic *état social* is highly conducive to centralized administration.[22]

To begin with, Tocqueville contended, "the idea of secondary powers, placed between the sovereign and the subjects," is as alien to the democratic social condition as it is natural where there is an aristocracy. Then, he remarked that, where equality is the norm, the idea that there should be intermediary powers can be introduced only by artifice (*artificiellement*) and that it is not normally retained except with considerable difficulty (II.iv.2, p. 240). Where equality is the rule, Tocqueville explains, complexity seems an intolerable offense: men naturally "conceive the idea of a power, single [*unique*] and central, that by itself conducts the citizens," and they have a natural preference for "uniform legislation," for it is hard for men who are "little different from their neighbors" to understand "why the rule that is applicable to one man should not be equally applicable to all the others." All privileges, even the least, such a man regards as "repugnant to reason," and "the faintest dissimilarities [*les plus légères dissemblances*] in the political institutions of the same people wound him." In time, Tocqueville tells us, intellectual propensities of this sort become "instincts so blind and habits so invincible that they still direct activities" even when "particular facts" demand the opposite. In France, he adds, "these same opinions have taken full possession of the intellect," and none of the existing parties is in any way opposed. Of course, those out of power tend to judge that the government is directing things badly, "but all nonetheless think that the government should act without cessation and take everything in hand." The salient feature of every new political scheme is the same—whether it comes from the left or the right: "the unity, the ubiquity, the omnipotence of the social power" and "the uniformity of its rules" (II.iv.2).

To make matters worse, "the sentiments of democratic peoples" tend in precisely the same direction—toward "concentrating power." This is in part a consequence of social isolation, for men in democratic societies have "neither superiors nor inferiors nor habitual and necessary associates," and it is reinforced by their lack of time. It is only "with effort" that men of this sort "tear themselves from their particular affairs to occupy themselves with common affairs; their natural penchant is to abandon to the State, the sole visible and permanent representative of the collective interests, the care" of such affairs. "In democratic times," Tocqueville observes, "private life is so active, so agitated, so full of desires and work, that it is almost the case that there is no longer any energy or leisure left to each man for political life" (II.iv.3, pp. 242–43).

This is part of the story, and there is more. In democratic ages, men are especially concerned with their own well-being, and they are rendered anxious by property's mobility. In consequence, "the love of public tranquillity is often the only political passion" that they feel, and it leads them to strengthen the only power capable of maintaining public order. Moreover, democratic societies are animated by a fierce hatred of privilege and inequality, and this causes democratic peoples to provide strong support to a central government eager, for reasons all its own, to enforce social and political uniformity (II.iv.3, pp. 243–44).

It is also natural, Tocqueville adds, that, in the absence of individuals and corporate bodies of any real substance, men intent on new enterprises look to the central power for help. Such men may well "admit, as a general principle, that the public power should not intervene in private affairs, but, as an exception, each of them desires that it aid him in the special affair that preoccupies him." In practice, Tocqueville explains, there is "a multitude of people" who entertain "this particular view with regard to a crowd of different objects at the same time"; and in consequence of this fact, "the sphere of the central power extends itself insensibly in every direction," even when every individual involved actually "wishes to restrain it" overall. The older the democratic society, Tocqueville suggests, the more centralized it will be. "Time works on its behalf; all accidents are to its profit; individual passions come to its aid without [anyone] being aware of it" (II.iv.3, pp. 243–44, n. 1).

In short, equality not only suggests "to men the thought of a government alone [*unique*], uniform, and strong"; at the same time, "it gives them a taste for it." It is to this end that "the natural propensity of mind and heart leads them, and for them to arrive" at this point it would simply "suffice that they not be held back" (II.iv.3, p. 245). In England, he indicates, and in America, there really is that which holds men back (II.iv.4). But this is not true on the continent of Europe. There, "the privileges of the nobles, the liberties of cities, and provincial administrations have been or will be destroyed." There, one could say that "every step" which men "take towards equality brings them nearer to despotism." There, "all the diverse rights—which have been wrenched successively in our time from classes, corporations, and men—have not served to raise up on a foundation more democratic new secondary powers, but invariably these rights have been concentrated in the hands of the sovereign." In Europe, we are told, virtually all the old charitable establishments "have fallen more or less into dependence on the sovereign," and "it is the State that has undertaken almost alone to give bread to those who are hungry, help and asylum to the sick, work to the idle"; and, in most places, education has also become "a national matter: the State receives and often takes the child from the arms of its mother in order to entrust it to its agents; it takes charge of inspiring sentiments in each [new] generation and of furnishing it with ideas. Uniformity reigns in studies as in all the rest; diversity, like liberty, disappears from it day by day." According to Tocqueville, religion is in a similar state in countries Catholic and Protestant alike. The rulers may not care very much about doctrine, but they are intent on "laying hold of the will of the man who explains" this doctrine. First, "they take from the clergy their property." Then, "they assign to each a salary"; and, finally, "they divert and use for their advantage alone the influence the priest possesses." In effect, "they make of him one of their functionaries and often one of their servants, and with his assistance they penetrate the ultimate depths of each man's soul" (II.iv.5, pp. 252–53).

Tocqueville could also foresee that the development of the industrial economy would provide ever more occasion for government intervention, and he recognized as well that Europe's governments would soon take over the savings
banks that had been founded to serve the poor. Even more to the point, he noticed that, as Europe's rulers steadily gathered the resources of each of the various nations into their hands, they became more ambitious. To his horror, they
had gotten into the habit of "judging themselves responsible for the actions and
for the individual destiny of their subjects," and they had "undertaken to guide
and enlighten each of them in the different activities of his life." If the "need"
were to present itself, he feared that they would be perfectly prepared "to render
him happy despite himself." In the process, "public administration has become
not only more centralized, but more inquisitive and more detailed; everywhere
it penetrates further into private affairs now than before; it regulates in its manner more actions, and smaller actions, and with every passing day it establishes itself more fully beside, around, and above each individual for the purpose of assisting him, counseling him, and constraining him" (II.iv.5, pp. 253–63).[23]

Such was the direction in which Europe was tending; and if nothing was done
to hold men back, democratic despotism would soon be their fate (II.iv.6). "Our
fathers," wrote Tocqueville, "showed how a people could organize an immense
tyranny in its bosom at the very moment in which it was escaping the authority of
the nobles and flouting the power of all the kings, revealing at the same time to
the world the way to win its independence and the way to lose it" (II.iv.5, p. 263).
Our fathers had done this, he thought, and we, in our ignorance and folly, are exceedingly apt to do the like again—and of course, in the wake of the revolution
of 1848, when Louis Napoleon was elected president of France and mounted a
coup d'état to make himself emperor, Alexis de Tocqueville was once again, to
his great chagrin, proven right.

TOCQUEVILLE'S LEGACY

With *Democracy in America*, Tocqueville achieved something of that at which
he aimed. He caught the attention of the political class in France, and he caused
many of those within it, on both left and right, to pause for a time and reflect.
They quoted him in the press and in the Chamber of Deputies, and they welcomed him into their ranks. In early January 1838, he was inducted into the Academy of Moral and Political Sciences; he was elected a deputy in early March 1839;
and, in late December 1841, the Immortals voted to make him a member of the
Académie française. As an author, Tocqueville enjoyed considerable acclaim.

As a statesman, however, Tocqueville failed. Despite a valiant effort, he did not in the end succeed in persuading his colleagues to recast the institutions and practices put in place by the Revolution and perfected by Napoleon; and even before the coup d'état staged by the great man's nephew on 2 December 1851—after having helped frame the constitution of the Second Republic, and after having completed a brief stint as foreign minister of France—Tocqueville came to the conclusion that his political career had been sterile and that he was better suited to literary pursuits and to the world of thought than to the world of practical politics.[24] Well aware of what was in the offing for France, he redirected his hopes to posterity and set out to write for his own use memoirs focused on the revolution of 1848, followed by a grand thematic study, which was intended for publication, of the French Revolution, the rise of the first Napoleon, and the character and significance of Bonapartist rule. Mindful that *Democracy in America* had failed to effect the radical transformation of French thinking concerning public policy that he had sought, Tocqueville intended on this occasion to abandon his policy of literary indirection and to tell his compatriots directly, bluntly, and even dogmatically that which it was suitable that they think concerning the direction in which they were tending. In the latter and more important of his two new works, which he intended to model on Montesquieu's *Considerations on the Causes of the Greatness of the Romans and their Decline*, his aim was to chart what he regarded as the point of departure for modern France, to clarify thereby the country's subsequent trajectory, and to elucidate its failure to find a proper footing for liberty. In this fashion, he hoped to prepare the way for the discovery of an antidote for the malady that beset his country.[25]

When Louis Napoleon carried out his coup, Tocqueville looked on with resignation and dismay as the majority of his compatriots, many of his fellow legitimists, and even his brothers rallied in support of a military dictatorship that he himself detested with a hatred that knew no bounds, and in the aftermath he came to feel very much alone.[26] In a letter to a friend, written some six months after this event, he wrote:

> I imagine that the spiritual predicament [*situation d'esprit*] in which people like us find ourselves must resemble to a degree that of the Jews in the Middle Ages when they felt themselves strangers everywhere, wherever they went: obstinate sectarians of a religion which was no longer believed in, still hoping for a Messiah whom no one around them awaited. If we resemble them in this particular, we must resemble them in another; their isolation on the earth rendered them dearer to one other; they sought one another out from one end of the world to the other, and they made for themselves a species of movable fatherland [*patrie mobile*], which they carried with them everywhere, wherever they found themselves in company together.[27]

Tocqueville once again experienced acclaim when he published the first part of his study of the French Revolution — *The Ancien Régime and the Revolution* — in 1856; and when he died three years later, in the spring of 1859, he was exceedingly well-known. Among those hostile to the Second Empire, he was even considered a great man of sorts. But in France, once the Third Republic found its feet, his fame quickly waned, and until the 1950s, when his compatriots had occasion to reflect at leisure on Europe's ongoing *Auseinandersetzung* with a particularly virulent form of democratic despotism, he was for the most part regarded as a figure of antiquarian interest. In his native land, his was a life almost without consequence.[28]

It is easy to see why. From a French perspective, Tocqueville's way of thinking was decidedly strange. Within the party system that existed, there was no place for someone of so idiosyncratic an outlook.[29] Earlier on, to be sure, before he published his magnum opus, there had been considerable speculation concerning the need for administrative decentralization and for the reestablishment of intermediary powers in one or another form. In practice, however, the programs espoused by the ultra-royalists and the liberals when in opposition were abandoned when they came to power.[30] Had there been a modicum of political consensus and social trust among the French, devolution might at this time have taken place. But the French had never been blessed with the latter;[31] the Revolution had shattered what there was of both; and those in office thereafter consistently harbored a well-founded fear of insurrection. In France, where, tellingly, the state had always been the State, the left thought it morally obligatory and the right, politically expedient to embrace "the unity, the ubiquity, the omnipotence of the social power" and "the uniformity of its rules," precisely as Tocqueville claimed.

After the appearance of *Democracy in America*, despite its author's best efforts and ongoing discussion of devolution in some circles, these attitudes remained predominant and this pattern of governance persisted;[32] and, despite the contributions that the passage of time and the deliberate efforts of Charles de Gaulle and François Mitterand made to healing the divisions that had for so long afflicted France, these attitudes and this pattern of governance have not yet lost their purchase[33] — for Tocqueville was surely right when he argued in *The Ancien Régime and the Revolution*, toward the end of his life, that the true victors in the French Revolution were the intellectual heirs of Anne-Robert-Jacques Turgot and of the Physiocrats.[34] In the years intervening between his day and our own, as in the immediately preceding time, France has oscillated between brief moments of hopefulness and even euphoria, extended periods of stagnation and immobility, and times of profound instability and wrenching change. In the period since 1789, the country has known five republics, two monarchies, two empires, and a dictatorship far more popular initially than anyone in postwar France was inclined to admit.[35] Moreover, in this period, the French have lived under so many different constitutions—some say sixteen—that it is hard to keep count. Under each and every one of these regimes and constitutions, however, there has been one crucial element of continuity. Through thick and thin the administrative apparatus of the State has steadily grown in weight, in power, and scope.[36] Today, more than one-quarter of those in the French laboring force work for the State, and the functionaries of that entity regulate daily life in minute detail.

THE TUTELARY STATE

At the time of the French Revolution, no one foresaw this development in all of its ramifications. But, from the outset, *abbé* Emmanuel Joseph Sieyès, the architect of the Revolution, sought to combine government by an enlightened elite with popular sovereignty. In the three pamphlets that he published late in 1788 and in 1789, he not only demanded an end to corporate privilege and the formal empowerment of the Third Estate; he also applied Adam Smith's notion of the division of labor to political life, distinguishing active from passive citizens, calling for governance by specialists who make a profession of politics, and outlining for the achievement of this end an elaborate constitutional scheme based on indirect elections and graduated promotion. He did not succeed in persuading his colleagues in the Constituent Assembly to adopt this scheme in all of its complexity, and he failed a second time in 1795 when, in part at his instigation, the Directory was established. But, on both occasions, those in control went part way, opting for indirect elections and distinguishing active from passive citizens on the basis of property-holding or the payment of taxes; and in 1799, after the 18th of Brumaire, Sieyès managed to persuade Napoleon Bonaparte to put in place much of his complex scheme. It was not until the Restoration that there were direct elections in France, and they were anything but democratic.[37] Moreover, the restored monarchy continued to support the École polytechnique and what is now called the École normale supérieure, which were founded in the course of the Revolution with an eye to producing an enlightened governing elite.

Nor did the July Monarchy alter anything essential. In fact, in the 1840s, after Tocqueville had published the second *Democracy*, France actually came to be ruled by a narrow oligarchy of self-styled experts, modeled on the corps of rational administrators envisaged by Turgot, and these were to a considerable degree drawn from among those labeled by their opponents the *Doctrinaires* and led by François Guizot[38]—a man whom Tocqueville had long since ceased to admire,[39] and against whom in the second *Democracy* he had directed many an oblique attack.[40] Moreover, the same spirit was in evidence under the Second Empire, the Third Republic, Vichy, and the Fourth Republic as well;[41] and today, although the Fifth Republic is formally democratic in a fashion in which the July Monarchy was not, France is nonetheless ruled by an oligarchy no less narrow and hardly less doctrinaire than the one over which Guizot presided. The main difference is that this time the narrow elite constituting the country's political class is drawn from the roughly one hundred individuals who graduate each year from the École nationale d'administration founded by Charles de Gaulle in 1945.

The *énarques*, as they are called, form an aristocracy of sorts. They are educated in common, and they exhibit an esprit de corps; they read the same books, and as one would expect, in each new generation they tend to think the same thoughts. As is only natural, they tend to pair off, if not to intermarry, and later those who bother to procreate carefully groom their children for entrance in turn into the *grandes écoles*. Many of the *énarques* come to live lives of great privilege at public expense; and as recent scandals have repeatedly made clear, in practice, to a very considerable extent, they are above the law. In France, the *énarques* run the major corporations, many of which are partially owned by the State. They dominate the civil service and the political parties; they head many of the ministries; and they effortlessly move back and forth between the corporations, the civil service, and high office. One can become foreign minister, interior minister, and even prime minister of France without ever having faced the voters, as Dominique de Villepin recently proved. But with rare exceptions—exemplified by the current president of France—one has little chance of securing any one of these three offices or, for that matter, any other prominent post if one is not, as is Villepin, an *énarque*.

One fact is illustrative. Arabs make up anywhere from 8 to 13 percent of the French population, but to date no Arab living in metropolitan France has ever held a seat in the National Assembly—not, as some suggest, because France is profoundly racist (which it is not), but because there has never been an Arab *énarque*. It says a great deal that, when adverse circumstances finally brought home to the French the dire long-term implications for France of the exclusion of its Arab citizens from the country's ruling order, they initially discussed rectifying the matter—not by recruiting candidates for elective office from within the Arab population (as would have been the case almost anywhere else), but by introducing into the selection process for the *grandes écoles* an element of discrimination along ethnic lines of the sort practiced in the United States. In France, there may no longer be a *noblesse de l'épée* and a *noblesse de la robe*, but there is what some tellingly call a *noblesse de l'État*.[42]

Of course, in the century and a half since Tocqueville's death, a great deal has changed. Except, perhaps, with regard to Islam, it is no longer the case that in France the spirit of religion and the spirit of liberty are profoundly at odds. This is due, however, not to a reconciliation between the two of the sort that Tocqueville had sought, but, rather, to the fact that by excluding religion from the public sphere and by monopolizing education over a considerable span of time under the Third Republic, the State eventually managed to suffocate genuine Christian faith.[43]

In similar fashion, there is now in France a Constitutional Council capable of setting aside legislation that contravenes the constitution of the Fifth Republic, the preamble of the constitution of the Fourth Republic, the Declaration of the Rights of Man and the Citizen, the European Convention on Human Rights, or one of the various treaties that France has signed. The members of this council are not, however, fully independent, and its purview is, to say the least, strictly confined. Apart from former presidents, those on the Constitutional Council are beholden to the president of the republic and to the presiding officers of the National Assembly and Senate for appointment and serve in office for a limited term of only nine years. The council itself has jurisdiction with regard to ordinary statutes only in the brief period after a law has been passed and before it has been signed by the president of the republic; and, even more to the point, it cannot sit in judgment except at the instigation of the president or prime minister, of the presiding officer of the National Assembly or Senate, or of sixty members of the National Assembly or Senate. In short, against abuses on the part of the legislative and executive powers, the ordinary citizen who has not been inducted into the *noblesse de l'État* has no recourse in a court of law. If the Constitutional Council is not quite a sham, it nonetheless comes close.

In France, there have been other changes as well, and they are significant. In the 1860s, commercial corporations with limited liability were sanctioned, and thereafter they grew.[44] In 1884, after a long struggle and an extended period of intense debate, labor unions were formally recognized as an instrument necessary for social accommodation and legally sanctioned as a means of social control. Over time, as they gained in importance and weight, they were given the freedom to engage in collective bargaining, to collect dues, own property, receive bequests, establish mutual-aid societies, build low-cost housing, administer charitable trusts, and agitate.[45] But while the industrial working class was allowed civic agency and the means of collective self-defense and white-collar unions eventually emerged as well, all other groupings were denied this privilege. It has been legal to form civil associations without explicit permission from the government for more than a century now. But the French state makes registration a prerequisite for the possession of civil personality and the ownership of property; it restricts property possession on the part of associations that it does not itself sponsor, subsidize, and openly guide; it denies them the right to receive bequests; and, at least in principle, it closely oversees them all.[46]

Moreover, to this day, the French make an exception of religious orders and confraternities. For a time, because these *congrégations* were regarded as states within the state, as instruments of a foreign power, and as "partial societies" of the very sort that Rousseau thought a threat to the general will (CS 1.7–2.3), the French state actively sought their suppression. Today, though it is no longer a crime to join the Jesuits, the Dominicans, or even Opus Dei, the *congrégations* are still denied civil personality and the capacity to own property.[47] For similar reasons, the State reserves for itself a right to suppress associations hostile to what it calls "republicanism,"[48] and in France there is no legal provision for the establishment of private foundations. In practice, though administrative authorization can be sought from the Council of State, very few applications receive the requisite approval; and on the board of every private foundation that is authorized, lest it even contemplate breaking ranks, there sits a representative of the ubiquitous State.[49] Despite all of the changes that have occurred, the spirit of 1789, that of 1793, and that of 1799 still govern France.[50]

In similar fashion, although—to the chagrin of ideologues hysterically hostile to markets[51]—the French state has cut taxes and sold off large blocks of stock in many of the major corporations that it once owned outright, in every case of any real significance, it has retained a stake in the enterprise sufficient to enable it to provide guidance when it sees fit. Here, it is crucial that one keep in mind, as the promoters of privatization within the Gaullist and the Socialist parties certainly did,[52] Tocqueville's recognition that the socialists of his day were at odds with Turgot and the Physiocrats of Malesherbes' time less in their aims than in their resolute refusal to acknowledge that laissez-faire economics is not only compatible with rational administration but absolutely essential to its success.[53]

In France, the State is everywhere to be found. It runs all of the universities; the various religious sects are closely supervised; and the police still keep extensive dossiers on the public and private comportment of everyone who is thought to be of any importance, as they have under every government since the time of Robespierre. Two centuries have passed, adjustments have been made, and a great deal has changed, but the spirit of the laws remains the same.

In the early 1980s, to be sure, Tocqueville was once again for a brief moment in vogue—thanks in part to the influence of Raymond Aron, François Furet, and Pierre Rosanvallon.[54] At that time, to his very great credit, François Mitterand made an attempt at decentralization, creating regions with elected officials and restoring a measure of autonomy to cities, towns, and villages, which in the past had always been regarded as consultative bodies, as instruments of central administration, and as nothing more. But this effort at devolution, like its predecessors under the July Monarchy and the Third Republic,[55] was half-hearted, to say the least—and soon enough it stalled. Education and what the French call *police* were reserved for the central government; next to no responsibilities of any real significance were handed over to the localities; and, in the regions and large cities, the principal posts soon came to be monopolized by *énarques*, most of them former civil servants who did double duty in the National Assembly as well. For all practical purposes, the government and administration of France are as centralized today as they were in Tocqueville's time.[56]

It does not help that the Fifth Republic—a resolutely presidential regime from the outset—has come to look more and more like an elective monarchy. Before 2002, perhaps because of an oversight on the part of Charles de Gaulle and his advisors, there existed a serious possibility at times that there would be divided power [*cohabitation*]—that one party would control the presidency, and another party would preside over the National Assembly—and, on more than one occasion, such a situation actually developed. A corrupt bargain that year between the Socialist Party leader Lionel Jospin and the Gaullist leader Jacques Chirac obviated the danger that the National Assembly might in consequence gradually become something more lively than a rubber stamp. By shortening the presidential term to five years, they ensured not only that legislative elections would follow immediately upon presidential elections and reflect the outcome of the latter but also that, except in extremis, legislative elections would not again be needed until after the next presidential poll.

As one would expect, oligarchical entrenchment has once again had as its consequence political stagnation. Since 1980, it has become evident that, in the face of an aging population and a persistently high level of structural unemployment (especially among the young and among Arab and Berber immigrants), the guarantees for employment security, the generous welfare provisions, the stipulation of a grossly inflated minimum wage, and the government pension system that exist in France cannot be sustained. A grave crisis, conducive to violence and civil strife and threatening the future material well-being of nearly everyone in the country, looms on the horizon, and everyone within the political class has known about it for quite some time. In the quarter century prior to 2007, however, despite the economic liberalization that took place, nothing of any substance was done to confront this challenge, and legislation made matters markedly worse. The work week was cut from thirty-nine to thirty-five hours; railway employees retained the right to retire at the age of fifty-five; the number of paid holidays was raised to a level higher than ever; the minimum wage was set at a level surpassing that in every other European state; public spending came to account for 55 percent of the national income; and the national debt grew to 65 percent of the gross domestic product. Moreover, prior to 2007, no one with any political capital dared to argue the necessity that employers be allowed to hire and fire at will, that the age of retirement be raised, that the work week be extended, that the minimum wage be lowered, that welfare payments be curtailed, and that pension commitments be reduced.

During these same years, as a consequence of underinvestment and slow growth, France gradually fell behind. In gross domestic product per head, it dropped over the course of twenty-five years from the eighth most prosperous nation in the world to the nineteenth. In the six years preceding 2007, its share of world exports fell by 20 percent, and even within the Eurozone its share of trade dropped by 15 percent. It is no wonder that two million of its most talented young people went abroad to seek their fortunes and that the numbers continued to grow. Prior to 2007, no one of any stature, in any of the major political parties, had the courage to address the question honestly and forthrightly and to acknowledge that, unless something genuinely drastic was done, younger workers who stayed in France would be saddled with an unbearable tax burden and the promises made to the generation on the verge of retirement would never be kept.[57]

As a consequence, France now hovers on the brink of an economic precipice, as did Great Britain on the eve of Margaret Thatcher's election as prime minister. Whether Nicholas Sarkozy—who, in 2007, had the courage to tell his compatriots part of the truth and who is evidently intent on doing at least part of what is needed to turn the French economy around—will be able to duplicate her remarkable feat, whether, by pushing through and implementing the necessary reforms, he can pull his country back from the brink, remains an open question. For, as he no doubt knows as well as anyone, what he proposed in his campaign for the presidency falls well short of the radical surgery that is required, and his compatriots may not be willing to stomach even the modest reforms that he is attempting to implement. The French have long been suspicious of the free market and, in the state-run high schools, this prejudice is systematically reinforced. From the textbook that everyone is made to read, students learn not only that capitalism is "brutal" and "savage," but that "economic growth" is a great evil, which "imposes" on those whom it befalls "a hectic form of life, producing overwork, stress, nervous depression, cardiovascular disease, and, according to some, even the development of cancer." In the past two decades, they are told therein, though wealth has doubled, this development has brought in its train "doubled unemployment, poverty, and exclusion, whose ill effects constitute the background for a profound social malaise."[58]

On occasion, to be sure, the French still display a heartening spirit of *indocilité*. By means of insurrection, they can bring the narrow oligarchy of putative experts that rules them to a screeching halt, and like the citizens in the various communities of ancient Crete (I.2, above), they kick up their heels and do just that from time to time. One might even describe insurrection as a permanent, extra-legal feature of the Fifth Republic, and one might also entertain the possibility that it serves as an antidote of sorts—as a check on abuse by the *noblesse de l'État* and as a means for overcoming the recurrent political sclerosis that oligarchical rule tends in the long run to produce in France. This possibility one might entertain, and, of course, there are those who do.[59] But it would be a mistake to bank on it, for as a presumption, in this case, it is almost certainly wrong. To judge by what happened in 1995, in 1998, and, most recently, in the spring of 2006, insurrection now serves merely to reinforce stagnation, for, outside the ghettoes to which North African immigrants have been relegated, the only thing that will set off an uprising these days is the prospect that the French government will make a halting, far less than half-hearted attempt at liberalizing labor markets or at confronting the impending crisis of the French welfare state. If Sarkozy's program of reform is insufficiently radical, if he proves to be as feckless and undisciplined as his immediate predecessor, or if his effort is in any significant way blocked, as is altogether possible, the Fifth Republic will have reached an impasse.

Even, however, if Sarkozy succeeds gloriously, in the manner in which Thatcher did, even if he resurrects the French economy and pares the welfare state, it is hard to imagine that he would move decisively beyond what she achieved—in the direction of dismantling the administrative state or dramatically reducing it in size and scope.[60] For what Tocqueville discerned in embryo long ago is now a matter of brute fact. Over the people of France today, as he feared would someday be the case, there "is elevated an immense, tutelary power, which takes sole charge of assuring their enjoyment and of watching over their fate," and it threatens to reduce this astonishingly talented nation "to nothing more than a herd of timid and industrious animals, of which the government is the shepherd" (II.iv.6, pp. 265–66).[61] It is truly an astonishing sight.

In short, in France, Tocqueville's worst nightmare has largely come true; and, as he also foresaw, it has come true elsewhere in Europe as well—for, as he understood from the outset, the French disease is infectious. In Tocqueville's day, the other states on the continent of Europe, even those never subject to the *Code Napoléon*, were drifting in precisely the same direction as France,[62] and nothing has happened in the interim to slow them down. If anything, by occasioning an astonishing concentration of power in the state, World War I, the Great Depression, World War II, and the long Cold War accelerated the progress of the malady.[63]

UNIVERSAL MONARCHY

Moreover, in the last half century, by way of the Common Market and its successor the European Union, the French elite has once again, in its tiresome way, attempted to establish a universal monarchy in Europe; and, in the process, its members have managed to export their self-consciously *Étatiste, dirigiste* model of minute bureaucratic rule to Europe as a whole, imposing on their neighbors and on themselves something very much like what Malesherbes and his colleagues on the *Cour des aides* long ago denounced in the *Grandes Remonstrances* as a "despotism of Administrators." Today, as a consequence, 80 percent of the legislation passed by the National Assembly in Paris originates in Brussels, and there is at this stage little if any prospect that the powerful mandarins entrenched in the latter city will ever be reined in, much less that they will ever be made genuinely responsible to a legislature directly elected by the various peoples they govern. Technocratic rule and centralized administration on the model envisaged by Turgot and the Physiocrats were sanctioned by Georg Wilhelm Friedrich Hegel in his *Philosophy of Right*, and, thanks to his influence, they were adopted as an ideal in the German-speaking world and elsewhere.[64] In any case, this combination suits perfectly the tastes and ambitions of those within the larger political class now dominant in nearly all of the countries of Europe, virtually all of whom belong to a highly educated elite that has never harbored any great affection for a genuine participation in governance by ordinary folk. In the press, especially in Great Britain, one occasionally encounters articles criticizing the European Union for its "democratic deficit," but next to no one within the political class cares passionately about the problem.[65]

In the massive, 450-page draft constitution produced by the constitutional convention chaired not long ago by Valéry Giscard d'Estaing, this "democratic deficit" was given scant notice; and, by determining all questions of genuine consequence in advance, that document, had it been ratified, would have permanently denied the European Parliament any real legislative scope. The fact that this constitution was rejected in a plebiscite by the French and the Dutch was a setback for the heirs of Turgot, as was the subsequent refusal of Irish voters to sanction the mildly truncated version of that constitution contained within the Treaty of Lisbon. But this left the overall situation unchanged, for no one of any authority has emerged to articulate an alternative model of governance, and we can be confident that the powers-that-be will eventually get their way. In Europe, there may never again be a genuine redress of grievances. On the continent (with the honorable exception of Switzerland), the administrative state reigns unchallenged and supreme, and, to an increasing extent, this is true in Great Britain and Ireland as well.[66]

It could hardly be otherwise. Genuine political participation is an acquired taste; the petty pleasures associated with private life within bourgeois society are enticing in the extreme; and, as Tocqueville foresaw, they leave ordinary folk with little, if any, time or inclination for public pursuits. It is possible, of course, that a renewal will some day take place. It is still conceivable that the various peoples of Europe will awaken from their self-induced slumber, shoulder aside their elites, establish themselves once again as self-governing nations, and re-claim the municipal liberties that once were theirs—and outsiders sympathetic to their plight can only hope and pray that this they will do.[67] But the hour is late, the mores and manners to which centralized administration and democratic despotism give rise are now firmly entrenched, and it is increasingly unlikely that such an event will ever take place.

To the peoples of Europe, one can now apply, with considerable justification, Montesquieu's description of the "libertine life [*libertinage*]" attendant on "the spirit of extreme equality." In virtually every country within the European Union, for some time now, the people have made the public treasury their "object" and have sold their votes to the highest bidder. Moreover, after having "been corrupted with a bribe of silver," they became, as one would expect, "cold-blooded." Today, "for silver, they display an affection, but they no longer have any affection for public affairs: without care for the government & concern re-garding the proposals it entertains, in tranquillity they await their pay" (*EL* 1.2.2, 8.2–3).

Europe's progress is painful to watch. It drives one back to the notes that Tocqueville penned while wrestling with the composition of the first *Democracy*—notes in which he expressed his concern that within the democratic *état social*, men might eventually become a mere "mass—floating in the middle, in-ert, egoistic, without energy, without patriotism, sensual, sybaritic—which has only instincts, which lives from day to day, which becomes in turn a plaything for all the others." He worried that men would come to display "moderation without virtue or courage, a moderation born from cowardice of heart and not from virtue—from exhaustion, from fear, from egoism." He was convinced that this would be accompanied by "a tranquillity derived not from well-being but from a lack of the courage and energy necessary for seeking something better." If allowed to proceed unimpeded, the process of depoliticization already under way would eventuate, he feared, in "a debasement of souls" in which men would exhibit "the passions of old men, which have as their conclusion impotence" (*DA* I.Intr., p. 11, n. e).[68]

The day is fast approaching when Tocqueville's prognostications, extreme though they may seem, will be considered all too apt. Already, our European friends seem entirely mired in the present and disinclined to think beyond the day after tomorrow, and we are left to wonder whether European society can even be sustained. France is hardly unique. Nearly everywhere on the continent of Europe the pattern is the same: sclerosis, political stagnation, and an incapacity to fully confront the bankruptcy of the social democratic model, joined not only with a breathtaking propensity for wishful thinking, an inclination to think of themselves as victims, and a posture of *ressentiment* but also with an unwillingness to provide for their own defense and an instinct for appeasement so abject that it would make Neville Chamberlain blush.[69]

Moreover, in Europe generally, thanks largely to mockery in the media and to disdain on the part of the continent's highly educated elite, religious faith is in steep decline; marriage is on the wane; and in most countries, as a matter of personal convenience, women nonchalantly arrange for the extermination of their offspring as yet unborn. Indeed, if we are to judge by the current birthrate, the various peoples of Europe appear to lack even the minimal energy and ambition needed for the procreation and rearing of the next generation.[70]

This last fact should give one pause, for demography is destiny, and the European birthrate falls well below that required for sustaining the continent's population. Montesquieu, who regarded population growth as an infallible sign of good government, had Usbek argue in the *Persian Letters* that "gentleness [*douceur*] in Government contributes marvelously to the propagation of the species" (*LP* 118/122),[71] but Rousseau, who shared Montesquieu's conviction that population growth presupposes political health (*CS* 3.9), doubted whether *douceur* was a sufficient guarantee of either. He worried that, as the Enlightenment took hold, "atheism" and something on the lines of "philosophical indifference" would come to characterize ordinary men, and he warned that, if this should ever come about, it would produce a "tranquillity" not unlike that "of the State under despotism" as Montesquieu had conceived it. This condition he denounced as a "tranquillity of death . . . more fatal than war itself," arguing that it would prevent human beings from even "being born by destroying" in the living "the mores that cause them to multiply, by detaching them from their species, by reducing all of their affections to a secret egoism as fatal to the population as it is to virtue" itself (É 4.632n — 35n). In similar fashion, Tocqueville expressed a fear that, within the democratic *état social*, there would come a time when men would "allow themselves to become so fully possessed by a cowardly love of present enjoyments that their interest in their own future and in that of their descendants will disappear" (*DA* II.iii.21, p. 219).

In Europe, to this, it has now at long last finally come. Moreover, to all appearances, the Europeans are proud of their sophistication and eager to export their mores, their manners, and their apolitical ways. In their passivity, they take comfort, and, with their personal lot, they are by and large content. It seems evident that they really do "prefer listlessly following the course of their destiny to making a sudden and energetic effort at redress in time of need" (II.iii.21, p. 219). On a continent that a short time ago dominated the world, history actually appears to have come to an end — not, however, with a bang, as once seemed likely, but with a whimper, a belch, and a self-satisfied sigh.[72]

Four

A DESPOTISM OF ADMINISTRATORS

Every measure which establishes legal charity on a permanent basis and gives to it an administrative form creates thereby a class unproductive and idle, living at the expense of the class which is industrious and given to work. . . . Such a law is a poisonous germ, deposited in the bosom of the legal code, . . . and if the current generation escapes its influence, it will devour the well-being of generations to come.

—*Alexis de Tocqueville*

In the face of Europe's decline, Americans should not gloat or be smug—for, unless something dramatic is done in the near future, the odds are good that we will follow our European cousins on the path that leads to servitude. After all, in the course of the last century, we, too, contracted the French disease;[1] and among us today, under Democrats and Republicans alike, the malady advances at a quickening pace.[2]

This development Alexis de Tocqueville did not foresee. His worries concerning the United States were of another sort. He was a great proponent of administrative decentralization and local self-government, but it would be a grave error to think of him, in American terms, as an Anti-Federalist.[3] In the 1830s, when he pondered the American prospect, he worried far less about the dangers attendant on centralized administration than about the possibility that the American union would eventually come apart.[4] Like Alexander Hamilton,[5] for whose political perspicacity he evidently had great admiration,[6] he was sensitive to the fact that state and local governments were present to the populace in a way that the national government was not and inspired a measure of loyalty that it could not match, and he was acutely aware of the tensions generated between the South and the North by the presence of slavery in the former and its gradual disappearance from the latter. At the time in which he penned the first great section of *Democracy in America*, he was firmly convinced that the bonds of the Union were weakening (*DA* I.ii.10, pp. 278–301),[7] and he recognized from afar what to this very day many historians fail to discern in retrospect: that the passage of the Kentucky Resolutions and the Virginia Resolutions, the defeat of the Federalist Party, and the so-called Revolution of 1800, eventuating in the election of Thomas Jefferson as president, had in fact dangerously weakened the Union.[8] Had Tocqueville and Gustave de Beaumont sojourned in Charleston, South Carolina, for some weeks, as they had originally planned; had they encountered in South Carolina prominent individuals prepared to argue that slavery is a positive good, as they surely would have, the former, who was generally quite sensitive to the close correlation between convictions concerning justice and the *état social*, would not have been as oblivious as he was to the profound differences emerging in public opinion between southerners and northerners. He would not have reported that, in Jacksonian America, one could no longer see any sign of the presence of "great political parties" at odds with one another on questions of fundamental political principle (I.ii.2, pp. 135–38), and he would have been even more fully alarmed concerning America's prospects than, in fact, he was.[9] He might, then, have attended to the growing significance for Americans outside the South of the stirring preamble to the Declaration of Independence,[10] which had been read out in public ceremony in the presence of both young men when they stopped in Albany, New York, on 4 July 1831.[11]

The failure of the Confederacy in what might variously, with equal accuracy, be called the War for Southern Independence and the War to Save the Union settled the question of the United States' permanence. Moreover, the administration of Abraham Lincoln, with full support from what was left of Congress after the secession of the Confederate states, transformed the American government in a fashion that would have fully satisfied Alexander Hamilton. To win the war, they reestablished a national bank, issued a federal currency, provided for an expansion of the national debt, and passed an elaborate, emergency program of federal taxation, including a progressive income tax. In its early stages, moreover, they imposed a tariff aimed at encouraging industrialization, and they instituted a program designed to promote the long-term economic well-being of the American people, including the Homestead Act, which made it easy for individuals to acquire federal land for farming in the West; the Morrill Act, which provided for the establishment of land-grant colleges in the various states; and legislation that made possible the building of America's first transcontinental railroad.[12] From this time on, the Union was a real and continuing presence in the lives of ordinary Americans. But, except temporarily under Reconstruction, and then only with regard to the old Confederacy, it would be an error to speak of administrative centralization.

THE PROGRESSIVE IMPULSE

The foundations for the administrative state were laid later on, in and after the 1870s and 1880s, in the thinking of a group of exceptional individuals, for the most part university professors, who regarded the separation of powers, the system of checks and balances, the federalist system, and the primacy of local government—the very features in American institutions that had most powerfully elicited Tocqueville's admiration—as hopelessly archaic.[13] Nearly all of these men stemmed from the Republican Party and the liberal wing of evangelical Protestantism. They were, in the conventional sense, high-minded. With regard to African Americans and other people of color, they adopted the pseudo-scientific racism fashionable within the academy at the time. For Roman Catholicism, for Protestants who thought the "higher criticism" of the Bible a threat to the Christian faith, and for others who looked to tradition and past experience for guidance, they exhibited withering contempt. A number of them had been educated in Germany; many of them powerfully felt the force of the vision of a secularized salvation history that had been propagated in *The Phenomenology of Spirit* and elsewhere by Georg Wilhelm Friedrich Hegel, and they found confirmation for this historicist vision in the evolutionary theory of Charles Darwin and in the positivism promoted by Turgot's admirer Auguste Comte.[14] Moreover, they tended to share Hegel's conviction that Tocqueville's Americans were not really citizens at all because America lacked a developed state and a genuine, ethically satisfactory public life.[15] They were among the first of their compatriots to suppose that Europe with all of its sophistication should set the standard for America, and their aim was to correct the fault identified by Hegel and to make of their backward nation something like a secular church.[16] If the clergymen in their number preached the Social Gospel, it was because the salvation they sought was to be found in the here and now.

The progressives had an argument. They pointed to the new means of communication and transportation—the telegraph, the telephone, the high-speed press, and the railroad. They noted the appearance of great cities and the isolated individuals who resided in them. They paid close attention to the great corporations and to labor unions, and they looked askance at mass immigration and at the political machines that grew up in its shadow. They took in all of this, and they came to the conclusion that the small communities hitherto dominant in America were doomed. But they did not abandon the rhetoric of community.

They merely transferred it from the township, the county, and the state to the nation as a whole. Nationalism was their cry, and rational administration was their aim.[17]

The importance of the Americans who came to be called the progressives was twofold. To begin with, they created the modern American university, and they gave to the academic profession then emerging the shape that it retains to this day, especially in the social sciences. They played a crucial role in founding the American Economic Association, the American Sociological Society, and the American Academy of Political and Social Science. They dominated the American Historical Association in its early years. But, even more important, they set the agenda for the social sciences and for the pursuit of learning more generally, charting a vision of unending social progress—to be achieved not just by advances in science and technology, but also by rational administration and social engineering, especially at the national level, and it is their vision of social progress that to this very day provides the rationale for the expenditure of vast sums of money on higher education in the United States.[18]

With regard to the significance of what the progressives taught, one could repeat what Tocqueville said in his celebrated address to the Academy of Moral and Political Sciences in Paris regarding the political sciences in general. In America, the thinking of the progressives gave "birth or at least form to the general ideas from which [would] emerge in turn both the particular facts in the midst of which the politicians operate and the laws that they believe they have invented" themselves. Around the society in which we now live, the "ideas" that they and their spiritual heirs propagated "form an intellectual atmosphere of sorts—from which the minds of the governed and the governors draw breath, whence the one and the other, often without knowing it, sometimes without wishing it, derive their principles of conduct."[19]

The progressives expressed great admiration for Abraham Lincoln, and they tended to justify their endeavor with an appeal to the American Founding Fathers and to speak of their aim as the achievement of Jeffersonian ends by Hamiltonian means.[20] But the truth is that Herbert Croly, Walter Lippmann, David Francis Bacon, Albion Small, John Bates Clark, Franklin Giddings, Richard Ely, Seth Low, Simon N. Patten, Benjamin Parke De Witt, William T. Stead, Shailer Matthews, Walter Weyl, Charles Horton Cooley, Edward Alsworth Ross, Henry Carter Adams, Roscoe Pound, Adolf A. Berle, Robert Park, John Dewey, and their associates aimed at the foundation of a new political regime, distinct from and, in certain critical respects, opposed to the one that had gradually taken shape in the period stretching from 1776 to 1789, which Lincoln later strove so mightily to defend. To this end, they abandoned not only Jefferson but Hamilton and Lincoln as well, dismissing as outdated the concern with individual, natural rights that the three men shared; rejecting as wrongheaded and outmoded Jefferson's argument for the virtues of political jealousy and his insistence that vigorous local self-government is essential to the maintenance of liberty; and substituting for Hamilton's notion of statesmanship and for that of Lincoln an account—grounded in Hegel's confidence in the inevitability of human progress, owing a great deal to his discussion of the civil service as a "universal class" in his *Philosophy of Right,* and informed by a truncated reading of Rousseau's *Social Contract*—which was incompatible with the principle of limited government and closely akin in its practical aspects to the vision of rational administration once projected in France by Anne-Robert-Jacques Turgot and by the Physiocrats.[21] To America from Germany, the progressives brought an especially virulent strain of the French disease.

By the turn of the century, the handwriting was on the wall. In 1900, E. L. Godkin, founder and longtime editor of *The Nation,* lamented that "the Declaration of Independence no longer arouses enthusiasm; it is an embarrassing instrument which requires to be explained away. The Constitution is said to be 'outgrown.'" He complained that laissez-faire economics was out of fashion, and he added that those who once "boasted that it had secured for the negro the rights of humanity and of citizenship" now listen "in silence to the proclamation of white supremacy" and make "no protest against the nullifications of the Fifteenth Amendment."[22] That progressivism's acceptance of white supremacy and its abandonment of the Declaration of Independence and the Constitution were of a piece Godkin understood, for he comprehended what the progressives were inclined to forget—that those who repudiate the notion of natural rights abandon thereby the principles dictating that government be limited in the ends it may pursue and in the means it may employ, and he recognized that in the name of a largely imaginary public interest—divorced from a concern with individual interests and rights, inspired by Rousseau's notion of the general will, and grounded in Hegel's vision of an ethically satisfactory public life—such men would be apt to commit what would hitherto have been recognized as monstrous crimes.

THE NEW FREEDOM AND THE NEW DEAL

Theodore Roosevelt reflected the trend. Like most Republicans in his generation, he revered Lincoln. In the face of Jim Crow, the disenfranchisement of African Americans in the South, and southern resistance to the appointment of blacks to federal offices in that region, he expressed dismay, and he was more than willing to restate the principles of the Declaration of Independence. In 1901, he even made a point of inviting Booker T. Washington to dine at the White House. But Roosevelt respected what passed in his day as science, and like the progressives in the universities, whom he greatly admired, he took for granted the racial inferiority of African Americans and other peoples of color. He was also eager to bind up the wounds that divided North from South; he hoped to put an end to the Democratic Party's dominance in the old Confederacy; and to this end, in and after 1904, he reluctantly signaled his willingness to acquiesce in Jim Crow.[23] Moreover, in 1912, when the Republican Party once again nominated William Howard Taft for the presidency and Roosevelt bolted and helped establish the Progressive Party as a vehicle for his own presidential ambitions, he found himself forced to decide which of the rival delegations from the South the party convention should seat—the "lily whites," as they were called, or those to which his African American supporters belonged—and he opted for the "lily whites." In consequence, not a word was said in the socially radical platform of the Progressive Party about protecting the rights of the former slaves.[24]

On this question, Roosevelt was, like many northern progressives, ambivalent. Woodrow Wilson was not. Although he lived in the North and had served as governor of New Jersey, he was a southerner, born and bred, and a Democrat. He was no friend to secession, and, in politic fashion, he professed a reverence for Lincoln. But he was no admirer of the principles enshrined in the Declaration of Independence and celebrated in the Gettysburg Address. Wilson thought of himself as a progressive and as a man of science, and he had good reason to do so. He had done graduate work at Johns Hopkins University, the chief conduit for German learning in the United States, and he had been a professor and a university president. He had authored various distinguished studies of American government and a multivolume history of the United States, in which he played down the moral significance of the Declaration of Independence as a founding document, treated the African American presence in America as a calamity, denounced Reconstruction, and expressed sympathy for the Ku Klux Klan.[25] Moreover, like many another progressive, Wilson was a supporter of eugenics. In 1907, he had lent his support to a successful campaign in Indiana aimed at the compulsory sterilization of criminals and the retarded, and in 1911, as governor of New Jersey, he had signed such a bill into law.

Wilson was a canny politician. He was more than willing to exploit African American unhappiness with Taft and Roosevelt, and to attract black voters in the North he promised that he would look after their interests.[26] But though willing to stoop to deceit, he was no mere opportunist. He was a man of principle, who knew what he was about. In April 1913, within a few weeks of his having become

president, he sanctioned the introduction of racial segregation within federal offices; in the aftermath, he connived in a dramatic reduction in the number of
African Americans appointed to federal posts and hired by the civil service; and,
when challenged by his erstwhile black supporters, he publicly defended Jim
Crow.[27] He followed up on 4 July 1913, the fiftieth anniversary of the Gettysburg
Address, by giving a speech at a reunion of fifty thousand Union and Confederate veterans held in Pennsylvania on the battlefield—in which he was ostentatiously silent concerning the principles that Lincoln had articulated on that hal-
lowed spot half a century before.[28]

Like the elder Roosevelt, as his endeavor on this festive occasion suggests, Wilson sought a reconciliation of North and South, but his aim was to achieve this
on white supremacist terms, and he knew that he had in progressive opinion a
silent—if, in some quarters, mildly embarrassed—ally. It was with this in mind
that he sought to exploit the release of D. W. Griffith's motion picture *The Birth
of a Nation*. This silent film was based on a best-selling novel published in 1905
by Thomas Dixon, who had been a classmate of Wilson's at Johns Hopkins. Entitled *The Clansman: An Historical Romance of the Ku Klux Klan*, it restated in
crude, simplistic, melodramatic, and highly exaggerated terms the argument of
Wilson's *History of the American People* concerning Reconstruction and the role
played by African Americans in American life, and on the ornate title cards used
in the movie to introduce its depiction of Reconstruction and the foundation of
the Ku Klux Klan, Griffith quoted selectively from Wilson's account. When, at
Dixon's suggestion, Wilson invited his staff and his cabinet to preview the film
with him in the East Room of the White House on 18 February 1915 and, by his
example, tacitly encouraged justices of the U. S. Supreme Court and members
of Congress to attend the separate showing held at the National Press Club the
following night, he cannot have been ignorant of the controversy stirred by
Dixon's novel, which had sold more than a million copies, and by the popular
play from it derived. It is unclear whether, as was later claimed, Wilson ever actually said of the film, "It is like writing history with lightning; my only regret is
that it is all so terribly true." But, when the movie was released two weeks after
the White House showing, it was widely presumed that it had a presidential im-
primatur. Although the furor that attended the release of the wildly popular motion picture prompted the president to prudently distance himself from Griffith's masterpiece, and ultimately from Dixon as well, we need not doubt his
enthusiasm at the time. This high-minded southern Presbyterian had an agenda,
and he was among the first to grasp the capacity of film to shape public opinion.
Dixon certainly had no doubts with regard to his old friend's aims. Six months after the movie's release, he wrote Wilson that two million had already seen it, that

fifty million more would, and that it was "transforming the entire population of the North and West into Sympathetic Southern voters." It would take a confrontation with Adolf Hitler to shake Americans from their embrace of this aspect of the Social Darwinism at the heart of the progressive impulse.[29]

There were other regards as well in which events proved Godkin's fears just. In keeping with his larger purpose, Wilson took his presidential campaign in 1912 as an opportunity to educate the American public in progressive doctrine. "We are in the presence of a new organization of society," he told his compatriots. Our time marks "a new social stage, a new era of human relationships, a new stage-setting for the drama of life," and "the old political formulas do not fit the present problems: they read now like documents taken out of a forgotten age." What Thomas Jefferson once taught is now, he insisted, quite out of date. It is "what we used to think in the old-fashioned days when life was very simple." As a university president, persuaded that the older generation was "out of sympathy with the creative, formative and progressive forces of society," he had tried "to make the young gentlemen of the rising generation as unlike their fathers as possible." Now he hoped to do something similar as president of the United States. Above all else, he hoped to persuade his compatriots to get "beyond the Declaration of Independence." That document "did not mention the questions of our day," he told them. "It is of no consequence to us." After all, "it is an eminently practical document, meant for the use of practical men; not a thesis for philosophers, but a whip for tyrants; not a theory of government, but a program of action" — once of use, outdated now.

For Montesquieu — the only figure, apart from Jefferson, whom he mentioned by name — Wilson had no use, and the constitution drafted under the Frenchman's influence — with its separation of powers, checks and balances, and distribution of authority between nation and state — he regarded as hopelessly passé. "Government," he argued,

> is not a machine; but a living thing. It falls, not under the theory of the universe, but under the theory of organic life. It is accountable to Darwin, not to Newton. It is modified by its environment, necessitated by its tasks, shaped to its functions by the sheer pressure of life. No living things can have its organs offset against each other, as checks, and live. On the contrary, its life is dependent upon their quick co-operation, their ready response to the commands of instinct or intelligence, their amicable community of purpose. . . . There can be no successful government without the intimate, instinctive co-ordination of the organs of life and action. . . . Living political constitutions must be Darwinian in structure and in practice.
>
> All that progressives ask or desire is permission — in an era when "develop-

ment," "evolution," is the scientific word—to interpret the Constitution according to Darwinian principle.

It is by no means fortuitous that the model that this future president recommended to his compatriots was the Third Republic of France.[30]

Wilson gave white supremacy a tremendous boost, and he popularized the notion that America's founding principles were false and its institutions, an anachronism. Otherwise, however, his domestic accomplishments were modest. In his day, as he understood as well as anyone, there were limits to the willingness of the Democratic Party to trample upon states' rights. Wilson did manage to establish the Federal Reserve Board, but, by March 1920, when he left office, his popularity had waned, and in the aftermath, his immediate successors, William G. Harding and Calvin Coolidge, sought a return to what the former called "normalcy"—above all by celebrating the principles enshrined in the Declaration of Independence and the Constitution. In late October 1921—in a speech delivered to a large audience, estimated at one hundred thousand, in Woodrow Wilson Park in Birmingham, Alabama, on the occasion of that city's fiftieth anniversary—Harding bluntly denounced black disenfranchisement and defended the notion that there should be political and economic equality for both black and white, remarking to the sullen white supremacists in the crowd, "Whether you like it or not, unless our democracy is a lie, you must stand for that equality."[31]

Seven months later, on Memorial Day in 1922, Harding spoke briefly at the dedication of the Lincoln Memorial. During his presidency, William Howard Taft had promoted the building of the memorial, and he had chaired the commission that oversaw the project. In effect, as everyone at the time understood, its construction was intended as a political statement. Lincoln was seated on the curule chair reserved for a Roman consul. On one wall, in a side chamber, was inscribed the Gettysburg Address; on the wall in the side chamber opposite was Lincoln's Second Inaugural Address. At the dedication, Taft, by then chief justice of the U.S. Supreme Court, and Harding spoke briefly to a crowd of fifty thousand. But, as was only appropriate, the keynote address was delivered by an African American, Dr. Robert Russa Moton, Booker T. Washington's successor as principal of the Tuskegee Institute.[32]

In time, Coolidge also entered the fray, seizing upon the occasion of the 150th anniversary of the Declaration of Independence to strike a counterblow at the arguments advanced by Wilson in 1912. In a speech delivered in Philadelphia at Independence Hall on 5 July 1926, he celebrated the fact that "amid all the clash of conflicting interests, amid all the welter of partisan politics, every American can turn for solace and consolation to the Declaration of Independence and the

Constitution of the United States with the assurance and confidence that those two great charters of freedom and justice remain firm and unshaken." What was at issue 150 years before, he explained, was not just the birth of a new nation but its establishment "on new principles"—the doctrine "that all men are created equal, that they are endowed with certain inalienable rights, and that therefore the source of the just powers of government must be derived from the consent of the governed." Because it embodies "these immortal truths," he argued, the Declaration of Independence was then and remains now "the most important civil document in the world." About it, he insisted, "there is a finality that is exceedingly restful," and then, without mentioning Wilson by name, he turned his attention to the progressive argument:

> It is often asserted that the world has made a great deal of progress since 1776, that we have had new thoughts and new experiences which have given us a great advance over the people of that day, and that we may therefore very well discard their conclusions for something more modern. But that reasoning can not be applied to this great charter. If all men are created equal, that is final. If they are endowed with inalienable rights, that is final. If governments derive their just powers from the consent of the governed, that is final. No advance, no progress can be made beyond these propositions. If anyone wishes to deny their truth or their soundness, the only direction in which he can proceed historically is not forward, but backward toward the time when there was no equality, no rights of the individual, no rule of the people.

In summing up his argument, Coolidge did not mince words. "Those who wish to proceed in that direction can not lay claim to progress. They are," he charged, "reactionary."

To this, Coolidge added one last telling point—that "it was in the contemplation of these truths that the fathers made their declaration and adopted their Constitution." Their aim "was to establish a free government" that would not "degenerate into the unrestrained authority of a mere majority or the unbridled weight of a mere influential few." To this end, "they undertook to balance these interests against each other and provide the three separate independent branches, the executive, the legislative, and the judicial departments of the Government, with checks against each other" so that none of the three could encroach upon the prerogatives accorded the others. Coolidge did not contend that the Constitution was beyond improvement, but he did warn against making "radical changes" in a framework that had stood the test of time, and he called, instead, for a close study of the political science of the American founders. "Before we can understand their conclusions," he wrote, "we must go back and review the course which they followed. We must think the thoughts which they thought."[33]

If Coolidge did not mention by name Montesquieu, the great champion of the separation of powers, it was because there was no need to do so.

Had there been no Great Depression, the effort undertaken by Taft, Hoover, and Coolidge might have succeeded in stemming and even reversing the progressive tide. But, in the 1920s and the early 1930s—with encouragement from Andrew Mellon, secretary of the treasury under Harding, Coolidge, and Herbert Hoover—the Federal Reserve Board mismanaged the money supply, initially by stoking an economic boom with an easy-money policy, and then by suddenly, radically, reversing course in such a fashion as to produce and then deepen a severe credit crunch, cause a stock market crash, produce deflation, and transform what might have been a brief and shallow recession into a deep depression.[34] This provided Franklin Delano Roosevelt, Wilson's secretary of the navy and a great admirer of the man, with an unprecedented political opportunity; and though inclined to keep his cards close to his chest, at one point in his presidential campaign, he signaled his adherence to the progressive cause in an address to the Commonwealth Club of San Francisco entitled "Of Progressive Government," which he had Adolf A. Berle draft on his behalf.[35]

Had Berle or the younger Roosevelt been willing to seek out the best economic advice available, had they attended to the cries of businessmen, small and large, cut off from the credit that was the lifeblood of their enterprise, they would have attacked Wilson's Federal Reserve Board, Andrew Mellon, and the three Republican presidents whom he served for mismanaging the money supply; and when they took Harding to task for signing a restrictive tariff that invited retaliation, they would have attacked him as well for dramatically raising taxes in the midst of an economic downturn. Instead, however, of imputing blame where blame was due, and instead of reflecting on the havoc that centralized administration can so easily wreak, they vilified the businessmen, the financiers, and the speculators caught up in the economic debacle, and they took up the arguments advanced by Wilson twenty years before and proposed as a cure an intensification of the disease. As a consequence of central planning, which is inevitably ill-informed, of policies hostile to investment and growth, of confiscatory taxation, and of macroeconomic blunders on the part of Roosevelt and his advisors, the depression went on and on; conditions in 1938 were worse than in 1932; and it took a world war and demand from abroad to put Americans back to work and bring the downturn to an end.[36] The regime of confiscatory taxation remained in place until the early 1960s, and it was not until the 1980s that taxes were reduced to a level conducive to the species of entrepreneurship and risk-taking that gives rise to dramatic increases in productivity and prosperity of the sort, not seen since the 1920s, that characterized the past quarter century.

There was this difference between Wilson and the younger Roosevelt. Instead of dismissing the Declaration of Independence, the latter sought to appropriate it and to present himself as Jefferson's heir. The world in which the sage of Monticello had lived was gone, he observed. The frontier had closed, and the United States was no longer a land of "equal opportunity for all." Americans now lived in a world of "large combinations." Theodore Roosevelt's attempt to turn back the clock by busting up the trusts had failed, and "opportunity" in the world of business "has narrowed." No one "saw the situation more clearly" than had Wilson. "Where Jefferson had feared the encroachment of political power on the lives of individuals," the twenty-eighth president of the United States had recognized "that the new power was financial," that "the highly centralized economic system" was "the despot of the 20th century, on whom great masses of individuals relied for their safety and their livelihood, and whose irresponsibility and greed (if it were not controlled) would reduce them to starvation and penury."

In this speech, the younger Roosevelt was not as demagogic as he would later be. He did not cast himself as a secular Messiah driving "the money-changers from their high seats in the temple of our civilization," as he would in his First Inaugural Address. He thought it sufficient on this occasion to say that what was needed now, in a time of depression, was not the "discovery or exploitation of natural resources, nor necessarily" the production of "more goods." It was "the soberer, less dramatic business of administering resources and plants already in hand, of seeking to reestablish foreign markets for our surplus production, of meeting the problem of underconsumption, of adjusting production to consumption, of distributing wealth and products more equitably, of adapting existing economic organizations to the service of the people." In short, the younger Roosevelt pointedly argued, "the task of statesmanship" required a profound "redefinition" of rights. "The old 'rights of personal competency,'" valued by Jefferson, "the right to read, to think, to speak, to choose, and live a mode of life must be respected at all hazards," but "property rights" would have to give way, for, he proudly announced, "the day of enlightened administration has come."[37]

No one saw the consequences as clearly as did Walter Lippmann, for no one was as well-positioned as he. Lippmann had been a leading progressive. At Harvard College, he had dabbled in socialism. Some four years after his graduation, he had joined Herbert Croly and Walter Weyl in founding *The New Republic*, and in 1914, he had published the influential progressive tract *Drift and Mastery: An Attempt to Diagnose the Current Unrest*. For a brief time, during the First World War, Lippmann had been an advisor to Woodrow Wilson. After the war, in which he witnessed the effectiveness of propaganda, Lippmann began to harbor doubts about the progressive conviction that popular sovereignty and governance by experts can easily be reconciled. In *Public Opinion*, published in 1922, he called into question the capacity of ordinary citizens to discern what was going on; and in *The Phantom Public*, published five years later, he expressed doubts as to whether it made any sense at all to speak of the public interest in the manner in which the progressives did: as something radically distinct from and in tension with individual rights and the diverse private interests of the citizens.

In 1932, thinking that there was no alternative, Lippmann voted for Franklin Delano Roosevelt. But by 1937 he had come to entertain grave misgivings. He had noticed that, while

> the partisans who are now fighting for the mastery of the modern world wear shirts of different colors, their weapons are drawn from the same armory, their doctrines are variations of the same theme, and they go forth to battle singing the same tune with slightly different words. . . .
>
> Throughout the world, in the name of progress, men who call themselves communists, socialists, fascists, nationalists, progressives, and even liberals, are unanimous in holding that government with its instruments of coercion must by commanding the people how they shall live, direct the course of civilization and fix the shape of things to come. . . . [T]he premises of authoritarian collectivism have become the working beliefs, the self-evident assumptions, the unquestioned axioms, not only of all the revolutionary regimes, but of nearly every effort which lays claim to being enlightened, humane, and progressive.
>
> So universal is the dominion of this dogma over the minds of contemporary men that no one is taken seriously as a statesman or a theorist who does not come forward with proposals to magnify the power of public officials and to extend and multiply their intervention in human affairs. Unless he is authoritarian and collectivist, he is a mossback, a reactionary, at best an amiable eccentric swimming hopelessly against the tide. It is a strong tide. Though despotism is no novelty in human affairs, it is probably true that at no time in twenty-five hundred years has any western government claimed for itself a jurisdiction over men's lives comparable with that which is officially attempted in totalitarian states. . . .
>
> But it is even more significant that in other lands where men shrink from the ruthless policy of these regimes, it is commonly assumed that the movement of events must be in the same direction. Nearly everywhere the mark of a progressive is that he relies at last upon the increased power of officials to improve the condition of men.

What worried Lippmann the most—what had worried Coolidge, and what should worry us still—was the failure of those who considered themselves progressives to "remember how much of what they cherish as progressive has come by emancipation from political dominion, by the limitation of power, by the release of personal energy from authority and collective coercion." He cited "the whole long struggle to extricate conscience, intellect, labor, and personality from the bondage of prerogative, privilege, monopoly, authority." It was, he said, "the gigantic heresy of an apostate generation" to suppose that "there has come into the world during this generation some new element which makes it necessary for us to undo the work of emancipation, to retrace the steps men have taken to limit the power of rulers, which compels us to believe that the way of enlightenment in affairs is now to be found by intensifying authority and enlarging its scope."[38] It is with Lippmann's warning in mind that we should resume our attempt to understand the present discontents in light of what we can learn from Montesquieu, Rousseau, and Tocqueville.

THE ADMINISTRATIVE STATE

The progressive movement, as such, never quite managed to translate the intellectual hegemony that it achieved into political power. Like Guizot, Thiers, and Tocqueville himself, the progressive exponents of the science of politics never fully mastered the art of government. In their way stood the American founding, the institutions established between 1776 and 1789, the mores and manners generated by the political settlement worked out between 1776 and 1800 and readjusted in the period stretching from 1861 to 1876, and the entrenched party system to which those developments had given rise. Americans were used to managing their own affairs by way of local and state governments; they had forged political parties for this purpose, and they were instinctively reluctant to cede control to a centralized administration dominated by a distant and patronizing intellectual elite.

In fits and starts, however, under the influence of progressive political science, the administrative state began to take shape in the last decades of the nineteenth century and in the first two decades of the twentieth century—at first, locally, and, then, at the national level.[39] Since then, under the tutelage of the progressives and their successors, those who govern us have gotten into the habit, deplored by Tocqueville, of "judging themselves responsible for the actions and for the individual destiny" of those they rule. To an ever increasing degree they have taken it upon themselves "to guide and enlighten each of" us "in the different activities of his life"; and, where they think it necessary, they are ready, willing, and even eager "to render" the citizen "happy despite himself." Moreover, as the outlook of the progressives took hold, "public administration" in America became "not only more centralized, but more inquisitive and more detailed."

Everywhere in the United States, as in Tocqueville's Europe, it "penetrates further into private affairs now than before; it regulates in its manner more actions, and smaller actions, and with every passing day it establishes itself more fully beside, around, and above each individual for the purpose of assisting him, counseling him, and constraining him" (II.iv.5, pp. 253–63).

At the national level, this development first fully took flight with Theodore Roosevelt, who turned the office of the president into what he called "a bully pulpit,"[40] and it gained ground under Woodrow Wilson, who exploited to the hilt the opportunities afforded by the First World War for a demonstration of the virtues of centralized administration.[41] The process accelerated and underwent a profound transformation under Franklin Delano Roosevelt, who managed to link a massive expansion of the administrative state with the formation of constituencies dependent on particular services delivered or income transferred and to do so in such a manner as to confer apparent immortality on a considerable array of government programs aimed at redistributing wealth. Under his heirs Lyndon Baines Johnson and Richard Milhous Nixon, the administrative state made even more dramatic gains.[42]

Strictly speaking, none of these men—except, in 1912, the elder Roosevelt and arguably Wilson as well[43]—could be classed as a progressive. They were partisan politicians of a familiar sort, operating within an inherited frame, and the younger Roosevelt, Johnson, and Nixon doled out favors and exploited special interests in a manner that the progressives of an earlier time, with their high-minded disdain for patronage and partisan politics, would have heartily disliked. These presidents faced genuine crises—among them, not just World War I, but also the Great Depression, World War II, the Cold War, and a long-overdue reckoning with regard to the place that was to be accorded African Americans in American life—and, when there was not a crisis ready to hand, they invented one.[44] In their eagerness to regiment the larger society, these presidents and their epigone were forever in quest for what William James once described with a felicitous phrase as "the moral equivalent of war."[45] They seized upon political opportunities, and in every case they thought it to their advantage, and perhaps even to that of the country as a whole, that they respond to these crises, genuine and imaginary, and exploit these opportunities by strengthening and extending the scope of the central administration in something akin to the fashion that the old progressives had once advised. From war, depression, and other crises, real or imagined, the administrative state has drawn strength.[46]

This process was accelerated immensely by a shift that began taking place in the late nineteenth century as populist reformers within the states, some of them influenced by the progressives, found ways to get around the provision in the

Constitution stipulating that U.S. senators be elected by the state legislatures. This shift was completed in April 1913 with the ratification of the Seventeenth Amendment to the Constitution—which, by establishing the direct, popular election of senators, severed, once and for all, the dependence of the U.S. Senate on the state legislatures and thereby eliminated the principal safeguard the state governments possessed against federal encroachment on their prerogatives. When matched with the Sixteenth Amendment to the Constitution, ratified in February of that same year, which legalized federal taxation of income, this shift in electoral practice paved the way for a massive expansion of the federal government in size and in scope and for the gradual transformation of local and state governments into instruments for the implementation of policies and programs devised in Washington, D.C.[47]

In the United States, there never has been a rationalizing revolutionary regime dedicated to wiping the slate clean, capable of abolishing the states in the way that abbé Emmanuel Joseph Sieyès and the Constituent Assembly eliminated the ancient provinces of France, and intent, as Sieyès and his associates had been, on establishing departments or the like, geometrically identical, more or less equal in population, and ideally suited to the exigencies of central administration.[48] Nor has there been a Napoleon Bonaparte, prepared to appoint prefects to manage local affairs and eager and able to impose on all and sundry a rational, uniform code of laws. We live, as a consequence, with an untidy compromise. The localities and the states still exist, just as they did in Tocqueville's day. Elections take place. There are school boards; town, city, county, and state governments; and they still matter—even if, on a great and growing variety of subjects, they take their orders from a national government that offers them vast sums in funding in return for strict compliance with its every whim. It is a hodgepodge, but with every passing year the burden of regulation becomes more intolerable and the number of mandates with increasing rapidity grows. Moreover, nearly all of the regulations imposed are devised by unelected civil servants and political appointees to whom Congress, undeniably in breach of the Constitution's separation of powers, has delegated both legislative and executive responsibilities;[49] and next to nothing with regard to these is examined and voted on by elected officials who can be held responsible by the voting public for the consequences of what has been done. We have private corporations, but they, too, to a remarkable degree, are dependent on federal largess, and with public contracts and participation in interstate commerce comes massive regulation. We possess private universities and colleges, but, if a single student in attendance at one of these takes a dime in federally guaranteed loans, it, too, must submit to federal regulation; and, under the administration of George W. Bush, there was an abortive move on the part of the secretary of education to deny accreditation to institutions of higher learning that refuse to fall in line. With every passing year, in every sphere of life, uniformity becomes more pervasive, and individual Americans have less and less control over the decisions that shape their lives. If local newspapers have slowly been dying out for half a century or more, it is merely a symptom of a much larger trend. Why should anyone bother to read about local shenanigans that do not signify?

A DRIFT TOWARD OLIGARCHY

There is in the United States no *noblesse de l'État*. We possess nothing quite like the École nationale d'administration, and we do not regard the state as the State. The greatest of our universities play a highly significant role in preparing men and women for public life, but they turn out tens of thousands of graduates every year, and they do not possess a monopoly. We draw our public officials, our civil servants, and our corporate leaders from a considerable number of disparate sources. They have attended a great variety of universities. Some, in fact, have attended none. They come from all walks of life. This is our strength. If our polity evidences oligarchical features—and all representative democracies do—we can at least take pride in the fact that no one can easily predict who is likely to rise and who is likely to fall; and because our political parties generally choose their candidates for local and state office, for the U. S. House of Representatives, and for the Senate in primaries, developments cannot easily be controlled from the top, and no one really knows what the outcome will be.

Even here, however, there is serious reason for concern. The citizen-legislator disappeared long ago. We are now ruled by women and men who make a profession of politics, and reelection is all too often their overriding concern. In recent years, thanks to computers, gerrymandering, once an art, has become a science; and, to an increasing degree, constituencies are groomed for candidates rather than vice versa. In similar fashion, what is euphemistically called "campaign finance reform"—which was aimed initially, or so it was said, at eliminating corruption, and which is now putatively aimed also at reducing the influence of wealth on politics more generally[50]—has made it much more difficult for insurgencies to develop within the parties and much easier for incumbents to secure their own reelection (beginning, precisely as one would expect, with the self-interested, bipartisan cadre of incumbents who passed the pertinent law). The effect is a species of sclerosis, in which next to no one, once elected to the federal House of Representatives, is ever voted out. In effect, these elections are fixed.[51]

At the same time, the courts have grown increasingly assertive. With the tacit connivance of senators subject to election in constituencies which cannot be gerrymandered and desperate to avoid taking sides on controversial measures, the judges have taken up Woodrow Wilson's challenge, and they now treat our frame of government as a "living Constitution." In the process, they have twisted the original document beyond recognition, and time and again they have substituted their will in a fashion utterly transparent for that of legislators who are genuinely accountable to the voters. It is difficult to think of any major issue dividing Americans in the past sixty years—apart from those pertaining to taxation, war, and peace—in which Congress has resolutely taken the lead. Thanks in large part to the timidity natural to those intent on making a living from politics, we live in an age of judicial supremacy.[52]

The reforms introduced over the past forty years by the major parties with regard to presidential selection, seconded by "campaign finance reform," have in a similar fashion restricted the free play of politics and public debate. It was once possible for a relative unknown, eager to take up a set of issues neglected by those in power, to raise money from a handful of wealthy individuals and to mount a campaign aimed at persuading party stalwarts and elected officials from within his party that he was a plausible candidate. Now one must be fabulously rich at the outset, a celebrity already well-known, a favorite of the media elite, vice president of the United States, or a former president's son, sibling, or spouse before one even stands a chance. The consequence is a marked narrowing of choices well before the intraparty campaign has even begun, a dependence on certain well-known families, and great difficulty in winnowing out those discovered in the course of the campaign to be unsuitable.

Despite all of the obstacles, then—thanks largely to the professionalization and nationalization of American politics, to the direct election of Senators, to refinements in the science of gerrymandering, to legislative acquiescence in the establishment of judicial supremacy, to the proliferation of presidential primaries, and to "campaign finance reform"—there is now in America a tolerably cohesive and stable governing elite. Virtually every piece of legislation its members devise and virtually every decision handed down by those from within its ranks who serve on the U.S. Supreme Court have as their witting or unwitting consequence an expansion of the administrative state and a tightening on us of the federal government's grasp. That so much of this is now done in the name of newly minted "rights" is testimony to Franklin Delano Roosevelt's astonishing mastery of what Tocqueville called "the art of government."[53]

THE PRICE OF PROGRAMMATIC RIGHTS

In private, if not in public, the bulk of those within our bipartisan political elite would find little to quarrel with in the annual message sent to Congress by President Roosevelt on 11 January 1944, wherein he asserted that the vision which had informed the American founding was an anachronism and then set out to redeem his promise to redefine our rights:

> This Republic had its beginning, and grew to its present strength, under the protection of certain inalienable political rights—among them the right of free speech, free press, free worship, trial by jury, freedom from unreasonable searches and seizures. They were our rights to life and liberty.
>
> As our Nation has grown in size and stature, however—as our industrial economy expanded—these political rights proved inadequate to assure us equality in the pursuit of happiness.
>
> We have come to a clear realization of the fact that true individual freedom cannot exist without economic security and independence. "Necessitous men are not free men." People who are hungry and out of a job are the stuff of which dictatorships are made.
>
> In our day these economic truths have become accepted as self-evident. We have accepted, so to speak, a second Bill if Rights under which a new basis of security and prosperity can be established for all.

This "second Bill of Rights," which aims, as Roosevelt tellingly put it, to "assure us equality in the pursuit of happiness," was never made a formal part of the Constitution, but, in effect, it has been read into that document by succeeding administrations and by the federal and state courts, and it now serves as an extralegal standard by which our government and its policies are judged. The list of "rights" that must be guaranteed is long, and it is meant in stages to grow and grow, for Roosevelt intimates that it is incomplete:

> The right to a useful and remunerative job in the industries, or shops or farms or mines of the nation;
>
> The right to earn enough to provide adequate food and clothing and recreation;
>
> The right of every farmer to raise and sell his products at a return which will give him and his family a decent living;
>
> The right of every business man, large and small, to trade in an atmosphere of freedom from unfair competition and domination by monopolies at home or abroad;
>
> The right of every family to a decent home;

The right to adequate medical care and the opportunity to achieve and enjoy good health;

The right to adequate protection from the economic fears of old age, sick-
ness, accident, and unemployment;

The right to a good education.[54]

Every item on this list that Roosevelt denominated a right is, of course, something intrinsically desirable and good; every item is arguably an element within
the "happiness" that the Founding Fathers expected most Americans to pursue.
But in their day, and in Tocqueville's as well, it was taken for granted that no one
had a "right" to such goods. They were not a matter for public provision; their
achievement was a task for individuals, acting on their own and in cooperation
with their families, their neighbors, and friends. These good things were not
items to which anyone was simply entitled; they had to be earned, and with the
earning came a certain dignity and pride. Moreover, it was up to individuals, acting on their own behalf, to determine for themselves what "happiness" meant.
Liberty consisted to a considerable degree in taking responsibility for one's own
well-being and for that of one's family. It was in possessing this liberty and in being saddled with this responsibility that men were deemed equal, and it was their
possession of this liberty and the allocation to them of this responsibility that government was established to protect.[55]

Moreover, at the time of the founding, Americans believed—and no one
more fervently than Thomas Jefferson—that the expansion in centralized administration necessary to guarantee "equality in the pursuit of happiness" and
requisite for the provision of such goods was incompatible with the protection of
the "political rights" that Roosevelt would later list in his message to Congress.[56]
Tocqueville was of the same opinion. In September 1848, when the Constituent
Assembly considered writing into the constitution of the Second Republic a provision guaranteeing to every French citizen "the right to work," he rose to issue a
stern warning. Inherent in such a commitment to programmatic rights, he argued, there was a "fatal necessity" which would ultimately require the sacrifice
of liberty. To make good on the promise implicit in this guarantee, he contended, the state would itself have to become the employer of last resort, in
which case it would itself become an industrial power, "gradually accumulating
in its own hands the capital of individuals." Or if it somehow managed to escape
this "fatal necessity," it would "be drawn" no less "fatally into attempting" a general and systematic "regimentation of industry." In the end, it would become either "the sole owner of all property" or "the great and unique organizer of work."

Behind this particular constitutional proposal, and the socialist program more generally, Tocqueville discerned "a profound mistrust of liberty, of human reason," and "a profound contempt for the individual taken on his own, for the human condition" itself. This hijacking of the rhetoric of rights was, he asserted, part and parcel of a larger "attempt—continuous, varied, incessant—to maim, to curtail, to impair human liberty in every fashion." Behind it, he found "the idea that the State ought not to be the director of the society only, but that it ought to be, so to speak, the master of every man—what do I say?—his master, his preceptor, his pedagogue; for fear of allowing him to fail, the State should situate itself unceasingly beside him, above him, around him to guide him, protect him, restrain him, sustain him." In a word, he said, this idea demands "confiscation"—not just of property, but "to a greater or lesser degree the confiscation of human liberty" as well. Socialism was, in his opinion, "a new formula for servitude," and in the battle against it, he was not prepared to give an inch.[57]

On this point, Tocqueville and our forebears were surely right. For in the course of the past seventy-five years, as our government has conferred on its citizens the extensive array of programmatic rights now called "entitlements," there has been a steady erosion of our political and our private rights.[58] To grasp why this is so, one must begin with the recognition that there is one great—one might even say, insuperable—obstacle to guaranteeing the citizens of a nation "equality in the pursuit of happiness," and that obstacle is what Tocqueville calls "the inequality of intellect." As we have already noted (III.1, above), the equality for which democratic peoples hunger cannot be achieved. No matter how "democratic the *état social* and the political constitution of a people may be," thanks to the natural "inequality of intellect," the equality that they desire "retreats before them every day without ever concealing itself from view; and in withdrawing, it draws them on in pursuit. Unceasingly, they believe that they are going to lay hold of it, and it escapes unceasingly from their grasp. They see it close enough to know its charms, they do not approach it close enough to enjoy it, and they die before having fully savored its sweetness." It is democratic envy, Tocqueville claims, that accounts for "the singular melancholy" displayed by the inhabitants of democratic countries "in the bosom of their abundance," and it explains as well "the disgust with life that comes at times to lay hold of them in the midst of an easy and tranquil existence" (*DA* II.ii.13, p. 125).

It is envy also that explains the democratic propensity to impose punitive taxation. In Jacksonian America, as Tocqueville noticed, wealth was regarded as suspect, and the wealthy were virtually banned from the political arena (I.ii.2, pp. 139–40). If their property was nonetheless safe, it was because impecunious Americans hoped to become prosperous someday themselves (II.iii.21, p. 214). If, however, as Roosevelt insisted, it really is the task of the government to "assure" its citizens "equality in the pursuit of happiness," property cannot be sacrosanct. If the government is to give, first it must take. For one's talent, diligence, discipline, parsimony, and prudence, if one possesses these attributes, one must be made to pay; and for one's incompetence, laziness, self-indulgence, extravagance, and folly, if one exhibits these defects, one is entitled to receive compensation. In this fashion, that which in the past would have been called theft came, in the United States, to be denominated *social* justice. Persons, we are now frequently told, have rights; property has none. But, of course, the attack on property rights is, in fact, an attack on persons who happen to be property-holders, and it is an assault as well on the industriousness and the ingenuity that enabled them to acquire. We have forgotten what James Madison so clearly understood—that it is from "the diversity in the faculties of men" that "the rights of property originate," and that "the protection of these faculties is the first object of Government"[59]—and with the growth in what are euphemistically called "transfer payments," our democracy has step by step become a giant kleptocracy. In 2006, at a time when there was a great clamor for tax hikes on the well-to-do and we were repeatedly told that the wealthy were not paying their fair share, the top 1 percent in income paid 40 percent; the top 10 percent, 71 percent; and the top 50 percent, 97.1 percent of the federal income taxes collected in the United States.[60]

Moreover, punitive taxation is merely the beginning. As a consequence of the demand for equality, our right to speak freely at election time has now been abridged. In the two months before the vote, we can—at least for the time being—still shout, march about, and demonstrate in the streets. But as individuals or by banding together into groups—lest, we are told, at the only moment when voters actually pay close attention to what is going on, some should have more influence than others—we can no longer purchase time on television, spots on the radio, or space in the press in which to praise one candidate or draw attention to the defects of another. For all practical purposes, at this juncture, ordinary Americans are gagged. The only exceptions belong to our new aristocracy the media elite: those who own or have easy access to newspapers, television stations, or radio outlets.[61]

Of course, we still have recourse to the Internet, at least for the time being, and we have not yet outlawed advocating certain controversial opinions, as have the French and others on the continent of Europe. Nor do we haul journalists before kangaroo courts parading as human rights commissions and try them for the crime of directing our attention to deeply unpleasant truths, as do our nearest neighbors to the north. The United States has proved to be a haven for outspoken Europeans and Canadians such as Oriana Fallaci and Mark Steyn. But this may be short-lived. On our campuses, both public and private, though they see themselves as bastions of academic freedom, there are now speech codes restricting conversation, discussion, and debate lest someone take umbrage; and instructors who risk offense by raising genuinely controversial questions in class and by considering them from all sides court public humiliation, if not prompt dismissal as well. That which Tocqueville once wrote concerning America is now doubly true of its universities. Within them, "the majority draws a formidable circle around thought." Within its limits, an instructor and scholar "is free, but misfortune awaits the man who dares to go beyond these. It is not that he has to fear an *auto-da-fé*," but if he offends progressive opinion, he can expect to be "an object of aversion in every form and the butt of everyday persecution" (I.ii.7, p. 200).[62] In consequence, among those accorded the privilege of teaching at our leading colleges and universities, the range of acceptable opinion is now so narrow that, when something untoward happens that strikes a nerve, it is all too easy for them to conduct themselves more in the manner of a lynch mob than a faculty dedicated to a dispassionate search for the truth.[63]

Nor is this modern inquisition restricted to the academy. Everywhere in the United States, to an increasing degree, compassion trumps candor. Like those who teach and study in our institutions of higher learning, employees in large corporations are routinely put through sensitivity training. Such is the petty tyranny with which we are now accustomed to live.

This erosion of rights extends into every sphere. In the name of child protection, we allow the coaching of witnesses, and we deny defendants the right to confront their accusers;[64] we encourage neighbors to become police informants and to report on those who fail to strap their offspring into car seats; we subject parents of young children who have accidents to close questioning in separate rooms and to humiliation and harassment at the hands of state officials belonging to the "caring" professions; and we send SWAT teams to pry children loose from parents wrongly accused of abuse or neglect. As a consequence of the so-called war on drugs, we are no longer protected from unreasonable searches and seizures.[65] For the putative purpose of promoting equality, we are required systematically to practice racial and sexual discrimination in hiring.[66] One price we paid for the civil rights revolution was an evisceration of the constitutional guarantee against double jeopardy.[67] And for similar reasons, local and state governments, the only governments that lie within the reach of ordinary citizens, have been deprived of the autonomy that they once possessed. The presiding presumption is that we Americans are vicious, corrupt, depraved, and incompetent—not to be trusted with the civil liberties guaranteed in the Bill of Rights, unworthy of equal treatment under the law, and utterly incapable of properly rearing our offspring and governing ourselves.

There is much greater freedom and decentralization in the United States of America than there is France, to be sure. Moreover, in the United States, we have not yet put a straitjacket on our economy. In fact, thanks in part to the critique of central planning articulated by Ludwig von Mises and Friedrich Hayek,[68] and thanks in part to Ronald Reagan and the collapse of communism in Europe, there was a measure of deregulation at the federal level; in modest ways tax rates were actually reduced; and the vision of regimentation and rational administration projected under the New Deal and revived forty years ago by John Kenneth Galbraith in *The New Industrial State* came to seem not just quaint and anachronistic but faintly embarrassing as well.[69] It nonetheless became harder and harder for a company to fire employees, especially if they belonged to "protected categories"; the burden of regulation grew apace; and market entry, though much easier than on the continent of Europe, became increasingly difficult. Large corporations now spend enormous sums on regulatory compliance. The owners of small businesses find that they can very easily break the law without having a clue that they are doing so.

THE EROSION OF MORES, MANNERS, AND RELIGION

Many of the moral obstacles to majority tyranny identified in *Democracy in America* have also now disappeared. In the United States, the legal profession and the courts were once, as Tocqueville observed, a restraint on the populist impulse. Today, their game is demagoguery, and their aim is to anticipate, strengthen, guide, and profit from the impulse that they once restrained. In the name of democracy, legal activists and politicized judges are willing to sweep away forms and formalities; in the name of progress, they are prepared to run roughshod over the legislative branch, especially in the states and localities; and, in the name of compassion, they are prepared to sanction systematic theft.[70] Whether genuinely responsible for a tort or not, the defendant who has deep pockets is made to pay.[71]

Civil associations still exist, to be sure. But, within the administrative state, the only ones that really flourish are lobbying operations, staffed at the national level, with little local presence and virtually no civic engagement. Moreover, to an increasing degree, civil associations subsist as shells for the sole purpose of securing federal grants and subsidies. As such, they are instruments of the administrative state and not of civic agency.[72] In effect, what Tocqueville once said with France in mind now pertains to the United States as well. Most Americans may still "admit, as a general principle, that the public power should not intervene in private affairs, but, as an exception, each of them desires that it aid him in the special affair that preoccupies him," and for this reason "the sphere of the central power extends itself imperceptibly in every direction" despite the fact that many individuals wish "to restrain it" overall. Our country has aged and, as Tocqueville predicted, it has steadily become more centralized. "Time works on behalf" of this process, he wrote. "All accidents are to its profit; individual passions come to its aid without [anyone] being aware of it" (II.iv.3, pp. 243–44, n. 1). In consequence, where once we were citizens, we have become clients, and ours is the age of the lobbyist.

As a people, if we are to judge solely by attendance in church, Americans are still comparatively religious. But no one today would describe religion as "the first" of our "political institutions," as Tocqueville once did (II.ii.9, p. 227), for it is no longer generally the case that our churches provide us with a moral anchor and impress upon us a severity in morals. Most of the mainline Protestant sects now fiercely advocate a toleration and compassionate embrace of that which they once regarded as abhorrent: if sanctimony is sustained, it is solely in offering succor to sin.[73] Those Catholic priests and evangelical Protestant ministers who are genuinely unsympathetic with the culture of self-indulgence all too frequently lack the moral authority required for persuasion. In our day, as in Tocqueville's time, they fear their flocks, and they tailor their sermons to accommodate current fashion. The American Catholic Church is quick to hand out annulments, and the evangelical Protestants wink at serial monogamy punctuated by a recurrence of divorce.[74]

Moreover, in the course of the past sixty years the courts have interpreted the First Amendment to the Constitution in such a fashion as to ban religion from the public sphere in a manner reminiscent of the militant *laïcisme* that has long formed the basis for public policy in France; and in keeping with the logic underpinning these court decisions, some states have excised the phrase "under God" from the version of the Pledge of Allegiance recited in public schools. It is as if the First Amendment were designed to provide Americans with freedom from religion and to protect the polity from contamination at its hands. During the same period, elite opinion, especially as situated within the universities,[75] Hollywood, and the national media, gradually became virulently hostile to and contemptuous of religious faith; and, in certain highly influential quarters, strong religious convictions are now treated publicly as a disqualification for election or appointment to high office. Religious Americans who feel threatened by these developments may be inclined to push back, but they are thwarted at every turn. If the present trend continues, they will eventually come to occupy in America the pariah status to which they are to an ever increasing degree consigned in many countries on the continent of Europe. At this point, Christians will sink into an embarrassed silence.

There is no need to dwell on the state of American sexual mores. It suffices to say that the sexual division of labor, so admired by Tocqueville, has gone by the boards; that young faculty members who wonder out loud whether its abandonment was a good thing risk having their careers brought to an untimely end; that stay-at-home mothers are quite commonly treated with condescension, if not open contempt, especially by women in the professions; that among sophisticates manliness and femininity are considered hopelessly passé;[76] that in public, as a matter of good manners, we are now required to pretend that, apart from the role that biology assigns the two sexes in procreation and nursing, the differences in conduct generally exhibited by women and men are no more reflective of the dictates of nature than is the assignment of gender to particular nouns in ancient Greek, Latin, German, Italian, and French; and that a university president, such as Larry Summers of Harvard, who fails in public to give lip service to this pious pretense courts immediate dismissal.[77] It goes without saying that chastity and fidelity are no longer as fashionable as they were in Tocqueville's day,[78] and the unavoidable consequence, which is of profound political significance, is that quite frequently, in America, the home is no longer the haven from *inquiétude* that it once was.

In the United States, divorce has become so commonplace that, by way of anticipation, couples on the verge of marrying often sign prenuptial agreements specifying its terms. Matrimony—the public ritual in which, as the word's etymology reminds us, motherhood is the aim, and, to that end, a man pledges to take responsibility for a particular woman's future offspring—is itself on the wane, especially among those not college-educated.[79] Moreover, to an increasing degree, ambitious young women in college, and high school girls who are college-bound, prefer casually "hooking up" to the rituals of courtship and romantic love;[80] and, within our educated elite, a species of serial concubinage called "partnership" is now in vogue. When one is introduced to someone's "partner," as often now takes place, one might be inclined, if one were mischievous, to ask what business the two are in, what are the terms of the contract between them, how long their partnership is expected to last, how many other partners they have, and precisely what it is that they share—but a frank exposure of the subterfuge would be thought unconscionably rude: so, out of politeness, we must pretend that nothing is amiss.[81]

In keeping with this new ethos, in which marriage delayed generally comes to be marriage denied, out-of-wedlock births have soared; the overall birthrate has plummeted, especially among those who are themselves native born; and the casual killing of children as yet unborn is anything but rare. Our euphemisms betray us. We have "adult bookstores" that no genuine adult would visit and "gentlemen's clubs" that no gentleman would frequent; and in the name of "reproductive rights," over the thirty-five years that have passed since the U.S. Supreme Court handed down its decision in *Roe v. Wade*, we have put a violent end to nearly 50 million human lives. With what we have sacrificed, one could populate a country of considerable size.[82]

Perhaps worst of all, many of the best educated among us—coarsened by a cowardly surrender to the fashionable conviction that killing a helpless human being for one's own convenience is a matter of right—have come to adopt what Tocqueville called the "impious maxim" that "everything is permitted in the interests of society." Just as, in the past, compulsory sterilization was commonplace and medical personnel associated with the Public Health Service, intent on improving our understanding of syphilis, were willing in the name of progress to deny proper medical treatment over a period of decades to ill-informed, comparatively helpless African Americans known to be infected with the disease,[83] so today their spiritual heirs think nothing of creating human beings in order to harvest from them, by way of premeditated murder, stem cells useful for medical research.[84] In our progressive age, we mistake wants for rights and talk of the latter incessantly, but no one who is not generally regarded as retrograde seriously holds it to be self-evident that "all men are created equal; that they are endowed by their Creator with certain inalienable rights; [and] that among these," the first and most important, the one that takes priority over all others, is the right to "life."[85] If we continue on the path that we now traverse, soon, like the Dutch,[86] we will casually kill the decrepit and old. After all, in Oregon, a progressive state which has always seen itself as a model for the nation, "physician-assisted suicide," as it is so delicately called, has been sanctioned by the law since 1994.

There are, indeed, a great many in America, especially among those who think of themselves as progressives, who share something akin to the conviction that Tocqueville attributed to his fellow Europeans, and that many educated Europeans still echo today—that "*the spirit of religion*" is incompatible with "*the spirit of liberty*" and that in the United States "the liberty and happiness of the human race fall short in nothing" apart from the fact that the Americans do not "believe with Spinoza in the eternity of the world and assert with Cabanis that the brain secretes thought" (I.i.6, pp. 35–36; ii.9, pp. 227–29). Moreover, the Americans who subscribe to something on the order of these propositions make up a high proportion of the 25 percent of the population who tell pollsters, such as Scott Rasmussen, that the country is not "generally fair and decent" and who express doubts as to whether the world would be better off if other nations were more like their own.[87] The more favorable one is to democracy's despotic drift, the greater one's present discontent.

In sum, the difference between the United States of America and France would now appear to be merely a matter of degree. In our mores and manners, in our attitudes with regard to religion and morality, as well as in our political institutions and practices, we are more like Tocqueville's compatriots than like the Americans of his day. And the fears that he expressed with regard to the French now apply with considerable force to us as well, for we have forgotten that human life is sacred, that it is unjust to take from one to give to another, that libertinism is fatal to liberty, and that strong, stable families and personal self-discipline are prerequisites for sustaining a government limited with regard to the ends it may pursue and the means it may employ. In the process, we have jettisoned much of the equipment—political, social, moral, and psychological—that in the past enabled us to join together, stand our ground, and resist liberal democracy's despotic drift; and now, denied the benefit of that equipment, we face a worldwide financial panic and an economic downturn more severe than any encountered since the stock market crashed in 1929.

Once again, rational administration has failed us. As in the 1920s, the Federal Reserve Board and the Department of the Treasury persistently pursued an easy-money policy bound to produce "irrational exuburance" in the markets and a bubble followed by a catastrophic decline in prices and a collapse of the credit markets. And we have responded precisely as we did in 1932 — by electing a president and choosing a Congress intent on dramatically increasing the scale and scope of the administrative state.

Our new masters have it in their power to deepen the economic crisis and worsen our distress in the manner of Hoover and the younger Roosevelt. By instituting a second New Deal, as they would very much like to do — by sharply raising taxes on fossil fuels, dividends, and capital gains; by targeting the earnings of the well-to-do; by pursuing protectionism, expanding the regime of programmatic rights, and forcing workers into labor unions — they can discourage investment, curb entrepreneurship, reduce foreign trade, and decisively slow economic growth, or even bring it to a lasting halt, while offering to those consigned to the dole thereby a dependence upon the generosity of an all-encompassing state. Just how ruthless they will prove to be on this occasion, just how far they intend to hustle us down the path we tread, remains as yet undetermined.

The only thing that is crystal clear is the direction of our drift and the nature of the threat we face. Walter Lippmann's warning is as apt today as it was in 1937 —

for "the premises of authoritarian collectivism" are once again, as they were then, "the working beliefs, the self-evident assumptions, the unquestioned axioms" behind "nearly every effort which lays claim to being enlightened, humane, and progressive," and hardly anyone today "is taken seriously as a statesman or a theorist who does not come forward with proposals to magnify the power of public officials and to extend and multiply their intervention in human affairs." Like the younger Roosevelt, our new leader poses as a secular Messiah; his minions believe, as did the progressives of an earlier time, that there has recently come into the world "some new element which makes it necessary for us to undo the work of emancipation" achieved by our forebears and "to retrace the steps men have taken to limit the power of rulers"; and in the ranks of our compatriots they will find many prepared to sacrifice self-reliance and personal independence for a promise of security no government can keep. The hour is, indeed, late.

To those caught up in the maelstrom, recent developments may well seem dramatic, but, in truth, they serve merely to highlight the plight that we have been in for more than three quarters of century. In consequence of our abandonment of our religious and moral heritage, of our rejection of the spirit of individual responsibility and the principles of limited government, over our own people today, as over the French, there "is elevated an immense, tutelary power," whose aim is to take "sole charge of assuring their enjoyment and of watching over their fate." In America, as in France and in Europe more generally, this power is "absolute, attentive to detail, regular, provident, and gentle." It works willingly for our "happiness," but it exacts a price, for "it wishes to be the only agent and the sole arbiter of that happiness." It provides for our security, it foresees and supplies our needs, it guides us in our principal affairs, it directs our industry, it regulates our testaments, it divides our inheritances, and it covers the "surface" of our society "with a network of petty regulations—complicated, minute, and uniform." Generally, it is gentle; almost never is it harsh. "It does not break wills; it softens them, bends them, and directs them." Only on the rarest of occasions "does it force one to act, but it constantly opposes itself to one's acting on one's own; it does not destroy, it prevents things from being born; it does not tyrannize, it gets in the way: it curtails, it enervates, it extinguishes, it stupefies." And, step by step, relentlessly, with every passing day, as we gradually succumb to the spirit of irresponsibility and self-indulgence, this power grows in influence and scope, making us more and more like "a herd of timid and industrious animals, of which the government is the shepherd" (II.iv.6, pp. 265–66).

CONCLUSION

All honor to Jefferson—to the man who, in the concrete pressure of a struggle for national independence by a single people, had the coolness, forecast, and capacity to introduce into a merely revolutionary document, an abstract truth, applicable to all men and all times, and so to embalm it there, that to-day, and in all coming days, it shall be a rebuke and a stumbling-block to the very harbingers of re-appearing tyranny and oppression.

—*Abraham Lincoln*

As should by now be evident, the danger that the world's liberal democracies face today was long ago foreseen. Three hundred years ago, by decisively defeating Louis XIV's France in a series of battles, John Churchill, duke of Marlborough, announced the presence on the world stage of a new species of government, capable of demonstrating that under modern circumstances, Carthage is apt to outpace Rome. In the aftermath, Voltaire, then Montesquieu, visited Great Britain and drew the attention of their compatriots to the virtues of its commercial republican regime. In *The Spirit of Laws*, the latter even intimated that monarchy on the French model was doomed, and he provided a brief, but dense analysis of the workings of the English polity that was consoling and alarming at the same time.

Subsequent events justified the confidence that Montesquieu reposed in England. On more than one occasion, it was appropriate to recall his prediction that "in Europe the last sigh of liberty will be heaved by an Englishman." On more than one occasion, Britain managed to "slow down the velocity" with which "other nations" made their way to "total collapse." And the like could in turn be said of the United States. But the concerns that Montesquieu hinted at seem increasingly apt as well.

The best-constituted of the liberal, commercial republics formed in modern times can claim to provide their citizens with what Montesquieu called "political liberty in its relation with the constitution." Thanks to the separation of powers, they are able to guarantee the rule of law so that "no one will be constrained to do things that the law does not require or prevented from doing those which the law permits him to do." But they lack intermediary powers capable of resisting the central authority, and they do not inspire in those who live under their rule the sense of security and the attendant tranquillity of soul that he called "liberty in relation to the citizen." Instead, in liberal, commercial man, they give rise to a profound sense of _inquiétude_, which renders him uneasy, restless, anxious, and apt to become irrationally afraid. This was, in Montesquieu's opinion, the Achilles heel of the modern republic, for he could easily imagine _inquiétude_ giving way to a species of fear conducive to despotic rule. If, nonetheless, he was sanguine, it was because he was convinced that in England the ongoing struggle between the executive and the legislative powers had the effect of transforming _inquiétude_ into a salutary jealousy of government. As long as government played only a modest role in providing for the economic well-being of its citizens, as long as the patronage it had on offer held little interest for the larger body of citizens, Montesquieu thought English liberty secure.

Jean-Jacques Rousseau was less sanguine than Montesquieu. He accepted the overall analysis presented in _The Spirit of Laws_, and with regard to the poor prospects for European monarchy — where Montesquieu had been reticent — he was breathtakingly frank. But he was by no means optimistic. _Inquiétude_ he took to be an inevitable consequence of man's entry into society, and he was convinced that scientific and technological progress, commercial growth, and a flourishing of the arts — all of which Montesquieu welcomed with open arms — would serve to heighten _amour propre_, to intensify _inquiétude_'s hold on mankind, and to promote human misery thereby. He argued, moreover, that, within commercial society, public opinion is a threat to freedom of the intellect — that in this setting men of surpassing intelligence and ability are exceedingly apt to debase themselves, as had Voltaire, by a vulgar pursuit of popular acclaim. In Rousseau's judgment, religious belief and romantic love might serve to reduce _inquiétude_, and in his political works he presented citizenship on the ancient model as the only plausible remedy.

Of those who sought guidance from Montesquieu and Rousseau in the aftermath of the French Revolution, no one was more acute than Alexis de Tocqueville. He was alert to Montesquieu's muted misgivings, and he recognized the force of Rousseau's critique of bourgeois society. But he was by no means confident that the state would refrain from invading the economic realm; he did not think citizenship on the ancient model any longer a possibility; and scientific and technological progress, commercial growth, and a flourishing of the arts he took as a given. In his judgment, the *inquiétude* so evident within liberal, commercial societies was a product of the democratic social condition, and this equality of condition, which was made manifest to all in the course of the French Revolution, he took to be just and an irreversible fact. He worried—as had Montesquieu before him—that the elimination of the intermediary powers that had given European monarchy its distinctive character might open the way for a descent into despotism, as had happened in France when Napoleon Bonaparte burst upon the scene. He feared, moreover, that, as isolated individuals retreated into their families and into circles of friends, surrendered to majority opinion, focused their attention narrowly on material well-being, and sought help and support from the state, centralized administration would gradually become the norm, and men would ultimately submit to tutelage at the hands of an administrative class not unlike the mandarins who paralyzed imperial China.

In America, to his great delight, Tocqueville discovered a people who had managed to fend off the democratic despotism he saw threatening Europe. Through participation in local government, they gained a sense of their own strength and significance, and they learned how to act in concert. By establishing civil associations at the local level, they became practiced in an art that enabled them to band together for the purpose of achieving ends that they could not have accomplished on their own. The lawyers among them restrained the populist impulse and taught them a salutary respect for forms and formalities. They were sheltered in some measure from *inquiétude* by religious convictions that protected them from moral anarchy; they found comfort and strength in marriages made stable by a sexual division of labor and by the firm adherence of American women to the code of chastity and the dictates of feminine modesty—and all of this instilled in them a fortitude that enabled them to take responsibility for their own well-being.

We live today in the world first discovered by Voltaire and Montesquieu. We profit from the accomplishments of liberal, commercial republicanism, and we grapple with the difficulties first discerned in turn by Montesquieu, Rousseau, and Tocqueville. That our cousins on the European continent should succumb to administrative centralization and democratic despotism is as understandable as it is regrettable. They at least have the excuse that the monarchical absolutism decried by Montesquieu paved the way and that they suffered more grievously in the course of World War I, the Great Depression, World War II, and the Cold

War than did we. In our case, there can be no excuse. Step by step, gradually, and to a considerable degree unwittingly, we have sold our birthright for a mess of pottage.

The fact that we still possess local governments and state governments, civil associations, and vibrant churches, the fact that most of us still marry and pro-create suggests, however, that there is still hope. What would require of the French, and of the Europeans more generally, a revolution far more profound than anyone now contemplates demands of us merely that we firmly resist democracy's drift, and this we can easily enough do if we come to a crystal-clear understanding of the inexorable logic unfolding within our regime and set out—under the guidance of the political science fashioned by Montesquieu and Rousseau and reconfigured by Tocqueville—to reverse the tide. On our part, this will require a great deal of thought concerning particular laws, programs, and policies and concerning mores and manners as well. It will require of us a systematic attempt to bring home to our fellow citizens the dangers they face, a level of civic engagement not recently seen, and a great effort at persuasion—aimed at reminding our compatriots of the central importance that must be ac-corded within a republican polity such as ours to chastity and fidelity, marriage and family, and religious faith; to local and state autonomy; to the maintenance of a firm and fast distinction between legislating, executing, and judging; to the system of checks and balances; to free public debate and freedom of inquiry; and to the right to life, the rights of those suspected or accused, and the right to retain that which one has earned. Above all else, however, we must impress upon our fellow Americans the profound dignity and the crucial importance of citizenship in the broadest sense.

The progressives within our midst, those who are wedded to the administra-tive state and find in its expansion a focus for their ambitions, will hint that all of this is an anachronism, and they will tell us that the concentration of power in Washington is a product of necessity—and, of course, with regard to the second claim, in some measure they have a case. The United States is too large a pres-ence within the world, too powerful, too wealthy, and, as such, too much an ob-ject of envy and resentment, for it to be able to withdraw. As we learned on 7 De-cember 1941, when the Japanese attacked Pearl Harbor, and relearned on 11 September 2001, when Al Q'aeda destroyed the Twin Towers in New York and damaged the Pentagon in Washington, D.C., isolationism is not for us a viable policy. When in the larger world things go badly awry, ultimately we will be a tar-get whether we have opted for the sidelines or not. For our own safety, we must, then, attempt to shape the larger security environment in which we live and trade, and this demands on our part a sizable defense and intelligence establishment; careful planning and provision with regard to defense industries, strategic materials, and technological development; and a genuine and unmistakable readiness to resort to force.

Given the character of our regime, it is doubly important that care be taken in this particular matter. What Montesquieu says concerning the English applies as well to us: "other nations have made their commercial interests give way to their political interests: this one has always made its political interests give way to the interests of its commerce" (*EL* 4.20.7). Moreover, Tocqueville was correct when he warned that "the same interests, the same fears, the same passions, which divert democratic peoples from revolutions, distance them from war," adding that "the *esprit militaire* and the *esprit révolutionnaire* weaken at the same time and because of the same causes." Men of property are now more numerous, he explains, and they are "lovers of peace." There is now a great deal of "movable wealth, which war devours so rapidly"; and in men, "equality inspires indulgence with regard to mores, a softness of heart, a disposition for pity," as well as "a coldness of reason that renders men relatively insensitive [*peu sensible*] to the poetic and violent emotions born among arms—all of these causes join together to extinguish the *esprit militaire*" (*DA* II.iii.22, p. 220). Tocqueville feared, moreover, that where there is an "equality of conditions" and "each citizen" plays next to no role in public affairs, where "all are independent and have goods to lose," men will fear "conquest" far less than the rigors of "war"; and, for this and other reasons, he thought it "necessary to give to peoples rights and an *esprit politique*, which suggests to each citizen some of those interests that induce the nobles within aristocracies to act" (II.iii.26, p. 234).

The advantage that commercial polities gain from this aversion to armed conflict is that they rarely fight unnecessary wars. The disadvantage is that they are reluctant to go to war even when vital interests are at stake. Moreover, after a great struggle, they tend to disarm and to attempt thereafter to provide for their defense on the cheap; and, in doing so, they frequently squander the fruits of victory. The British did this in Montesquieu's youth after the War of the League of Augsburg, and this helped bring on the War of the Spanish Succession; all of the western powers did so in the wake of World War I, and, subsequently, they were resistant to facing up to the untoward consequences of their wishful thinking and neglect—which opened the way for the Nazi juggernaut. In recent years, after the end of the Cold War, our European cousins have once again succumbed to wishful thinking on a preposterous scale; and, if recent polling data is to be trusted, a substantial part of our own population is similarly inclined.[1] If we are not vigilant, if we do not recover what Tocqueville calls the *esprit politique*, the odds are good that we will follow in our cousins' wake. If isolationism returns in the United States, however, it will not look like the isolationism of the 1920s and the 1930s. It will be clothed in the righteous rhetoric of internationalism and of multilateral defense. As our European cousins have discovered, the easiest way to evade responsibility is to refer everything to the Security Council and General Assembly of the United Nations. In this fashion, one can occupy the moral high ground while incurring no expense.

What is true with regard to national defense applies as well to the larger world of commerce. We cannot do without a national currency. Nor can we prosper if there is no national bank, no Federal Reserve Board, and no oversight with regard to fiduciary institutions. In like fashion, it is crucial that the federal government oversee aviation, railroads, interstate highways, and the like, and there may be no alternative to federal allocation of spectrum for radio and television. The fact that crime fairly often ignores state and even national boundaries dictates that there be a federal criminal code and a Federal Bureau of Investigation, and there are obviously other areas in which federal intervention is required.

But there is a great deal that the federal government does that could be handled on the state and local levels just as well, and there are a great many things that it does that do not need doing or that, in fact, do positive harm. Thus, to take the most obvious and important example, we do not need a Federal Election Commission; we do not need elaborate regulations concerning the financing of political campaigns; and we do not need any rules at all restricting when, how, and under what circumstances American citizens may be allowed to speak up with regard to political issues and the merits and demerits of political candidates. The First Amendment was designed to protect political, not commercial, speech, and public debate, not pornography posing as art. Its aim was to rule out the possibility that—in the name of law and order, public integrity, justice, equality, or some other recognized good—Congress and the executive branch would conspire, as they now have, to shut down, restrict, or manage public debate. Its purpose was to guarantee in perpetuity our freedom to seek a redress of grievances, to pursue public office, to support another's candidacy, and to speak our minds on issues of common concern through any available medium. Without this freedom, the framers of the First Amendment feared, we would be helpless when confronted with public authority. The first thing that we should do is to recover what really does constitute our first freedom by repealing all of the pertinent federal legislation and by abolishing the Federal Election Commission in its entirety.

There is, of course, much more to be done. We must restore the separation of powers and put an end to legislating from the bench; we must restore the balance between the federal government and the states. To this end, we must put an end to federal mandates, and we must reduce the size and scope of the federal government. It is, for example, an open question whether we still need a department of agriculture. Farming in America is now largely a matter for agribusiness, which can perfectly well take care of itself. The agricultural price-support programs are a national disgrace—a patronage operation which encourages farmers to till land that should not be cultivated, which transfers wealth from poor Americans to those already prosperous, and which makes it exceedingly hard for farmers in the Third World to find a market for their produce in the United States.

Education is an even more egregious case. There is not now and never has been a justification for there being a department of education. Education may well need public support, but not from the federal government. Public schools are best managed on the local level by teachers accountable to parents—the only individuals guaranteed in the aggregate to care for the genuine well-being of those in school. Under federal guidance—thanks to thousands of mandates having little, if anything, to do with education per se—our schools have gone steadily downhill for decades. Their only hope is local funding and full local control.

What applies to public schools applies with even greater force to higher education. Our colleges and universities became the finest in the world when they were left to their own devices. It is in the years of federal regulation and superintendence that they became top heavy with bureaucracy and ridiculously expensive, fiercely ideological and unwilling to give grades that would distinguish the goats from the sheep, and increasingly hostile to the very idea of liberal education. The only conceivable justification for federal regulation of education is the preposterous conviction, entertained by our administrative class, that ordinary human beings are simply unfit to manage their own affairs.

I limit myself to these examples for a reason. In effecting a general reform, one should begin with what is most obvious, and one should proceed slowly and steadily in well-considered steps, restating one's argument at every turn. If we are to resist the malign effects of democracy's drift, if we are not to become permanent wards of the state, our first operating principle with regard to politics should be that government intervention—wherever it is evidently unjust, as it is in the case of the ethnic spoils system that is euphemistically called "affirmative action,"[2] or tyrannical, as it is in the case of court-mandated busing for the sake of racial balance—should simply be stopped: it is far better to do nothing than to do genuine harm. Our second principle should be that of subsidiarity—if a matter can be handled at the local level, it should be dealt with there and not at the level of the state or federal government. And our third should be that the principle of subsidiarity applies to individuals as well and that there are a great many matters that individual human beings should manage for themselves. Although the Tenth Amendment to the U.S. Constitution, which specifies that "the powers not delegated to the United States by the Constitution, nor prohibited by it to the States, are reserved to the States respectively, or to the people," is now widely regarded as a dead letter, it has not been repealed, and it can and should be revived.

As Tocqueville recognized long ago, human dignity is bound up with taking responsibility for conducting one's own affairs. Every single item mentioned as a "right" on Franklin Delano Roosevelt's list—from useful and remunerative jobs to adequate medical care and a good education—is a matter for personal achievement and provision. A serious attempt on the part of the government to guarantee that absolutely everyone has a useful and remunerative job, adequate medical care, and a good education is certain to result in a tyrannical denial to many of each and every one of these goods. As schoolteachers can testify, the effectual truth of the program entitled "No Child Left Behind" is that in the public schools no child blessed with talent and drive is allowed to get ahead. To the discrepancy between human beings, to what Tocqueville termed "the inequality of intellect," the administrative state is profoundly hostile. In mass society, one size must be made to fit all. It is impossible to "assure" everyone "equality in the pursuit of happiness," but one can pretend to do so, and to this end there has to be social promotion (even at the college level), and we must dumb everything down (as we now systematically do), for the natural inequalities that we refuse to acknowledge really do preclude our leveling up.

Toward the end of his message to Congress, immediately after proposing his "second Bill of Rights," Roosevelt issued an admonition against "the grave dangers" that would be attendant on a "'rightist reaction' in this Nation," arguing that if such a "reaction should develop—if history were to repeat itself and we were to return to the so-called 'normalcy' of the 1920's—then it is certain that even though we shall have conquered our enemies on the battlefields abroad, we shall have yielded to the spirit of Fascism here at home."[3] It was a moment of pure demagoguery, and, as a claim, it was patently false. In fact, something like the opposite was the case, for, as Roosevelt and his advisors knew perfectly well, the New Deal owed a great deal to the fascist example, and the "rights" on his list were all goods that Benito Mussolini and Adolf Hitler had attempted, by way of systematic government intervention, to guarantee to the people of Italy and Germany.[4]

Of course, behind Roosevelt's disgraceful rhetoric, there was a real point: we cannot re-create the small-town America of the 1920s, much less the small-town

America that so impressed Tocqueville in the early 1830s. But this does not mean, as Roosevelt suggested, that we must or should abandon the American ideal of limited government and local self-rule.

For wisdom in these matters, we can turn back to our country's founding documents. Woodrow Wilson to the contrary notwithstanding (III.4, above), the Declaration of Independence is and always will be of "consequence to us," for it contains "a thesis for philosophers" and embodies "a theory of government," precisely as Abraham Lincoln and Calvin Coolidge contended; and the "abstract truth, applicable to all men and all times," that both discerned therein, can be for us, as it was in his day, "a rebuke and a stumbling-block to the very harbingers of re-appearing tyranny and oppression,"[5] for it specifies what we take to be the ends of government, and in doing so it points to the grounds of our dignity as human beings. As, in Lincoln's day, it proved to be an obstacle to Americans' acceptance of slavery as a matter indifferent, to be judged in each separate locality solely with regard to its convenience, so, in our day, it makes it impossible for Americans to make their peace with the modern-day slaughter of the innocents legislated for us by an intellectually bankrupt and morally corrupt Supreme Court.

In the same fashion, the Constitution of 1787 and the original Bill of Rights direct us to the means by which the ends specified in the Declaration of Independence are to be achieved. They specify that our federal government is limited in scope, they specify that there be a genuine separation of powers, and they stipulate that prerogatives not granted to the federal government belong to the states or to individuals. As long as these remain our founding documents, as long as we as a people remain familiar with our own history, Americans even minimally instructed in their import will have a sneaking suspicion, if not, alas, a firm conviction, that in their country something has gone seriously awry, and they will be profoundly uncomfortable with the administrative state in a fashion in which the French are not now and have not been in more than two hundred years.

As Tocqueville understood long ago, it is this instinctive discomfort—rooted in the ordinary and honorable human desire to take responsibility for one's own well-being and that of one's family and local community—that is man's only bulwark against the soft despotism that is modern democracy's drift. As he puts it in his last published work:

> That which, in all times, has so strongly attached the hearts of certain men to liberty is its intrinsic attractions [*ses attraits mêmes*], the charm that it possesses in and of itself, independent of its benefits. It is the pleasure of being able to

speak, act, breathe without constraint, under the government of God and the laws alone. He who seeks in liberty anything other than itself is made for servitude.

Certain peoples pursue liberty obstinately in the face of all sorts of perils and misfortunes. It is not the material goods that it offers them that these peoples then love in it; they consider it itself as a good so precious and so necessary that no other good could console them for its loss and that they find, in tasting it, consolation for everything that occurs. Other peoples tire of it in the midst of their prosperity; they allow it to be snatched from their hands without resistance, for fear of jeopardizing by such an effort the very well-being they owe to it. What do they lack with regard to remaining free? What, indeed? The taste itself for being free. Do not ask me to analyze this sublime taste, it is necessary to experience it. It enters of its own accord into the great hearts that God has prepared to receive it; it fills them, it inflames them. One must renounce making mediocre souls understand what they have never felt.[6]

The great storms have come and gone; the horrors of the twentieth century recede now into the past. But tyrannical ambition and servile temptation will always be with us, as they are most emphatically now. The choice is, nonetheless, ours. We can be what once we were, or we can settle for a gradual, gentle descent into servitude. It is high time that we reclaim what is, after all, our legacy as Americans, for the genuine self-government that we once enjoyed in plenitude is a possession wholly consonant with our dignity as human beings and with our rights as women and men. Let our motto be, as once it was, "Don't tread on me!" And let our virtue be individual responsibility.

NOTES

INTRODUCTION

1. In this connection, see Alan Charles Kors, "Can There Be an 'After Socialism'?" *Social Philosophy & Policy* 20:1 (Winter 2003): 1–17.

2. See Francis Fukuyama, "The End of History?" *National Interest* 16 (Summer 1989): 3–18, and *The End of History and the Last Man* (New York: Free Press, 1992). Note also *After History? Francis Fukuyama and His Critics*, ed. Timothy Burns (Lanham, MD: Rowman & Littlefield, 1994).

3. Compare Samuel P. Huntington, "The Clash of Civilizations," *Foreign Affairs* 72:3 (Summer 1993): 22–49, and "The West: Unique, Not Universal," *Foreign Affairs* 75:6 (November/December 1996): 28–46, as well as *The Clash of Civilizations and the Remaking of the World Order* (New York: Simon and Schuster, 1996), with Neil McInnes, "The Great Doomsayer (Oswald Spengler's *The Decline of the West*)," *National Interest* 47 (Summer 1997): 65–77.

4. Richard Ned Lebow and Janice Gross Stein, *We All Lost the Cold War* (Princeton, NJ: Princeton University Press, 1994). Compare John Lewis Gaddis, *We Now Know: Rethinking Cold War History* (Oxford, UK: Oxford University Press, 1997).

5. See Tony Judt, "A Story Still to Be Told," *New York Review of Books* 53:5 (23 March 2006): 11–13, reviewing John Lewis Gaddis, *The Cold War: A New History* (New York: Penguin Press, 2005).

6. The utopian vision underpinning the criticism directed at Gaddis is made manifest in Tony Judt, *Postwar: A History of Europe Since 1945* (New York: Penguin, 2005).

7. See, for example, Ernest Gellner, *Conditions of Liberty: Civil Society and Its Rivals* (New York: Penguin, 1994); *Democratization in Eastern Europe: Domestic and International Perspectives*, ed. Geoffrey Pridham and Tatu Vanhanen (London: Routledge, 1994); Marina Ottaway, *Democratization and Ethnic Nationalism: African and Eastern European Experiences* (Washington, DC: Overseas Development Council, 1994); Christopher McMahon, *Authority and Democracy: A General Theory of Government and Management* (Princeton, NJ: Princeton University Press, 1994); *Developing Democ-*

racy, ed. Ian Budge and David McKay (London: Sage, 1994); *The Politics of Democrati-*
zation: Generalizing East Asian Experiences, ed. Edward Friedman (Boulder, CO:
Westview, 1994); Joan M. Nelson et al., *Intricate Links: Democratization and Market*
Reforms in Latin America and Eastern Europe (New Brunswick, NJ: Transaction, 1994);
Politics, Society, and Democracy: Comparative Studies, ed. H. E. Chehabi and Alfred
Stepan (Boulder, CO: Westview, 1995); *Political Culture and Constitutionalism: A*
Comparative Approach, ed. Daniel P. Franklin and Michael J. Baun (Armonk, NY:
M. E. Sharpe, 1995); Robert Amerson, *How Democracy Triumphed over Dictatorship:*
Public Diplomacy in Venezuela (Washington, DC: American University Press, 1995);
Robert Strausz-Hupé, *Democracy and American Foreign Policy: Reflections on the Legacy*
of Alexis de Tocqueville (New Brunswick, NJ: Transaction, 1995). Many more could be
listed.

8. See Matthew Continetti, "The Peace Party vs. the Power Party: The Real Divide in
American Politics," *Weekly Standard* 12:16 (1–8 January 2007): 17–19, 22–24.

9. See Robin Abcarian, "Michelle Obama in Spotlight's Glare," *Los Angeles Times*, 21
February 2008, and Lauren Collins, "The Other Obama," *New Yorker*, 10 March 2008.

10. "Circular to the Governors of the States," 8 June 1783, in *The Writings of George Wash-*
ington, ed. John C. Fitzpatrick (Washington, DC: U. S. Government Printing Office,
1931–1944), XXVI 485–86.

11. See Alexander Hamilton, John Jay, and James Madison, *The Federalist*, ed. Jacob E.
Cooke (Middletown, CT: Wesleyan University Press, 1961) no. 47, p. 324; no. 78,
p. 523n.

12. See Donald S. Lutz, "The Relative Influence of European Writers on Late Eighteenth-
Century American Political Thought," *American Political Science Review* 78:1 (March
1984): 189–97. See also James W. Muller, "The American Framers' Debt to Montesquieu," in *The Revival of Constitutionalism*, ed. James W. Muller (Lincoln: University of Nebraska Press, 1988), 87–102; Matthew P. Bergman, "Montesquieu's Theory of Government and the Framing of the American Constitution," *Pepperdine*
Law Review 18:1 (1990): 1–42; and Bernard Manin, "Checks, Balances and Boundaries: The Separation of Powers in the Constitutional Debate of 1787," in *The Inven-*
tion of the Modern Republic (Cambridge, UK: Cambridge University Press, 1994),
27–62.

13. *The Federalist* no. 47, pp. 324–25. See also Edmund Burke, *An Appeal from the New to*
the Old Whigs (1791), in *The Writings and Speeches of the Right Honourable Edmund*
Burke (Boston: Little, Brown, 1901), IV 211–12.

14. See James Madison, "Helvidius, No. 1," 24 August 1793, in *The Papers of James Madison*,
ed. William T. Hutchinson, William M. E. Rachal et al. (Chicago: University of
Chicago Press, 1962–1977; Charlottesville: University Press of Virginia, 1977–1991), XV
68.

BOOK ONE, PREFACE

1. This preface summarizes the argument first presented in Paul A. Rahe, "The Book That
Never Was: Montesquieu's *Considerations on the Romans* in Historical Context," *His-*

tory of Political Thought 26:1 (Spring 2005): 43–89, and articulated in greater detail in Rahe, M I, where full annotation is provided.

2. Compare Niccolò Machiavelli, Dell'arte della guerra 2.302–9, in Machiavelli, Tutte le opere, ed. Mario Martelli (Florence: G. C. Sansoni, 1971), 332–33, with Machiavelli, Dell'arte della guerra 5.93–104, in ibid., 359–60, and see Istorie fiorentine 5.1 and 6.1, in ibid., 738–39, 765–66, and note Machiavelli, Discorsi sopra la prima deca di Tito Livio 2.6, in ibid., 155–56. For a discussion of the place of this particular argument within Machiavelli's overall analysis of modern politics, see Rahe, ATA 56–100 (esp. 83–100).

3. See Charles de Secondat, "Mémoire pour servir a l'éloge historique de M. de Montesquieu," in Louis Vian, Histoire de Montesquieu: Sa Vie et ses œuvres (Geneva: Slatkine Reprints, 1970), 396–407 (at 401).

4. [Montesquieu], Two Chapters of a celebrated French work, intitled De l'Esprit des loix, translated into English. One, treating of the constitution of England; another of the character and manners which result from this constitution (Edinburgh: Hamilton and Balfour, 1750).

5. After consulting EL 1.8.17, 19, 21, p. 367, 2.9.6–7, 13.17, 3.17.6, 4.21.21, p. 642, 22, pp. 645–47, where Montesquieu lifts entire passages from RMU 8, 10, 15–17, 19–22, 24, and considering, more generally, EL 1.8.17–21, 2.9.6, 9–10.16, 11.19, 13.18, 3.17.3–4, 6, where Montesquieu elaborates on themes first developed in RMU 1–8, 14, 18–22, 25, see Montesquieu, EL 2.11.5–20.

BOOK ONE, CHAPTER ONE. PRINCIPLES

1. For a more fully elaborated and annotated statement of the argument presented in this chapter, see Rahe, M II.1

2. Note Blaise Pascal, Pensées sur la religion et sur quelques autres sujets, qui ont esté trouvées après sa mort parmy ses papiers, 3rd ed., ed. Étienne Périer (Paris: Guillaume Desprez, 1671), 184–86 (XXV.4–6, in the expanded edition published in 1678 and frequently republished thereafter), where the epigraph to this chapter is to be found.

3. Compare Polyb. 6.3.5–10.14 with Xen. Mem. 4.6.12, Oec. 21.9–12; Pl. Pol. 291d–303b, Leg. 3.689e–702d, 4.712c–715d, 8.832b–d; Arist. Eth. Nic. 1160a31–1161b10, Pol. 1278b30–1280a5, 1284b35–1285b33, 1295a7–24, Rh. 1365b21–1366a22, and see Pl. Leg. 6.756e–758a, Arist. Pol. 1281b22–38 (esp. 28–31), 1295a25–1297a12 (esp. 1296b14–16), 1297b1–27, 1329a2–17, 1332b12–41. Note, in this connection, Pind. Pyth. 2.86–88, Hdt. 3.80–83, and Thuc. 8.97.2.

4. See Thomas Hobbes, The Elements of Law Natural and Politic, 2nd ed., ed. Ferdinand Tönnies (London: Frank Cass, 1969) II.i.3; De Cive: The Latin Version, ed. Howard Warrender (Oxford, UK: Clarendon Press, 1983) II.vii.1–17, x.2; and Leviathan, ed. Edwin Curley (Indianapolis, IN: Hackett, 1994) II.xix.1–2.

5. The pertinent passage was initially included in and eventually excised from EL 1.3.9: see "Dossier de L'Esprit des lois," in Pléiade II 996.

6. See Rahe, RAM II.v.12, n. 173, and Paul Carrese, "The Machiavellian Spirit of Montesquieu's Liberal Republic," in Machiavelli's Liberal Republican Legacy, ed. Paul A. Rahe (New York: Cambridge University Press, 2006), 121–42 (esp. 137–40).

7. See Montesquieu, "Réponses et explications données à la faculté de théologie," in Pléiade II 1174–95 (at 1181).
8. I first set out much of the pertinent evidence in Paul A. Rahe, "The Primacy of Politics
   in Classical Greece," *American Historical Review* 89:2 (April 1984): 265–93; I restate
   and amplify my argument and then explore its consequences for our understanding of
   classical civilization in Rahe, *RAM* I.
9. See Paul A. Rahe "Situating Machiavelli," in *Renaissance Civic Humanism Reappraisals and Reflections,* ed. James Hankins (Cambridge, UK: Cambridge University
   Press, 2000), 270–308; "In the Shadow of Lucretius: The Epicurean Foundations of
   Machiavelli's Political Thought," *History of Political Thought* 28:1 (Spring 2007): 30–
   55; and *ATA* 19–55.
10. Compare Pl. *Rep.* 443d–e, Rom. 6:17–18, and Thomas Aquinas, *Summa theologiae,* ed.
    Thomas Gilby, O.P., et al. (New York: McGraw-Hill, 1964–1976) Ia q.77 a.4.
11. Consider Arist. *Eth. Nic.* 1103a4–b25 in light of 1097b28–1098a18, 1098b22–99a21.
12. Montesquieu's elaborate comparison of republican Sparta, despotic China, and early
    Rome in this regard deserves attention: consider *EL* 3.19.16–21 with an eye to 1.5.19,
    p. 306; note 1.6.9 (esp. n. a), 7.6–7, and 8.21; and see Rahe, *M* II.3–4.
13. In this connection, note Montesquieu, *LP* 61/63, 96–97/99–100; see *EL* 3.16.11–12.
    Note also Montesquieu, *MP* 1062, 1491, 1625, and see Rahe, *M* III.1, 3.
14. See Vickie B. Sullivan, *Machiavelli's Three Romes: Religion, Human Liberty, and Poli-
    tics Reformed* (Dekalb: Northern Illinois University Press, 1996), passim (esp. 15–59,
    119–90), and Rahe, *ATA* 56–100.
15. Consider Montesquieu, *EL* 4.21.20, pp. 640–41, in light of Vickie B. Sullivan, "Against
    the Despotism of a Republic: Montesquieu's Correction of Machiavelli in the Name of
    the Security of the Individual," *History of Political Thought* 27:2 (Summer 2006): 263–
    88.
16. Consider Montaigne, "De la Cruauté" and "De la Vertu," in *Les Essais de Michel de
    Montaigne,* ed. Pierre Villey and V.-L. Saulnier (Paris: Presses Universitaires de
    France, 1978), 2.11, 29, in light of Rahe, *RAM* II.i.3–4.
17. See also *EL* 1.3.10, 2.12.29, 5.26.2
18. Consider Montesquieu's failure to discuss the aristocratic republic in *EL* 1.4 in light of
    the first paragraph of 1.5.8.
19. Compare Sir Isaac Newton, *Philosophiæ naturalis principia mathematica* (London:
    Joseph Streater, 1687) 1.23.
20. Compare Adam Smith, *The Theory of Moral Sentiments* IV.i.10 and *An Inquiry into the
    Nature and Causes of the Wealth of Nations* IV.ii.9, with "The History of Astronomy"
    III.2, in *Essays on Philosophical Subjects*—all to be found in *The Glasgow Edition of the
    Works and Correspondence of Adam Smith* (Oxford, UK: Oxford University Press, 1976).
21. Note, in this connection, *EL* 1.5.19, p. 304.
22. Compare Montesquieu, *EL* 1.6.5, with Niccolò Machiavelli, *Discorsi sopra la prima
    deca di Tito Livio* 1.7, in *Tutte le opere,* 87–88.
23. In his notebooks, Montesquieu remarks that in England "money is accorded sovereign
    esteem" while "honor and virtue" are accorded but "little." See *NA* 878.

BOOK ONE, CHAPTER TWO. UNEASINESS

1. This chapter is an abbreviated version of Rahe, *M* II.2–4.
2. For a further exploration of this point, see *EL* 5.26.15, 20. Compare 5.24.2.
3. On the latter point, see also *EL* 2.11.18.
4. See Keith Michael Baker, "Politics and Public Opinion under the Old Regime: Some Reflections," in *Press and Politics in Pre-Revolutionary France*, ed. Jack R. Censer and Jeremy. Popkin (Berkeley: University of California Press, 1987), 204–46 (at 214–21), which is revised, expanded, and reprinted as Baker, "Public Opinion as a Political Invention," in Baker, *Inventing the French Revolution* (Cambridge, UK: Cambridge University Press, 1990), 167–99 (at 173–78).
5. Note François Duverger Véron de Forbonnais, *Un Extrait chapitre par chapitre du livre de l'Esprit des Lois: Des Observations sur quelques endroits particuliers de ce livre, & une idée de toutes les critiques qui en ont été faites, avec quelques remarques de l'éditeur* (Amsterdam: Arkstée and Merkus, 1753), 173–212 (at 182).
6. After considering *EL* 2.11.6 and 2.12.1–2 with an eye to 1.5.6 and 4.20.5, see 1.5.14, 8.21, 2.11.5, 3.16.9, 18.1, 19.16, 19–20, 5.25.15, 6.29.18.
7. Note Montesquieu, *MP* 5.
8. Note Paul A. Rahe, "In the Shadow of Lucretius: The Epicurean Foundations of Machiavelli's Political Thought," *History of Political Thought* 28:1 (Spring 2007): 30–55, and *ATA* 22–55, and see Paul Carrese, "The Machiavellian Spirit of Montesquieu's Liberal Republic," in *Machiavelli's Liberal Republican Legacy*, ed. Paul A. Rahe (New York: Cambridge University Press, 2006), 121–42 (esp. 131–41).
9. Compare Machiavelli, *Discorsi sopra la prima deca di Tito Livio* 1.6, 37, 2 Proemio, in Machiavelli, *Tutte le opere*, ed. Mario Martelli (Florence: G. C. Sansoni, 1971), 84–87, 119–20, 144–46, with Thomas Hobbes, *Leviathan*, ed. Edwin Curley (Indianapolis, IN: Hackett, 1994) I.iii.3–5, viii.14–16, and with David Hume, *A Treatise of Human Nature*, ed. L. A. Selby-Bigge (Oxford, UK: Clarendon Press, 1888) II.iii.
10. Consider *EL* 1.1.2, 5.12, 2.11.3, 5.24.5, 26.15 with an eye to 5.24.2.
11. See also *EL* 5.24.2, 5, and *MP* 1625.
12. Compare Blaise Pascal, *Pensées: Édition établie d'après la copie référence de Gilberte Pascal*, ed. Philippe Sellier (Paris: Classiques Garnier, 1999) nos. 1–414, with Michel de Montaigne, "De la Vanité," *Essais* 3.9, in Montaigne, *Œuvres complètes*, ed. Albert Thibaudet and Maurice Rat (Paris: Bibliothèque de la Pléiade, 1962), 922–80 (esp. 966).
13. See John Locke, *An Essay concerning Human Understanding*, ed. Peter H. Nidditch (Oxford, UK: Clarendon Press, 1979) II.x.9.
14. Compare Locke, *An Essay concerning Human Understanding* II.xxi.55, with Hobbes, *Leviathan* I.xi.1.
15. Compare Locke, *An Essay concerning Human Understanding* II.vii.1–2, xx.6, 15, xxi.29–71, with Blaise Pascal, *Pensées sur la religion et sur quelques autres sujets, qui ont esté trouvées après sa mort parmy ses papiers*, 3rd ed., ed. Étienne Périer (Paris: Guillaume Desprez, 1671), 62, 159–64, 179–81 (where this chapter's epigraph is to be

found), 192–210, 242–46, 266–72, 275–76 (VIII.1, XXI.1–4, XXIV.12, XXVI.1–4, XXVIII.35–36, XXIX.11, 18, 23, 29, 39, in the expanded edition published in 1678 and frequently republished thereafter).

16. John Locke, *Essai philosophique concernant l'entendement humain: où l'on montre quelle est l'étendue de nos connoissances certaines, et la manière dont nous y parvenons,* tr. Pierre Coste (The Hague: Pierre Husson, 1714), 267n. This edition was originally published in 1700.

17. See Jean Deprun, *La Philosophie de l'inquiétude en France au XVIIIe siècle* (Paris: Librairie philosophique J. Vrin, 1979).

18. See *Catalogue de la bibliothèque de Montesquieu à La Brède,* ed. Louis Desgraves and Catherine Volpilhac-Auger (Oxford, UK: Voltaire Foundation, 1999) no. 1489.

19. See Pascal, *Pensées sur la religion et sur quelques autres sujets,* 294–95 (XXX.3, in the expanded edition published in 1678 and frequently republished thereafter). Note also the reference to *libido sentiendi, libido sciendi, libido dominandi* in ibid., 254–55 (XXVIII.55, in the expanded edition published in 1678 and frequently republished thereafter).

20. See Pascal, *Pensées: Édition établie d'après la copie référence de Gilberte Pascal* nos. 150, 243–44.

21. See August. *In epistolam Joannis ad Parthos tractatus decem* 8.9.

22. See Pierre Nicole, "De la charité et de l'amour-propre," in Nicole, *Essais de morale,* ed. Laurent Thirounin (Paris: Presses Universitaires de France, 1999), 381–415 (esp. 406–7, where the passage from Augustine is cited and paraphrased). The same theme is developed in Nicole, "De la grandeur," in ibid., 197–243 (at 212–17).

23. Note Jean Starobinski, "La Rochefoucauld et les morales substitutives," *La nouvelle Revue française* 163 (July 1966): 16–35, 164 (August 1966): 211–29, and see Keith Michael Baker, "Enlightenment and the Institution of Society: Notes for a Conceptual History," in *Main Trends in Cultural History: Ten Essays,* ed. Willem Melching and Wyger Velema (Amsterdam: Rodopi, 1994), 95–120.

24. See Pascal, *Pensées sur la religion et sur quelques autres sujets,* 176 (XXIV.1, in the expanded edition published in 1678 and frequently republished thereafter).

25. Note [Jean Le Rond d'Alembert], "Éloge de M. le President de Montesquieu," in *Encyclopédie, ou Dictionnaire raisonné des sciences, des arts, et des métiers,* ed. Denis Diderot and Jean Le Rond d'Alembert (Paris: Briasson, 1751–1772; Neufchastel: S. Faulche & Compagnie: 1765; Amsterdam: M. M. Rey, 1776–1777; Paris: Panckoucke, 1777–1780), V iii–xviii (at vii).

26. For a full discussion of Montesquieu's analysis of the difficulties facing Europe's monarchies, see Rahe, M I.1–3, II.1, 4, III.3.

27. In this connection, see also Montesquieu, *EL* 2.11.19.

28. I have articulated this argument more fully in Rahe, M III.4.

29. See Robert Shackleton, "John Nourse and the London Edition of *L'Esprit des Lois,*" in *Studies in the French Eighteenth Century Presented to John Lough,* ed. D. J. Mossop, G. E. Rodmell, and D. B. Wilson (Durham, UK: University of Durham, 1978), 248–59, and Cecil Patrick Courtney, "Montesquieu et ses relations anglaises: Autour de sa correspondance des années 1749–1750 sur deux éditions britanniques et deux traductions

de *L'Esprit des lois,"* in *Montesquieu, Oeuvre ouverte?* (*1748–1755*): *Actes du Colloque de Bordeaux* (*6–8 décembre 2001, Bordeaux, bibliothèque municipale*), ed. Catherine Larrère (Oxford, UK: Voltaire Foundation, 2005), 147–62.

30. See Letter from William Domville to Montesquieu on 4 June 1749, in Nagel III 1235–37.

31. Note, in this connection, *LP* 99/102.

32. See Paul Langford, *The Excise Crisis: Society and Politics in the Age of Walpole* (Oxford, UK: Clarendon Press, 1975).

33. See Letter from Montesquieu to William Domville on 22 July 1749, in Nagel III 1244–45.

34. In consequence, it would be completely inappropriate for an admirer of English liberty to share the disdain that, in his guise as a Roman republican, Cicero quite rightly expressed for "men of commerce . . . for whom all governments are equal as long as they are tranquil": note Cic. *Att.* 7.7–8, and cf. Montesquieu, *EL* 2.18.1 with *MP* 1960 (À Monsieur Domville), p. 600.

35. Montesquieu touches on the question of executive patronage in *EL* 3.19.27, p. 575.

36. See *EL* 3.19.27, pp. 576–77.

37. Elsewhere in his discussion of England Montesquieu treats elections as an antidote to corruption: *EL* 2.11.6, p. 402.

38. See also *EL* 1.8.6, and cf. Montesquieu, *CR* 15.100–103.

BOOK TWO, PREFACE

1. See *Lettres familières de M. le président de Montesquieu*, ed. l'abbé Ottaviano, comte di Guasco (Florence: n.p., 1767), 45n.

2. In compiling the bibliographical data, Cecil Patrick Courtney has done yeoman work: on the *Persian Letters*, see Courtney, "Bibliographie II. Editions," in VF I 84–131, which should be read in conjunction with Edgar Mass, *Literatur und Zensur in der frühen Aufklärung: Produktion, Distribution und Rezeption der Lettres persanes* (Frankfurt am Main: Vittorio Klostermann, 1981), 139–271; and on Montesquieu's other two works, see Courtney, "Introduction à *Considérations sur les causes de la grandeur des Romains et de leur décadence* VI. Manuscrits et éditions," in VF II 48–85, and Courtney, "*L'Esprit des lois* dans la perspective d l'histoire du livre (1748–1800)," in *Le Temps de Montesquieu: Actes du colloque international de Genève* (*28–31 octobre 1998*), ed. Michel Porret and Catherine Volpilhac-Auger (Geneva: Droz, 2002), 66–96.

3. Note Frank T. H. Fletcher, *Montesquieu and English Politics, 1750–1800* (London: E. Arnold, 1939), and William Stewart, "Montesquieu vu par les Anglais depuis deux siècles," in *Actes du congrès Montesquieu réuni à Bordeaux du 23 au 26 mai 1955* (Bordeaux: Impriméries Delmas, 1956), 339–48; then see Cecil Patrick Courtney, *Montesquieu and Burke* (Oxford, UK: Blackwell, 1963); Paul O. Carrese, *The Cloaking of Power: Montesquieu, Blackstone, and the Rise of Judicial Activism* (Chicago: University of Chicago Press, 2003); Paul E. Chamley, "The Conflict between Montesquieu and Hume: A Study of the Origins of Adam Smith's Universalism," in *Essays on Adam Smith*, ed. Andrew S. Skinner and Thomas Wilson (Oxford, UK: Clarendon Press,

1975), 274–305; David Carrithers, "The Enlightenment Science of Society," in *Inventing Human Science: Eighteenth-Century Domains*, ed. Christopher Fox, Roy Porter, and Robert Wokler (Berkeley: University of California Press, 1995), 232–70; Sheila M. Mason, "Les Héritiers écossais de Montesquieu: Continuité d'inspiration et métamorphose de valeurs," in *La Fortune de Montesquieu: Montesquieu écrivain* (Bordeaux: Bibliothèque Municipale, 1995), 143–54; and James Moore, "Montesquieu and the Scottish Enlightenment," in *Montesquieu and His Legacy*, ed. Rebecca E. Kingston (Albany: State University of New York Press, 2008), 179–95.

4. Note Paul Merrill Spurlin, *Montesquieu in America, 1760–1801* (Baton Rouge: Louisiana State University Press, 1940), and see James W. Muller, "The American Framers' Debt to Montesquieu," in *The Revival of Constitutionalism*, ed. James W. Muller (Lincoln: University of Nebraska Press, 1988), 87–102; Anne M. Cohler, *Montesquieu's Comparative Politics and the Spirit of American Constitutionalism* (Lawrence: University Press of Kansas, 1988); Matthew P. Bergman, "Montesquieu's Theory of Government and the Framing of the American Constitution," *Pepperdine Law Review* 18:1 (1990): 1–42; Rahe, *RAM* II.iii.4, III.Prologue, i.3–7, ii.2, iii.4–5, iv.3–5, 7, 9, v.3, 6; Bernard Manin, "Checks, Balances and Boundaries: The Separation of Powers in the Constitutional Debate of 1787," in *The Invention of the Modern Republic* (Cambridge, UK: Cambridge University Press, 1994), 27–62; and Jacob Levy, "Montesquieu's Constitutional Legacies," in *Montesquieu and His Legacy*, 115–37.

5. See Catherine Larrère, "Droit de punir et qualification des crimes de Montesquieu à Beccaria," in *Beccaria et la culture juridique des lumières*, ed. Michel Porret (Geneva: Droz, 1997), 89–108, and David W. Carrithers, "Montesquieu's Philosophy of Punishment," *History of Political Thought* 19:2 (Summer 1998): 213–40.

6. See Michael A. Mosher, "The Particulars of a Universal Politics: Hegel's Adaptation of Montesquieu's Typology," *American Political Science Review* 78:1 (March 1984): 179–88, and Yoshie Kawade, "La Liberté civile contre la théorie réformiste de l'État souverain: Le Combat de Montesquieu," in *Le Travail des lumières: Pour Georges Benrekassa*, ed. Caroline Jacot Grapa, Nicole Jacques-Lefèvre, Yannick Séité, and Carine Trevisan (Paris: Honoré Champion, 2002), 203–23.

7. See Roberto Romani, "All Montesquieu's Sons: The Place of *Esprit Général, Caractère National*, and *Moeurs* in French Political Philosophy, 1748–1789," *Studies on Voltaire and the Eighteenth Century* 362 (1998): 189–235, whose reading of Montesquieu and of his critics and heirs nonetheless leaves something to be desired. The case of Denis Diderot is of special interest: see Arthur M. Wilson, "The Concept of *Moeurs* in Diderot's Social and Political Thought," in *The Age of the Enlightenment: Studies Presented to Theodore Besterman*, ed. W. H. Barber et al. (Edinburgh: Oliver & Boyd, 1967), 188–99.

8. In this connection, see the essays collected in the two-volume study *Montesquieu e i suoi interpreti*, ed Domenico Felice (Pisa: Edizioni ETS, 2005). Note also Catherine Volpilhac-Auger, "*L'Esprit des lois*, une lecture *ad usum Delphini?*" in *Le Travail des lumières*, 137–71.

9. See Élie Carcassonne, *Montesquieu et le problème de la constitution française au XVIIIe siècle* (Paris: Presses Universitaires de France, 1927), and J. H. Shennan, *The Parlement*

of Paris (London: Eyre & Spottiswoode, 1968), 285–325 (esp. 308–25), along with Daniel Roche, *France in the Enlightenment*, tr. Arthur Goldhammer (Cambridge, MA: Harvard University Press, 1998), 252–57, 268, 277–80, 308–19, 408, 449–82; and Michael A. Mosher, "Monarchy's Paradox: Honor in the Face of Sovereign Power," in *Montesquieu's Science of Politics: Essays on the Spirit of Laws (1748)*, ed. David Carrithers, Michael A. Mosher, and Paul A. Rahe (Lanham, MD: Rowman & Littlefield, 2001), 159–229 (esp. 183–203).

10. See Rahe, *M* III.3–4.

11. See Julian Swann, "'Fauteurs de toutes les maximes qui sont contraires à la monarchie': Le Gouvernement face aux magistrats jansénists sous Louis XV," in *Jansénisme et Révolution*, ed. Catherine-Laurence Maire (Paris: Bibliothèque Mazarine, 1990), 163–72.

12. After reading Dale K. Van Kley, *The Jansenists and the Expulsion of the Jesuits from France, 1757–1765* (New Haven, CT: Yale University Press, 1975), *The Damiens Affair and the Unraveling of the Ancien Régime, 1750–1770* (Princeton, NJ: Princeton University Press, 1984), and *The Religious Origins of the French Revolution: From Calvin to the Civil Constitution, 1560–1791* (New Haven, CT: Yale University Press, 1996); Keith Michael Baker, "Memory and Practice: Politics and the Representation of the Past in Eighteenth-Century France," *Representations* 11 (Summer 1985): 134–64, which is reprinted in Baker, *Inventing the French Revolution* (Cambridge, UK: Cambridge University Press, 1990), 31–58, along with Baker, "Controlling French History: The Ideological Arsenal of Jacob-Nicolas Moreau," in ibid., 59–85; and Jeffrey W. Merrick, *The Desacralization of the French Monarchy in the Eighteenth Century* (Baton Rouge: Louisiana State University Press, 1990), see John Rogister, *Louis XV and the Parlement of Paris, 1737–1755* (Cambridge, UK: Cambridge University Press, 1995), and Julian Swann, *Politics and the Parlement of Paris under Louis XV, 1754–1774* (Cambridge, UK: Cambridge University Press, 1995). Note, in this connection, Montesquieu, *MP* 426.

13. In this connection, see Pierre Grosclaude, *Malesherbes: Témoin et interprète de son temps* (Paris: Librairie Fischbacher, 1961).

14. For an extended discussion of Malesherbes, the *Cour des aides*, the tendencies evident in the remonstrances that he drafted, and his debt to Montesquieu, see Elizabeth Badinter, *Les 'Remonstrances' de Malesherbes, 1771–1775* (Paris: Union Général des Éditions, 1978), 11–147.

15. See Rahe, *M* III.3.

16. See "Trés-humbles et trés-respectueuses Remonstrances que présentent au Roi notre trés honoré Souverain & Seigneur, les Gens tenans sa Cour des Aides à Paris," 6 May 1775, ed. James Harvey Robinson, in *Translations and Reprints from the Original Sources of European History* V:2 (Philadelphia: Department of History of the University of Pennsylvania, 1912), 1–74, and in Badinter, *Les 'Remonstrances' de Malesherbes*, 169–276. Note also the somewhat free English translation provided by Grace Reade Robinson in *Translations and Reprints from the Original Sources of European History*, V:2 77–153.

17. Consider *LP* 2–4, 6–7, 9, 19–20/20–21, 24–25/26–27, 39–41/41–43, 45/47, 51/53, 60/62, 62–63/64–65, 68–69/70–71, 77/79, 93/96, 139–48/147–56, 149/159, 150/161 in light of 35.10–25/37, 86.5–16/88, and 104/107, and see Corey Robin, "Reflections on Fear:

Montesquieu in Retrieval," *American Political Science Review* 94:2 (June 2000): 347–60, which should be read in light of Rahe, *M* I.3, notes 15–16.

18. See "Trés-humbles et trés-respectueuses Remonstrances que présentent au Roi notre trés honoré Souverain & Seigneur, les Gens tenans sa Cour des Aides à Paris," 6 May 1775, in *Translations and Reprints from the Original Sources of European History*, V:2 23–27, 62, 70–72, and in Badinter, *Les 'Remonstrances' de Malesherbes*, 202–10, 265–66, 269–73.

19. See Keith Michael Baker, "French Political Thought at the Accession of Louis XVI," *Journal of Modern History* 50:2 (June 1978): 279–303, which is reprinted in *Inventing the French Revolution*, 109–27.

20. See Rahe, *M* III.1–2.

21. See Anne-Robert-Jacques Turgot, "Discours sur les avantages que la religion chrétienne a procurés au genre humain, prononcé en latin à l'ouverture des Sorboniques," 3 July 1750, and "Tableau philosophique des progrès successifs de l'esprit humain, discours prononcé en latin, dans les écoles de la Sorbonne, pour la clôture des Sorboniques," 11 December 1750, in *Œuvres de Turgot et documents le concernant*, ed. Gustave Schelle (Paris: Librairie Felix Alcan, 1913–1923), I 194–235. The latter of the two can be found in English translation, along with extensive selections from a slightly later fragmentary work in which Turgot lays out his argument in considerably greater detail, in *Turgot on Progress, Sociology and Economics*, ed. and tr. Ronald L. Meek (Cambridge, UK: Cambridge University Press, 1973), 41–118. For the latter work in its entirety in the original French, see Anne-Robert-Jacques Turgot, "Sur l'Histoire universelle," in *Œuvres de M^r. de Turgot, ministre d'État, precedées et accompagnées de mémoires et de notes sur la vie, son administrations et ses ouvrages*, ed. Pierre Samuel du Pont de Nemours (Paris: A. Belin, 1808; Paris: Delance, 1808–1811), II 209–352.

22. See Frank E. Manuel, *The Prophets of Paris* (Cambridge, MA: Harvard University Press, 1962), 11–51, and Ronald L. Meek, *Social Science and the Ignoble Savage* (Cambridge, UK: Cambridge University Press, 1976), 5–98, who underestimates the young Turgot's intellectual dependence on Montesquieu's *Spirit of Laws* and who takes Turgot's simplification of Montesquieu's subtle and complex analysis and his subordination of it to a scheme of secular salvation history as an advance. Compare Henry C. Clark, *Compass of Society: Commerce and Absolutism in Old Regime France* (Lanham, MD: Lexington Books, 2007), 222–24, who thinks Turgot no less respectful of contingency than Montesquieu.

23. For an astute appreciation of Turgot's qualities as an economist and an attempt to situate him vis-à-vis his immediate predecessors and successors, see Murray N. Rothbard, *An Austrian Perspective on the History of Economic Thought I: Economic Thought before Adam Smith* (Cheltenham, UK: Edward Elgar, 1995), 211–534 (esp. 383–413). See also Peter Groenewegen, *Eighteenth-Century Economics: Turgot, Beccaria and Smith and Their Contemporaries* (London: Routledge, 2002), 3–47, 282–378, and Michael Sonenscher, *Before the Deluge: Public Debt, Inequality, and the Intellectual Origins of the French Revolution* (Princeton, NJ: Princeton University Press, 2007), 281–90, which can profitably be read in conjunction with Mario Einaudi, *The Physiocratic Doctrine of Judicial Control* (Cambridge, MA: Harvard University Press, 1938); Elizabeth Fox-Gen-

ovese, *The Origins of Physiocracy* (Ithaca, NY: Cornell University Press, 1976); Clark, *Compass of Society*, 153–91; and Michael Sonenscher, "Physiocracy as Theodicy," *History of Political Thought* 23:2 (Summer 2002): 326–39, and *Before the Deluge*, 199–222. For a biography of the one economist, after Turgot, to give proper attention to the contribution of entrepreneurship, see Thomas K. McCraw, *Prophet of Innovation: Joseph Schumpeter and Creative Destruction* (Cambridge, MA: Belknap Press, 2007).

24. See Gerald J. Cavanaugh, "Turgot: The Rejection of Enlightened Despotism," *French Historical Studies* 6:1 (Spring 1969): 31–58, and Clark, *Compass of Society*, 109–256.

25. See Dominique-Joseph Garat, *Mémoires sur la vie de M. Suard, sur ses écrits, et sur le XVIIIe siècle* (Paris: A. Belin, 1820), I 330, and Amable-Guillaume-Prosper Brugière de Barante, *Histoire de la convention nationale* (Brussels: Méline, Cans et Comp., 1851–53), II 247.

26. See Rahe, *M* III.4.

27. For overviews, see Douglas Dakin, *Turgot and the Ancien Régime in France* (New York: Octagon Books, 1980); Jean-Pierre Poirier, *Turgot: Laissez-faire et progrès social* (Paris: Perrin, 1999); and Pierre Rétat, "Turgot réformateur," in *Le Travail des lumières*, 481–95.

28. See Turgot, "Mémoire sur les municipalités," in *Œuvres de Turgot et documents le concernant*, IV 568–621. Note also the extract from Condorcet's biography of Turgot that Schelle appends to this document: ibid., IV 621–26.

29. Consider Jean-Antoine-Nicolas de Caritat, marquis de Condorcet, "Observations on the Twenty-Ninth Book of *The Spirit of Laws*," in [Antoine Louis Claude Destutt, comte de Tracy], *A Commentary and Review of Montesquieu's Spirit of Laws*, [tr. Thomas Jefferson] (Philadelphia: William Duane, 1811), 261–82, in light of Turgot's criticism of Montesquieu in Letter to Pierre Samuel du Pont de Nemours on 13 March 1771, in *Œuvres de Turgot et documents le concernant*, III 476–78 (at 477), and see Keith Michael Baker, *Condorcet: From Natural Philosophy to Social Mathematics* (Chicago: University of Chicago Press, 1975), esp. 197–386.

30. See Keith Michael Baker, "The Language of Liberty in Eighteenth-Century Bordeaux: Early Writings of Guillaume-Joseph Saige," in *L'età dei lumi: Studi storici sul settecento Europeo in onore di Franco Venturi* (Naples: Casa Editrice Jovene, 1985), I 331–70, which is reprinted as "A Classical Republican in Eighteenth-Century Bordeaux: Guillaume-Joseph Saige," in *Inventing the French Revolution*, 128–52.

31. This shift had various dimensions: see David A. Bell, *Lawyers and Citizens: The Formation of a Political Elite in Old Regime France* (New York: Oxford University Press, 1994), 139–94; then consider Dale Van Kley, "New Wine in Old Wineskins: Continuity and Rupture in the Pamphlet Debate of the French Prerevolution, 1787–1789," *French Historical Studies* 17:2 (Fall 1991): 447–65, and Sarah Maza, *Private Lives and Public Affairs: The Causes Célèbres of Prerevolutionary France* (Berkeley: University of California Press, 1993), which should be read with an eye to ibid., 313–24.

32. See Jules Flammermont, *Le Chancelier Maupeou et les Parlements* (Paris: Alphonse Picard, 1883); William Doyle, "The Parlements of France and the Breakdown of the Old Régime, 1771–1788," *French Historical Studies* 6:4 (Autumn 1970): 415–58; Durand Echeverria, *The Maupeou Revolution: A Study in the History of Libertarianism: France,*

1770–1774 (Baton Rouge: Louisiana State University Press, 1985), 1–34; and Swann, *Politics and the Parlement of Paris under Louis XV*, 250–368.

33. See Carcassonne, *Montesquieu et le problème de la constitution française au XVIIIᵉ siècle*, 401–17.

34. See "Très humbles et très respectueuses Remonstrances de la cour des aides de Paris, du 18 février 1771, sur l'édit de décember 1770, et l'état actuel du parlement de Paris," in Badinter, *Les 'Remonstrances' de Malesherbes*, 151–65.

35. See David Hudson, "In Defense of Reform: French Government Propaganda during the Maupeou Crisis," *French Historical Studies* 8:1 (Spring 1973): 51–76; Echeverria, *The Maupeou Revolution*, 37–304; Dale Van Kley, "The Religious Origins of the Patriot and Ministerial Parties in Pre-Revolutionary France," in *Belief in History: Innovative Approaches to European and American Religion*, ed. Thomas Kselman (Notre Dame, IN: Notre Dame University Press, 1991), 173–236; and Shanti-Marie Singham, "*Vox populi vox Dei*: Les Jansénistes pendant la révolution Maupeou," in *Jansénisme et Révolution*, 183–93, and "The *Correspondance Secrète*: Forging Patriotic Opinion during the Maupeou Years," *Historical Reflections/Refléxions Historiques* 18:2 (Summer 1992): 65–101. Additional material can be found in Singham's unpublished dissertation: "'A Conspiracy of Twenty Million Frenchmen': Public Opinion, Patriotism, and the Assault on Absolutism during the Maupeou Years, 1770–775," Princeton University, 1991.

36. See Ferdinando Galiani and Louise d'Épinay, *Correspondance*, ed. Georges Dulac and Daniel Maggetti (Paris: Desjonquères, 1992–1997), II 88 n.2, where this letter is described as being "apocryphal without a doubt." Unfortunately, no argument is offered on behalf of this claim.

37. See Letter of Madame d'Épinay to Abbé Ferdinando Galiani on 11 April 1771, in Ferdinando Galiani, *Correspondance*, new edition, ed. Lucien Perey and Gaston Maugras (Paris: Calman Lévy, 1881–1882), I 371–76 (at 374–76).

38. See Denis Diderot, "Essai historique sur la police de la France depuis son origine jusqu'à son extinction actuelle," in Diderot, *Œuvres politiques*, ed. Paul Vernière (Paris: Garnier, 1963), 221–56 (at 238–41).

39. See Doyle, "The Parlements of France and the Breakdown of the Old Régime," 415–58, along with William Doyle, *The Parlement of Bordeaux at the End of the Old Regime, 1771–1790* (London: Ernest Benn, 1974), the two books by Bailey Stone: *The Parlement of Paris, 1774–1789* (Chapel Hill: University of North Carolina Press, 1981), and *The French Parlements and the Crisis of the Old Regime* (Chapel Hill: University of North Carolina Press, 1986); and Bell, *Lawyers and Citizens*, 139–94 (esp. 181–94).

40. In this connection, note Gabriel Dominique Bonno, *La Constitution brittanique devant l'opinion française de Montesquieu à Bonaparte* (New York: Burt Franklin, 1971).

41. After reading Harold T. Parker, *The Cult of Antiquity and the French Revolutionaries: A Study in the Development of the Revolutionary Spirit* (Chicago: University of Chicago Press, 1937), and Claude Mossé, *L'Antiquité dans la Révolution française* (Paris: Albin Michel, 1989), see Bernard Manin, "Montesquieu," in *A Critical Dictionary of the French Revolution*, ed. François Furet and Mona Ozouf, tr. Arthur Goldhammer (Cambridge, MA: Belknap Press, 1989), 728–41 (at 730–31); Marco Platania, "Virtù,

repubbliche, rivoluzione: Saint-Just e Montesquieu," in *Poteri, democrazia, virtù: Montesquieu nei movimenti repubblicani all'epoca della Rivoluzione francese,* ed. Domenico Felice (Milan: Franco Angeli, 2000), 11–44, along with Catherine Larrère, "Montesquieu et *l'exception française,*" in ibid., 51–64, and Cristina Passetti, "Temi montesquieuiani in Louis de Saint-Just," in *Montesquieu e i suoi interpreti,* I 413–31.

42. See Robert Shackleton, *Montesquieu: A Critical Biography* (Oxford, UK: Oxford University Press, 1961), 276–77; Wyger R. E. Velema, "Republican Readings of Montesquieu: *The Spirit of Laws* in the Dutch Republic," *History of Political Thought* 18:1 (Spring 1997): 43–63; and the essays as yet uncited from *Poteri, democrazia, virtù,* as well as Catherine Larrère, "Montesquieu républicain? De l'Interprétation universitaire pendant la IIIᵉ République," *XVIIIᵉ siècle* 21 (1989): 150–62, and "Montesquieu and the Modern Republic: The Republican Heritage in Nineteenth-Century France," in *Montesquieu and the Spirit of Modernity,* ed. David W. Carrithers and Patrick Coleman (Oxford, UK: Voltaire Foundation, 2002), 235–49. For current scholarship reflective of the same propensity, see Rahe, *M* II.1, note 40.

43. See Anicet Sénéchal, "Jean-Jacques Rousseau, secrétaire de Madame Dupin d'après des documents inédits avec an inventaire des papiers Dupin dispersés en 1957 et 1958," *Annales de la Société Jean-Jacques Rousseau* 36 (1963–1965): 173–288, with Bernard Gagnebin, "Notes sur la dispersion des papiers Dupin," ibid., 289–90.

44. See Corrado Rosso, *Montesquieu moraliste: Des Lois au bonheur* (Paris: Editions Ducros, 1971), 283–316; Robert Shackleton, "Montesquieu, Dupin and the Early Writings of Rousseau," in *Reappraisals of Rousseau: Studies in Honour of R. A. Leigh,* ed. Simon Harvey, Marian Hobson, David Kelley, and Samuel S. B. Taylor (Manchester, UK: Manchester University Press, 1980), 234–49, which is reprinted in Shackleton, *Essays on Montesquieu and on the Enlightenment,* ed. David Gilson and Martin Smith (Oxford, UK: Voltaire Foundation, 1988), 183–96; Jean Ehrard, "Rousseau et Montesquieu: Le mauvais Fils réconcilié," *Annales de la société Jean-Jacques Rousseau* 41 (1997): 57–77, reprinted as "Le Fils coupable," in Ehrard, *L'Esprit des mots: Montesquieu en lui-même et parmi les siens* (Geneva: Droz, 1998), 256–75; and Charles Porset, "Madame Dupin et Montesquieu, ou Les Infortunes de la vertu," in *Actes du colloque international tenu à Bordeaux, du 3 au 6 décembre 1998,* ed. Louis Desgraves (Bordeaux: Académie de Bordeaux, 1999), 287–306. Note, however, Sonenscher, *Before the Deluge,* 222–39.

45. There are exceptions to this rule. Leo Strauss, "On the Intention of Rousseau," *Social Research* 14 (1947): 455–87, which is reprinted in *Hobbes and Rousseau: A Collection of Critical Essays,* ed. Maurice Cranston and Richard S. Peters (Garden City, NY: Doubleday, 1972), 254–90, recognized the connection, apparently without being aware of the work in this regard done by Rousseau for the Dupins, as did Alexis François, "Rousseau, Les Dupins, Montesquieu," *Annales de la société Jean-Jacques Rousseau* 30 (1943–1945): 47–64; Michel Launay, "Le *Discours sur les sciences et les arts*: Jean-Jacques entre Mᵐᵉ Dupin et Montesquieu," in *Jean-Jacques Rousseau et son temps: Politique et littérature au XVIIIᵉ siècle,* ed. Michel Launay (Paris: A.-G. Nizet, 1969), 93–103, and *Jean-Jacques Rousseau: Écrivain politique,* 2nd ed., reviewed and aug-

mented with a preface by Jean Starobinski (Geneva: Éditions Slatkine, 1989), 158–62; Bernard Yack, *The Longing for Total Revolution: Philosophic Sources of Social Discontent from Rousseau to Marx and Nietzsche* (Princeton, NJ: Princeton University Press, 1986), 35–60; and Sonenscher, *Before the Deluge*, 222–39, who all had the benefit of being aware of the extensive notes on *De l'Esprit des lois* taken by Rousseau.

BOOK TWO, CHAPTER ONE.
THE ENLIGHTENMENT INDICTED

1. For the details, see Arthur M. Wilson, *Diderot* (New York: Oxford University Press, 1972), 103–16, and Maurice Cranston, *Jean-Jacques: The Early Life and Work of Jean-Jacques Rousseau, 1712–1754* (New York: W. W. Norton, 1982), 226–70. In this connection, note Raymond Trousson, *Socrate devant Voltaire, Diderot, et Rousseau: La Conscience en face du mythe* (Paris: Minard, 1967), 105–24.

2. For the advertisement, which appeared in *Mercure de France* (October 1949): 153–55, see Rousseau, *DSA* 91.

3. Letter to Chrétien Guillaume de Lamoignon de Malesherbes on 12 January 1762, in JJR I 1134–38 (at 1135–36).

4. See Wilson, *Diderot*, 113–15, and Cranston, *Jean-Jacques*, 227–70.

5. Rousseau's claim that Madame Dupin "never employed" him "except to write under her dictation and for research of pure erudition" is, to say the least, misleading: see C 7.341–42.

6. See Alexis François, "Rousseau, Les Dupins, Montesquieu," *Annales de la société Jean-Jacques Rousseau* 30 (1943–1945): 47–64; Michel Launay, "Le *Discours sur les sciences et les arts*: Jean-Jacques entre Mme Dupin et Montesquieu," in *Jean-Jacques Rousseau et son temps: Politique et littérature au XVIIIe siècle*, ed. Michel Launay (Paris: A.-G. Nizet, 1969), 93–103; and *Jean-Jacques Rousseau: Écrivain politique*, 2nd ed., reviewed and augmented with a preface by Jean Starobinski (Geneva: Éditions Slatkine, 1989), 158–62; Bernard Yack, *The Longing for Total Revolution: Philosophic Sources of Social Discontent from Rousseau to Marx and Nietzsche* (Princeton, NJ: Princeton University Press, 1986), 35–60; Michael Sonenscher, *Before the Deluge: Public Debt, Inequality, and the Intellectual Origins of the French Revolution* (Princeton, NJ: Princeton University Press, 2007), 222–39; then consider Jean Ehrard, "Rousseau et Montesquieu: Le mauvais Fils réconcilié," *Annales de la société Jean-Jacques Rousseau* 41 (1997): 57–77, reprinted as "Le Fils coupable," in Ehrard, *L'Esprit des mots: Montesquieu en lui-même et parmi les siens* (Geneva: Droz, 1998), 256–75.

7. See Montesquieu, *Voyage de Gratz a La Haye*, in Pléiade I 863–64, 873–74.

8. See *EL* 3.14.10, 16.11, 19.5–9.

9. For a more elaborate discussion of this issue than is possible here, see Rahe, *M* II.2–4, III.2–4.

10. In many of his works, Rousseau highlighted—and even exaggerated—his ties to Geneva, and much of what he had to say in his political works was directed to his compatriots: note Arthur M. Melzer, *The Natural Goodness of Man: On the System of*

Rousseau's Thought (Chicago: University of Chicago Press, 1990), 253–82, and see Helena Rosenblatt, *Rousseau and Geneva: From the First Discourse to the Social Contract, 1749–1762* (Cambridge, UK: Cambridge University Press, 1997). Whether it was aimed exclusively at them is, of course, another question. Rousseau was after all a dramatist with a keen sense of how comedies and operas would play on the stage.

11. Consider Rousseau, *LS* 31–43, in light of Voltaire, *Lettres philosophiques*, ed. Gustave Lanson, 3rd ed. (Paris: Société des Textes Français Modernes, 1924), II 184–226, esp. 185, and see Arnoux Straudo, *La Fortune de Pascal en France au dix-huitième siècle* (Oxford, UK: Voltaire Foundation, 1997), 77–104, 179–88, 227–39, 301–29, 362–70; then, ibid., 215–26; and Mark Hulliung, "Rousseau, Voltaire, and the Revenge of Pascal," in *The Cambridge Companion to Rousseau*, ed. Patrick Riley (Cambridge, UK: Cambridge University Press, 2001), 57–77.

12. That Rousseau's peculiar temperament was a powerful spur to his ruminations he makes clear in his biographical works. In the process, he virtually demands that his thinking be interpreted in this light. For exceedingly intelligent attempts to do so, see Jean Starobinski, *Jean-Jacques Rousseau: Transparency and Obstruction* (1957), tr. Arthur Goldhammer (Chicago: University of Chicago, 1988), and Ronald Grimsley, *Jean-Jacques Rousseau: A Study in Self-Awareness* (Cardiff, UK: University of Wales Press, 1961). Although the Marxist interpretation articulated by Launay, *Jean-Jacques Rousseau*, passim, suffers from all of the usual defects, it has the great virtue of paying close and intelligent attention both to the society in which Rousseau lived and to contemporary events. See also John McManners, "The Social Contract and Rousseau's Revolt against Society," in *Hobbes and Rousseau: A Collection of Critical Essays*, ed. Maurice Cranston and Richard S. Peters (Garden City, NY: Doubleday, 1972), 291–317, and Georges May, "Rousseau and France," *Yale French Studies* 28 (1961): 122–35.

13. Consider Rousseau, *C* 9, 404–5, in light of what can be inferred from Rousseau, *Dépêches de Venise*, ed. Jean-Daniel Candaux, in JJR III 1043–1234.

14. See Leo Strauss, "On the Intention of Rousseau," *Social Research* 14 (1947): 455–87, which is reprinted in *Hobbes and Rousseau*, 254–90, along with François, "Rousseau, Les Dupin, Montesquieu," 47–64; Launay, "Le *Discours sur les sciences et les arts*," 93–103, and *Jean-Jacques Rousseau*, 158–62; Yack, *The Longing for Total Revolution*, 35–60; and Sonenscher, *Before the Deluge*, 222–39.

15. See Denis Diderot, *Réfutation suivie de l'ouvrage d'Helvétius intitulé L'Homme* (ca. 1773–74), in *Œuvres complètes de Diderot*, ed. Jules Assézat and Maurice Tourneux (Paris: Garnier, 1875–1877), II 275–456 (at 285–87).

16. That he was, even then, a republican, he expressly indicated in Letter to François-Marie Arouet de Voltaire on 30 January 1750 (no. 149), in CCJJR II 123–26, which, as it happens, is the first letter he is known ever to have signed "Citoyen de Genève."

17. If one neglects the circumstances in which Rousseau was writing, one will be likely to underestimate the continuity between the analysis that he lays out in his *First Discourse* and that which appears in his *Discourse on the Origin and Foundations of Inequality among Men*: see, for example, Robert Wokler, "The *Discours sur les sciences et les arts* and its Offspring: Rousseau in Reply to His Critics," in *Reappraisals of Rousseau: Stud-*

ies in Honour of R. A. Leigh, ed. Simon Harvey et al. (Manchester, UK: Manchester University Press, 1980), 250–78, and John Hope Mason, "Reading Rousseau's *First Discourse,*" *Studies on Voltaire and the Eighteenth Century* 249 (1987): 251–66.

18. In describing and analyzing Rousseau's dilemma, Launay, *Jean-Jacques Rousseau,* 158–61, is especially perceptive.

19. See Strauss, "On the Intention of Rousseau," 455–87, reprinted in *Hobbes and Rousseau,* 254–90; Victor Gourevitch, "Rousseau on the Arts and Sciences," *Journal of Philosophy* 69 (1972): 737–54; Clifford Orwin, "Rousseau's Socratism," *Journal of Politics* 60:1 (February 1998): 174–87; and Sally Howard Campbell and John T. Scott, "Rousseau's Politic Argument in the *Discourse on the Sciences and Arts,*" *American Journal of Political Science* 49:4 (October 2005): 818–28. In this connection, see *Jean-Jacques entre Socrate et Caton: Textes inédits de Jean-Jacques Rousseau (1750–1753),* ed. Claude Pichois and René Pintard (Paris: José Corti, 1972). Note also Laurence D. Cooper, "Human Nature and the Love of Wisdom: Rousseau's Hidden (and Modified) Platonism," *Journal of Politics* 64:1 (February 2002): 108–25.

20. See Mark Hulliung, *The Autocritique of Enlightenment: Rousseau and the Philosophes* (Cambridge, MA: Harvard University Press, 1994).

21. See II.2–3, below.

22. Note, for example, Rousseau, DSA 1, DOI 109, and the title pages of *LS,* in JJR V 1, and of *CS,* in JJR III 347; then consider Rousseau, *Julie* Seconde Préf., p. 27, where Rousseau explains why in some works he calls himself a "Citizen of Geneva" and why in others he does not. In this connection, see Graeme Garrard, *Rousseau's Counter-Enlightenment: A Republican Critique of the Philosophes* (Albany: State University of New York Press, 2003), passim (esp. 87–101).

23. In this connection, see Victor Goldschmidt, *Anthropologie et politique: Les Principes du système de Rousseau* (Paris: Vrin, 1974), 45–104.

24. See Antoine Adam, "De quelques Sources de Rousseau dans la littérature philosophique (1700–1750)," in *Jean-Jacques Rousseau et son oeuvre: Problèmes et recherches* (Paris: Librarie C. Klincksieck, 1964), 125–32 (at 127–28).

25. See Denise Leduc-Fayette, *Jean-Jacques Rousseau et le mythe de l'antiquité* (Paris: J. Vrin, 1974).

26. For the significance given the word *police* and its cognates at this time, see Peter France, "Polish, police, *polis,*" in his *Politeness and Its Discontents: Problems in French Classical Culture* (Cambridge, UK: Cambridge University Press, 1992), 53–73, and Daniel Gordon, *Citizens without Sovereignty: Equality and Sociability in French Thought, 1670–1789* (Princeton, NJ: Princeton University Press, 1994), 18–23.

27. In this connection, consider the epigraph to II.Pref., above: Rousseau, PN 968.

28. In this connection, see Pierre Manent, *An Intellectual History of Liberalism,* tr. Rebecca Balinski (Princeton, NJ: Princeton University Press, 1994), 53–79 (esp. 63–72).

29. For the origins and import of the phrase *l'esprit fort,* see Rahe, ATA 155–68, 297–312.

30. Elsewhere, by way of a discussion of playwrights and the theater, Rousseau explores more fully the social and political import of the artist's dependence on his audience: see Rousseau, LS 1–125 (esp. 14–84).

31. Compare the note at the end of Rousseau, *CS* 3.9, in which he takes an oblique shot at Voltaire, with Montesquieu, *LP* 46.59–69/48. Note also the indictment leveled in Jean-Jacques Rousseau, *Lettre à M. de Voltaire*, 18 August 1756, ed. Henri Gouhier, in JJR IV 1059–75.

32. Compare Montesquieu, *EL* 1.4.6, 7.8–9, 14, 3.19.12, with *MP* 1062; consider Rahe, *M* III.1; and see Rousseau, *DOI* 119–20. Then see Rousseau, *Julie* II.xxi; note Montesquieu, *LP* 61/63, 96–97/99–100; and consider Ursula Vogel, "'But in a Republic, Men Are Needed': Guarding the Boundaries of Liberty," in *Rousseau and Liberty*, ed. Robert Wokler (Manchester, UK: Manchester University Press, 1995), 213–30.

33. See Antoine Lilti, "The Writing of Paranoia: Jean-Jacques Rousseau and the Paradoxes of Celebrity," *Representations* 103 (Summer 2008): 53–83.

34. Rousseau's attempt to disguise his point was so maladroit, as he must have recognized in the end, that it could never have passed muster: see the critical edition of Bibliothèque publique et universitaire de Genève MS. fr. 228, fol. 39 recto–40 verso, and Bibliothèque de la ville de Neuchâtel MS R.N. a. 9 fol. 1, which is printed in Jean-Jacques Rousseau, *Diskurs über die Ungleichheit/Discours sur l'inégalité: Kritische Ausgabe des integralen Textes, mit sämtlichen Fragmenten und ergänzenden Materialien nach den Originalausgaben und den Handschriften neu ediert, übersetzt, und kommentiert*, 5th ed., ed. Heinrich Meier (Paderborn: Ferdinand Schöningh, 2001), 386–403, and consider Robert Shackleton, "Censure and Censorship: Impediments to Free Publication in the Age of Enlightenment," *Library Chronicle of the University of Texas at Austin* n.s. 6 (December 1973): 25–41, reprinted in Shackleton, *Essays on Montesquieu and on the Enlightenment* (Oxford, UK: Voltaire Foundation, 1988), 405–20, and William Hanley, "The Policing of Thought: Censorship in Eighteenth-Century France," *Studies on Voltaire and the Eighteenth Century* 183 (1980): 265–95. Note also Edgar Mass, *Literatur und Zensur in der frühen Aufklärung: Produktion, Distribution und Rezeption der Lettres persanes* (Frankfurt am Main: Vittorio Klostermann, 1981), 5–68, 139–205.

35. See Mark Goldie, "The Civil Religion of James Harrington," in *The Languages of Political Theory in Early-Modern Europe*, ed. Anthony Pagden (Cambridge, UK: Cambridge University Press, 1987), 197–222. With regard to the history and character of the early modern crusade against priestcraft, see Rahe, *ATA* passim.

36. In this connection, see François Furet, "La *Librairie* du royaume de France au 18ᵉ siècle," in *Livre et société dans la France du XVIIIᵉ siècle*, ed. Geneviève Bollème et al. (Paris: Mouton, 1965–1970), I 3–32, which is reprinted in translation as "Book Licensing and Book Production in the Kingdom of France in the Eighteenth Century," in Furet, *In the Workshop of History*, tr. Jonathan Mandelbaum (Chicago: University of Chicago Press, 1984), 99–124.

37. Note Christopher Kelly, *Rousseau as Author: Consecrating One's Life to the Truth* (Chicago: University of Chicago Press, 2003), and see Pierre Grosclaude, *Malesherbes: Témoin et interprète de son temps* (Paris: Librairie Fischbacher, 1961), 63–186, and Maurice Cranston, *The Noble Savage: Jean-Jacques Rousseau, 1754–1762* (Chicago: University of Chicago Press, 1991), 6–7, 133–39, 151, 203–4, 215–16, 220, 226, 232–53, 266–69, 278–362.

38. See Maurice Cranston, *The Noble Savage,* 323–62, and *The Solitary Self: Jean-Jacques Rousseau in Exile and Adversity* (Chicago: University of Chicago Press, 1997).

39. For a brief introduction to this neglected work, see Christopher Kelly and Roger D. Masters, "Rousseau on Reading 'Jean-Jacques': *The Dialogues,*" *Interpretation: A Journal of Political Philosophy* 17:2 (Winter 1989–1990): 239–53.

40. For a more detailed discussion than is possible here, see Arthur M. Melzer, "The Origin of the Counter-Enlightenment: Rousseau and the New Religion of Sincerity," *American Political Science Review* 90:2 (June 1996): 344–60 (esp. 344–51).

41. For a brief but telling discussion of the foundations for Rousseau's claim, see Judith N. Shklar, *Men and Citizens: A Study of Rousseau's Social Theory* (Cambridge, UK: Cambridge University Press, 1969), 95–99. Note also Melzer, "The Origin of the Counter-Enlightenment," 347 n. 7, and Garrard, *Rousseau's Counter-Enlightenment,* 11–27, 83–87.

BOOK TWO, CHAPTER TWO. SOCIABILITY AS A MALADY

1. In this connection, see Charles Edwyn Vaughan, "The Eclipse of Contract: Montesquieu," in *Studies in the History of Political Philosophy before and after Rousseau,* 2nd ed., ed. Andrew George Little (New York: Russell & Russell, 1960), I 253–302 (esp. 295–96), and Robert Derathé, "Montesquieu et Jean-Jacques Rousseau," *Revue internationale de philosophie* 33–34: 3–4 (1955): 366–86.

2. See Letter to Pastor Jean Pedriau on 20 February 1755 (no. 277), in CCJJR III 98–100.

3. See also Letter to the Gens de loi on 15 October 1758 (no. 712), in CCJJR V 177–81 (at 178).

4. Letter to Paul-Claude Moultou on 25 October 1762 (no. 2338), in CCJJR XIV 100–103 (at 101–2).

5. See Letter to Charles-François-Frédéric de Montmorency-Luxembourg, maréchal-duc de Luxembourg on 20 October 1761 (no. 1514), in CCJJR IX 189–90.

6. The last of these chapters should be read in light of Rousseau, *LM* 1.706–7.

7. Compare Jean Le Rond d'Alembert, "Discours préliminaire des editeurs" (1751), in *Encyclopédie, ou Dictionnaire raisonné des sciences, des arts, et des métiers,* ed. Denis Diderot and Jean Le Rond d'Alembert (Paris: Briasson, 1751–1772; Neufchastel: S. Faulche & Compagnie: 1765; Amsterdam: M. M. Rey, 1776–1777; Paris: Panckoucke, 1777–780), I i–liii (at xxxiii), with Jean-Jacques Rousseau, *Observations de Jean-Jacques Rousseau de Genève* (1751), ed. François Bouchardy, in JJR III 35–57 (at 42–43, 56–57).

8. Compare Montesquieu, *EL* 3.19, and see Roberto Romani, "All Montesquieu's Sons: The Place of *Esprit Général, Caractère National,* and *Moeurs* in French Political Philosophy, 1748–1789," *Studies on Voltaire and the Eighteenth Century* 362 (1998): 189–235 (esp. 213–18), and Fonna Forman-Barzilai, "The Emergence of Contextualism in Rousseau's Political Thought: The Case of Parisian Theatre in the *Lettre à d'Alembert,*" *History of Political Thought* 24:3 (Autumn 2003): 435–63. Compare John T. Scott, "Climate, Causation, and the Power of Music in Montesquieu and Rousseau," in *Musique et langage chez Rousseau,* ed. Claude Dauphin, *Studies on Voltaire and the Eighteenth*

Century 2004:08 (2004): 51–61, who fails to grasp the complexity of Montesquieu's analysis of national character, understates the role played in Montesquieu's scheme by moral causes, and thereby underestimates the scope of Rousseau's reliance on his predecessor's political science.

9. Compare Montesquieu, *EL* 1.1.3. Note the attention that Rousseau pays to modes of subsistence in Jean-Jacques Rousseau, *Fragments politiques* 10.1, ed. Robert Derathé, in JJR III 529–33.

10. See Letter from David Hume on 2 July 1762 (no. 1944), in CCJJR XI 196–98 and in *Letters of David Hume*, ed. J. Y. T. Greig (Oxford: Clarendon Press, 1932), I 364–65.

11. On the significance of this allusion, see Michel Launay, "Le *Discours sur les sciences et les arts*: Jean-Jacques entre Mme Dupin et Montesquieu," in *Jean-Jacques Rousseau et son temps: Politique et littérature au XVIIIe siècle*, ed. Michel Launay et al. (Paris: A.-G. Nizet, 1969), 93–103; and *Jean-Jacques Rousseau: Écrivain politique*, 2nd ed., reviewed and augmented with a preface by Jean Starobinski (Geneva: Éditions Slatkine, 1989), 158–62.

12. Compare Thomas Hobbes, *Leviathan*, ed. Edwin Curley (Indianapolis, IN: Hackett, 1994) I.x.16.

13. In this connection, see John T. Scott, "Rousseau and the Melodious Language of Freedom," *Journal of Politics* 59:3 (August 1997): 803–29, and "The Harmony between Rousseau's Musical Theory and His Philosophy," *Journal of the History of Ideas* 59:2 (April 1998): 287–308.

14. After reading the essay cited in note 36, this chapter, see Clifford Orwin, "Montesquieu's *Humanité* and Rousseau's *Pitié*," in *Montesquieu and His Legacy*, ed. Rebecca E. Kingston (Albany: State University of New York Press, 2008), 139–47.

15. Note Rousseau's depiction of the philosopher in *DOI* 156.

16. Compare Montesquieu, *Le Temple de Gnide* (1725), in Pléiade I 386–415, which should be read in conjunction with the material cut in 1743 from the original preface, which can be found in ibid. I 1602–3 (esp. 1603), and see Victor Gourevitch, "Rousseau on Lying: A Provisional Reading of the Fourth *Rêverie*," *Berkshire Review* 15 (1980): 93–107.

17. It is, as Gourevitch points out, "Rousseau on Lying," 105, n. 25, instructive to compare Montesquieu, *LP* Préf. 1–3, where the author chooses to remain anonymous, with Rousseau, *Julie* Préf., p. 5, where the author insists on taking responsibility for what he writes. In this connection, see Christopher Kelly, *Rousseau as Author: Consecrating One's Life to the Truth* (Chicago: University of Chicago Press, 2003).

18. Compare Niccolò Machiavelli, *Il principe* 15, in Machiavelli, *Tutte le opere*, ed. Mario Martelli (Florence: G. C. Sansoni, 1971), 280.

19. Letter to Pastor Jean Pedriau on 20 February 1755 (no. 277), in CCJJR III 98–100.

20. Note Rousseau, *CS* 4.9, and see Derathé, "Montesquieu et Jean-Jacques Rousseau," 371–76.

21. In this connection, see Pierre Manent, *An Intellectual History of Liberalism*, tr. Rebecca Balinski (Princeton, NJ: Princeton University Press, 1994), 53–64; Jean Ehrard, "Actualité d'un demi-silence: Montesquieu et l'idée de souveraineté," *Rivista di storia della filosofia* 49:1 (January–March 1994): 9–20, which is reprinted as "La Souve-

raineté," in Ehrard, *L'Esprit des mots: Montesquieu en lui-même et parmi les siens* (Geneva: Droz, 1998), 147–60; Catherine Larrère, "Montesquieu: L'Éclipse de la souveraineté," in *Penser la souveraineté à l'époque modern et contemporaine*, ed. Gian Mario Cazzaniga and Yves Charles Zarka (Paris: Vrin, 2001), 199–214; and Yoshie Kawade, "La Liberté civile contre la théorie réformiste de l'État souverain: Le Combat de Montesquieu," in *Le Travail des lumières: Pour Georges Benrekassa*, ed. Caroline Jacot Grapa, Nicole Jacques-Lefèvre, Yannick Séité, and Carine Trevisan (Paris: Honoré Champion, 2002), 203–23.

22. In this connection, see Vaughan, "The Eclipse of Contract: Montesquieu," 253–302, and Rahe, *M* III.4. This was a concern of David Hume as well: see Charles Edwyn Vaughan, "The Assault on Contract: Hume," in *Studies in the History of Political Philosophy before and after Rousseau*, I 303–64.

23. Consider Rousseau, *DR* 76, and Rousseau, *PN* 971–72, in light of *Observations de Jean-Jacques Rousseau de Genève*, in JJR III 52, 55–56; and see Rousseau, *D* 3.935. Note in this connection, Rousseau, *LM* 7.828.

24. See Jean-Jacques Rousseau, "Jugement sur la polysynodie" (ca. 1756–58), ed. Sven Stelling-Michaud, in JJR III 635–45 (at 637–38). In this connection, see Gordon H. McNeil, "The Anti-Revolutionary Rousseau," *American Historical Review* 58:4 (July 1953): 808–23.

25. Compare Montesquieu, *EL* 3.19, and see Rahe, *M* III.1. Note also *CP* 15.1041, where Rousseau speaks of the need "to follow the *esprit* of this Republic."

26. In this connection, see David Lowenthal, "Book I of Montesquieu's *Spirit of the Laws*," *American Political Science Review* 53:2 (June 1959): 485–98; Mark H. Waddicor, *Montesquieu and the Philosophy of Natural Law* (The Hague: Martinus Nijhoff, 1970), 65–99; Thomas L. Pangle, *Montesquieu's Philosophy of Liberalism: A Commentary on The Spirit of the Laws* (Chicago: University of Chicago Press, 1973), 20–47; George Klosko, "Montesquieu's Science of Politics: Absolute Values and Ethical Relativism in *L'Esprit des lois*," *Studies on Voltaire and the Eighteenth Century* 189 (1980): 153–77; Jean Goldzinck, "Sur le Chapitre 1, du livre 1, de *l'Esprit des lois* de Montesquieu," in *Analyses & réflexions sur Montesquieu, De l'Esprit des lois: La Nature et la loi* (Paris: Ellipses, 1987), 107–19; Pierre Rétat, "Les Ambiguïtés de la notion de loi chez Montesquieu: Analyse du livre I de *L'Esprit des lois*," in *De la Tyrannie au totalitarisme: Recherche sur les ambiguïtés de la philosophie politique* (Lyon: L'Hermès, 1986), 125–35; Michael Zuckert, "Natural Law, Natural Rights, and Classical Liberalism: On Montesquieu's Critique of Hobbes," in *Natural Law and Modern Moral Philosophy*, ed. Ellen Frankel Paul, Fred Miller Jr., and Jeffrey Paul (Cambridge, UK: Cambridge University Press 2001): 227–51; Stanley Rosen, "Politics and Nature in Montesquieu," in Rosen, *The Elusiveness of the Ordinary: Studies in the Possibility of Philosophy* (New Haven, CT: Yale University Press, 2002), 14–53; Kawade, "La Liberté civile contre la théorie réformiste de l'État souverain," 203–23; and Stuart D. Warner, "Montesquieu's Prelude: An Interpretation of Book I of *The Spirit of Laws*," in *Enlightening Revolutions: Essays in Honor of Ralph Lerner*, ed. Svetozar Minkov and Stephane Douard (Lanham, MD: Lexington Books, 2006), 159–87. Also pertinent are Sharon R. Krause, "History and the Human Soul in Montesquieu," *History of Political Thought* 24:2 (Summer 2003): 235–61 (at

235–52), and "Laws, Passion, and the Attractions of Right Action in Montesquieu," *Philosophy & Social Criticism* 32:2 (2006): 211–30.

27. See Rahe, *M* III.1.

28. See Simone Goyard-Fabre, *Montesquieu, adversaire de Hobbes* (Paris: Lettres Modernes, 1980).

29. Compare Thomas Hobbes, *Leviathan* I.xiv.31.

30. Note Montesquieu, *CR* 6.211–34, and see Rahe, *M* III.1–2.

31. See John T. Scott, "The Theodicy of the *Second Discourse*: The 'Pure State of Nature' and Rousseau's Political Thought," *American Political Science Review* 86:3 (September 1992): 696–711 (at 709–10, n. 7), who acknowledges Rousseau's debt but underestimates its extent, and Zuckert, "Natural Law, Natural Rights, and Classical Liberalism," 239–51 (esp. 240, 251).

32. Note also Rousseau, *É* 4.493, along with the passage that Rousseau cut from the end of the note in *É* 4.495 (which can be found at *JJR* IV 1459), and *D* 2.805, and see Patrick Riley, *The General Will before Rousseau: The Transformation of the Divine into the Civic* (Princeton, NJ: Princeton University Press, 1986), passim (esp. 138–250).

33. Note, in this connection, Rousseau, *Julie* Seconde Préf., p. 12.

34. Compare Rousseau, *EOL* 9.395–407 (esp. 396–400), where his debt to Montesquieu is even more obvious.

35. That he took note of the passage is clear: cf. Rousseau, *EOL* 9.402.

36. See Clifford Orwin, "Rousseau and the Discovery of Political Compassion," in *The Legacy of Rousseau*, ed. Clifford Orwin and Nathan Tarcov (Chicago: University of Chicago Press, 1997), 296–320.

37. For an extended rumination on the latter problem, see Judith N. Shklar, "Rousseau's Images of Authority," *American Political Science Review* 58:4 (December 1964): 919–32, which is reprinted in *Hobbes and Rousseau: A Collection of Critical Essays*, ed. Maurice Cranston and Richard S. Peters (Garden City, NY: Doubleday, 1972), 333–65, and in *The Cambridge Companion to Rousseau*, ed. Patrick Riley (Cambridge, UK: Cambridge University Press, 2001), 154–92. See also Judith N. Shklar, *Men and Citizens: A Study of Rousseau's Social Theory* (Cambridge, UK: Cambridge University Press, 1969), 127–65.

38. On the various stages in this process, see Arthur O. Lovejoy, "The Supposed Primitivism of Rousseau's *Discourse on Inequality*," *Modern Philology* 21 (1923): 165–86, which is reprinted in Lovejoy, *Essays in the History of Ideas* (Baltimore, MD: Johns Hopkins University Press, 1948), 14–37, and should be read alongside Arthur O. Lovejoy and George Boas, *Primitivism and Related Ideas in Antiquity* (Baltimore, MD: Johns Hopkins University Press, 1961), 103–367 (esp. 222–42). In this connection, see also Victor Goldschmidt, *Anthropologie et politique: Les Principes du système de Rousseau* (Paris: Vrin, 1974).

39. Note Rousseau, *DOI* 133, and then consider 122, 138–39, 151–57, 164, 168–79, 188–93, 202–8. For accounts of the argument of the *Second Discourse* far more detailed and systematic than it is possible to provide here, see Leo Strauss, *Natural Right and History* (Chicago: University of Chicago Press, 1953), 252–94; Marc F. Plattner, *Rousseau's State of Nature: An Interpretation of the Discourse on Inequality* (Dekalb: Northern Illi-

nois University Press, 1979); Heinrich Meier, "Rousseaus Diskurs über den Ursprung und die Grundlagen der Ungleichheit unter den Menschen: Ein einführender Essay über die Rhetorik und die Intention des Werkes," in Jean-Jacques Rousseau, *Diskurs über die Ungleichheit/Discours sur l'inégalité: Kritische Ausgabe des integralen Textes, mit sämtlichen Fragmenten und ergänzenden Materialien nach den Originalausgaben und den Handschriften neu ediert, übersetzt, und kommentiert*, 5th ed., ed. Heinrich Meier (Paderborn: Ferdinand Schöningh, 2001), xxi–lxvii, and "The *Discourse on the Origin and the Foundations of Inequality among Men:* On the Intention of Rousseau's Most Philosophic Work," *Interpretation: A Journal of Political Philosophy* 16:2 (Winter 1988–1989): 211–27; and Scott, "The Theodicy of the *Second Discourse*," 696–711.

40. Compare, however, Rousseau, *EOL* 9.395–407, where Rousseau provides an account, much closer to the one found in Montesquieu, in which something like the family and a measure of natural sociability appear to have existed from the start: see Victor Gourevitch, "'The First Times' in Rousseau's *Essay on the Origins of Languages*," *Graduate Faculty Philosophy Journal* 11:2 (1986): 123–46, and "The Political Argument of Rousseau's *Essay on the Origin of Languages*," in *Pursuits of Reason: Essays in Honor of Stanley Cavell*, ed. Ted Cohen, Paul Guyer, and Hilary Putnam (Lubbock: Texas Tech University, 1993), 21–35, along with Scott, "Rousseau and the Melodious Language of Freedom," 803–29. In keeping with this fact, and in contrast with all but the last of the scholars cited in note 39, this chapter, Gourevitch thinks that in the *Discourse on the Origin and Foundations of Inequality*, Rousseau's depiction of man in the pure state of nature as a radically solitary individual is conjectural: see Victor Gourevitch, "Rousseau's Pure State of Nature," *Interpretation: A Journal of Political Philosophy* 16:1 (Fall 1988): 23–59. For an elaborate argument along similar lines, see Jonathan Marks, *Perfection and Disharmony in the Thought of Jean-Jacques Rousseau* (New York: Cambridge University Press, 2005), 15–117.

41. In this connection, see Rousseau, *Lettre à M. de Voltaire*, 18 August 1756, ed. Henri Gouhier, in JJR IV 1059–75 (esp. 1062–63, 1069–70); note Arist. *Pol.* 1278b25–30; and see note 55, this chapter.

42. See Bernard Mandeville, "An Essay on Charity and Charity-Schools" (1723), in *The Fable of the Bees: or, Private Vices, Publick Benefits*, ed. F. B. Kaye (Oxford, UK: Clarendon Press, 1924), I 254–59.

43. Compare, however, Rousseau, *EOL* 9.395–96, and *RPS* 9.1094, where we are told that pity presupposes reflection, with Rousseau, *D* 2.798, 805–6, 864, where the opposite is suggested. In this connection, see also Rousseau, É 4.489–5.867 (esp. 4.502–18, 522–37, 543–48, 594–606).

44. Note Jean Morel, "Recherches sur les sources du *Discours sur l'inegalité*," *Annales de la Société Jean-Jacques Rousseau* 5 (1910): 119–98, and see James H. Nichols Jr., *Epicurean Political Philosophy: The De rerum natura of Lucretius* (Ithaca, NY: Cornell University Press, 1976), 179–210 (esp. 198–207), who highlights the link between Lucretius' antipolitical outlook and the critical evaluation of the significance of sociability that dictates the peculiar slant of Rousseau's political philosophy. In this connection, see the running commentary in Heinrich Meier's notes to Rousseau, *Diskurs über die Ungleichheit/Discours sur l'inégalité*, esp. 79, n. 96; 91, n. 114; 92–94, n. 116; 109–10, n. 139a; 119,

n. 152; 122–24, n. 156; 126–27, n. 160; 180, n. 222; 183, n. 227; 185, n. 229; 188–89, n. 232; 194–95, n. 240; 198–99, n. 247; 203–4, n. 251; 217–18, n. 265; 366–67, n. 451, which document the unspoken connection in detail. Note also the crucial paragraph prudently omitted from Rousseau, *Lettre à M. de Voltaire*, in JJR IV 1059–75 (at 1071).

45. See Rousseau, *Lettre de J. J. Rousseau à Monsieur Philopolis*, ed. Jean Starobinski, in JJR III 230–36 (at 232).

46. Consider Rousseau, *DOI* 219–20, in light of Nannerl O. Keohane, *Philosophy and the State in France: The Renaissance to the Enlightenment* (Princeton, NJ: Princeton University Press, 1980), 183–97, 262–82, 294–311, 420–442; the epigraph to I.2, above; and the discussion which follows in that chapter; then see John Plamenatz, "Pascal and Rousseau," *Political Studies* 10:3 (October 1962): 248–63; Harvey Mitchell, "Reclaiming the Self: The Pascal-Rousseau Connection," *Journal of the History of Ideas* 54:4 (October 1993): 637–58, and Mark Hulliung, *The Autocritique of Enlightenment: Rousseau and the Philosophes* (Cambridge, MA: Harvard University Press, 1994), 9–37, and "Rousseau, Voltaire, and the Revenge of Pascal," in *The Cambridge Companion to Rousseau*, 57–77; Arnoux Straudo, *La Fortune de Pascal en France au dix-huitième siècle* (Oxford, UK: Voltaire Foundation, 1997), 215–26; Christopher Brooke, "Rousseau's Political Philosophy: Stoic and Augustinian Origins," in *The Cambridge Companion to Rousseau*, 94–123; and Matthew W. Maguire, *The Conversion of Imagination: From Pascal through Rousseau to Tocqueville* (Cambridge, MA: Harvard University Press, 2006), 17–158.

47. See Blaise Pascal, *Pensées sur la religion et sur quelques autres sujets, qui ont esté trouvées après sa mort parmy ses papiers*, 3rd ed., ed. Étienne Périer (Paris: Guillaume Desprez, 1671), 62, 159–64, 179–81, 192–210, 242–46, 266–72, 275–76 (VIII.1, XXI.1–4, XXIV.12, XXVI.1–4, XXVIII.35–36, XXIX.11, 18, 23, 29, 39, in the expanded edition published in 1678 and frequently republished thereafter).

48. See Pascal, *Pensées sur la religion et sur quelques autres sujets*, 176, 254–55, 294–95 (XXIV.1, XXVIII.55, XXX.3, in the expanded edition published in 1678 and frequently republished thereafter), and Pierre Nicole, "De la charité et de l'amour-propre," in Nicole, *Essais de morale*, ed. Laurent Thirounin (Paris: Presses Universitaires de France, 1999), 381–415.

49. See Marks, *Perfection and Disharmony in the Thought of Jean-Jacques Rousseau*, 54–88, who makes a powerful case that the advantages associated with this stage in human development serve as a standard that in his various thought experiments Rousseau seeks to approximate.

50. In this connection, see the passage from which the epigraph for this chapter is drawn in the second chapter of the first book of the so-called Geneva manuscript, which was an early draft of *The Social Contract*: see Jean-Jacques Rousseau, *Du Contract social; ou, Essai sur la forme de la république (Première version)*, ed. Robert Derathé, 1.2, in JJR III 281–82.

51. See Rousseau, *Fragments politiques* 2.1, in JJR III 475.

52. Consider *LP* 2–4, 6–7, 9, 19–20/20–21, 24–25/26–27, 39–41/41–43, 45/47, 51/53, 60/62, 62–63/64–65, 68–69/70–71, 77/79, 93/96, 139–48/147–56, 149/159, 150/161 in light of 35.10–25/37, 86.5–16/88, and 104/107, and see Corey Robin, "Reflections on Fear:

Montesquieu in Retrieval," *American Political Science Review* 94:2 (June 2000): 347–60, which should be read in light of Rahe, *M* I.3, notes 15–16.

53. This is a theme to which Rousseau will return: see, for example, *LM* 8.842n.

54. In this connection, see E. J. Hundert, *The Enlightenment's Fable: Bernard Mandeville and the Discovery of Society* (Cambridge, UK: Cambridge University Press, 2003), 62–115 (esp. 105–15).

55. For a meditation on the significance of this shift, see Eve Grace, "The Unbearable Restlessness of 'Being': Rousseau's Protean *Sentiment of Existence,*" *History of European Ideas* 27:2 (2001): 133–51.

56. With regard to "the foolish pride of the bourgeois," see Rousseau, *PC* 911.

57. For a more extensive discussion of the role played by political psychology in Rousseau's thought than is possible here, see Arthur M. Melzer, "Rousseau and the Problem of Bourgeois Society," *American Political Science Review* 74:4 (December 1980): 1018–33, and *The Natural Goodness of Man: On the System of Rousseau's Thought* (Chicago: University of Chicago Press, 1990), 59–85.

BOOK TWO, CHAPTER THREE.
CITIZENSHIP AS A REMEDY

1. For a systematic overview, see Roger D. Masters, *The Political Philosophy of Rousseau* (Princeton, NJ: Princeton University Press, 1968), and Arthur M. Melzer, *The Natural Goodness of Man: On the System of Rousseau's Thought* (Chicago: University of Chicago Press, 1990), 1–252.

2. In this connection, consider Rousseau, *Julie* Seconde Préf., and see Joel Schwartz, *The Sexual Politics of Jean-Jacques Rousseau* (Chicago: University of Chicago Press, 1984), along with Allan Bloom, *Love and Friendship* (New York: Simon and Schuster, 1993), 39–156 (esp. 140–56). Note also H. Gaston Hall, "The Concept of Virtue in *La Nouvelle Héloise,*" *Yale French Studies* 28 (Fall–Winter, 1961–1962): 20–33; Lester G. Crocker, "Julie, ou La nouvelle Duplicité," *Annales de la société Jean-Jacques Rousseau* 36 (1963–1965): 105–52; Judith N. Shklar, "Rousseau's Images of Authority," *American Political Science Review* 58:4 (December 1964): 919–32 (esp. 925–30), which is reprinted in *Hobbes and Rousseau: A Collection of Critical Essays,* ed. Maurice Cranston and Richard S. Peters (Garden City, NY: Doubleday, 1972), 333–65 (esp. 348–61), and in *The Cambridge Companion to Rousseau,* ed. Patrick Riley (Cambridge, UK: Cambridge University Press, 2001), 154–92 (esp. 156–79), along with Shklar, *Men and Citizens: A Study of Rousseau's Social Theory* (Cambridge, UK: Cambridge University Press, 1969), 127–65; and Mark S. Cladis, "Rousseau and the Redemptive Mountain Village: The Way of Family, Work, Community, and Love," *Interpretation: A Journal of Political Philosophy* 29:1 (Fall 2001): 35–54.

3. See Bertrand de Jouvenel, "Essai sur la politique de Rousseau," in Jean-Jacques Rousseau, *Du Contrat social,* ed. Bertrand de Jouvenel (Geneva: Éditions du Cheval Aile, 1947), 15–160; Lester G. Crocker, *Rousseau's Social Contract: An Interpretive Essay* (Cleveland, OH: Case Western Reserve University Press, 1968); John McManners, "The Social Contract and Rousseau's Revolt against Society," in *Hobbes and Rousseau,*

291–317; and Hilail Gildin, *Rousseau's Social Contract: The Design of the Argument* (Chicago: University of Chicago Press, 1983).

4. See Allan Bloom, "Introduction," in Jean-Jacques Rousseau, *Émile, or On Education* (New York: Basic Books, 1979), 3–28, which is reprinted as Bloom, "*Emile*," in Bloom, *Giants and Dwarfs: Essays, 1960–1990* (New York: Simon and Schuster, 1990), 177–207, along with Bloom, *Love and Friendship*, 39–140. Note also Geraint Parry, "*Émile*: Learning to Be Men, Women, and Citizens," and Susan Meld Shell, "*Émile*: Nature and the Education of Sophie," in *The Cambridge Companion to Rousseau*, 247–301, as well as Eve Grace, "The Unbearable Restlessness of 'Being': Rousseau's Protean *Sentiment of Existence*," *History of European Ideas* 27:2 (2001): 133–51, and Jeffrey A. Smith, "Natural Happiness, Sensation, and Infancy in Rousseau's *Emile*," *Polity* 35:1 (Fall 2002): 92–120.

5. Consider the passage cited and Rousseau, *D* 2.822, in light of Jean-Jacques Rousseau, *Lettre à M. de Voltaire*, 18 August 1756, ed. Henri Gouhier, in *JJR* IV 1059–75 (esp. 1062–63, 1069–70), and Rousseau, *Julie* III.xxii, pp. 388–90, which suggest that this sentiment is almost never fully stifled, and see Charles E. Butterworth, "Interpretive Essay," in Jean-Jacques Rousseau, *The Reveries of the Solitary Walker*, tr. Charles E. Butterworth (New York: New York University Press, 1979), 145–241. In this connection, note also Arist. *Pol.* 1278b25–30. Compare, however, Rousseau, *É* 2.306, 4.588, and see Grace, "The Unbearable Restlessness of 'Being,'" 133–51.

6. See Letter to Nicolas-Bonaventure Duchesne on 23 May 1762 (no. 1790), in *CCJJR* X 280–82. In keeping with this fact, Rousseau provides within *Émile*, quite near the end, an epitome of *The Social Contract*: see *É* 5.836–49.

7. For an extended rumination on the significance of this fact, see Arthur M. Melzer, "Rousseau's Moral Realism: Replacing Natural Law with the General Will," *American Political Science Review* 77:3 (September 1983): 633–51.

8. For a systematic attempt to situate Rousseau vis-à-vis this literature, see Robert Derathé, *Jean-Jacques Rousseau et la science politique de son temps*, 2nd ed. (Paris: J. Vrin, 1979).

9. For a detailed discussion of Harrington, emphasizing the centrality of this concern for him, his predecessor Machiavelli, and their successors among the English Whigs and the luminaries of the Scottish Enlightenment, as well as their American heirs, see Rahe, *RAM* II.v (with II.i.3, 5, iv.6, vi, vii.9, Epilogue, III.Prologue, i.3, 6, iv.4–7, v.6), and *ATA* 321–46.

10. See Letter to David Hume on 25 March 1767, in *Œuvres de Turgot et documents le concernant*, ed. Gustave Schelle (Paris: Librairie Felix Alcan, 1913–1923), II 658–65 (esp. 659–62), where Turgot disparages Rousseau's first and second discourses and carefully circumscribes the praise he bestows on *The Social Contract* and on the educational doctrine presented in *Émile*.

11. Note Rousseau, *DOI* 118, and *C* 1.9, and see George Pire, "Du bon Plutarque au Citoyen de Genève," *Revue de littérature comparée* 32 (1958): 510–47, and Denise Leduc-Fayette, *Rousseau et le mythe de l'antiquité* (Paris: J. Vrin, 1974).

12. See Jean-Jacques Rousseau, *Les Lettres morales* (1757–58), ed. Henri Gouhier II, in *JJR* IV 1089–90. Note also Rousseau, *CP* 2.956–59.

13. See Montesquieu, *EL* 3.19.16–21 with an eye to 1.5.19, p. 306; note 1.6.9 (esp. n. a), 7.6–7, and 8.21; and see Rahe, *M* II.

14. See I, above. For a more elaborate discussion, see Rahe, *M* II.1–4, III.3–4.

15. Note the manner in which Rousseau paraphrases Montesquieu's formula: see Rousseau, *CP* 1.955.

16. See Shklar, *Men and Citizens*, 184–97; Melzer, "Rousseau's Moral Realism," 633–51, as well as Melzer, *The Natural Goodness of Man*, 114–99; Patrick Riley, "Rousseau's General Will: Freedom of a Particular Kind," in *Rousseau and Liberty*, ed. Robert Wokler (Manchester, UK: Manchester University Press, 1995), 1–28, which is reprinted without the subtitle in *The Cambridge Companion to Rousseau*, 124–53; and Gopal Sreenivasan, "What Is the General Will?" *Philosophical Review* 109:4 (October 2000): 545–81. For the theological and philosophical background to Rousseau's deployment of this concept—which, in Pascal, has a political dimension—see Patrick Riley, *The General Will before Rousseau: The Transformation of the Divine into the Civic* (Princeton, NJ: Princeton University Press, 1986).

17. In this connection, cf. J. L. Talmon, *The Origins of Totalitarian Democracy* (New York: Praeger, 1960), 38–49, and Lester G. Crocker, "Rousseau et la voie du totalitarisme," *Annales de philosophie politique* 5 (1965): 99–136, with John Plamenatz, "'Ce qui ne signifie autre chose sinon qu'on le forcera d'être libre,'" ibid., 137–52, which is reprinted in *Hobbes and Rousseau*, 318–32. Note also John Hope Mason, "'Forced to Be Free,'" in *Rousseau and Liberty*, 121–38.

18. Compare, however, *DEP* 262–64.

19. Note also Rousseau, *DEP* 258.

20. In this connection, see Bertrand de Jouvenel, "Théorie des formes de gouvernement chez Rousseau," *Le Contrat social* 6 (November–December 1962): 343–51, and "Rousseau's Theory of the Forms of Government," in *Hobbes and Rousseau*, 484–97. Compare John P. McCormick, "Rousseau's Rome and the Repudiation of Populist Republicanism," *Critical Review of International Social and Political Philosophy* 10:1 (March 2007): 3–27, who denies that there is any need to temper democratic sovereignty with aristocratic governance in the interests of prudence and reliability, and who regards the arrangements embraced by Rousseau as a betrayal of the democratic impulses that he has unleashed.

21. Consider Montesquieu, *EL* 2.11.12–19, which should be read in conjunction with Montesquieu, *CR* 8.92–94, 11.29–31, and *EL* 1.2.2–3, 3.3, 5.3, 6–8, 15, 17–19, 6.3–5, 8, 11, 15, 17, 7.2, 4, 10–14, 8.5, 7, 11–14, 2.9.1, 8, 10.3, 6, 14, 16–17, and see I, above. For a more elaborate discussion of the evidence, see Rahe, *M* I–II.

22. Compare Montesquieu, *EL* 3.19.27, p. 582–83, and see I.2, above. This juxtaposition is entirely consistent with the very different assessment reached in their published works by these two with regard to the relations between the two sexes in Paris. Compare Montesquieu, *EL* 1.7.8–9, 14, 3.16.11–12, 19.5–6, 8–9, 12, 14–15, 6.28.22, with Rousseau, *DOI* 119–20, and see Rousseau, *Julie* II.xxi. In this connection, however, see Montesquieu, *LP* 61/63, 96–97/99–100. Note also Rahe, *M* III.1.

23. See Rousseau, *Julie* I.xlv, lx, lxii, II.ii, ix, III.xxii–xxiii, V.i.

24. See Jean-Jacques Rousseau, *Extrait du projet de paix perpétuelle de Monsieur l'abbé de Saint Pierre* (1761), ed. Sven Stelling-Michaud, in JJR III 563–89 (at 573n).

25. In this connection, see Shklar, "Rousseau's Images of Authority," 919–32, reprinted in *Hobbes and Rousseau*, 333–65, and in *The Cambridge Companion to Rousseau*, 154–92, as well as Shklar, *Men and Citizens*, 127–214.

26. In this connection, see Richard Fralin, "Rousseau and Community: The Role of *Moeurs* in Social Change," *History of Political Thought* 7:1 (Spring 1986): 131–50.

27. See also Rousseau, *DEP* 251–62.

28. In this connection, see Christopher Kelly and Rogert D. Masters, "Human Nature, Liberty and Progress: Rousseau's Dialogue with the Critics of the *Discours sur l'inégalité*," in *Rousseau and Liberty*, 53–69.

29. Consider Rousseau's defense of salutary fictions in *RPS* 4, in light of Victor Gourevitch, "Rousseau on Lying: A Provisional Reading of the Fourth *Rêverie*," *Berkshire Review* 15 (1980): 93–107.

30. See Christopher Kelly, "'To Persuade without Convincing': The Language of Rousseau's Legislator," *American Journal of Political Science* 31:2 (May 1987): 321–35. In this connection, see Rahe, *ATA* 56–100 (esp. 59–83), 139–74 (esp. 155–68).

31. See John T. Scott, "Rousseau and the Melodious Language of Freedom," *Journal of Politics* 59:3 (August 1997): 803–29. In this connection, see also Scott, "The Harmony between Rousseau's Musical Theory and His Philosophy," *Journal of the History of Ideas* 59:2 (April 1998): 287–308.

32. Note the epigraph to this chapter, which is drawn from the second chapter of the first book of the so-called Geneva manuscript, an early draft of *The Social Contract*: see Jean-Jacques Rousseau, *Du Contract social; ou, Essai sur la forme de la république (Première version)*, ed. Robert Derathé, 1.2, in JJR III 288, and see Jean Starobinski, "The Antidote in the Poison: The Thought of Jean-Jacques Rousseau," in Starobinski, *Blessings in Disguise; or, The Morality of Evil*, tr. Arthur Goldhammer (Cambridge, MA: Harvard University Press, 1993), 118–68, and Graeme Garrard, *Rousseau's Counter-Enlightenment: A Republican Critique of the Philosophes* (Albany: State University of New York Press, 2003), 55–68. Compare Arthur O. Lovejoy, "The Supposed Primitivism of Rousseau's *Discourse on Inequality*," *Modern Philology* 21 (1923): 165–86 (at 185–86), which is reprinted in Lovejoy, *Essays in the History of Ideas* (Baltimore, MD: Johns Hopkins University Press, 1948), 14–37 (at 36–37), who errs grievously when he accuses Rousseau of having failed to "realize fully how strongly *amour propre* tends to assume a collective form."

33. Compare Montesquieu, *MP* 1062, 1491.

34. See Fonna Forman-Barzilai, "The Emergence of Contextualism in Rousseau's Political Thought: The Case of Parisian Theatre in the *Lettre à d'Alembert*," *History of Political Thought* 24:3 (Autumn 2003): 435–63.

35. Compare Montesquieu, *EL* 1.4.6–7, where the familial model is also mentioned.

36. Note the manner in which Rousseau warns that in corrupt societies an attempt at genuine revolution is likely to do more harm than good while nonetheless holding it open as a remote possibility that it might in fact succeed: see Jean-Jacques Rousseau, *Obser-*

vations de Jean-Jacques Rousseau de Genève (1751), ed. François Bouchardy, in JJR III 35–57 (at 52, 55–56).

37. Compare Niccolò Machiavelli, *Il principe* 6, in Machiavelli, *Tutte le opere*, ed. Mario Martelli (Florence: G. C. Sansoni, 1971), 264–65, who mentions in this connection "Moses, Cyrus, Romulus, Theseus, and the like."

38. Compare Montesquieu, *EL* 1.4.6–7; 5.19, p. 306; 6.9, n. a; 7.6–7; 8.21; 3.19.16–21; 4.23.7, 17, and see I.1–2, above. For a more elaborate discussion, see Rahe, M II.1, 4, III.2.

39. See Garrard, *Rousseau's Counter-Enlightenment*, 69–82.

40. See Rahe, ATA 56–100, 139–74.

41. At the end of this passage, Rousseau deploys language meant to remind readers of the Roman practice of *devotio* and of the stipulation in the Twelve Tables that those guilty of certain infractions be made *sacer*. In this connection, see Jean-Jacques Rousseau, *Fragments politiques* 4.12, ed. Robert Derathé, in JJR III 495.

42. In this connection, consider Jean-Jacques Rousseau, "[Fiction, ou Merceau allégorique sur la révélation]," ed. Henri Gouhier, in JJR IV 1044–54, in light of Christopher Kelly, "Rousseau's Philosophic Dream," *Interpretation: A Journal of Political Philosophy* 23:3 (Spring 1996): 417–35.

43. See Alfred B. C. Cobban, *Rousseau and the Modern State* (London: G. Allen & Unwin, 1934), 151–91; Alexandre Choulguine, "Les Origines de l'esprit national moderne et Jean-Jacques Rousseau," *Annales de la société Jean-Jacques Rousseau* 26 (1937): 1–283 (esp. 188–283); Robert Derathé, "Patriotisme et nationalisme au XVIIIᵉ siècle," *Annales de la philosophie politique* 8 (1969): 69–84; and F. M. Barnard, "National Culture and Political Legitimacy: Herder and Rousseau," *Journal of the History of Ideas* 44:2 (April–June 1983): 231–53. Compare, however, Mauro Barberis, "Quel che resta dell'universale: L'idea di nazione da Rousseau a Renan," *Filosofia politica* 7 (1993): 5–28.

44. See also Rousseau, *Lettre à M. de Voltaire*, in JJR IV 1059–75 (esp. 1073–74). For the context within which this more or less open letter was composed, see Ralph A. Leigh, "Rousseau's Letter to Voltaire on Optimism," *Studies on Voltaire and the Eighteenth Century* 30 (1964): 247–309. For the intellectual framework within which Rousseau's discussion of religion is properly to be understood, note John T. Scott, "The Theodicy of the *Second Discourse*: The 'Pure State of Nature' and Rousseau's Political Thought," *American Political Science Review* 86:3 (September 1992): 696–711, and "Pride and Providence: Religion in Rousseau's *Lettre à Voltaire sur la providence*," in *Rousseau and l'Infâme: Religion, Toleration, and Fanaticism*, ed. Ourida Mostefai and John T. Scott (Amsterdam: Rodopi, 2008), 115–36, and see Kelly and Masters, "Human Nature, Liberty and Progress," 53–69, and Victor Gourevitch, "Rousseau on Providence," *Review of Metaphysics* 53:3 (March 2000): 565–611, which is reprinted in *The Cambridge Companion to Rousseau*, 193–246.

45. Compare Machiavelli's poignant description of the religion of ancient Romans: see Niccolò Machiavelli, *Discorsi sopra la prima deca di Tito Livio* 2.2.2, in *Tutte le opere*, 196–97.

46. In this connection, see Jonathan Marks, *Perfection and Disharmony in the Thought of Jean-Jacques Rousseau* (New York: Cambridge University Press, 2005), 54–88.

47. In this connection, consider Rousseau, *Julie* passim, see Judith N. Shklar, "Rousseau's Two Models: Sparta and the Age of Gold," *Political Science Quarterly* 81:1 (March 1966): 25–51; Shklar, *Men and Citizens*, 1–32; and the secondary literature cited in note 2, this chapter.

48. Compare the reasonable Christianity that Rousseau attributes to Julie in *Julie* VI.xi, pp. 714–16, and the apolitical profession of faith he attributes to the Savoyard vicar in *É* 4.565–635, and consider Arthur M. Melzer, "The Origin of the Counter-Enlightenment: Rousseau and the New Religion of Sincerity," *American Political Science Review* 90:2 (June 1996): 344–60 (esp. 351–59). It would, of course, be a mistake to confuse convictions expressed by the characters that Rousseau fashioned with those privately entertained by Rousseau himself: see Rousseau, *D* 1.750–51 and *RPS* 3.1018–19, and consider the discussion of lying in *RPS* 4, in light of Gourevitch, "Rousseau on Lying," 93–107; Jean Starobinski, "The Motto *Vitam Impendere Vero* and the Question of Lying," tr. Patrick Riley Jr., in *The Cambridge Companion to Rousseau*, 365–96; and Christopher Kelly, *Rousseau as Author: Consecrating One's Life to the Truth* (Chicago: University of Chicago Press, 2003), and see Jeffrey Macy, "'God Helps Those Who Help Themselves': New Light on the Theological-Political Teaching in Rousseau's *Profession of Faith of the Savoyard Vicar*," *Polity* 24:4 (Summer 1992): 615–32.

49. Compare Robert Shackleton, "Montesquieu, Dupin and the Early Writings of Rousseau," in *Reappraisals of Rousseau: Studies in Honour of R. A. Leigh*, ed. Simon Harvey, Marian Hobson, David Kelley, and Samuel S. B. Taylor (Manchester, UK: Manchester University Press, 1980), 234–49, which is reprinted in Shackleton, *Essays on Montesquieu and on the Enlightenment*, ed. David Gilson and Martin Smith (Oxford, UK: Voltaire Foundation, 1988), 183–96, with Jean Ehrard, "Rousseau et Montesquieu: Le mauvais Fils réconcilié," *Annales de la société Jean-Jacques Rousseau* 41 (1997): 57–77, reprinted as "Le Fils coupable," in Ehrard, *L'Esprit des mots: Montesquieu en lui-même et parmi les siens* (Geneva: Droz, 1998), 256–75.

50. See Letter from Charles-Jean-François Hénault on 13 February 1752, in Nagel III 1421.

51. See Letter from Jean-Vincent Capperonnier de Gauffecourt on 9 December 1764 (no. 3728), in CCJJR XXII 204. I see no reason to share Robert Shackleton's skepticism as to whether Gauffecourt was acquainted with Montesquieu: in such a case, an absence of evidence can hardly be taken as evidence of absence, and Gauffecourt had no obvious motive for lying to his friend Rousseau. Indeed, the letter presupposes that Rousseau knows perfectly well that Gauffecourt was acquainted with Montesquieu. Compare Shackleton, *Montesquieu: A Critical Biography* (Oxford, UK: Oxford University Press, 1961), 187 n. 3, with Ehrard, "Rousseau et Montesquieu," 59–60, reprinted as "Le Fils coupable," 259–60.

52. Compare Shackleton, *Montesquieu*, 358–59, who is arguably too quick to credit Dupin's subsequent claim that, in suppressing the first of his two critiques, he had acted entirely of his own volition, with Charles Porset, "Madame Dupin et Montesquieu, ou Les Infortunes de la vertu," in *Actes du colloque international tenu à Bordeaux, du 3 au 6 décembre 1998*, ed. Louis Desgraves (Bordeaux: Académie de Bordeaux, 1999), 287–306 (esp. 293–306 and the attendant notes). Dupin can hardly have been eager to advertise his pusillanimity.

53. See Roger Barny, *Prélude idéologique à la Révolution française: Le Rousseauisme avant 1789* (Paris: Les Belles Lettres, 1985), *Rousseau dans la Révolution: Le Personnage de Jean-Jacques et les débuts du culte révolutionnaire, 1787–1791* (Oxford: Voltaire Foundation, 1986), and *Le Comte d'Antraigues: Un Disciple aristocrate de J.-J. Rousseau: De la Fascination au reniement, 1782–1797* (Oxford: Voltaire Foundation, 1991). It is, of course, possible that Rousseau profoundly misapprehended the impact that his writings would have: cf. Arthur M. Melzer, "Rousseau's 'Mission' and the Intention of His Writings," *American Journal of Political Science* 27:2 (May 1983): 294–320, and Melzer, *The Natural Goodness of Man*, 253–82, with Matthew W. Maguire, *The Conversion of Imagination: From Pascal through Rousseau to Tocqueville* (Cambridge, MA: Harvard University Press, 2006), 256–57, n. 192. But how likely is this?

54. In this connection, note Irving Babbitt, *Rousseau and Romanticism* (Boston: Houghton Mifflin, 1919), along with Robert Darnton, "Readers' Response to Rousseau: The Fabrication of Romantic Sensitivity," in *The Great Cat Massacre and Other Episodes in French Cultural History* (New York: Basic Books, 1984), 215–56, and Maurice Cranston, *The Romantic Movement* (London: Blackwell, 1994); then see Choulguine, "Les Origines de l'esprit national moderne et Jean-Jacques Rousseau," 1–283, and Allan Bloom, "Rousseau—The Turning Point," in *Confronting the Constitution: The Challenge to Locke, Montesquieu, Jefferson, and the Federalists from Utilitarianism, Historicism, Marxism, Freudianism, Pragmatism, Existentialism . . . ,* ed. Allan Bloom (Washington, DC: AEI Press, 1990), 211–34, which is reprinted in Bloom, *Giants and Dwarfs*, 208–32, as well as *The Legacy of Rousseau*, ed. Clifford Orwin and Nathan Tarcov (Chicago: University of Chicago Press, 1997), and Richard L. Velkley, *Being after Rousseau: Philosophy and Culture in Question* (Chicago: University of Chicago Press, 2002), especially the last.

55. In this connection, see Bernard Yack, *The Longing for Total Revolution: Philosophic Sources of Social Discontent from Rousseau to Marx and Nietzsche* (Princeton, NJ: Princeton University Press, 1986).

56. Today, to a remarkable degree, these arguments infect contemporary scholarship on republican thought before Rousseau, much of which consists in an ill-conceived attempt to read Rousseau's distinctive moral vision back into Machiavelli, the republican thought of the English interregnum, and English Whiggery more generally: see, for one such attempt, J. G. A. Pocock, *The Machiavellian Moment: Florentine Political Thought and the Atlantic Republican Tradition* (Princeton, NJ: Princeton University Press, 1975), and "Historical Introduction," in *The Political Works of James Harrington*, ed. J. G. A. Pocock (Cambridge, UK: Cambridge University Press, 1977), 1–152; and for another, consider the various works by Quentin Skinner examined in Paul A. Rahe, "Situating Machiavelli," in *Renaissance Civic Humanism: Reappraisals and Reflections*, ed. James Hankins (Cambridge, UK: Cambridge University Press, 2000), 270–308. This propensity is especially visible in Skinner's summary statement on this question: see Skinner, *Liberty before Liberalism* (Cambridge, UK: Cambridge University Press, 1998). Nowhere, however, is it more obvious than in the work of his student Maurizio Viroli.

BOOK THREE, PREFACE

1. In this connection, see Alan B. Spitzer, *The French Generation of 1820* (Princeton, NJ: Princeton University Press, 1987).

2. After perusing Steven Holmes, *Benjamin Constant and the Making of Modern Liberalism* (New Haven, CT: Yale University Press, 1984), and Biancamaria Fontana, *Benjamin Constant and the Post-Revolutionary Mind* (New Haven, CT: Yale University Press, 1991); Larry Siedentop, "Two Liberal Traditions," in *The Idea of Freedom*, ed. Alan Ryan (Oxford, UK: Oxford University Press, 1979), 153–74, and "Introduction," in François Guizot, *The History of Civilization in Europe*, tr. William Hazlitt, ed. Larry Siedentop (London: Penguin, 1997), vii–xxxvii; Pierre Rosanvallon, *Le Moment Guizot* (Paris: Gallimard, 1985); Pierre Manent, *An Intellectual History of Liberalism*, tr. Rebecca Balinski (Princeton, NJ: Princeton University Press, 1994), 80–102; Aurelian Craiutu, *Liberalism under Siege: The Political Thought of the French Doctrinaires* (Lanham, MD: Lexington Books, 2003); and Annelien de Dijn, *French Political Thought from Montesquieu to Tocqueville: Liberty in a Levelled Society?* (Cambridge, UK: Cambridge University Press, 2008), 40–128, see George Armstrong Kelly, *The Humane Comedy: Constant, Tocqueville, and French Liberalism* (Cambridge, UK: Cambridge University Press, 1992); Larry Siedentop, *Tocqueville* (Oxford, UK: Oxford University Press, 1994), 20–43, 71–72, 83–84, 98–100; Aurelian Craiutu, "Tocqueville and the Political Thought of the French *Doctrinaires* (Guizot, Royer-Collard, Rémusat)," *History of Political Thought* 20:3 (Autumn 1999): 456–93; Cheryl B. Welch, *De Tocqueville* (Oxford, UK: Oxford University Press, 2001), 13–42; and Dijn, *French Political Thought from Montesquieu to Tocqueville*, 129–84.

3. These notes survive, at least in part: see Tocqueville, "Notes sur le cours d'histoire de la civilisation en France de Guizot," in *ATG* XVI 439–534. Tocqueville used Beaumont's lecture notes when, for one reason or another, he had none of his own: see Letter to Gustave de Beaumont on 18 March 1829, in *ATG* VIII:1 76–78.

4. The character of Tocqueville's appropriation and critique of Guizot's account of the medieval *commune* is already evident in Letter to Gustave de Beaumont on 5 October 1828, in *ATG* VIII:1 47–71 and *LC* 114–35. With regard to his reading in Guizot, see Letters to Gustave de Beaumont on 30 August and 15 September 1829, in *ATG* VIII:1 78–85 (at 80–81, 83). For his reference to Guizot's *esprit analytique*, see Letter to Gustave de Beaumont on 25 October 1829, in *ATG* VIII:1 91–96 (esp. 91, 93) and *LC* 136–41 (esp. 136, 138). On Tocqueville's *Auseinandersetzung* with the thinking of Guizot, see François Furet, "Tocqueville et le problème de la Révolution française," in *Science et conscience de la société: Mélanges en l'honneur de Raymond Aron*, ed. Jean-Claude Casanova (Paris: Calmann-Lévy, 1971), I 309–43 (esp. 309–19), which appears in translation as François Furet, "De Tocqueville and the Problem of the French Revolution," in Furet, *Interpreting the French Revolution*, tr. Elborg Forster (Cambridge, UK: Cambridge University Press, 1981), 132–63 (esp. 132–40); "Naissance d'un paradigme: Tocqueville et le voyage en Amérique (1825–1831)," *Annales: Économies, Sociétés, Civilisations* 39:2 (March–April 1984): 225–39; and "The Intellectual Origins of Tocqueville's Thought," *The Tocqueville Review/La Revue Tocqueville* 7 (1985–1986): 117–29 (esp.

120–25); Pierre Manent, "Guizot et Tocqueville devant l'ancien et le nouveau," in *François Guizot et la culture politique de son temps,* ed. Marina Valensise (Paris: Gallimard, 1991), 147–59, and *An Intellectual History of Liberalism,* 93–113; John Marini, "Centralized Administration and the 'New Despotism,'" in *Interpreting Tocqueville's Democracy in America,* ed. Ken Masugi (Savage, MD: Rowman & Littlefield, 1991), 255–86; Ralph C. Hancock, "The Modern Revolution and the Collapse of Moral Analogy: Tocqueville and Guizot," *Perspectives on Political Science* 30:4 (Fall 2001): 213–27, which is reprinted in *Democracy and Its Friendly Critics: Tocqueville and Political Life Today,* ed. Peter Augustine Lawler (Lanham, MD: Lexington Books, 2004), 49–58; Robert T. Gannett Jr., *Tocqueville Unveiled: The Historian and His Sources for the Old Regime and the Revolution* (Chicago: University of Chicago Press, 2003), 1–3, 17–27; and Melvin Richter, "Tocqueville and Guizot on Democracy: From a Type of Society to a Political Regime," *History of European Ideas* 30:1 (March 2004): 61–82. Note also Tocqueville, *DA* I.Intr., p. 10, n. a.

5. In this connection, see François Furet, "Le Systeme conceptuel de la *Démocratie en Amérique,*" in *Alexis de Tocqueville — Zur Politik in der Demokratie: Symposion zum 175. Geburtstage von Alexis de Tocqueville,* ed. Michael Hereth and Jutta Höffken (Baden-Baden: Nomos Verlagsgesellschaft, 1981), 19–60, which is reprinted in translation as "The Conceptual System of Democracy in America," in Furet, *In the Workshop of History,* tr. Jonathan Mandelbaum (Chicago: University of Chicago Press, 1984), 167–96; and "Naissance d'un paradigme," 225–39, along with Siedentop, *Tocqueville,* 20–43, 71–72, 98–100; Marini, "Centralized Administration and the 'New Despotism,'" 255–86; and Hancock, "The Modern Revolution and the Collapse of Moral Analogy," 213–27, which is reprinted in *Democracy and Its Friendly Critics,* 49–58.

6. See Manent, *An Intellectual History of Liberalism,* 93–102, and Rosanvallon, *Le Moment Guizot,* passim.

7. See Letter to Charles Stöffels on 21 April 1830, in *LC* 145–48 and *DA* II 322–24.

8. See André Jardin, *Tocqueville: A Biography,* tr. Lydia Davis and Robert Hemenway (New York: Farrar, Straus, and Giroux, 1988), 3–7.

9. See "Très-humbles et très-respectueuses Remonstrances de la Cour des aides de Paris, du 18 février 1771, sur l'édit de décembre 1770, et l'état actuel du parlement de France," in Elisabeth Badinter, *Les 'Remonstrances' de Malesherbes, 1771–1775* (Paris: Union Générale des Éditions, 1978), 151–65.

10. In this connection, see Pierre Grosclaude, *Malesherbes: Témoin et interprète de son temps* (Paris: Librairie Fischbacher, 1961), esp. 703–16.

11. See Grosclaude, *Malesherbes,* 717–52.

12. See Jardin, *Tocqueville,* 7–36.

13. Note Eduardo Nolla, "Introduction de l'éditeur," in *DA* I xiii–lxxxi (at xiv–xv, with particular reference to the letter penned by Hervé de Tocqueville on 15 January 1827 that is quoted in n. 6), and Françoise Mélonio, *Tocqueville and the French,* tr. Beth G. Raps (Charlottesville: University Press of Virginia, 1998), 2; and see Otto Vossler, *Alexis de Tocqueville: Freiheit und Gleichheit* (Frankfurt am Main: Klostermann, 1973), 13–63 (esp. 13–43); Roger L. Williams, "From Malesherbes to Tocqueville: The Legacy of

Liberalism," *Journal of the Historical Society* 6:3 (September 2006): 443–63; and David A. Bell, "Malesherbes et Tocqueville: Les Origines parlementaires du libéralisme français," *The Tocqueville Review/La Revue Tocqueville* 27:2 (2006): 273–82, as well as the material cited in III.3, note 8, below.

14. For surveys of the literature produced by Chateaubriand and his colleagues, see Bernard Faÿ, *L'Esprit révolutionnaire en France et aux États-Unis à la fin du XVIIIᵉ siècle* (Paris: E. Champion, 1925), and Durand Echeverria, *Mirage in the West: A History of the French Image of American Society to 1815* (Princeton, NJ: Princeton University Press, 1957), with François Furet, "De l'Homme sauvage à l'homme historique: L'Expérience américaine dans la culture française," *Annales: Économies, Sociétés, Civilisations* 33:4 (July–August 1978): 729–39, which is reprinted in *La Révolution Américaine et l'Europe*, ed. Claude Fohlen and Jacques Godechot (Paris: Centre national de la recherche scientifique, 1979), 91–108, and in translation as "From Savage Man to Historical Man: The American Experience in Eighteenth-Century French Culture," in Furet, *In the Workshop of History*, 153–66.

15. See Jardin, *Tocqueville*, 7–9, 88–107.

16. See Letter to Ernest Chabrol on 18 May 1831, quoted in Edward T. Gargan, "The Formation of Tocqueville's Historical Thought," *Review of Politics* 24:1 (January 1962): 48–61 (at 54), and Tocqueville, *DA* I.Intr., p. 10, n. a.

17. See George Wilson Pierson, *Tocqueville and Beaumont in America* (New York: Oxford University Press, 1938), which is the classic work on the subject and remains unsurpassed, along with Jardin, *Tocqueville*, 107–77.

18. See Roger Boesche, "The Prison: Tocqueville's Model for Despotism," *Western Political Quarterly* 33:4 (December 1980): 550–63, which is reprinted in Boesche, *Tocqueville's Road Map: Methodology, Liberalism, Revolution, and Despotism* (Lanham, MD: Lexington Books, 2006), 149–68.

19. In time, the two would play a role in the introduction of prison reform: see Seymour Drescher, *Dilemmas of Democracy: Tocqueville and Modernization* (Pittsburgh, PA: University of Pittsburgh Press, 1968), 124–50.

20. See Jardin, *Tocqueville*, 178–93.

21. See Jardin, *Tocqueville*, 194–200.

22. See Jardin, *Tocqueville*, 200–240.

23. This can be inferred from the fact that, in the first great section of *Democracy in America*, Tocqueville more than once issues a promise presupposing that he will publish a second great section very much like the one he did eventually publish, pledging that in due course he will "attempt to determine the influence exercised by the freedom of the press on civil society within the United States" and that he will find "occasion, later, to speak of the effects produced by associations in [American] civil life." Compare *DA* I.ii.3–4, pp. 140 and 146, with II.ii.2–8.

24. See Jardin, *Tocqueville*, 239.

25. See Gustave Auguste de Beaumont de La Bonnière, *L'Irlande sociale, politique et religieuse* (Paris: Gosselin, 1839), which was immediately translated into English: see Gustave de Beaumont, *Ireland: Social, Political, and Religious*, ed. William Cooke

Taylor ([London]: R. Bentley, 1839). A new translation has recently been issued: see Gustave de Beaumont, *Ireland: Social, Political, and Religious,* tr. Tom Garvin and Andreas Hess (Cambridge, MA: Belknap Press, 2006).

26. See Letter to Louis de Kergorlay on 10 November 1836, in *ATG* XIII:1 415–18 (at 418). The same fears are evident in Letter to John Stuart Mill on 24 June 1837, in *ATG* VI:1 324–36.

27. See Jardin, *Tocqueville,* 239–42. This last effort would eventually bear fruit: see Drescher, *Dilemmas of Democracy,* 151–95.

28. See Alexis de Tocqueville, *Mémoire sur le paupérisme* (1835) and *Deuxième article sur le paupérisme* (ca. 1837), in *ATP* I 1155–97. In this connection, see Drescher, *Dilemmas of Democracy,* 51–123.

29. See Alexis de Tocqueville, *L'État social et politique de la France avant et depuis 1789* (1836), in *ATP* III 1–40, which appeared as [Alexis de Tocqueville], "Political and Social Condition of France," [tr. John Stuart Mill], *London and Westminster Review* 25:1 (April 1836): 75–92, in light of Furet, "Tocqueville et le problème de la Révolution française," 309–43 (esp. 309–19), which is printed in translation as Furet, "De Tocqueville and the Problem of the French Revolution," 132–63 (esp. 132–39).

30. See Tocqueville, *Deux lettres sur l'Algérie,* 23 June and 22 August 1837, in *ATG* III:1 129–53.

31. See Jardin, *Tocqueville,* 242–50.

32. In this connection, see Pierre Rosanvallon, "The History of the Word 'Democracy' in France," *Journal of Democracy* 6:4 (1995): 140–54 (esp. 148–51)

33. See Bernard E. Brown, "Tocqueville and Publius," in *Reconsidering Tocqueville's Democracy in America,* ed. Abraham S. Eisenstadt (New Brunswick, NJ: Rutgers University Press, 1988), 43–74.

34. See James T. Schleifer, *The Making of Tocqueville's Democracy in America,* 2nd ed. (Indianapolis, IN: Liberty Fund, 2000), 3–22.

35. See Robert Nisbet, "Tocqueville's Ideal Types," in *Reconsidering Tocqueville's Democracy in America,* 171–91.

36. See Schleifer, *The Making of Tocqueville's Democracy in America,* 23–45.

BOOK THREE, CHAPTER ONE. DEMOCRATIC DESPOTISM

1. See Letter to Louis de Kergorlay on 10 November 1836, in *ATG* XIII:1 415–18 (at 418). Tocqueville appears to have first read Montesquieu and Rousseau in his father's library while he was a student at school at Metz: note Conversation with Nassau W. Senior on 10 February 1851, in *Correspondence and Conversations of Alexis de Tocqueville with Nassau William Senior from 1834 to 1859,* ed. M. C. M. Simpson (London: Henry S. King, 1872), I 222–23, and *ATG* VI:2 346, and see André Jardin, *Tocqueville: A Biography,* tr. Lydia Davis and Robert Hemenway (New York: Farrar, Straus, and Giroux, 1988), 61–64.

2. For the opinion that Tocqueville entertained with regard to his great predecessor, see Letter to Pierre Freslon on 29 December 1855, in *LC* 1139–41.

3. Compare Wilhelm Hennis, "Tocquevilles 'Neue Politische Wissenschaft,'" in *Aspekte*

der Kultursoziologie: Aufsätze zur Soziologie, Philosophie, Anthropologie und Geschichte der Kultur: Zum 60. Geburtstag von Mohammed Rassem, ed. Justin Stagl (Berlin: Dietrich Reimer Verlag, 1982), 385–407, and "Tocqueville's Perspective: *Democracy in America:* In Search of the 'New Science of Politics,'" *Interpretation: A Journal of Political Philosophy* 16:1 (Fall 1988): 61–86, the latter of which is reprinted in *Interpreting Tocqueville's Democracy in America,* ed. Ken Masugi (Savage, MD: Rowman & Littlefield, 1991), 27–62, and in *Tocqueville's Political Science: Classic Essays,* ed. Peter Augustine Lawler (New York: Garland, 1992), 59–90, whose attempt to drive a wedge between Montesquieu and Tocqueville is based on a caricature of the former, and George Wilson Pierson, *Tocqueville and Beaumont in America* (New York: Oxford University Press, 1938), 768–69, who greatly underestimates the depth of Tocqueville's theoretical acumen, with the more appreciative accounts of the two provided by Raymond Aron, *Main Currents of Sociological Thought,* tr. Richard Howard and Helen Weaver (New York: Basic Books, 1965–1967) I: *Montesquieu, Comte, Marx, Tocqueville, The Sociologists and the Revolution of 1848,* 11–56, 181–231; Melvin Richter, "Comparative Political Analysis in Montesquieu and Tocqueville," *Comparative Politics* 1:2 (January 1969): 129–60, "The Uses of Theory: Tocqueville's Adaptation of Montesquieu," in *Essays in Theory and History: An Approach to the Social Sciences,* ed. Melvin Richter (Cambridge, MA: Harvard University Press, 1970), 74–102, and "Modernity and Its Distinctive Threats to Liberty: Montesquieu and Tocqueville on New Forms of Illegitimate Domination," in *Alexis de Tocqueville — Zur Politik in der Demokratie: Symposion zum 175. Geburtstage von Alexis de Tocqueville,* ed. Michael Hereth and Jutta Höffken (Baden-Baden: Nomos Verlagsgesellschaft, 1981), 61–80; François Furet, "The Intellectual Origins of Tocqueville's Thought," *The Tocqueville Review/La Revue Tocqueville* 7 (1985/86): 117–29; Anne M. Cohler, *Montesquieu's Comparative Politics and the Spirit of American Constitutionalism* (Lawrence: University Press of Kansas, 1988); Jean-Claude Lamberti, *Tocqueville and the Two Democracies,* tr. Arthur Goldhammer (Cambridge, MA: Harvard University Press, 1989); and Annelien de Dijn, *French Political Thought from Montesquieu to Tocqueville: Liberty in a Levelled Society?* (Cambridge, UK: Cambridge University Press, 2008). In this connection, note also James T. Schleifer, "Tocqueville as Historian: Philosophy and Methodology in the *Democracy,*" in *Reconsidering Tocqueville's Democracy in America,* ed. Abraham S. Eisenstadt (New Brunswick, NJ: Rutgers University Press, 1988), 146–67 (esp. 161–64).

4. See Pierson, *Tocqueville and Beaumont in America,* 3–4; John Stuart Mill, "Bentham" (August 1838), in *Dissertations and Discussions Political, Philosophical, and Historical* (New York: Haskell House, 1973), I 330–92 (at 382); and Letter from Henry Reeve to Mrs. Reeve on 25 February 1835, in *Memoirs of the Life and Correspondence of Henry Reeve,* ed. John Knox Laughton (London: Longmans, Green, 1898), I 42. In this connection, note Georgios Varouxakis, "Guizot's Historical Works and J. S. Mill's Reception of Tocqueville," *History of Political Thought* 20:2 (Summer 1999): 292–312.

5. See Alexis de Tocqueville, *L'Ancien Régime et la Révolution* (1856) I.4, in *ATP* III 67–68.

6. Compare Richter, "The Uses of Theory," 74–102, who insists that Tocqueville was a "careless" reader, thinker, and writer who simply failed to comprehend the pertinence

of Montesquieu's discussion of England for understanding the modern, liberal, commercial democracy that had emerged in North America, with Tocqueville, *DA* I.ii.2, where great emphasis is placed on "the point of departure" of those whom he pointedly refers to as "the Anglo-Americans," and see Seymour Drescher, *Tocqueville and England* (Cambridge, MA: Harvard University Press, 1964), 18–151, and Aron, *Main Currents in Sociological Thought,* I 188–89.

7. In this connection, see Drescher, *Tocqueville and England,* 18–34.

8. See Rahe, *M* III.1.

9. Note Tocqueville, *DA* II.i.20, and cf. Tocqueville, *Souvenirs* (1850–51) II.1, in *ATP* III 776, with Montesquieu, *CR* 18.52–60, and see Rahe, *M* III.1. In this connection, note Jon Elster, "Tocqueville on 1789: Preconditions, Precipitants, and Triggers," in *The Cambridge Companion to Tocqueville,* ed. Cheryl B. Welch (Cambridge, UK: Cambridge University Press, 2006), 49–80.

10. See David Hume, "Of National Characters" (1748), in Hume, *Essays Moral, Political, and Literary,* rev. ed., ed. Eugene F. Miller (Indianapolis, IN: Liberty Fund, 1985), 197–215.

11. Earlier, Tocqueville had been inclined to give climate and terrain more weight: note Letter to Gustave de Beaumont on 25 October 1829, in *ATG* VIII:1 91–96 (at 93–94) and *LC* 136–40 (at 138); and Letter to Ernest de Chabrol on 16 January 1832, quoted in *DA* I.ii.9, p. 216, n. f, and see James T. Schleifer, *The Making of Tocqueville's Democracy in America,* 2nd ed. (Indianapolis, IN: Liberty Fund, 2000), 49–111.

12. In this connection, see Pierre Manent, *Tocqueville and the Nature of Democracy,* tr. John Waggoner (Lanham, MD: Rowman & Littlefield, 1996). Note also Michael P. Zuckert, "On Social State," in *Tocqueville's Defense of Human Liberty: Current Essays,* ed. Peter Augustine Lawler and Joseph Alulis (New York: Garland, 1993), 1–17, which, though penetrating, neglects Tocqueville's debt to Guizot in this particular, exaggerates the sociological character of his understanding of the *état social,* and in keeping with this latter propensity, exhibits the defect identified in III.2, note 36, below.

13. If Tocqueville owes the idea of the *état social* to his predecessors among the French *Doctrinaires*—as Aurelian Craiutu suggest in "Tocqueville and the Political Thought of the French *Doctrinaires* (Guizot, Royer-Collard, Rémusat)," *History of Political Thought* 20:3 (Autumn 1999): 456–93 (at 483–91), and *Liberalism under Siege: The Political Thought of the French Doctrinaires* (Lanham, MD: Lexington Books, 2003), 104–12–he nonetheless pointedly gave the notion a political twist all his own. In this connection, note Melvin Richter, "Guizot and Tocqueville on Democracy: From a Type of Society to a Political Regime," *History of European Ideas* 30:1 (March 2004): 61–82, and Cheryl B. Welch, "Tocqueville's Resistance to the Social," *History of European Ideas* 30:1 (March 2004): 83–107.

14. When placed in a comparable position, Americans are similarly ill at ease: cf. Tocqueville, *DA* II.iii.3.

15. Compare Arist. *Pol.* 1263b36–37 with 1276a8–b15, and see Paul A. Rahe, *RAM* I.Prologue, and "Aristotle and the Study of History: A Manifesto," in *Reconstructing History: The Emergence of the Historical Society,* ed. Elizabeth Fox-Genovese and Elisabeth Lasch-Quinn (New York: Routledge, 1999), 202–13.

16. In this connection, see Aron, *Main Currents in Sociological Thought*, I 13–56.

17. Note Aron, *Main Currents of Sociological Thought*, I 203–4, and see Marvin Zetterbaum, *Tocqueville and the Problem of Democracy* (Stanford, CA: Stanford University Press, 1967), 137–44; Robert P. Kraynak, "Tocqueville's Constitutionalism," *American Political Science Review* 81:4 (December 1987): 1175–95; Stephen Salkever, *Finding the Mean: Theory and Practice in Aristotelian Political Philosophy* (Princeton, NJ: Princeton University Press, 1990), 245–62; Sheldon S. Wolin, *Tocqueville between Two Worlds: The Making of a Political and Theoretical Life* (Princeton, NJ: Princeton University Press, 2001), 210–11; Harvey C. Mansfield and Delba Winthrop, "Tocqueville's New Political Science," in *The Cambridge Companion to Tocqueville*, 81–107; and Aristide Tessitore, "Tocqueville and Gobineau on the Nature of Modern Politics," *Review of Politics* 67:4 (Fall 2005): 631–57.

18. Note Peter Augustine Lawler, "Tocqueville's Elusive Moderation," *Polity* 22:1 (Autumn 1989): 181–89, and see Lawler, "Was Tocqueville a Philosopher?" *Interpretation: A Journal of Political Philosophy* 17:3 (Spring 1990): 401–14, and "Tocqueville and Revolution in His *Souvenirs*," *Intercollegiate Review* 26:2 (Spring 1991): 25–34; then consider with the care that it deserves Peter Augustine Lawler, *The Restless Mind: Alexis de Tocqueville on the Origin and Perpetuation of Human Liberty* (Lanham, MD: Rowman & Littlefield, 1993), passim (esp. 11–100), along with Agnès Antoine, *L'Impensé de la démocratie: Tocqueville, la citoynneté, et la religion* (Paris: Fayard, 2003).

19. As Lawler, *The Restless Mind*, 101–24, is clearly aware, it is difficult, if not impossible, to reconcile Tocqueville's assertion of the primacy of political life with a thoroughgoing commitment on his part to the political psychology elaborated by Pascal. Politics may be diverting—and, as Lawler shows, Tocqueville experienced it as such. But if, at the same time, Tocqueville regarded it as more than mere *divertissement*—and he surely did so—he must have embraced a species of natural teleology, which means that he had more in common with Aristotle and less in common with Pascal than Lawler is inclined to admit. Note Salkever, *Finding the Mean*, passim (esp. 245–62), whose depiction of Aristotle as a crypto-Platonist who elaborates a politically salutary but false public teaching concerning moral virtue and the intrinsic dignity of politics needs correction in light of the more plausible account advanced by Mary P. Nichols, *Citizens and Statesmen: A Study of Aristotle's Politics* (Savage, MD: Rowman & Littlefield, 1992); then see James W. Ceaser, *Liberal Democracy and Political Science* (Baltimore, MD: Johns Hopkins University Press, 1990), passim (esp. 26–69, 143–76).

20. For the manner in which civil society came to be distinguished from and juxtaposed with the state, see Charles Taylor, "Civil Society in the Western Tradition," in *The Notion of Tolerance and Human Rights: Essays in Honor of Raymond Klibansky*, ed. Ethel Groffier and Michel Paradis (Ottawa: Carleton University Press, 1991), 117–34. Note in this connection Melvin Richter, "Montesquieu and the Concept of Civil Society," *European Legacy* 3:6 (1998): 33–41, and Yoshie Kawade, "La Liberté civile contre la théorie réformiste de l'État souverain: Le Combat de Montesquieu," in *Le Travail des lumières: Pour Georges Benrekassa*, ed. Caroline Jacot Grapa, Nicole Jacques-Lefèvre, Yannick Séité, and Carine Trevisan (Paris: Honoré Champion, 2002), 203–23. Though helpful and lucid, none of these pieces does full justice to the role played in this process

by the articulation of a theory of spontaneous social order by Pierre Nicole, Pierre Bayle, and Bernard Mandeville.

21. See Letter to Claude-François (Francisque) de Corcelle on 17 September 1853, in *ATG* XV:2 79–83 (at 80–81) and *LC* 1080–83 (at 1081–82).

22. Whether Tocqueville had access to the fragmentary political ruminations of Pascal, which were at this time as yet unpublished, remains unclear, but this may not in the end matter, for Pascal's skepticism with regard to politics is visible even in the Port-Royal edition. On the character of this skepticism, see Erich Auerbach, "On the Political Theory of Pascal," in *Blaise Pascal: Modern Critical Views*, ed. Harold Bloom (New York: Chelsea House, 1989), 17–35.

23. See Cheryl B. Welch, *De Tocqueville* (Oxford, UK: Oxford University Press, 2001), 13–31.

24. If one fails to reflect on the fact that *nómos* in Greek, which is ordinarily translated as "law," means "custom" as well, and if one fails to recognize just how inclusive the ancient understanding of what constitutes a *politeía* is, one will fall into the trap of eliding the regime-oriented political science of the ancients with the institutional political science of the early moderns; one will attribute to the latter the explanatory power possessed by the former; and one will conclude, from the fact that Tocqueville thinks mores, inherited practices, and civil law generally more influential than political institutions narrowly understood, that he gives primacy to the subpolitical: cf., for example, Thomas G. West, "Misunderstanding the American Founding," in *Interpreting Tocqueville's Democracy in America*, 155–77 (esp. 157–60), with Welch, "Tocqueville's Resistance to the Social," 83–107, and see Rahe, *RAM* I.Prologue, and "Aristotle and the Study of History," 202–13. The fact that Tocqueville displayed a keen interest in accurate statistical information deserves attention, but it has no bearing on the question discussed here: cf., however, Michael Drolet, "Tocqueville's Interest in the Social: Or How Statistics Informed His 'New Science of Politics,'" *History of European Ideas* 31:4 (November 2005): 451–71.

25. In this connection, note Letter to Louis de Kergorlay on 29 June 1831, in *ATG* XIII:1 225–36 (at 231–35) and *LC* 191–202 (at 198–201), and see Tocqueville, *DA* I.i.3, pp. 37–44.

26. See Lucien Jaume, *L'Individu effacé, ou Le Paradoxe du libéralisme français* (Paris: Fayard, 1997), 119–77, and Pierre Rosanvallon, *La Démocratie inachevée: Histoire de la souveraineté du peuple en France* (Paris: Gallimard, 2000), 93–126.

27. See Alexis de Tocqueville, "Discours prononcé a la séance publique annuelle de L'Académie des Sciences Morales et Politiques," 3 April 1852, in *ATP* I 1215–26 (esp. 1215–17), which should be read in light of Alexis de Tocqueville, *Souvenirs* (1850–51) III.1–4, in *ATP* III 886–950, and Letter to Louis de Kergorlay on 15 December 1850, in *ATG* XIII:2 229–34 and *LC* 700–705. In this connection, see Edward Gargan, *Alexis de Tocqueville: The Critical Years, 1848–1851* (Washington, DC: Catholic University of America Press, 1955); Maurice Agulhon, *The Republican Experiment, 1848–1852*, tr. Janet Lloyd (Cambridge, UK: Cambridge University Press, 1983); and Saguiv A. Hadari, "Unintended Consequences in Periods of Transition: Tocqueville's *Recollections* Revisited," *American Journal of Political Science* 33:1 (February 1989): 136–49.

28. See Tocqueville, "Discours prononcé a la séance publique annuelle de L'Académie des Sciences Morales et Politiques," 1217–20.

29. In this connection, Tocqueville's fiercely critical response to the racialist theories advanced by his former secretary Arthur de Gobineau is quite revealing: consider Letters Exchanged with Arthur de Gobineau on 29 April and 15 May 1852, 11 October, 17 November, and 20 December 1853, 8 January, 20 March, 1 May, 30 July, and 29 November 1856, 24 January and 20 May 1857, and 16 September 1858, in *ATG* IX 194–206, 244–46, 257–84, 296–98, the most important of which can be found in *LC* 1091–96, 1179–83, 1227–32, 1318–20; and see James W. Ceaser, *Reconstructing America: The Symbol of America in Modern Thought* (New Haven, CT: Yale University Press, 1997), 87–161 (esp. 136–61). Note also Larry Siedentop, *Tocqueville* (Oxford, UK: Oxford University Press, 1994), 125–30.

30. See Letter to Jean-Jacques Ampère on 26 August 1656, in *ATG* XI 340–42 (at 342).

31. See the passage from a letter written by Pierre-Paul Royer-Collard to a friend, which is quoted by André Jardin, "Introduction," in *ATG* XI i–xxviii (at v).

32. Consider Arist. *Pol.* 1274b32–1288b6 (esp. 1280a7–31, 1281a42–b38) in light of Arist. *Top.* 100a18–101b4 (esp. 100b21–23), which should be read with *Eth. Nic.* 1098b9–12, 27–31, 1145b2–7, 1153b25–28; *Eth. Eud.* 1216b26–1217a18, 1235b13–18; *Rh.* 1355a14–18, 1361a25–27, 1398b20–1399a6, 1400a5–14; *Metaph.* 993a30–b19. Note in this connection Aristotle's attitude regarding that which has been sanctioned by time: *Pol.* 1264a1–10, *Metaph.* 1074b1–15. The stated principle of Aristotle is entirely in keeping with the practice of Socrates in the Platonic dialogues. In this connection, one should consider the significance of Socrates' "taking refuge in rational speech (*lógous*)": cf. Pl. *Phd.* 96a–100b with *Resp.* 5.473a, and see *Leg.* 12.950b–c; note *Pol.* 262a–263b; and see Leo Strauss, *The Political Philosophy of Hobbes: Its Basis and Its Genesis* (Chicago: University of Chicago Press, 1952), 142–45; Ronna Burger, *The Phaedo: A Platonic Labyrinth* (New Haven, CT: Yale University Press, 1984), 135–60; and Seth Benardete, *Socrates' Second Sailing: On Plato's Republic* (Chicago: University of Chicago Press, 1989). The task of political science as Aristotle understood it was identical with that of science in general as understood by Plato and his followers: both aimed at making sense of the ordinary man's perceptions; both sought, in this way, "to save *tà phainómena*." Consider Arist. *Eth. Eud.* 1216b26–1217a18, 1235b13–18, *Eth. Nic.* 1145b2–7 in conjunction with the famous claim of Eudemus recorded by Simplicius, *De Caelo* 488.18–24 (Heiberg), and see Harold Cherniss, "The Philosophical Economy of the Theory of Ideas," *American Journal of Philology* 57:4 (1936): 445–56; G. E. L. Owen, "*Tithenai ta phainomena*," in *Aristote et les problèmes de méthode*, ed. Suzanne Mansion (Louvain: Publications Universitaires, 1961), 83–103; and Martha Craven Nussbaum, "Saving Aristotle's Appearances," in Nussbaum, *The Fragility of Goodness: Luck and Ethics in Greek Tragedy and Philosophy* (Cambridge, UK: Cambridge University Press, 1986), 240–63. Compare Jonathan Barnes, "Aristotle and the Methods of Ethics," *Revue internationale de la philosophie* 34 (1981): 490–511.

33. Consider Letter to Eugène Stöffels on 12 January 1833, in *LC* 284–85, in light of Leo Strauss, "On Classical Political Philosophy," in Strauss, *What Is Political Philosophy? and Other Studies* (New York: Free Press, 1959), 78–94 (esp. 81n), and see Robert Eden,

"Tocqueville and the Problem of Natural Right," *Interpretation: A Journal of Political Philosophy* 17:3 (Spring 1990): 389–400, which is reprinted in *Tocqueville's Political Science*, 3–11. For a defense of the species of political science that Tocqueville had in mind, see Ceaser, *Liberal Democracy and Political Science*, passim.

34. See James W. Ceaser, "Alexis de Tocqueville on Political Science, Political Culture, and the Role of the Intellectual," *American Political Science Review* 79:3 (September 1985): 656–72, which is reprinted in *Interpreting Tocqueville's Democracy in America*, 287–325.

35. See John C. Koritansky, *Alexis De Tocqueville and the New Science of Politics: An Interpretation of Democracy in America* (Durham, NC: Carolina Academic Press, 1986), 89–90.

36. To get a sense of the intellectual atmosphere in which Tocqueville grew up, one need only consult the two books that his father eventually published: see Hervé Louis François Joseph Bonaventure, comte Clérel de Tocqueville, *Histoire philosophique du règne de Louis XV par le comte de Tocqueville* (Paris: Amyot, 1847), and *Coup d'oeil sur le règne de Louis XVI depuis son avènement à la couronne jusqu'à la séance royale du 23 juin 1789, pour faire suite à l'Histoire philosophique du règne de Louis XV, par le comte de Tocqueville* (Paris: Amyot, 1850). With regard to the difference in outlook between father and son, see *The Two Tocquevilles, Father and Son: Hervé and Alexis de Tocqueville on the Coming of the French Revolution*, ed. Robert R. Palmer (Princeton, NJ: Princeton University Press, 1987). Compare Annelien de Dijn, *French Political Thought from Montesquieu to Tocqueville: Liberty in a Levelled Society?* (Cambridge, UK: Cambridge University Press, 2008), who, in her account of the ultra-royalists and liberals of the Restoration period and of their successors under the Orléanist monarchy and the Second Empire, is strangely silent with regard to the specter of Napoleon Bonaparte.

37. In addition to the secondary literature collected in III.Pref., notes 2–4, above, see Robert T. Gannett Jr., *Tocqueville Unveiled: The Historian and His Sources for the Old Regime and the Revolution* (Chicago: University of Chicago Press, 2003).

38. See Alexis de Tocqueville, *Considérations sur la Révolution* (1850–58) III, in *ATP* III 635–36, whence comes the epigraph for this chapter.

39. Note Richter, "Modernity and Its Distinctive Threats to Liberty," 61–80, and see Melvin Richter, "Tocqueville, Napoleon, and Bonapartism," in *Reconsidering Tocqueville's Democracy in America*, 110–45, along with Gannett, *Tocqueville Unveiled*, 15–17, 27–38. For a discussion of the setting within which Tocqueville developed his critique of Bonapartism, see Melvin Richter, "Toward a Concept of Political Illegitimacy: Bonapartist Dictatorship and Democratic Legitimacy," *Political Theory* 10:2 (May 1982): 185–214. Note also Melvin Richter, "Tocqueville and French Nineteenth-Century Conceptualizations of the Two Bonapartes and their Empires," in *Dictatorship in History and Theory*, ed. Peter Baehr and Melvin Richter (Cambridge, UK: Cambridge University Press, 2004), 83–102.

40. See Craiutu, "Tocqueville and the Political Thought of the French *Doctrinaires*," 469–79, and *Liberalism under Siege*, 93–104, and the secondary literature cited in III.Pref., note 4, above, especially Tocqueville, *DA* I.Intr., p. 10, n. a, and Ralph C. Hancock, "The Modern Revolution and the Collapse of Moral Analogy: Tocqueville and Gui-

zot," *Perspectives on Political Science* 30:4 (Fall 2001): 213–27, which is reprinted in *Democracy and Its Friendly Critics: Tocqueville and Political Life Today*, ed. Peter Augustine Lawler (Lanham, MD: Lexington Books, 2004), 49–58.

41. See Letter to Louis de Kergorlay on 29 June 1831, in *ATG* XIII:1 225–36 (at 231–35) and *LC* 191–202 (at 198–201).

42. It was this last concern, which was profound, that gave to Tocqueville's political moderation a paradoxical character: see Aurelian Craiutu, "Tocqueville's Paradoxical Moderation," *Review of Politics* 67:4 (Fall 2005): 599–629.

43. Compare William Henry George, "Montesquieu and de Tocqueville and Corporative Individualism," *American Political Science Review* 16:1 (February 1922): 10–21, with Siedentop, *Tocqueville*, 20–43, and Craiutu, "Tocqueville and the Political Thought of the French *Doctrinaires*," 479–8, and see Rudolf von Thadden, *Restauration und napoleonisches Erbe: Der Verwaltungszentralismus als politisches Problem in Frankreich (1814–1830)* (Wiesbaden: Franz Steiner, 1972); Pierre Rosanvallon, *The Demands of Liberty: Civil Society in France since the Revolution*, tr. Arthur Goldhammer (Cambridge, MA: Harvard University Press, 2007), 13–146; and Dijn, *French Political Thought from Montesquieu to Tocqueville*, passim, who trace the debate over intermediary bodies from the *ancien régime* through the French Revolution to Tocqueville's day. Royer-Collard, who meant in all seriousness what he said, Tocqueville held in high regard to the end of his days: see Letter to Pierre Freslon on 8 July 1858, in *LC* 1310–11.

44. In this connection, see Letter to Louis de Kergorlay, ca. January 1835, in *ATG* XIII:1 373–75 (at 373).

45. In this connection, see J.-P. Mayer, "Alexis de Tocqueville: Sur la Démocratie en Amérique. Fragments inédits," *La Nouvelle Revue Française* 76 (April 1959): 761–68 at (766–68), and Gannett, *Tocqueville Unveiled*, 173, n. 58.

46. See Rahe, *M* II.4.

47. See I.2, above.

48. Tocqueville's argument for democracy's inevitability in the passages cited above; in *DA* II.*Avertissement*, p. 8, and iv.8; and in *L'Ancien Régime et la Révolution* (1856) Avant-propos, in *ATP* III 48, should be taken with more than a grain of salt: note *DA* II.i.10, pp. 49–50, and Letter to Eugène Stöffels on 21 February 1835, in *LC* 314–15; then consider *DA* II.i.20; Letter to Harriet Grote on 25 June 1850, in *ATG* VI:3 134–36; *Souvenirs* (1850–51) II.1, in *ATP* III 776; Letter to Arthur de Gobineau on 17 November 1853, in *ATG* IX 201–4 and *LC* 1091–94; and Letter to Claude-François (Francisque) de Corcelle on 22 July 1854, in *ATG* XV:2 105–9 (esp. 107–9) and *LC* 1103–6 (esp. 1104–5), in light of Zetterbaum, *Tocqueville and the Problem of Democracy*, 1–21; and see Robert Kraynak, "Alexis de Tocqueville on Divine Providence and Historical Progress," in *Political Philosophy and the Human Soul: Essays in Memory of Allan Bloom*, ed. Michael Palmer and Thomas L. Pangle (Lanham, MD: Rowman & Littlefield, 1995), 203–27, who suggests that, behind Tocqueville's various treatments of this theme, there lurks something very much like Rousseau's doctrine of Providence: on which, see II.3, above.

49. As Michael Bressolette pointed out some time ago in "Tocqueville et le paupérisme: L'Influence de Rousseau," *Littératures: Annales publiées par la Faculté des lettres et sciences humaines de Toulouse* 16 (1969): 67–78, Tocqueville's dependence on Rousseau's

Discourse on the Origins and Foundations of Inequality among Men in his *Mémoire sur le paupérisme* is unmistakable: see *Mémoire sur le paupérisme* (1835), in *ATP* I 1155–80, which recapitulates Rousseau's argument and even echoes his language; note Lawler, *The Restless Mind*, 16–17; and then consider, in context, note 77, this chapter.

50. Note, for example, Arist. *Pol.* 1292a4–38, 1292b41–1293a10, and see Rahe, *RAM* I.vii.

51. See Thomas Jefferson, *Notes on the State of Virginia*, ed. William Peden (New York: W. W. Norton, 1972), 120–21 (Query 13).

52. See Alexander Hamilton, James Madison, and John Jay, *The Federalist*, ed. Jacob E. Cooke (Middletown, CT: Wesleyan University Press, 1961) nos. 10, 51.

53. In this connection, see James T. Schleifer, "Jefferson and Tocqueville," in *Interpreting Tocqueville's Democracy in America*, 178–203.

54. See Tocqueville, "Notes sur les *Pensées* de Pascal," in *ATG* XVI 551–54 (at 551, n. 1)

55. See Tocqueville, "Notes sur les *Pensées* de Pascal," in *ATG* XVI 551–54.

56. After reading Letter to Louis de Kergorlay on 6 July 1835, in *ATG* XIII:1 375–78 and *LC* 333–35; Letter to Édouard de Tocqueville on 2 September 1840, in *ATG* XIV 213–15 and *LC* 464–66; Letter to Jean-Jacques Ampère on 10 August 1841, in *ATG* XI 151–52 and *LC* 482–83; and Letters to Mme. Sophie Swetchine on 4 August 1856 and on 26 February 1857, in *ATG* XV:2 284–86, 313–16, and *LC* 1187–89, 1242–45, as well as Letter to Mme. Sophie Swetchine on 11 February 1857, in *ATG* XV:2 308–11 (at 309), and Letter to A. E. V. Childe on 23 January 1858, in *ATG* VII 221–24 (at 222–23), note Jardin, *Tocqueville*, 373, 451; consider the self-portrait provided in Alexis de Tocqueville, *Souvenirs* (1850–51), passim (esp. II.3. III.4), in *ATP* III 727–984 (esp. 789–98, 922–24), in light of Lawler, "Tocqueville and Revolution in his *Souvenirs*," 25–34, reprinted in *Tocqueville's Political Science*, 361–78, and ponder Peter Augustine Lawler, "The Restless Mind," in *Tocqueville's Defense of Human Liberty*, 63–81; then see Luiz Díez del Corral, "El liberalismo de Tocqueville (La influencia de Pascal)," *Revista de Occidente* 3:26 (1965): 133–53; Lawler, *The Restless Mind*, passim (esp. 11–124); Antoine, *L'Impensé de la démocratie*, passim; and Matthew W. Maguire, *The Conversion of Imagination: From Pascal through Rousseau to Tocqueville* (Cambridge, MA: Harvard University Press, 2006), 17–223 (esp. 185–220). Note also Kraynak, "Alexis de Tocqueville on Divine Providence and Historical Progress," 203–27.

57. Note Rahe, *M* III.3, and see Maguire, *The Conversion of Imagination*, 185–220, who, though silent regarding Tocqueville's debt to Montesquieu, does a fine job of charting his keen awareness that the aristocratic ethos rests on illusions that can no longer be sustained.

58. See Regina Pozzi, "Guizot et Tocqueville face à l'histoire anglaise," *The Tocqueville Review/La Revue Tocqueville* 22:2 (2001): 155–72.

59. See Letter to William Naussau Senior on 27 July 1851, in *LC* 714–17.

60. See Letter to Henry Reeve on 11 February 1857, in *ATG* VI:1 211–15 (at 212) and *LC* 1235–39 (at 1236). The words in italics appear underlined in English in the original.

61. In this connection, see Rahe, *ATA* 219–44.

62. See Seymour Drescher, *Tocqueville and England*, passim, and "Tocqueville's Comparative Perspectives," in *The Cambridge Companion to Tocqueville*, 21–48 (esp. 27–31, 36–41).

63. Consider Montesquieu, *EL* 3.19.27, in light of I.2, above.

64. Note Zetterbaum, *Tocqueville and the Problem of Democracy*, 21–40, and see Melvin Richter, "Rousseau and Tocqueville on Democratic Legitimacy and Illegitimacy," in *Rousseau and Liberty*, ed. Robert Wokler (Manchester, UK: Manchester University Press, 1995), 70–95.

65. Consider Zuckert, "On Social State," 3–17, who is arguably right in the emphasis that he puts on Tocqueville's conviction regarding the central role that man's awareness of death plays in defining the human condition, in light of III.2, note 36, below, and see Peter Augustine Lawler, "Tocqueville on Human Misery and Human Liberty," *Social Science Journal* 28:2 (April 1991): 243–57, and *The Restless Mind*, 11–124, as well as Maguire, *The Conversion of Imagination*, 70–220.

66. After reading II.1–2, above, see Zetterbaum, *Tocqueville and the Problem of Democracy*, 41–84, and Sanford Lakoff, "Liberty, Equality, Democracy: Tocqueville's Response to Rousseau," in *Lives, Liberties, and the Public Good: New Essays in Political Theory for Maurice Cranston*, ed. George Feaver and Frederick Rosen (New York: St. Martin's Press, 1987), 101–20, who underestimates just how close Rousseau is to Montesquieu and who therefore understates somewhat Tocqueville's debt to Rousseau.

67. Compare Arist. *Pol.* 1281a11–1282b6, 1286a7–b2.

68. See Siedentop, *Tocqueville*, 69–95.

69. The material found in Tocqueville, *DA* II.iv, had initially been drafted for deployment in the preface he intended to write for the second *Democracy*: see II.*Avertissement*, p. 7, n. b.

70. See Jon Elster, *Political Psychology* (Cambridge, UK: Cambridge University Press, 1993), 101–91.

71. See Manent, *Tocqueville and the Nature of Democracy*, 53–65, and Lawler, "Tocqueville on Human Misery and Human Liberty," 243–57, and *The Restless Mind*, 11–124.

72. In this connection, see Wolin, *Tocqueville between Two Worlds*, 76–91.

73. See Koenrad W. Swart, "Individualism in the Mid-Nineteenth Century, 1826–1860," *Journal of the History of Ideas* 23 (1962): 77–86; Schleifer, *The Making of Democracy in America*, 305–22; and Rosanvallon, *The Demands of Liberty*, 96–98.

74. In this connection, see Jean-Claude Lamberti, *Tocqueville and the Two Democracies*, tr. Arthur Goldhammer (Cambridge, MA: Harvard University Press, 1989), 168–90.

75. Compare Letter to Louis de Kergorlay on 5 August 1836, in *ATG* XIII:1 387–91 (at 389) and *LC* 355–60 (at 358), where Tocqueville appears to be less worried by *matérialisme honnête*, and see Roger Boesche, "Why Did Tocqueville Fear Abundance? On the Tension between Commerce and Citizenship," *History of European Ideas* 9:1 (February 1988): 25–45, which is reprinted in Boesche, *Tocqueville's Road Map: Methodology, Liberalism, Revolution, and Despotism* (Lanham, MD: Lexington Books, 2006), 59–84.

76. See II.2–3, above.

77. Note Zuckert, "On Social State," 3–17, and consider Lawler, "Tocqueville on Human Misery and Human Liberty," 243–57, and *The Restless Mind*, 11–50, 73–87, with an eye to note 49, this chapter.

78. Note Montesquieu, *EL* 3.19.27, and see I.2, above.

79. See Melvin Richter, "Tocqueville's Contribution to the Theory of Revolution," in *Revolution*, ed. Carl J. Friedrich (New York: Atherton, 1966), 75–121, and Seymour Drescher, "'Why Great Revolutions Will Become Rare': Tocqueville's Most Neglected Prognosis," *Journal of Modern History* 64:3 (September 1992): 429–54.

80. See Letter to Eugène Stöffels on 5 October 1836, in *LC* 364–66, and consider Roger Boesche, "Why Did Tocqueville Think a Successful Revolution Was Impossible?" in *Liberty, Equality, Democracy*, ed. Eduardo Nolla (New York: New York University Press, 1992), 165–85, which is reprinted in Boesche, *Tocqueville's Road Map*, 85–107.

81. See Alexis de Tocqueville, *Souvenirs* (1850–51) II.3, III.4, in *ATP* III 789–98 (esp. 793–95), 922–50 (at 922–24).

82. See Alexis de Tocqueville, "De la classe moyenne et du peuple" (October 1847), in *ATG* III:2 738–41 and *ATP* I 1121–24.

83. See Tocqueville, "De la classe moyenne et du peuple," in *ATG* III:2 740–41 and *ATP* I 1123–24.

84. See Alexis de Tocqueville, "Discours prononcé à la chambre des députés dans le 27 janvier 1848 dans la discussion du projet d'adresse en réponse au discours de la Couronne," in *ATG* III:2 745–58 and *ATP* I 1125–38.

85. Note Drescher, "'Why Great Revolutions Will Become Rare,'" 448–54, and see Alexis de Tocqueville, *Souvenirs* (1850–51) I.1, II.1, in *ATP* III 727–39, 779–80, and *L'Ancien Régime et la Révolution* (1856) III.2, in *ATP* III 185, along with Letter to Eugène Stöffels on 21 July 1848, in *LC* 634–36, and Letters to Louis de Kergorlay on 15 December 1850 and 16 May 1858, in *ATG* XIII:2 229–34, 336–38 and *LC* 700–705, 1305–7.

86. In this connection, see Zetterbaum, *Tocqueville and the Problem of Democracy*, 147–60.

87. Note also Tocqueville, *DA* II.iii.19, p. 206.

88. For a close study of the process by which Tocqueville came to this conclusion, and for an account of its implications for his startling and original depiction of the species of despotism most likely to prevail within the democratic *état social*, see Gannett, *Tocqueville Unveiled*, 1–10. Note the manner in which his ultimate conclusions in this regard are foreshadowed in the last sentence in Tocqueville, *DA* I.i.5, p. 75, n. 50.

89. See John Marini, "Centralized Administration and the 'New Despotism,'" in *Interpreting Tocqueville's Democracy in America*, 255–86; Françoise Mélonio, "Tocqueville et le despotisme moderne," *Revue française d'histoire des idées politiques* 6 (1997): 339–54; and Cristina Cassina, "Alexis de Tocqueville e il dispotismo 'di nuova specie,'" in *Dispotismo: Genesi e sviluppi di un concetto filosofico-politico*, ed. Domenico Felice (Naples: Liguori, 2001–2002), II 515–43.

90. For a thoughtful discussion, see Martin Malia, "Did Tocqueville Foresee Totalitarianism?" *Journal of Democracy* 11:1 (2000): 179–86.

91. In this connection, consider Rosanvallon, *The Demands of Liberty*, passim, in light of the thoughtful review by David A. Bell, *The New Republic* 237:8 (22 October 2007): 52–55.

92. Compare *Habits of the Heart*, ed. Robert Bellah et al. (Berkeley: University of California Press, 1985), and Roger Boesche, *The Strange Liberalism of Alexis de Tocqueville* (Ithaca, NY: Cornell University Press, 1987), 133–34, who suppose the thrust of Tocque-

ville's thought compatible with social democracy, with Daniel J. Mahoney, "Tocqueville and Socialism," in *Tocqueville's Defense of Human Liberty*, 177–201, who shows why this cannot be so. Note also Bruce Frohnen, "Materialism and Self-Deification: Bellah's Misuse of Tocqueville," in ibid., 135–56.

93. With regard to Tocqueville's development of this analysis, see Letter to Gustave de Beaumont on 8 July 1838, in *ATG* VIII:1 309–12 and *LC* 418–20.

94. In this connection, see Letter to Claude-François (Francisque) de Corcelle on 31 December 1853, in *ATG* XV:2 87–90 (at 88–89), and consider Alexis de Tocqueville, *L'Ancien Régime et la Révolution* (1856) III.3, in *ATP* III 186–95 (esp. 190–91); and Tocqueville, *Esquisses de L'Ancien Régime et la Révolution*, in *ATP* III 359–417, 432–50, with an eye to Gannett, *Tocqueville Unveiled*, 99–106 (esp. 103).

BOOK THREE, CHAPTER TWO.
AMERICAN EXCEPTIONALISM

1. Tocqueville was, nonetheless, upset when an early reader of the first *Democracy* took it to be more pessimistic than he intended, and he worried that the original English translation of it might be seen by readers as hypercritical with regard to democracy: see Letter to Claude-François (Francisque) de Corcelle on 12 April 1835, in *ATG* XV:1 52–54 and *LC* 318–19, and Letter to Henry Reeve on 15 October 1839, in *ATG* VI:1 47–48.

2. See III.Pref., note 7, above.

3. Compare Seymour Drescher, "Tocqueville's Two *Démocraties*," *Journal of the History of Ideas* 25: 2 (April–June 1964): 201–16, and "More than America: Comparison and Synthesis in *Democracy in America*," in *Reconsidering Tocqueville's Democracy in America*, ed. Abraham S. Eisenstadt (New Brunswick, NJ: Rutgers University Press, 1988), 77–93, as well as Jean-Claude Lamberti, *Tocqueville and the Two Democracies*, tr. Arthur Goldhammer (Cambridge, MA: Harvard University Press, 1989), with James T. Schleifer, "How Many Democracies?" in *Liberty, Equality, Democracy*, ed. Eduardo Nolla (New York: New York University Press, 1992), 193–205, which is reprinted in Schleifer, *The Making of Tocqueville's Democracy in America*, 2nd ed. (Indianapolis, IN: Liberty Fund, 2000), 354–68, who demonstrates that the themes thought by some to be peculiar to the second *Democracy*, or to its fourth part and Tocqueville's subsequent writings, are present in the first *Democracy* or in the sketches he drew in preparation for writing it. The fact that Tocqueville did have considerable difficulty in working out the implications of the argument advanced in the first *Democracy* as it pertained to the intellectual propensities, sentiments, mores, and long-term prospects of men situated within the democratic *état social* and that he had to do a great deal of rewriting as his thinking progressed shows that he did not have his entire argument worked out in advance, as Robert T. Gannett Jr. points out in *Tocqueville Unveiled: The Historian and His Sources for the Old Regime and the Revolution* (Chicago: University of Chicago Press, 2003), 1–10. But it does not prove that the two great sections of *Democracy in America* are at odds. Nor does it justify the claim that in the second *Democracy*, Tocqueville "condemned the revolutionary legacy as being incompatible with liberty": cf. Annelien de Dijn, *French Political Thought from Montesquieu to Tocqueville: Liberty in*

a Levelled Society? (Cambridge, UK: Cambridge University Press, 2008), 178, which should be read in light of ibid., 135–54. In fact, the first *Democracy* presupposes the second: see III.Pref, note 23, above.

4. See Alexis de Tocqueville, "Mon instinct, mes opinions" (ca. October 1840?), in *ATG* III:2 87. In this connection, note Peter Augustine Lawler, "Tocqueville's Elusive Moderation," *Polity* 22:1 (Autumn 1989): 181–89.

5. Compare John C. Koritansky, *Alexis De Tocqueville and the New Science of Politics: An Interpretation of Democracy in America* (Durham, NC: Carolina Academic Press, 1986), 23–47, who notes and exaggerates the strength of Tocqueville's dissatisfaction with the institutions in place in the United States, with Tocqueville's account of his own efforts as a member of the committee appointed by the Constituent Assembly in 1848 to prepare a constitution for the Second Republic, which reveals his thinking with regard to just how well those institutions, if properly adapted, might suit France: see Alexis de Tocqueville, *Souvenirs* (1850–51) II.11, in *ATP* III 870–85, where the virtues of administrative decentralization, bicameralism, the electoral college, and an independent judiciary loom large.

6. In the first *Democracy*, Tocqueville had made the same point from a slightly different perspective: *DA* I.i.3, pp. 44–45

7. Compare Martin Diamond, "The Separation of Powers and the Mixed Regime," *Publius: The Journal of Federalism* 8:3 (1978): 33–43, with Harvey C. Mansfield, "Separation of Powers in the American Constitution," in Mansfield, *America's Constitutional Soul* (Baltimore, MD: Johns Hopkins University Press, 1991), 115–27, and see William Kristol, "The Problem of the Separation of Powers: *Federalist* 47–51," in *Saving the Revolution: The Federalist Papers and the American Founding*, ed. Charles R. Kesler (New York: Free Press, 1987), 100–130; then see Paul A. Rahe, *RAM* III.i (esp. III.i.6–8), and "Between Trust and Distrust: *The Federalist* and The Emergence of Modern Republican Constitutionalism," *1650–1850: Ideas, Aesthetics, and Inquiries in the Early Modern Era* 11 (2005): 375–406.

8. That Tocqueville had Montesquieu's discussion of republican virtue in mind is evident from the arguments that he sketched while working on the pertinent chapters of the second *Democracy*: see Schleifer, *The Making of Tocqueville's Democracy in America*, 290–304 (esp. 301–2).

9. See Robert T. Gannett Jr., "Bowling Ninepins in Tocqueville's Township," *American Political Science Review* 97:1 (February 2003): 1–16, who shows, among other things, that Tocqueville had been obsessed with the history of the *commune* in Europe since at least 1828. Note also Larry Siedentop, *Tocqueville* (Oxford, UK: Oxford University Press, 1994), 41–68.

10. In this connection, see Mark Goldie, "The Unacknowledged Republic: Officeholding in Early Modern England," in *The Politics of the Excluded, ca. 1500–1850*, ed. Tim Harris (Houndsmills, UK: Palgrave, 2001), 153–94. Tocqueville's impressions in this regard were strongly reinforced on his second visit to England: see Seymour Drescher, *Tocqueville and England* (Cambridge, MA: Harvard University Press, 1964), 74–104.

11. See Letter to Ernest de Chabrol on 16 July 1831, in *LC* 203–6. In this connection, see

Notes to Pages 196–99   327

George Wilson Pierson, *Tocqueville and Beaumont in America* (New Haven, CT: Yale University Press, 1938), 179–84.

12. See Alexander Hamilton, James Madison, and John Jay, *The Federalist*, ed. Jacob E. Cooke (Middletown, CT: Wesleyan University Press, 1961) no. 9.

13. See Rahe, *RAM* III.

14. In this connection, consider Martin Diamond, "The Ends of Federalism," *Publius: The Journal of Federalism* 3 (1973): 121–51, and Ralph C. Hancock, "Tocqueville on the Good of American Federalism," *Publius: The Journal of Federalism* 20 (1990): 89–108, which are reprinted in *Tocqueville's Political Science: Classic Essays*, ed. Peter Augustine Lawler (New York: Garland, 1992), 107–53, which should be read in conjunction with John Marini, "Centralized Administration and the 'New Despotism,'" in *Interpreting Tocqueville's Democracy in America*, ed. Ken Masugi (Savage, MD: Rowman & Littlefield, 1991), 255–86.

15. See Robert H. Wiebe, *Self-Rule: A Cultural History of American Democracy* (Chicago: University of Chicago Press, 1995).

16. See Marvin Zetterbaum, *Tocqueville and the Problem of Democracy* (Stanford, CA: Stanford University Press, 1967), 85–109, 145–60; Koritansky, *Alexis De Tocqueville and the New Science of Politics*, passim; and Siedentop, *Tocqueville*, 64–68.

17. See Sheldon S. Wolin, *Tocqueville between Two Worlds: The Making of a Political and Theoretical Life* (Princeton, NJ: Princeton University Press, 2001), 210–11.

18. Compare Arist. *Pol.* 1252b27–1253a39, 1278b15–30, 1280a25–1281a10, 1283b42–1284a3; *Eth. Nic.* 1097a15–1098b8, 1169b16–18, and see I.1–2, II.2–3, above.

19. See I.2, II.2, above.

20. Compare Koritansky, *Alexis De Tocqueville and the New Science of Politics*, 72–77, 86–88, 148.

21. In this connection, see Lamberti, *Tocqueville and the Two Democracies*, 188.

22. Compare *Cod. Iust.* 5.59.5.2 with *Dig.* 39.3.8, and see Gaines Post, "Corporate Community, Representation, and Consent," in *Studies in Medieval Legal Thought* (Princeton, NJ: Princeton University Press, 1964), 27–238. See also Yves M.-J. Congar, "Quod omnes tangit ab omnibus tractari et approbari debet," *Revue historique du droit français et étranger*, 4th series, 36 (1958): 210–59; Peter N. Riesenberg, "Civism and Roman Law in Fourteenth-Century Italian Society," *Explorations in Economic History* 7 (1969): 237–54; and Riesenberg, "Citizenship at Law in Late Medieval Italy," *Viator* 5 (1974): 333–46.

23. After reading Peter Riesenberg, *Citizenship in the Western Tradition: Plato to Rousseau* (Chapel Hill: University of North Carolina Press, 1994), 85–199, consider David Bien, "Old Regime Origins of Democratic Liberty," in *The French Idea of Freedom: The Old Regime and the Declaration of Rights of 1789*, ed. Dale K. Van Kley (Stanford, CA: Stanford University Press, 1994), 23–71, and Gail Bossenga, "Status, *Corps*, and Monarchy: Roots of Modern Citizenship in the Old Regime," in *Tocqueville and Beyond: Essays on the Old Regime in Honor of David D. Bien*, ed. Robert M. Schwartz and Robert A. Schneider (Newark: University of Delaware Press, 2003), 127–54.

24. The *pólis* did not appear spontaneously; its establishment required artifice: see Arist.

Pol. 1252b27–1253a39. See also Arist. *Pol.* 1278b15–30, 1280a25–1281a10, 1283b42–1284a3; *Eth. Nic.* 1097a15–1098b8, 1169b16–18; then consider Gannet, "Bowling Ninepins in Tocqueville's Township," 8, n. 11.

25. Tocqueville could, perhaps, have gleaned all that was required from the one letter in which Jefferson made his argument—the one written to Samuel Kercheval on 12 July 1816—that is printed in full in translation in the volumes that Tocqueville is known to have employed while working on *Democracy in America* and from the letter directed to Kercheval on 5 September 1816 that the editor of these volumes quoted at length in his notes thereon: see *Mélanges politiques et philosophiques extraits des mémoires et de la correspondance de Thomas Jefferson*, ed. and tr. L.-P. Conseil (Paris: Paulin, 1833), II 273–90 (esp. 280–83). Nearly all of the letters in which Jefferson laid out his argument were available in the fourth volume of *Memoir, Correspondence, and Miscellanies, from the Papers of Thomas Jefferson*, ed. Thomas Jefferson Randolph (Charlottesville,VA: F. Carr, 1829), which Tocqueville may well have came across in the libraries that he visited during his sojourn in the United States.

26. See Rahe, *RAM* III.iv.4–9 (esp. III.iv.8, with nn. 142–44, where I cite the letters in which Jefferson articulates his argument).

27. See Letter from Thomas Jefferson to Samuel Kercheval on 12 July 1816, in *Mélanges politiques et philosophiques*, II 273–90 (esp. 280–83). Note also Letter from Thomas Jefferson to Joseph C. Cabell on 2 February 1816, in *The Writings of Thomas Jefferson*, ed. H. A. Washington (New York: J. C. Riker, 1853–1855), VI 540–44, which is even more emphatic but which was as yet unpublished in the 1830s when Tocqueville wrote *Democracy in America.*

28. It is by no means fortuitous that Tocqueville makes no mention of *Marbury v. Madison* and treats judicial review as if it were deliberately implied within the Constitution. In his day, for good reason, this was the common sense of the matter: see Paul A. Rahe, "Background to *Marbury v. Madison:* The Debate Concerning Judicial Review at the Federal Convention and during the Ratification Period," in *Marbury v. Madison: 1803–2003: Un Dialogue franco-américain/A French-American Dialogue*, ed. Élisabeth Zoller (Paris: Dalloz, 2003), 19–36.

29. See Faustin Adolphe Thomas Hélie, *Les Constitutions de la France* (Paris: Marescq ainé, 1875), 288.

30. Nothing has happened to invalidate the observation, advanced more than a century ago by Brinton Coxe, that the original constitution's "restriction of judicial power. . . . has unquestionably prevailed in France from 1791 to the present day under all forms of government." See Coxe, *An Essay on Judicial Power and Unconstitutional Legislation* (Philadelphia: Kay & Brother, 1893), 77–78.

31. In this connection, see Harvey C. Mansfield, "The Forms and Formalities of Liberty," *Public Interest* 70 (1983): 121–31, which is reprinted in *Tocqueville's Political Science*, 25–36, and in Mansfield, *America's Constitutional Soul* (Baltimore, MD: Johns Hopkins University Press, 1991), 193–208.

32. See III.1, above.

33. See Rahe, *RAM* II.i.4. See also David Lewis Schaefer, *The Political Philosophy of Montaigne* (Ithaca, NY: Cornell University Press, 1990).

34. Note Zetterbaum, *Tocqueville and the Problem of Democracy*, 109–23, and see Pierre Manent, *Tocqueville and the Nature of Democracy*, tr. John Waggoner (Lanham, MD: Rowman & Littlefield, 1996), 83–107, and Ralph C. Hancock, "The Uses and Hazards of Christianity in Tocqueville's Attempt to Save Democratic Souls," in *Interpreting Tocqueville's Democracy in America*, 348–93, from which I have learned a great deal. See also Catherine Zuckert, "Not by Preaching: Tocqueville on the Role of Religion in American Democracy," *Review of Politics* 43:2 (April 1981): 259–80, and "The Role of Religion in Preserving American Liberty: Tocqueville's Analysis 150 Years Later," in *Tocqueville's Defense of Human Liberty: Current Essays*, ed. Peter Augustine Lawler and Joseph Alulis (New York: Garland, 1993), 223–40; Koritansky, *Alexis De Tocqueville and the New Science of Politics*, 49–107; Peter Augustine Lawler, *The Restless Mind: Alexis de Tocqueville on the Origin and Perpetuation of Human Liberty* (Lanham, MD: Rowman & Littlefield, 1993), 141–58; Sanford Kessler, *Tocqueville's Civil Religion: American Christianity and the Prospects for Freedom* (Albany: State University of New York Press, 1994); Joshua Mitchell, *The Fragility of Freedom: Tocqueville on Religion, Democracy, and the American Future* (Chicago: University of Chicago Press, 1995), 162–214; Agnès Antoine, *L'Impensé de la démocratie: Tocqueville, la citoyenneté, et la religion* (Paris: Fayard, 2003); and Aristide Tessitore, "Tocqueville and Gobineau on the Nature of Modern Politics," *Review of Politics* 67:4 (Fall 2005): 631–57, which should be read in conjunction with Siedentop, *Tocqueville*, 96–112.

35. See, for example, Letter to Arthur de Gobineau on 5 September 1843, in *ATG* IX 45–48 (at 46–47) and *LC* 515–19 (at 517–18).

36. Compare Michael P. Zuckert, "On Social State," in *Tocqueville's Defense of Human Liberty*, 1–17, who, in dealing with the emergence of the democratic *état social*, ignores altogether the central role played by Christianity.

37. See, for example, Letter to Arthur de Gobineau on 5 September 1843, in *ATG* IX 45–48 (at 46–47) and *LC* 515–19 (at 517), and Letter to Louis de Kergorlay on 4 August 1857 in *ATG* XIII:2 326–28 and *LC* 1255–57.

38. For a detailed investigation of Montesquieu's argument, see Rahe, *M* III.1.

39. See David Hume, "Of National Characters" (1748), in Hume, *Essays Moral, Political, and Literary*, rev. ed., ed. Eugene F. Miller (Indianapolis, IN: Liberty Fund, 1985), 197–215.

40. With regard to the latter of the two figures mentioned, see Martin S. Staum, *Cabanis: Enlightenment and Medical Philosophy in the French Revolution* (Princeton, NJ: Princeton University Press, 1980).

41. See Lawler, *The Restless Mind*, 11–50.

42. In this connection, see Letter to Louis de Kergorlay on 29 June 1831, in *ATG* XIII:1 225–36 (at 225–31) and *LC* 191–202 (at 192–98).

43. In this connection, see Paul Thibaud, "Rousseau-Tocqueville: Un Dialogue sur la religion," *The Tocqueville Review/La Revue Tocqueville* 18:1 (1997): 47–59.

44. Consider Tocqueville, *DA* I.ii.9, pp. 232–33, in light of Letter to Arthur de Gobineau on 2 October 1843, in *ATG* IX 56–62 (at 57) and *LC* 525–29 (at 525), and see Letter to Mme. Sophie Swetchine on 26 February 1857, in *ATG* XV:2 313–16 (esp. 315) and *LC* 1242–45 (esp. 1244–45), which should perhaps be read in light of Conversation with

Nassau W. Senior on 10 February 1851, in *Correspondence and Conversation of Alexis de Tocqueville with Nassau William Senior from 1834 to 1859*, ed. M. C. M. Simpson (London: Henry S. King, 1872), I 222–23, and *ATG* VI:2 346. In this connection, see Siedentop, *Tocqueville*, 130–37.

45. See Lawler, *The Restless Mind*, 11–124, and Matthew W. Maguire, *The Conversion of Imagination: From Pascal through Rousseau to Tocqueville* (Cambridge, MA: Harvard University Press, 2006), 17–223 (esp. 185–220). Note also Robert Kraynak, "Alexis de Tocqueville on Divine Providence and Historical Progress," in *Political Philosophy and the Human Soul: Essays in Memory of Allan Bloom*, ed. Michael Palmer and Thomas L. Pangle (Lanham, MD: Rowman & Littlefield, 1995), 203–27.

46. In this connection, see Peter Augustine Lawler, "Was Tocqueville a Philosopher? The Distinctiveness of His View of Liberty," *Interpretation: A Journal of Political Philosophy* 17 (1990): 401–14, which is reprinted in *Tocqueville's Political Science*, 91–105.

BOOK THREE, CHAPTER THREE. THE FRENCH DISEASE

1. See Letter to Claude-François (Francisque) de Corcelle on 17 September 1853, in *ATG* XV:2 79–83 (at 80) and *LC* 1080–83 (1081).

2. See Letter to Hervé de Tocqueville on 24 January 1832, in *ATG* XIV 166–68 (at 166).

3. See Letter to Henry Reeve on 15 October 1839, in *ATG* VI:1 47–48.

4. See Letter to Louis de Kergorlay on 18 October 1847, in *ATG* XIII:2 207–12 (at 208–9) and *LC* 586–90 (587–88).

5. In this last connection, see Rahe, *RAM* III.Prologue.

6. Compare Peter Augustine Lawler, *The Restless Mind: Alexis de Tocqueville on the Origin and Perpetuation of Human Liberty* (Lanham, MD: Rowman & Littlefield, 1993), 135, who attributes his own opinion to Tocqueville, and Thomas G. West, "Misunderstanding the American Founding," in *Interpreting Tocqueville's Democracy in America*, ed. Ken Masugi (Savage, MD: Rowman & Littlefield, 1991), 155–77 (at 161–68), who rightly takes Tocqueville to task for failing to emphasize the significance for Americans of the Declaration of Independence but does so in so exaggerated a fashion that one is left thinking that he believes that their colonial heritage of local self-government somehow ceased to matter to Americans on 4 July 1776. It is important to recognize that the Constitution adopted in 1788 would never have been ratified had Americans not feared that, without it as a backstop, republican government in the states and localities would not long endure: see Rahe, *RAM* III.i–ii.

7. After consulting Steven L. Kaplan, *La Fin des corporations*, tr. Béatrice Vierne (Paris: Fayard, 2001), which has as its primary focus the guilds, and reading Pierre Rosanvallon, *The Demands of Liberty: Civil Society in France since the Revolution*, tr. Arthur Goldhammer (Cambridge, MA: Harvard University Press, 2007), 13–146, which is much broader in focus, note Donald J. Maletz, "The Spirit of Tocqueville's Democracies," *Polity* 30:3 (Spring 1998): 513–30, and consider in detail Robert T. Gannett Jr., "Bowling Ninepins in Tocqueville's Township," *American Political Science Review* 97:1 (February 2003): 1–16. From the outset, Tocqueville sought a gradual decentralization of administration in France: see Letter to Louis de Kergorlay on 29 June 1831, in *ATG* XIII:1

225–38 (at 233–34) and *LC* 191–202 (at 199–201), which was written with an eye to the law passed by the Chamber of Deputies under the July Monarchy on 21 March 1831, establishing elected municipal councils in the French communes; and, in context, see Letter from Édouard de Tocqueville on 15 June 1834, in *DA* I.i.5, p. 69, n. c, along with Letter to Louis de Kergorlay on 10 October 1836, in *ATG* XIII:1 407–12 (at 407–8) and *LC* 366–70 (at 367–68); Letter to Odilon Barrot on 16 September 1842, in *LC* 499–505 (at 504); and *Souvenirs* (1850–51) II.11, in *ATP* III 872–73. There was a moment, early in the July Monarchy, when he was prepared to entertain the notion that centralization and then a devolution of the very sort he favored was an element within "the natural, the instinctive, and . . . the inevitable progress, which those societies follow, which by their social condition, their ideas, and their manners, are travelling towards democracy." See Alexis de Tocqueville, *L'État social et politique de la France avant et depuis 1789* (1836), in *ATP* III 1–40 (at 27–30), which appeared as [Alexis de Tocqueville], "Political and Social Condition of France," [tr. John Stuart Mill], *London and Westminster Review* 25:1 (January–April 1836): 75–92 (at 86–88).

8. Had Tocqueville survived to finish his history of the French Revolution, he would have had much to say on the subject of the parlements: see Tocqueville, *Considérations sur la Révolution* (1850–58) I.3–4, in *ATP* III 471–90; note Tocqueville, *Souvenirs* (1850–51) II.11, in *ATP* III 882–83; and consider Robert Descimon, "Reading Tocqueville: Property and Aristocracy in Modern France," ed. Robert A. Schneider, tr. Mary Schwartz, in *Tocqueville and Beyond: Essays on the Old Regime in Honor of David D. Bien*, ed. Robert M. Schwartz and Robert A. Schneider (Newark: University of Delaware Press, 2003), 111–26 (esp. 121); Keith Michael Baker, "Tocqueville's Blind Spot? Political Contestation under the Old Regime," *The Tocqueville Review/La Revue Tocqueville* 27:2 (2006): 258–72; and David A. Bell, "Malesherbes et Tocqueville: Les Origines parlementaires du libéralisme français," *The Tocqueville Review/La Revue Tocqueville* 27:2 (2006): 273–82.

9. See Maurice Agulhon, *Le Cercle dans la France bourgeoise, 1810–1848* (Paris: Librairie Armand Colin, 1977); Jean-Pierre Chaline, *Sociabilité et érudition: Les Sociétés savantes en France, XIXᵉ–XXᵉ siècles* (Paris: Éditions du C. T. H. S., 1995); and Carol Harrison, *The Bourgeois Citizen in Nineteenth-Century France: Gender, Sociability, and the Uses of Emulation* (Oxford, UK: Oxford University Press, 1999).

10. It is an egregious error to suppose that Tocqueville was a Parisian, ignorant of the proliferation of clubs in the provinces, where he, in fact, spent a great deal of time in his youth and later in life; and it is a mistake to presume that the focus of his thinking with regard to civil associations was mere *sociability*. As Rousseau (*LS* 115–23; *CS* 1.7–2.3) and his disciples understood, there is all the difference in the world between harmless local clubs and tame societies tacitly sanctioned, if not in fact promoted, by the state, on the one hand, and "partial societies" freely formed that operate almost as states within the state and serve as instruments of agency on the part of citizens, on the other: cf. Carol Harrison, "Unsociable Frenchmen: Associations and Democracy in Historical Perspective," *The Tocqueville Review/La Revue Tocqueville* 17:2 (1996): 37–56, and Stefan-Ludwig Hoffmann, "Democracy and Associations: Towards a Transnational Perspective," *Journal of Modern History* 75:2 (June 2003): 269–99, who miss Tocqueville's

point, with Koritansky, *Alexis de Tocqueville and the New Science of Politics*, 109–19;
Gannett, "Bowling Ninepins in Tocqueville's Township," 1–16; and Dana Villa, "Tocqueville and Civil Society," in *The Cambridge Companion to Tocqueville*, ed. Cheryl B.
Welch (Cambridge, UK: Cambridge University Press, 2006), 216–44, who, in the manner of Hannah Arendt, *On Revolution* (New York: Viking Press, 1963), comes close to
asserting that civic agency was Tocqueville's only point; then see Rosanvallon, *The Demands of Liberty*, 186–207. On the relationship between Tocqueville and Arendt, see
Roger Boesche, "Tocqueville and Arendt on the Novelty of Modern Tyranny," in
Tocqueville's Defense of Human Liberty: Current Essays, ed. Peter Augustine Lawler
and Joseph Alulis (New York: Garland, 1993), 157–75, which is reprinted in Boesche,
Tocqueville's Road Map: Methodology, Liberalism, Revolution, and Despotism (Lanham, MD: Lexington Books, 2006), 169–88.

11. See Maurice Agulhon, "Vers une Histoire des associations," *Esprit* 6 (1978): 13–18, and
    "L'Histoire sociale et les associations," *La Revue de l'Économie Sociale* 14 (April 1988):
    35–44; Harrison, *The Bourgeois Citizen in Nineteenth-Century France*, 22–33; Ray-
    mond Huard, "Political Association in Nineteenth-Century France: Legislation and
    Practice," in *Before Civil Society: Lessons from Nineteenth-Century Europe*, ed. Nancy
    Bermeo and Philip Nord (Lanham, MD: Rowman & Littlefield, 2000), 135–53; and
    Rosanvallon, *The Demands of Liberty*, 13–146, 186–91, 231–46.

12. Consider Letter to Charles Stöffels on 21 April 1830, in *LC* 145–48 and *DA* II 322–24;
    Letter to Eugène Stöffels on 24 July 1836, in *LC* 352–55; Letters to Louis de Kergorlay
    on 18 October 1847 and 4 August 1857, in *ATG* XIII:2 207–12 (at 209–11), 326–28 and *LC*
    586–91 (at 588–90), 1255–57; and Letters to Claude-François (Francisque) de Corcelle
    on 13 May 1852, 17 September 1853, and 29 July 1857, in *ATG* XV:2 53–56, 79–83 (at 81),
    203–5 and *LC* 1036–39, 1080–83 (at 1082), 1252–54, in light of Alexis de Tocqueville,
    L'Ancien Régime et la Révolution (1856) I.2–3, in *ATP* III 56–63, and see Pierre Ma-
    nent, *Tocqueville and the Nature of Democracy*, tr. John Waggoner (Lanham, MD:
    Rowman & Littlefield, 1996), 83–107 (esp. 96–107), and Larry Siedentop, *Tocqueville*
    (Oxford, UK: Oxford University Press, 1994), 45–52.

13. See, for example, Jon Elster, *Political Psychology* (Cambridge, UK: Cambridge Univer-
    sity Press, 1993), 111–12.

14. In this connection, see Allan Bloom, "The Relation of the Sexes: Rousseauan Reflec-
    tions on the Crisis of Our Times," *Independent Journal of Philosophy* 5/6 (1987): 31–36,
    which is reprinted in *Tocqueville's Political Science: Classic Essays*, ed. Peter Augustine
    Lawler (New York: Garland, 1992), 233–44, along with John C. Koritansky, *Alexis de
    Tocqueville and the New Science of Politics*, 127–34, and "Alexis de Tocqueville's Hopes
    for the Education of Democratic Women," in *Tocqueville's Defense of Human Liberty*,
    283–96; Manent, *Tocqueville and the Nature of Democracy*, 83–88; Delba Winthrop,
    "Tocqueville's American Woman and 'the True Conception of Democratic Progress,'"
    Political Theory 14:2 (May 1986): 239–61; Sanford Kessler, "Tocqueville on Sexual
    Morality," *Interpretation: A Journal of Political Philosophy* 16 (1989): 465–80, which is
    reprinted in *Tocqueville's Political Science*, 247–64; and William Kristol, "Women's
    Liberation: The Relevance of Tocqueville," in *Interpreting Tocqueville's Democracy in*

America, 480–93. Tocqueville's knowledge of the anguish to which infidelity gives rise was more than merely academic: see Letter to Louis de Kergorlay on 27 September 1843, in *ATG* XIII:2 120–23 (esp. 120–22) and *LC* 521–23 (esp. 521–22). Compare Cheryl B. Welch, *De Tocqueville* (Oxford, UK: Oxford University Press, 2001), 190–207: if Tocqueville is inclined to follow Rousseau in this matter rather than to adopt the pose of Montesquieu, it is at least in part because he regards the world of monarchy described by the latter and the mores said to befit it as forever gone.

15. Consider Letters to Édouard de Tocqueville on 9 August 1829 and 15 and 24 March, 6 and 29 April, and 6 May 1830, in *ATG* XIV 49–51 (at 51), 55–69, and Tocqueville, *Souvenirs* (1850–51) II.1, in *ATP* III 779, in light of André Jardin, *Tocqueville: A Biography*, tr. Lydia Davis and Robert Hemenway (New York: Farrar, Straus, and Giroux, 1988), 84–87.

16. See Letter to Louis de Kergorlay on 10 November 1836, in *ATG* XIII:1 415–18 (at 416–17).

17. See Alexis de Tocqueville, "Discours prononcé à la chambre des députés dans le 27 janvier 1848 dans la discussion du projet d'adresse en réponse au discours de la Couronne," in *ATG* III:2 745–58 and *ATP* I 1125–38. This speech, which was appended to the thirteenth edition of *De la Démocratie en Amèrique*, published in 1850, has been translated into English and can be found in Alexis de Tocqueville, *Democracy in America*, tr. George Lawrence (New York: Harper & Row, 1966), 749–58.

18. See Letter to Henry Reeve on 9 January 1852, in *ATG* VI:1 132–34 (at 133) and *LC* 1011–13 (at 1012–13), along with Letter to Claude-François (Francisque) de Corcelle on 13 May 1852, in *ATG* XV:2 53–56 (at 54) and *LC* 1036–39 (at 1037).

19. Consider Tocqueville, *DA* II.ii.9, p. 240, in light of Letter to Eugène Stöffels on 5 October 1836, in *LC* 364–66, and Tocqueville, *Souvenirs* (1850–51) III.2, in *ATP* III 897–98.

20. See Tocqueville, "Note pour le comte de Chambord," 14 January 1852, in *ATG* III:3 465–70.

21. See Letter to Pierre-Paul Royer-Collard on 15 August 1838, in *ATG* XI 66–68.

22. In this connection, consider the story that James T. Schleifer has to tell in *The Making of Tocqueville's Democracy in America*, 2nd ed. (Indianapolis, IN: Liberty Fund, 2000), 159–322, concerning the manner in which Tocqueville found his way to this conclusion; note what Robert T. Gannett Jr. has to add to this picture in *Tocqueville Unveiled: The Historian and His Sources for the Old Regime and the Revolution* (Chicago: University of Chicago Press, 2003), 1–10; and see John Marini, "Centralized Administration and the 'New Despotism,'" in *Interpreting Tocqueville's Democracy in America*, 255–86.

23. The fact that in this passage Tocqueville echoes the notorious assertion of Rousseau, *CS* 1.7, p. 364, can hardly be an accident.

24. The grounds for Tocqueville's disappointment with regard to his own conduct as a statesman are visible in the memoirs he wrote concerning the revolution of 1848 and his service under the Second Republic: consider Tocqueville, *Souvenirs* (1850–51) III.1–4, in *ATP* III 886–950, in light of Edward Gargan, *Alexis de Tocqueville: The Critical Years, 1848–1851* (Washington, DC: Catholic University of America Press, 1955), and Maurice Agulhon, *The Republican Experiment, 1848–1852*, tr. Janet Lloyd (Cambridge,

UK: Cambridge University Press, 1983), and see Saguiv A. Hadari, "Unintended Consequences in Periods of Transition: Tocqueville's *Recollections* Revisited," *American Journal of Political Science* 33:1 (February 1989): 136–49.

25. Initially, his focus had been Napoleon and the empire: see Conversation with Nassau W. Senior on 19 August 1850, in *Correspondence and Conversation of Alexis de Tocqueville with Nassau William Senior from 1834 to 1859*, ed. M. C. M. Simpson (London: Henry S. King, 1872), I 112–19 (at 112–14), and *ATG* VI:2 285–90 (at 286–87); and Letter to Louis de Kergorlay on 15 December 1850, in *ATG* XIII:2 229–34 and *LC* 700–705. See also Letter to A. E. V. Childe on 23 January 1858, in *ATG* VII 221–24 (at 222–23). In this connection, see Delba Winthrop, "Tocqueville's *Old Regime*: Political History," *Review of Politics* 43 (1981): 88–111, which is reprinted in *Tocqueville's Political Science*, 335–60; Manent, *Tocqueville and the Nature of Democracy*, 109–27; Ralph Lerner, *Revolutions Revisited: Two Faces of the Politics of Enlightenment* (Chapel Hill: University of North Carolina Press, 1994), 112–28; Siedentop, *Tocqueville*, 113–25; Welch, *De Tocqueville*, 121–64; Gannett, *Tocqueville Unveiled*, 10–162; and David W. Carrithers, "Montesquieu and Tocqueville as Philosophical Historians: Liberty, Determinism, and the Prospects for Freedom," in *Montesquieu and His Legacy*, ed. Rebecca E. Kingston (Albany: State University of New York Press, 2008), 149–77.

26. See Letters to Mme. Sophie Swetchine on 7 January and 20 October 1856, in *ATG* XV:2 267–69, 296–99 (at 298–99), and *LC* 1143–45, 1216–19 (at 1218–19).

27. See Excerpts from a Letter dated 16 June 1852, in Albert Gigot, "M. de Tocqueville," *Le Correspondant* 51 (December 1860): 690–726 (at 715–16), and note Seymour Drescher, *Tocqueville and England* (Cambridge, MA: Harvard University Press, 1964), 222–23, who draws attention to its significance.

28. Compare Françoise Mélonio, *Tocqueville and the French*, tr. Beth G. Raps (Charlottesville: University Press of Virginia, 1998), who overstates the case, with Serge Audier, *Tocqueville retrouvé: Genèse et enjeux du renouveau tocquevillien français* (Paris: Librairie Philosophique Vrin, 2004), and Annelien de Dijn, *French Political Thought from Montesquieu to Tocqueville: Liberty in a Levelled Society?* (Cambridge, UK: Cambridge University Press, 2008), 155–84, which serve as a corrective.

29. For the political world into which Tocqueville did not fit and for some of the reasons why, see Roger Boesche, *The Strange Liberalism of Alexis de Tocqueville* (Ithaca, NY: Cornell University Press, 1987).

30. See François Burdeau, *Liberté, libertés locales chéries* (Paris: Éditions Cujas, 1983), 11–133 (esp. 69–133). Note also Dijn, *French Political Thought from Montesquieu to Tocqueville*, 40–128.

31. See Henry C. Clark, *Compass of Society: Commerce and Absolutism in Old Regime France* (Lanham, MD: Lexington Books, 2007).

32. See Tocqueville, *Souvenirs* (1850–51) II.11, in *ATP* III 872–73.

33. See Jack Hayward, *Fragmented France: Two Centuries of Disputed Identity* (Oxford, UK: Oxford University Press, 2007).

34. Consider Alexis de Tocqueville, *L'Ancien Régime et la Révolution* (1856) III.3, in *ATP* III 186–95, in light of Letter to Claude-François (Francisque) de Corcelle on 31 December 1853, in *ATG* XV:2 87–90 (at 88–89), and Tocqueville, *Esquisses de L'Ancien*

Régime et la Révolution, in *ATP* III 359–417, 432–50; and see Harvey Mitchell, "Tocqueville's Mirage or Reality? Political Freedom from Old Regime to Revolution," *Journal of Modern History* 60:1 (March 1988): 28–54; Gannett, *Tocqueville Unveiled*, esp. 101–6; and Hayward, *Fragmented France*, 71–89. On Tocqueville's last great literary project more generally, see François Furet, "Tocqueville est-il un historien de la Révolution française?" *Annales: Économies, Sociétés, Civilisations* 25:2 (March–April 1970): 434–51, which was reprinted in Furet, "Tocqueville et le problème de la Révolution française," in *Science et conscience de la société: Mélanges en l'honneur de Raymond Aron*, ed. Jean-Claude Casanova (Paris: Calmann-Lévy, 1971), I 309–43 (at 319–43), and has appeared in translation in "De Tocqueville and the Problem of the French Revolution," in Furet, *Interpreting the French Revolution*, tr. Elborg Forster (Cambridge, UK: Cambridge University Press, 1981), 132–63 (at 140–63).

35. It is good to remember that Philippe Pétain was installed in power by the National Assembly of the Third Republic, which then voted its own indefinite adjournment; that the civil service, the army, and the diplomatic corps quickly rallied to the new regime; and that in 1940 Charles de Gaulle, who was unknown to the larger public and had only recently been made a general, had no support. For an overview, see Philippe Burrin, "Vichy," in *Realms of Memory: Rethinking the French Past I: Conflicts and Divisions*, ed. Pierre Nora, tr. Arthur Goldhammer (New York: Columbia University Press, 1996), 181–202. For the details, which reveal a great deal about French divisiveness, see Marc Bloch, *Strange Defeat: A Statement of Evidence Written in 1940*, tr. Gerard Hopkins (New York: W. W. Norton, 1968), and Julian Jackson, *The Fall of France: The Nazi Invasion of 1940* (Oxford, UK: Oxford University Press, 2003); then, Robert O. Paxton, *Vichy France: Old Guard and New Order, 1940–1944*, 2nd ed. (New York: Columbia University Press, 2001), Julian Jackson, *France: The Dark Years, 1940–1944* (Oxford, UK: Oxford University Press, 2001), and Richard Vinen, *The Unfree French: Life under the Occupation* (New Haven, CT: Yale University Press, 2006); and, finally, Henry Rousso, *The Vichy Syndrome: History and Memory in France since 1944*, tr. Arthur Goldhammer (Cambridge, MA: Harvard University Press, 1991), and Éric Conan and Henry Rousseau, *Vichy: An Ever-Present Past*, tr. Nathan Bracher (Hanover, NH: University Press of New England, 1998).

36. Much of considerable intelligence has been written concerning the linkage between social divisiveness, political instability, sociopolitical immobility, and the predominance of the administrative state in France. First, see Michel Crozier, *The Bureaucratic Phenomenon* (Chicago: University of Chicago Press, 1964), which first appeared in France as *Le Phénomène bureaucratique: Essai sur les tendances bureaucratiques des systèmes d'organisations modernes et sur leurs relations en France avec le système social et culture* (Paris: Éditions du Seuil, 1963), and Stanley Hoffmann, "Paradoxes of the French Political Community," in Hoffmann et al., *In Search of France: The Economy, Society, and Political System in the Twentieth Century* (Cambridge, MA: Harvard University Press, 1963), 1–117. Then, cf. Hoffmann, *Decline or Renewal? France since the 1930s* (New York: Viking Press, 1974), esp. 61–184, 363–486, with Crozier, *La Société bloquée* (Paris: Éditions du Seuil, 1970), which appeared in English as *The Stalled Society* (New York: Viking Press, 1973); and see Alain Peyrefitte, *Le Mal français* (Paris:

Plon, 1976), which is translated as *The Trouble with France*, tr. William R. Byron (New York: Random House, 1981); Crozier, *On ne change pas la société par décret* (Paris: B. Grasset, 1979), which appeared in English as *Strategies for Change: The Future of French Society*, tr. William R. Beer (Cambridge, MA: MIT Press, 1982); Laurent Cohen-Tanugi, *Le Droit sans l'État: Sur la Démocratie en France et en Amérique* (Paris: Presses Universitaires de France, 1985); and Crozier, *État modeste, État moderne: Stratégies pour an autre changement* (Paris: Fayard, 1987).

37. After working one's way through Emannuel Joseph Sieyès, *Political Writings*, ed. and tr. Michael Sonenscher (Indianapolis, IN: Hackett, 2003), and reading Sonenscher's informative introduction, one should peruse Malcolm Crook, *Elections in the French Revolution* (Cambridge, UK: Cambridge University Press, 1996), and Patrice Gueniffrey, *Le Nombre et la raison: La Révolution française et les élections* (Paris: Éditions de l'École des Hautes Études en Sciences Sociales, 1993).

38. See Pierre Rosanvallon, *Le Moment Guizot* (Paris: Gallimard, 1985), and H. A. C. Collingham, with R. S. Alexander, *The July Monarchy: A Political History of France, 1830–1848* (London: Longman, 1988). For a discussion of the thinking of the *Doctrinaires*, a subject which deserves attention, see Aurelian Craiutu, *Liberalism under Siege: The Political Thought of the French Doctrinaires* (Lanham, MD: Lexington Books, 2003). For the thinking that underpinned Guizot's commitment to the rule of a natural aristocracy, see Pierre Manent, *An Intellectual History of Liberalism*, ed. Rebecca Balinski (Princeton, NJ: Princeton University Press, 1994), 93–102.

39. As Gannett points out in *Tocqueville Unveiled*, 1–3, 17–27, Tocqueville had identified what he took to be the defects in Guizot's thinking well before the latter had the opportunity to attempt a permanent political settlement along these lines in France: see Letter to Gustave de Beaumont on 5 October 1828, in *ATG* VIII:1 47–71 and *LC* 114–35. See, in context, Tocqueville, *DA* II.ii.5, p. 103, n. c.

40. See Claude Lefort, "Préface," in Alexis de Tocqueville, *Souvenirs*, ed. Luc Monnier, J. P. Mayer, and B. M. Wicks-Boisson (Paris: Gallimard, 1999), i–l (esp. xv–xix).

41. After reading Pierre Rosanvallon, *Le Peuple introuvable: Histoire de la répresentation démocratique en France* (Paris: Gallimard, 2002), and *Le Sacre du citoyen: Histoire du suffrage universel en France* (Paris: Gallimard, 2002), see Hayward, *Fragmented France*, 147–342.

42. See Michel Crozier, with Bruno Tilliette, *La Crise de l'intelligence: Essai sur l'impuissance des élites à se réformer* (Paris: InterEditions, 1995), who argue for the abolition of the École nationale d'administration, as have two of its most distinguished alumni, former prime ministers Laurent Fabius and Alain Juppé. With regard to the *énarques*, few observers are as acute as those who are associated with the reactionary left: see, for example, Perry Anderson, "La Dégringolade," *London Review of Books* 26:17 (2 September 2004): 3–9, and "Union Sucrée," *London Review of Books* 26:18 (23 September 2004): 10–16, which should be taken with the grains of salt offered in the letter to the editor written by David A. Bell, "Dégringolade," *London Review of Books* 26:19 (7 October 2004): 4, and in the article by Arthur Goldhammer, "Did Historians Make History?" *French Politics, Culture, & Society* 24:2 (Summer 2006): 102–14.

43. For a brief overview of the struggle and the aftermath, see Claude Langlois, "Catholics and Seculars," in *Realms of Memory*, I 109–43.

44. See Anne Lefebvre Teillard, *La Société anonyme au XIXe siècle* (Paris: Presses Universitaires de France, 1985), and Charles E. Freedeman, *Joint-Stock Enterprise in France, 1807–1867: From Privileged Company to Modern Corporation* (Chapel Hill: University of North Carolina Press, 1979), and *The Triumph of Corporate Capitalism in France, 1867–1914* (Rochester, NY: University of Rochester Press, 1993).

45. See Rosanvallon, *The Demands of Liberty*, 147–85, 208–13.

46. See Jean-François Merlet, *Une grande Loi de la IIIe République: La Loi du 1er juillet 1901* (Paris: LGDI, 2001).

47. Note Christian Sorrel, *La République contre les congrégations: Histoire d'une passion française (1899–1904)* (Paris: Editions du Cerf, 2003), which describes in detail the campaign to suppress the religious orders and confraternities, and see *Les Congrégations hors la loi? Autour de la loi du 1er juillet 1901*, ed. Jacqueline-Lalouette and Jean-Pierre Machelon (Paris: Letouzey et Ané, 2002). For an overview, see Paul Nourrisson, *Histoire légale des congrégations religieuses en France depuis 1789* (Paris: Recueil Sirey, 1928), and Jean-Paul Duran, *La Liberté des congrégations religieuses en France* (Paris: Editions du Cerf, 1999). For a meditation on the origins of the peculiarly anti-Christian character of the French Revolution and of French republicanism ever after, see Dale K. Van Kley, "Christianity as Casualty and Chrysalis of Modernity: The Problem of Dechristianization in the French Revolution," *American Historical Review* 108:4 (October 2003): 1081–1103.

48. See Agulhon, "L'Histoire sociale et les associations," 37–40.

49. See Michel Pomey, *Traité des fondations d'utilité publique* (Paris: Presses Universitaires de France, 1980).

50. See Rosanvallon, *The Demands of Liberty*, 186–265.

51. For an especially influential example, see Pierre Bourdieu, *Contre-feux: Propos pour servir à la résistance contre l'invasion néo-libérale* (Paris: Liber, 1998), which is translated into English as *Acts of Resistance: Against the Tyranny of the Market*, tr. Richard Nice (New York: New Press, 1998).

52. On the transformation in outlook that occurred within the Socialist Party in France after 1980, see Goldhammer, "Did Historians Make History?" 102–14.

53. Consider Tocqueville, *L'Ancien Régime et la Révolution* (1856) III.3, in *ATP* III 189–95 (esp. 191–92), in light of Daniel J. Mahoney, "Tocqueville and Socialism," in *Tocqueville's Defense of Human Liberty*, 177–201, and see Friedrich Hayek, "The Use of Knowledge in Society," *American Economic Review* 35:4 (September 1945): 519–30.

54. See Audier, *Tocqueville retrouvé*, passim, and Hayward, *Fragmented France*, 344–53. To get a sense of the sources of resistance in France to learning from Tocqueville, consider Claire Le Strat and Willy Pelletier, *La Canonisation libérale de Tocqueville* (Paris: Éditions Syllepse, 2006), in light of Philippe Raynaud, *L'Extrême Gauche plurielle: Entre Démocratie radicale et révolution* (Paris: Éditions Autrement, 2006).

55. See Rosanvallon, *The Demands of Liberty*, 220–30.

56. See Vivien Schmidt, *Democratizing France: The Political and Administrative History of*

Decentralization (Cambridge, UK: Cambridge University Press, 1990), and Jonah D. Levy, *Tocqueville's Revenge: State, Society, and Economy in Contemporary France* (Cambridge, MA: Harvard University Press, 1999).

57. See Timothy B. Smith, *France in Crisis: Welfare, Inequality, and Globalization since 1980* (Cambridge, UK: Cambridge University Press, 2004); "Survey of France," *Economist*, 26 October 2006; John Thornhill, "Why France May Find Its Social Model Exacts Too High a Price," *Financial Times*, 15 April 2007; and John Ward Anderson and Molly Moore, "A Paradoxical French Electorate: Voters in Presidential Race Demand, and Fear, Change," *Washington Post*, 21 April 2007.

58. See Stefan Theil, "Europe's Philosophy of Failure," *Foreign Policy* 164 (January–February 2008): 54–60, from whom I have taken material quoted from the third and last volume of Serge Berstein and Pierre Milza, *Histoire du XXe siècle* (Paris: Hatier, 1993–2005), which bears the subtitle: *Vers la mondialisation et le début du XXIe siècle*. No less revealing is Albertino Alesina and Edward L. Glaeser, *Fighting Poverty in the U.S. and Europe: A World of Difference* (New York: Oxford University Press, 2004).

59. See Anderson, "Union Sucrée," 10–16.

60. Late in his life, Tocqueville acknowledged that given the burden of France's past, he could see no way out: see Letter to Pierre Freslon on 11 September 1857, in *LC* 1260–61. The obstacles are immense: see Alan Charles Kors, "Can There Be an 'After Socialism'?" *Social Philosophy & Policy* 20:1 (Winter 2003): 1–17. Note, however, Michel Crozier, with Bruno Tilliette, *Nouveau regard sur la société française: S'écouter pour s'entendre* (Paris: Oldile Jacob, 2007).

61. For an elegant illustration of the entrenched mentality that sustains in France the tutelary state, see Alain Supiot, "The Condition of France," *London Review of Books* 28:11 (8 June 2006): 24–26.

62. For the suspicion with which virtually all states on the European continent regarded the formation of civil associations, see the first chapter of Joseph C. Bradley, *Voluntary Associations in Tsarist Russia: Science, Patriotism, and Civil Society* (Cambridge, MA: Harvard University Press, 2009). For a detailed discussion of Portugal, Russia, Italy, Germany, Belgium, and the Netherlands, see *Civil Society before Democracy: Lessons from Nineteenth-Century Europe*, ed. Nancy Bermeo and Philip Nord (Lanham, MD: Rowman & Littlefield, 2000), 3–108, 155–78. The Italian story, in all of its complexity, is especially revealing: see Robert D. Putnam, *Making Democracy Work: Civic Tradition in Modern Italy* (Princeton, NJ: Princeton University Press, 1993).

63. In this connection, see Paul Edward Gottfried, *After Liberalism: Mass Democracy in the Managerial State* (Princeton, NJ: Princeton University Press, 1999).

64. Tocqueville, who recognized in Hegel an apologist for the existing bureaucratic order, and who traced to his influence the socialist school, was instinctively hostile: see Letter to Claude-François (Francisque) de Corcelle on 22 July 1854, in *ATG* XV:2 105–9 (esp. 107–9) and *LC* 1103–6 (esp. 1104–5).

65. As one would expect, the thoughtful, systematic critique of the French model for European integration articulated by Larry Siedentop, *Democracy in Europe* (New York: Columbia University Press, 2001), on the basis of his own reflections on Montesquieu

and Tocqueville has had almost no influence on subsequent pan-European delibera-
tions.

66. Here, too, the reactionary left has been admirably alert: see Susan Watkins, "Continental Tremors," *New Left Review* 33 (May–June 2005): 5–21, and Perry Anderson, "European Hypocrisies," *London Review of Books* 29:18 (20 September 2007): 13–21.

67. For an eloquent, and philosophically subtle, call to arms, see Pierre Manent, *A World
beyond Politics? A Defense of the Nation State*, tr. Marc LePain (Princeton, NJ: Princeton University Press, 2006), and *Democracy without Nations? The Fate of Self-Government in Europe*, tr. Paul Seaton (Wilmington, DE: ISI Books, 2007).

68. As this passage should make clear, in his analysis of the dangers attendant on modern
egalitarianism, Tocqueville anticipated much of what Friedrich Nietzsche would later
say: see Roger Boesche, "Hedonism and Nihilism: The Predictions of Tocqueville and
Nietzsche," *The Tocqueville Review/La Revue Tocqueville* 8 (1987–1989): 165–84, reprinted in *Tocqueville's Political Science*, 37–58, and in Boesche, *Tocqueville's Road
Map*, 127–47.

69. On this last point, see Robert Kagan, *Of Paradise and Power: America and Europe in the
New World Order* (New York: Alfred A. Knopf, 2003), whose argument is confirmed by
Tony Judt, *Postwar: A History of Europe since 1945* (New York: Penguin, 2005). Note also
James J. Sheehan, *Where Have All the Soldiers Gone? The Transformation of Modern
Europe* (New York: Houghton Mifflin, 2008).

70. See Nicholas Eberstadt, "Population Power: Another Transatlantic Divergence?" *European Outlook*, AEI Online (November–December 2004), and "'Demographic Excep-
tionalism' in the United States: Tendencies and Implications," *Agir* (January 2007).

71. See David B. Young, "Libertarian Demography: Montesquieu's Essay on Depopula-
tion in the *Lettres persanes*," *Journal of the History of Ideas* 36:4 (October 1975): 669–82.

72. Compare Judt, *Postwar*, which nicely exemplifies the blind self-satisfaction that paralyzes Europe, with Walter Laqueur, *The Last Days of Europe: Epitaph for an Old Continent* (New York: St. Martin's Press, 2007). Note also Bruce S. Thornton, *Decline and
Fall: Europe's Slow Motion Suicide* (New York: Encounter Books, 2007).

BOOK THREE, CHAPTER FOUR.
A DESPOTISM OF ADMINISTRATORS

1. With the analysis presented here, one might wish to compare Michel Crozier, *The
Trouble with America: Why the System Is Breaking Down*, tr. Peter Heinegg (Berkeley:
University of California Press, 1984), who, on his second extended sojourn in the
United States, recognized that something was, indeed, amiss but failed to give due
weight to the contribution made to the American malady by the Great Society, and
Sheldon S. Wolin, *Democracy Incorporated: Managed Democracy and the Specter of In-
verted Totalitarianism* (Princeton, NJ: Princeton University Press, 2008), who has written a fine book on Tocqueville but is too wedded to the shibboleths of the 1960s to be
able to properly consider the present discontents in light of the Frenchman's analysis.

2. In this connection, see Paul Edward Gottfried, *After Liberalism: Mass Democracy in the*

Managerial State (Princeton, NJ: Princeton University Press, 1999), and John Lukacs, *A New Republic: A History of the United States in the Twentieth Century* (New Haven, CT: Yale University Press, 2004).

3. Compare David Broyles, "Tocqueville on the Nature of Federalism," in *Tocqueville's Defense of Human Liberty: Current Essays*, ed. Peter Augustine Lawler and Joseph Alulis (New York: Garland, 1993), 297–320, who fails to reflect sufficiently on the degree to which *Democracy in America* is pitched to the French and oriented to what Tocqueville took to be their needs.

4. See John C. Koritansky, *Alexis De Tocqueville and the New Science of Politics: An Interpretation of Democracy in America* (Durham, NC: Carolina Academic Press, 1986), 23–47, 83–86. These worries are even more visible in Tocqueville's research notes and in material within the working manuscript of *Democracy in America* that he ultimately omitted from the version sent to the printer: see James T. Schleifer, *The Making of Tocqueville's Democracy in America*, 2nd ed. (Indianapolis, IN: Liberty Fund, 2000), 115–48, who fails to appreciate Tocqueville's remarkable prescience in this regard.

5. See Rahe, *RAM* III.iii.

6. See Schleifer, *The Making of Tocqueville's Democracy in America*, 122–25.

7. Later, however, in 1838, when he was composing the second *Democracy*, Tocqueville briefly considered backing off from this last claim: consider Tocqueville, *DA* II. *Avertissement*, p. 7, n. b, in light of Schleifer, *The Making of Tocqueville's Democracy in America*, 37, 146–47.

8. Note Schleifer, *The Making of Tocqueville's Democracy in America*, 143–46, and see Rahe, *RAM* III.ii–vi.

9. Later, after the publication of *Democracy in America*, Tocqueville would become more alarmed—above all, with regard to slavery and the future of the Union, but also with regard to other matters as well: see Françoise Mélonio, "Tocqueville et les malheurs de la démocratie américaine (1831–1859)," *Commentaire* 38 (1987): 381–89; Hugh Brogan, "Alexis de Tocqueville and the Coming of the American Civil War," in *American Studies: Essays in Honour of Marcus Cunliffe*, ed. Brian Holden Reid and John White (New York: St. Martin's Press, 1991), 83–104; and Aurelian Craiutu and Jeremy Jennings, "The Third *Democracy*: Tocqueville's Views of America after 1840," *American Political Science Review* 98:3 (August 2004): 391–404.

10. Compare Thomas G. West, "Misunderstanding the American Founding," in *Interpreting Tocqueville's Democracy in America*, ed. Ken Masugi (Savage, MD: Rowman & Littlefield, 1991), 155–77 (at 166–68), who fails to recognize that Tocqueville mistook southerners, not northerners. West's contention that Tocqueville was unaware that in the United States equality was a political principle derives from his presumption that Tocqueville's political science is sociological in character.

11. See Letter to Ernest Chabrol on 16 July 1831, in *LC* 203–6.

12. See Leonard P. Curry, *Blueprint for Modern America: Non-Military Legislation of the First Civil War Congress* (Nashville, TN: Vanderbilt University Press, 1968); Barrington Moore Jr., *Social Origins of Dictatorship and Democracy: Lord and Peasant in the Making of the Modern World* (Boston: Beacon Press, 1966), 111–65; and Gabor S. Boritt, *Lincoln and the Economics of the American Dream* (Memphis, TN: Memphis State Uni-

versity Press, 1978). In this connection, see also James M. McPherson, *Abraham Lincoln and the Second American Revolution* (New York: Oxford University Press, 1991).

13. In this connection, see Eldon J. Eisenach, *The Lost Promise of Progressivism* (Lawrence: University Press of Kansas, 1994). Note also *Challenges to the American Founding: Slavery, Historicism, and Progressivism in the Nineteenth Century*, ed. Ronald J. Pestritto (Lanham, MD: Lexington Books, 2004).

14. After reading Jurgen Herbst, *The German Historical School in American Scholarship* (Cambridge, MA: Harvard University Press, 1965), consider John A. Marini, "Theology, Metaphysics, and Positivism: The Origins of the Social Sciences and the Transformation of the American University," in *Challenges to the American Founding*, 163–94, and Eldon J. Eisenach, "Progressivism as a National Narrative in Biblical-Hegelian Time," *Social Philosophy & Policy* 24:1 (Winter 2007): 55–83.

15. Note Georg Wilhelm Friedrich Hegel, *Die Vernunft in der Geschichte*, ed. J. Hoffmeister (Hamburg: F. Meiner, 1952), 207, and see George Armstrong Kelly, "Hegel's America," in Kelly, *Hegel's Retreat from Eleusis* (Princeton, NJ: Princeton University Press, 1978), 184–223.

16. Considerable light is cast on their attitudes by James A. Nuechterlein, "The Dream of Scientific Liberalism: *The New Republic* and American Progressive Thought, 1914–1920," *Review of Politics* 42:2 (April 1980): 169–90.

17. See Jean B. Quandt, *From the Small Town to the Great Community: The Social Thought of Progressive Intellectuals* (New Brunswick, NJ: Rutgers University Press, 1970).

18. After reading Louise L. Stevenson, *Scholarly Means to Evangelical Ends: The New Haven Scholars and the Transformation of Higher Learning in America, 1830–1890* (Baltimore, MD: Johns Hopkins University Press, 1986), see Marini, "Theology, Metaphysics, and Positivism," 163–94.

19. See Alexis de Tocqueville, "Discours prononcé a la séance publique annuelle de L'Académie des Sciences Morales et Politiques," 3 April 1852, in *ATP* I 1215–26 (esp. 1215–20).

20. For representative selections of their writings, see *The Social and Political Thought of American Progressivism*, ed. Eldon J. Eisenach (Indianapolis, IN: Hackett, 2006), and *American Progressivism: A Reader*, ed. Ronald J. Pestritto and William J. Atto (Lanham, MD: Rowman & Littlefield, 2008).

21. In this connection, see *The Progressive Revolution in Politics and Political Science: Transforming the American Regime*, ed. John A. Marini and Ken Masugi (Lanham, MD: Rowman & Littlefield, 2005). See also Gottfried, *After Liberalism*, 41–42, 49–71, who draws attention to the manner in which the thinking of Hegel's American student George Bancroft foreshadowed this development.

22. Consider Edwin Lawrence Godkin, "The Eclipse of Liberalism," *The Nation*, 9 August 1900, in light of C. Vann Woodward, *The Strange Career of Jim Crow*, 3rd ed. (New York: Oxford University Press, 1974), 3–110, and Lawrence J. Friedman, *The White Savage: Racial Fantasies in the Postbellum South* (Englewood Cliffs, NJ: Prentice-Hall, 1970), 3–149.

23. See Seth M. Scheiner, "Theodore Roosevelt and the Negro, 1901–1908," *Journal of Negro History* 47:3 (July 1962): 169–82. For a recent attempt to come to grips with the elder

Roosevelt's thinking as a whole, see Will Morrissey, "Theodore Roosevelt on Self-Government and the Administrative State," in *The Progressive Revolution in Politics and Political Science*, 35–71.

24. Consider "The Progressive Party Platform of 1912," in *American Progressivism*, 273–87, in light of Sidney M. Milkis and Daniel J. Tichenor, "'Direct Democracy' and Social Justice: The Progressive Party Campaign of 1912," *Studies in American Political Development* 8:2 (Fall 1994): 282–340.

25. See Woodrow Wilson, *A History of the American People* (New York: Harper and Bros., 1901–1902), esp. V 1–115.

26. See Arthur S. Link, "The Nego as a Factor in the Campaign of 1912," *Journal of Negro History* 32:1 (January 1947): 81–99.

27. See Kathleen Long Wohlgemuth, "Wilson's Appointment Policy and the Negro," *Journal of Southern History* 24:4 (November 1958): 457–71, and "Woodrow Wilson and Federal Segregation," *Journal of Negro History* 44:2 (April 1959): 158–73; Arthur S. Link, *Wilson: The New Freedom* (Princeton, NJ: Princeton University Press, 1956), 243–52; Henry Blumenthal, "Woodrow Wilson and the Race Question," *Journal of Negro History* 48:1 (January 1963): 1–21; Nicholas Patler, *Jim Crow and the Wilson Administration: Protesting Federal Segregation in the Early Twentieth Century* (Boulder: University Press of Colorado, 2004); and Bruce Barlett, *Wrong on Race: The Democratic Party's Buried Past* (New York: Palgrave Macmillan, 2008), 95–110. Compare Ray Stannard Baker, *Woodrow Wilson, Life and Letters: IV. President, 1913–1914* (Garden City, NY: Doubleday, Doran, 1931), 220–25.

28. Consider Woodrow Wilson, "Address at the Gettysburg Battlefield," 4 July 1913, in *The Papers of Woodrow Wilson*, ed. Arthur S. Link et al. (Princeton, NJ: Princeton University Press, 1966–1994), XXVIII 23–25, in light of David W. Bright, *Race and Reunion: The Civil War in American Memory* (Cambridge, MA: Harvard University Press, 2001), esp. 6–30, 383–91.

29. See Patler, *Jim Crow and the Wilson Administration*, 38–40, 76; Friedman, *The White Savage*, 150–72; and Bartlett, *Wrong on Race*, 111–68; then, see Melvyn Stokes, *D. W. Griffith's The Birth of a Nation: A History of "The Most Controversial Motion Picture of All Time"* (New York: Oxford University Press, 2007). For the view that Dixon tricked an unwitting president, see Link, *Wilson: The New Freedom*, 252–54. In this connection, see Letters from Thomas Dixon Jr. to Joseph Patrick Tumulty on 27 January 1915 and to Woodrow Wilson on 20 February 1915 (with the attendant notes), Letter from David Wark Griffith to Woodrow Wilon on 2 March 1915, Letter from Margaret Blaine Damrosch to Joseph Patrick Tumulty on 27 March 1915, Letter from Edward Douglass White to Joseph Patrick Tumulty on 5 April 1915, Exchange of Notes between Joseph Patrick Tumulty and Woodrow Wilson on 24 April 1915, Letter to Thomas Dixon Jr. on 7 September 1915, and Letter to Joseph P. Tumulty on 22 April 1918 (with the attendant notes), in *The Papers of Woodrow Wilson*, XXXII 142, 267, 310–11, 455, 486–87, XXXIII 68, XXXIV 426–27, XLVII 388. Unfortunately, Arthur Link chose not to print the highly revealing letter of thanks that Thomas Dixon Jr. wrote to Wilson on 4 September 1915, which Friedman, *The White Savage*, 171, cites.

30. Consider Woodrow Wilson, *The New Freedom: A Call for the Emancipation of the Generous Energies of a People* (New York: Doubleday, Page, 1913), passim (esp. 3–7, 19–22, 41–54), in light of Robert Eden, "Opinion Leadership and the Problem of Executive Power: Woodrow Wilson's Original Position," *Review of Politics* 57:3 (Summer 1995): 483–503, and "The Rhetorical Presidency and the Eclipse of Executive Power: Woodrow Wilson's *Constitutional Government in the United States*," *Polity* 28:3 (Spring 1996): 357–78, and see Paul Carrese, "Montesquieu, The Founders, and Woodrow Wilson: The Evolution of Rights and the Eclipse of Constitutionalism," in *The Progressive Revolution in Politics and Political Science*, 133–62, and Ronald J. Pestritto, *Woodrow Wilson and the Roots of American Liberalism* (Lanham, MD: Rowman & Littlefield, 2005).

31. See *The New York Times* (27 October 1921): 1, 11. Harding's speech was also published in *The Birmingham Post* on 27 October 1921 and discussed the next day, and his off-the-cuff remarks are quoted in Carl V. Harris, *Political Power in Birmingham, 1871–1921* (Knoxville: University of Tennessee Press, 1977), 33–35.

32. See Merrill D. Peterson, *Lincoln in American Memory* (New York: Oxford University Press, 1994), 206–16.

33. See Calvin Coolidge, "The Inspiration of the Declaration," in Coolidge, *Foundations of the Republic: Speeches and Address* (New York: Scribners, 1926), 441–54, which should be read in light of Thomas B. Silver, *Coolidge and the Historians* (Durham, NC: Carolina Academic Press, 1982). Compar Robert H. Ferrell, *The Presidency of Calvin Coolidge* (Lawrence: University Press of Kansas, 1998), who makes no mention of Coolidge's duel with Wilson.

34. See Benjamin M. Anderson, *Economics and the Public Welfare: A Financial and Economic History of the United States, 1914–1946* (New York: D. Van Nostrand, 1949), 47–297, and Milton Friedman and Anna Jacobson Schwartz, *A Monetary History of the United States, 1867–1960* (Princeton, NJ: Princeton University Press, 1963), 240–419.

35. See the seminal study by Robert Eden, "On the Origins of the Regime of Pragmatic Liberalism: John Dewey, Adolf A. Berle, and FDR's Commonwealth Club Address of 1932," *Studies in American Political Development* 7:1 (Spring 1993): 74–150.

36. See Amity Shlaes, *The Forgotten Man: A New History of the Great Depression* (New York: HarperCollins, 2007).

37. Consider Franklin Delano Roosevelt, "First Inaugural Address" (4 March 1933), in *Nothing to Fear: The Selected Addresses of Franklin Delano Roosevelt, 1932–1945*, ed. B. D. Zevin (Boston: Houghton Mifflin, 1946), 12–17, in light of Roosevelt, "Commonwealth Club Address" (23 September 1932), in *Franklin Delano Roosevelt, 1882–1945*, ed. Howard F. Bremer (Dobbs Ferry, NY: Oceana Publications, 1971), 99–107.

38. See Walter Lippmann, *An Inquiry into the Principles of the Good Society* (Boston: Little, Brown, 1937), 3–6. For background, see Ronald Steel, *Walter Lippmann and the American Century* (Boston: Little Brown, 1980), 3–326.

39. The Progressives did have a considerable impact, even in the early years: see Stephen Skowronek, *Building a New American State: The Expansion of National Administrative Capacities, 1877–1920* (New York: Cambridge University Press, 1982), and James Klop-

penberg, *Uncertain Victories: Social Democracy and Progressivism in European and American Thought* (New York: Oxford University Press, 1986).

40. See Jeffrey K. Tulis, *The Rhetorical Presidency* (Princeton, NJ: Princeton University Press, 1987), and Will Morrisey, "Theodore Roosevelt on Self-Government and the Administrative State," in *The Progressive Revolution in Politics and Political Science*, 35–72.

41. On the latter, see Ronald J. Pestritto, *Woodrow Wilson and the Roots of American Liberalism*, passim, and "The Progressive Origins of the Administrative State: Wilson, Goodnow, and Landis," *Social Philosophy & Policy* 24 (2007): 16–54. The Progressives were unhappy with Wilson only when, at the end of the war, he acquiesced in a partial dismantling of the vast administrative apparatus assembled during the course of the war: see Nuechterlein, "The Dream of Scientific Liberalism," 169–90.

42. For the history, see Michael Barone, *Our Country: The Shaping of America from Roosevelt to Reagan* (New York: Free Press, 1990), 3–534. For thoughtful meditation on the consequences, see Theodore J. Lowi, *The End of Liberalism: The Second Republic of the United States*, 2nd ed. (New York: W. W. Norton, 1979), and Jonathan Rauch, *Demosclerosis: The Silent Killer of American Government* (New York: New York Times Books, 1994), which is grounded on Mancur Olson, *The Logic of Collective Action: Public Goods and the Theory of Groups* (Cambridge, MA: Harvard University Press, 1971), and *The Rise and Decline of Nations: Economic Growth, Stagflation, and Social Rigidities* (New Haven, CT: Yale University Press, 1982).

43. Wilson's example is instructive: cf. Terri Bimes and Stephen Skowronek, "Woodrow Wilson's Critique of Popular Leadership: Reassessing the Modern-Traditional Divide in Presidential History," *Polity* 29:1 (Autumn 1996): 27–63, and Eisenach, *The Lost Promise of Progressivism*, 3, 31–36, 124–25, with Ronald J. Pestritto, "Woodrow Wilson, American History, and the Advent of Progressivism," in *Challenges to the American Founding*, 265–96.

44. The current hysteria concerning global warming is a case in point. Thirty years ago, meteorologists—who were then, as now, incapable of accurately predicting the weather in any given locality a week in advance—were not only trumpeting the grave dangers attendant on what they took to be a global cooling trend but insisting on the need for government action: see Peter Gwynne, "The Cooling World," *Newsweek* 85:17 (28 April 1975): 64. For a refreshingly sober discussion of the current controversy, see Freeman Dyson, "The Question of Global Warming," *New York Review of Books* 55:10 (12 June 2008): 43–45.

45. Note William James, "The Moral Equivalent of War" (1910), in James, *Pragmatism and Other Essays* (New York: Washington Square Press, 1963), 289–301, and see William E. Leuchtenburg, "The New Deal and the Analogue of War," in *Change and Continuity in Twentieth-Century America*, ed. John Braeman, Robert Bremner, and Everett Walters (Columbus: Ohio University Press, 1964), 81–143, who shows, before the fact, that the war on poverty, the war on inflation, the war against the energy crisis, the war on terrorism, and the war on global warming all go back rhetorically to the New Deal.

46. Consider Robert Higgs, *Crisis and Leviathan* (Oxford, UK: Oxford University Press, 1987), in light of Tocqueville, *DA* II.iii.22, pp. 223–24.

47. See Ralph A. Rossum, *Federalism, the Supreme Court, and the Seventeenth Amendment: The Irony of Constitutional Democracy* (Lanham, MD: Lexington Books, 2001). Compare Sara Brandes Cook and John R. Hibbing, "A Not-So-Distant Mirror: The 17th Amendment and Congressional Change," *American Political Science Review* 91:4 (December 1997): 845–53, who miss altogether what was at stake.

48. Consider Marie-Vic Ozouf-Marignier, *La Formation des départements: La Représentation du territoire français à la fin du XVIIIe siècle* (Paris: Editions de l'EHESS, 1989), in light of Pierre Rosanvallon, *The Demands of Liberty: Civil Society in France since the Revolution*, tr. Arthur Goldhammer (Cambridge, MA: Harvard University Press, 2007), 13–75.

49. See Gary S. Lawson, "The Rise of the Administrative State," *Harvard Law Review* 107:6 (April 1994): 1231–54.

50. See Tiffany R. Jones, "Campaign Finance Reform: The Progressive Reconstruction of Free Speech," in *The Progressive Revolution in Politics and Political Science*, 321–46.

51. In this connection, see James C. Miller III, *Monopoly Politics* (Stanford, CA: Hoover Institution Press, 1999).

52. See Raoul Berger, *Government by Judiciary: The Transformation of the Fourteenth Amendment* (Cambridge, MA: Harvard University Press, 1977); Robert H. Bork, *The Tempting of America: The Political Seduction of the Law* (New York: Free Press, 1990); and Matthew Franck, *Against the Imperial Judiciary: The Supreme Court vs. the Sovereignty of the People* (Lawrence: University Press of Kansas, 1996).

53. For a discussion of the transformation worked by Roosevelt, see Sidney M. Milkis, "The Presidency, Policy Reform, and the Rise of Administrative Politics," and R. Shep Melnick, "The Courts, Congress, and Programmatic Rights," in *Remaking American Politics*, ed. Richard A. Harris and Sidney M. Milkis (Boulder, CO: Westview Press, 1989), 146–212, along with David Plotke, *Building a Democratic Political Order: Reshaping American Liberalism in the 1930s and 1940s* (Cambridge, UK: Cambridge University Press, 1996), and Shlaes, *The Forgotten Man*, passim.

54. See Franklin Delano Roosevelt, Annual Message to Congress, 11 January 1944, in *Nothing to Fear*, 387–97 (at 395–97).

55. In this connection, consider the epigraph to this chapter: Alexis de Tocqueville, *Mémoire sur le paupérisme* (1835), in *ATP* I 1155–80 (at 1170), and see Delba Winthrop, "Rights, Interest, and Honor," in *Tocqueville's Defense of Human Liberty*, 203–22.

56. See Rahe, *RAM* III.iv–vi.

57. Consider Alexis de Tocqueville, "Discours prononcé à l'Assemblée Constituante dans la discussion du projet de constitution sur la question du droit au travail," 12 September 1848, in *ATP* I 1139–52, in light of *DA* II.iv.5, pp. 253–63 (esp. 254), where similar language is deployed, and see Daniel J. Mahoney, "Tocqueville and Socialism," in *Tocqueville's Defense of Human Liberty*, 177–201, and Harvey C. Mansfield, "Tocqueville and the Future of the American Constitution," in Mansfield, *America's Constitutional Soul* (Baltimore, MD: Johns Hopkins University Press, 1991), 176–92. Note also Seymour Drescher, *Dilemmas of Democracy: Tocqueville and Modernization* (Pittsburgh: University of Pittsburgh Press, 1968), 196–250; and on the relationship between the right to property and liberty more generally, consider the implications of Harvey C. Mansfield,

"On the Political Character of Property in Locke," in *Powers, Possessions, and Freedom: Essays in Honour of C. B. Macpherson*, ed. Alkis Kontos (Toronto: University of Toronto Press, 1979), 23–38.

58. See James Bovard, *Lost Rights: The Destruction of American Liberty* (New York: St. Martin's Griffin, 1995). For an example of extreme complacency, see Hugh Brogan, *Alexis de Tocqueville: A Life* (New Haven, CT: Yale University Press, 2007), 499–500, 523.

59. See Alexander Hamilton, James Madison, and John Jay, *The Federalist*, ed. Jacob E. Cooke (Middletown, CT: Wesleyan University Press, 1961) no. 10.

60. See *The Wall Street Journal* (21 July 2008): A12.

61. See Bradley A. Smith, *Unfree Speech: The Folly of Campaign Finance Reform* (Princeton, NJ: Princeton University Press, 2001); Rodney A. Smith, *Money, Power, and Elections: How Campaign Finance Reform Subverts American Democracy* (Baton Rouge: Louisiana State University Press, 2006); and John Samples, *The Fallacy of Campaign Finance Reform* (Chicago: University of Chicago Press, 2006). For an update, see Bradley A. Smith, "Campaign Finance Reform's War on Political Freedom," *City Journal*, 1 July 2007, available at http://www.city-journal.org.

62. See Alan Charles Kors and Harvey C. Silverglate, *The Shadow University: The Betrayal of Liberty on America's Campuses* (New York: Free Press, 1999). For updates, see Fire: Foundation for Individual Rights in Education, online at http://www.thefire.org.

63. See Stuart Taylor Jr. and K. C. Johnson, *Until Proven Innocent: Political Correctness and the Shameful Injustices of the Duke Lacrosse Rape Case* (New York: St. Martin's Press, 2007).

64. See Dorothy Rabinowitz, *No Crueler Tyrannies: Accusation, False Witness, and Other Terrors of Our Times* (New York: Free Press, 2003).

65. See Bovard, *Lost Rights*, 10–17.

66. See Terry Eastland, *Ending Affirmative Action: The Case for Colorblind Justice* (New York: Basic Books, 1996); Carl Cohen, *Naked Racial Preference: The Case against Affirmative Action* (Lanham, MD: Madison Books, 1995); and Bovard, *Lost Rights*, 165–98.

67. Consider the powerful case made on behalf of the double-jeopardy clause by David S. Rudstein, "A Brief History of the Fifth Amendment Guarantee against Double Jeopardy," *William & Mary Bill of Rights Journal* 14:6 (October 2005): 193–242, who is strangely silent concerning the so-called separate sovereigns exception under which the U.S. Supreme Court sanctions retrying in federal court criminal defendants already tried and acquitted in state courts for the same offense, in light of Montesquieu's discussion of the close relationship of liberty and criminal law in *EL* 2.12; then cf. Laurie L. Levenson, "Civil Rights Prosecutions and Double Jeopardy: The Future of State and Federal Civil Rights Prosecutions: The Lessons of the Rodney King Trial," *UCLA Law Review* 41 (February 1994): 509–608, and Paul Hoffman, "Double Jeopardy Wars: The Case for a Civil Rights 'Exception,'" ibid., 649–91, with Susan N. Herman, "Double Jeopardy All Over Again: Dual Sovereignty, Rodney King, and the ACLU," ibid., 609–47, and Paul G. Cassell, "Some Observations on Original Meaning and the ACLU's Schizophrenic Views of the Dual Sovereignty Doctrine," ibid., 693–720. In general, one can say that everyone favors paying particular attention to the rights of the

accused—except when he or she cares passionately about the crimes the accused putatively committed.

68. The best brief summary of their argument can be found in Friedrich Hayek, "The Use
of Knowledge in Society," *American Economic Review* 35:4 (September 1945): 519–30.

69. See John Kenneth Galbraith, *The New Industrial State* (Boston: Houghton, Mifflin,
1967). There are, of course, those who, in their eagerness to manage the lives of others,
know no such shame: see, for example, Paul Krugman, *The Conscience of a Liberal*
(New York: W. W. Norton, 2007).

70. In this connection, see Berger, *Government by Judiciary*, passim; Bork, *The Tempting of
America*, passim; and Franck, *Against the Imperial Judiciary*, passim.

71. On this particular point, see George L. Priest, "The Invention of Enterprise Liability: A
Critical History of the Intellectual Foundations of Modern Tort Law," *Journal of Legal
Studies* 14:3 (December 1985): 461–527, and "Procedural vs. Substantive Controls of
Mass Tort Actions," ibid. 26:2 (June 1997): 521–73; Walter K. Olson, *The Litigation Explosion: What Happened When America Unleashed the Lawsuit* (New York: Dutton,
1991), and *The Rule of Lawyers: How the New Litigation Elite Threatens America's Rule
of Law* (New York: St. Martin's, 2003); and Charles Sykes, *A Nation of Victims: The De-
cay of American Character* (New York: St. Martin's, 1992). In this connection, one may
also want to consider Paul Moreno, "*Placek v. Sterling Heights*: Civil Wrongs and the
Rights Revolution," *Michigan Bar Journal* 88:2 (February 2009).

72. Compare Theda Skocpol, "The Tocqueville Problem: Civic Engagement in American
Democracy," *Social Science History* 21:4 (Winter 1997): 455–79, and *Civic Engagement
in American Democracy*, ed. Theda Skocpol and Morris P. Fiorina (Washington, DC:
Brookings Institution Press, 1999), with Robert D. Putnam, "Bowling Alone: America's
Declining Social Capital," *Journal of Democracy* 6:1 (1995): 65–78, and *Bowling Alone:
The Collapse and Revival of American Community* (New York: Simon & Schuster,
2000); note Robert A. Nisbet, *The Quest for Community: A Study in the Ethics of Order
and Freedom* (Oxford, UK: Oxford University Press, 1953), and Robert T. Gannett Jr.,
"Bowling Ninepins in Tocqueville's Township," *American Political Science Review* 97:1
(February 2003): 1–16; and see William A. Schambra, "Is There Civic Life beyond the
Great National Community?" in *Civil Society, Democracy, and Civic Renewal*, ed.
Robert K. Fullinwider (Lanham, MD: Rowman & Littlefield, 1999), 89–125. Note also
Steven Rathgreb Smith, "Civic Infrastructure in America: The Interrelationship be-
tween Government and the Voluntary Sector," in ibid., 127–50; Gerald Gamm and
Robert D. Putnam, "The Growth of Voluntary Associations in America, 1840–1940,"
Journal of Interdisciplinary History 29:4 (Spring 1999): 511–57; and *Freedom of Associa-
tion*, ed. Amy Gutmann (Princeton, NJ: Princeton University Press, 1998).

73. On this subject, much more could be said: see, for example, Camille Paglia, "The Joy
of Presbyterian Sex," in Paglia, *Sex, Art, and American Culture: Essays* (New York: Vin-
tage Books, 1992), 26–37.

74. In this connection, see Sanford Kessler, "The Secularization Debate: A Tocquevillian
Perspective," in *Tocqueville's Defense of Human Liberty*, 265–82.

75. See George Marsden, *The Soul of the American University: From Protestant Establishment to Established Non-Belief* (New York: Oxford University Press, 1994).

76. For an extended meditation on this phenomenon, see Harvey C. Mansfield, *Manliness* (New Haven, CT: Yale University Press, 2006).

77. There is one clear indication that the public posture now required is pure hypocrisy: when it turns out that women are underrepresented in a prestigious profession, it is immediately taken as proof positive for the existence of prejudice and discrimination; when men are overrepresented in prison populations worldwide, no such conclusion is drawn.

78. For a Tocquevillean perspective, see Allan Bloom, *The Closing of the American Mind: How Higher Education Has Failed Democracy and Impoverished the Souls of Today's Students* (New York: Simon & Schuster, 1987), 47–137 (esp. 82–137).

79. In this connection, see Kay S. Hymowitz, *Marriage and Caste in America: Separate and Unequal Families in a Post-Marital Age* (Chicago: Ivan R. Dee, 2006).

80. See Laura Sessions Stepp, *Unhooked* (New York: Riverhead Press, 2007), whose findings are confirmed by the fact that there is a large audience for self-help books promoting such conduct: see, for example, Jessica Rozler, Andrea Lavinthal, and Cindy Luu, *The Hookup Handbook: A Single Girl's Guide to Living It Up* (New York: Simon Spotlight Entertainment, 2005), and Alexa Joy Sherman and Nicole Tocantins, *The Happy Hook-up: A Single Girl's Guide to Casual Sex* (Berkeley, CA: Ten Speed Press, 2004). That no such books exist for young men is telling: see George Gilder, *Sexual Suicide* (New York: Quadrangle, 1973).

81. The internal logic inherent in the radical individualism underpinning the principled rejection of matrimony as such and the preference for "partnership" points ultimately to the advantages of solitude: consider Rachel P. Mains, *The Technology of Orgasm: "Hysteria," the Vibrator, and Women's Sexual Satisfaction* (Baltimore, MD: Johns Hopkins University Press, 2001).

82. See Rachel K. Jones, Mia R. S. Zolna, Stanley K. Hinshaw, and Lawrence B. Finer, "Abortion in the United States: Incidence and Access to Services, 2005," *Perspectives on Sexual and Reproductive Health* 49 (2008): 6–16. For updates, see the Guttmacher Institute, online at http://www.guttmacher.org.

83. See James H. Jones, *Bad Blood: The Tuskegee Syphilis Experiment*, new and expanded ed. (New York: Free Press, 1993).

84. To comfort oneself in the face of what amounts to a Holocaust, one can always tell oneself that an unborn child is not "a person": see Michael Sandel, *The Case against Perfection: Ethics in the Age of Genetic Engineering* (Cambridge, MA: Harvard University Press, 2007). By this definition, newborn babies and the severely senile should be fair game as well.

85. See Ramesh Ponnuru, *The Party of Death: The Democrats, the Media, the Courts, and the Disregard for Human Life* (Washington, DC: Regnery, 2006), who readily acknowledges in the body of the text what his subtitle might be taken to deny—that some Democrats oppose "the party of death" and a great many Republicans belong to it.

86. See Raphael Cohen-Almagor, *Euthanasia in the Netherlands: The Policy and Practice of Mercy Killing* (Dordrecht: Kluwer Academic Publishers, 2004).

87. See Matthew Continetti, "The Peace Party vs. the Power Party: The Real Divide in American Politics," *Weekly Standard* 12:16 (1–8 January 2007): 17–19, 22–24.

CONCLUSION

1. See Matthew Continetti, "The Peace Party vs. the Power Party: The Real Divide in American Politics," *Weekly Standard* 12:16 (1–8 January 2007): 17–19, 22–24.
2. The resort to euphemism is a cover for deep embarrassment: see Harvey C. Mansfield, "Affirmative Action *versus* the Constitution," in *A Melting Pot, or a Nation of Minorities*, ed. W. Lawson Taitte (Austin: University of Texas Press, 1986), 89–110, which is reprinted in adapted form as "Pride and Justice in Affirmative Action," in Mansfield, *America's Constitutional Soul* (Baltimore, MD: Johns Hopkins University Press, 1991), 84–97.
3. See Franklin Delano Roosevelt, Annual Message to Congress, 11 January 1944, in *Nothing to Fear: The Selected Addresses of Franklin Delano Roosevelt, 1932–1945*, ed. B. D. Zevin (New York: Houghton Mifflin, 1946), 387–97 (at 396–97).
4. In this connection, see John P. Diggins, *Mussolini and Fascism: The View from America* (Princeton, NJ: Princeton University Press, 1972); Amity Shlaes, *The Forgotten Man: A New History of the Great Depression* (New York: HarperCollins, 2007); and Jonah Goldberg, *Liberal Fascism: The Secret History of the American Left, From Mussolini to the Politics of Meaning* (New York: Doubleday, 2008).
5. See Letter to Henry L. Pierce and Others on 6 April 1859, in *The Collected Works of Abraham Lincoln*, ed. Roy P. Basler (New Brunswick, NJ: Rutgers University Press, 1953) III 374–76 (at 376).
6. See Tocqueville, *L'Ancien Régime et la Révolution* (1856) III.3, in *ATP* 195.

INDEX